The Devils of ROME MADE ME DO IT!

By jackelin j. jarvis

Flip Wilson, you'll always be my inspiration.

Pathway to the Spanish Steps

Order this book online at www.trafford.com
or email orders@trafford.com

Most Trafford titles are also available at major online book retailers.

Narrative by Jackelin Joan Jarvis
Designed by Jackelin Joan Jarvis
Illustration by Tama and Jackelin Joan Jarvis
Punterelle Images provided by Mia Parsons and www.morguefile.com
CN Images provided by Clara Natoli and www.morguefile.com
CR Images provided by Cristina Rivera and www.cristinarivera.com.ar
MB Images provided by Marco Benini

Printed in Victoria, BC, Canada.

ISBN: 978-1-4251-6102-6 (sc)
ISBN: 978-1-4251-6103-3 (eb)

Our mission is to efficiently provide the world's finest, most comprehensive book publishing service, enabling every author to experience success. To find out how to publish your book, your way, and have it available worldwide, visit us online at www.trafford.com

Trafford rev. 6/22/2010

www.trafford.com

North America & international
toll-free: 1 888 232 4444 (USA & Canada)
phone: 250 383 6864 • fax: 812 355 4082

Table of Contents

Table of Contents

Disclaimer

During the very moment I put my pen onto paper for the creating of this book, things began to change. Permit me errors, being the impossibility to construct an accurate book under changing conditions, times, numbers, and owners.
DR. MMDIT will provide you with reference materials, cultural aspects expressed through stories, poems, and useful information blended with realistic facts. DR. MMDIT suggests, but it's entirely up to you, going by your intuition.
May this book enhance the joys of residents and travellers alike.

Acknowledgements

Thank you: Cristina Rivera for your photography contributions www.cristinarivera.com. ar,
Lopez photo services of Rocca Priora;
the Carabineri and their investigating on me and the permission to publish the calendar drawings and photos;
Marco Gazzoli for the SPQR recipes;
my Brazilian friend Fatima for her sweetness in explaining San Crispino's unique ice creams, I will never forget her gracious spirit;
Clara Natoli whose photos I admire and appreciate;
Susan Wheeler and associates in Rome at FORC Friends of Roman Cats;
Stuardt-Mikhail Clarke for the airport map;
Marco Benini for contributing photos;
TAMA my dear artist and nutty illustrator;
Mattia for contributing the specks of superb Roman churches, unique buildings and legends, I thank him for defining the true nature of my book".... . la natura un po' favolistica del tuo libro;
Nero my cat for his warmth and tenderness in my times of need;
the Glinni brothers: Raffaelo and Gianni for finding a 16th century Rome guide book hidden within their basement and allowing me to publish its pages - a book that could turn out to be the first Rome guide ever written;
José Neto a superb Brazilian designer;
and to all those that have contributed the small, but important things that helped enhance this book.
Roberto Mangosi for the befana witch drawing inspiration.

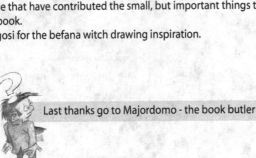

I

GIORNATA PRIMA.

Da Ponte S. Angelo à S. Pietro per Borgo Vaticano.

ESSENDO, per la moltitudine de gli alberghi notissima a' Forastieri la strada dell'Orso, e di Tor di Nona, lastricata già da Sisto IV. di mattoni, che perciò nel suo secolo si diceua Sestina, facilmente prende la maggior parte di essi l'habitatione in questa contrada; per il che da questa parmi necessario, che con la presente guida principiate, e terminate giornalmente, il vostro viaggio.

Nell'uscir dunque di casa, lasciando à dietro la Chiesa Parochiale, e Collegiata di S. Lucia della Tinta, e passando quella

A

Last thanks go to Majordomo - the book butler

Drawings by TAMA:

- Cover Drawing
- Maggiordomo
- Two dogs in Rome
- Bribery
- Miss Bugg-Eyes
- Roman scemi
- Superperstious
- Tamastein
- Dreams exiting the drawer
- ZZZZZ
- La Scarpetta
- Harlequin
- Elevator mash
- Espresso is for the birds
- Number mascarade
- Barefoot on a flat floor
- No sense of time
- Italian hands with a pen

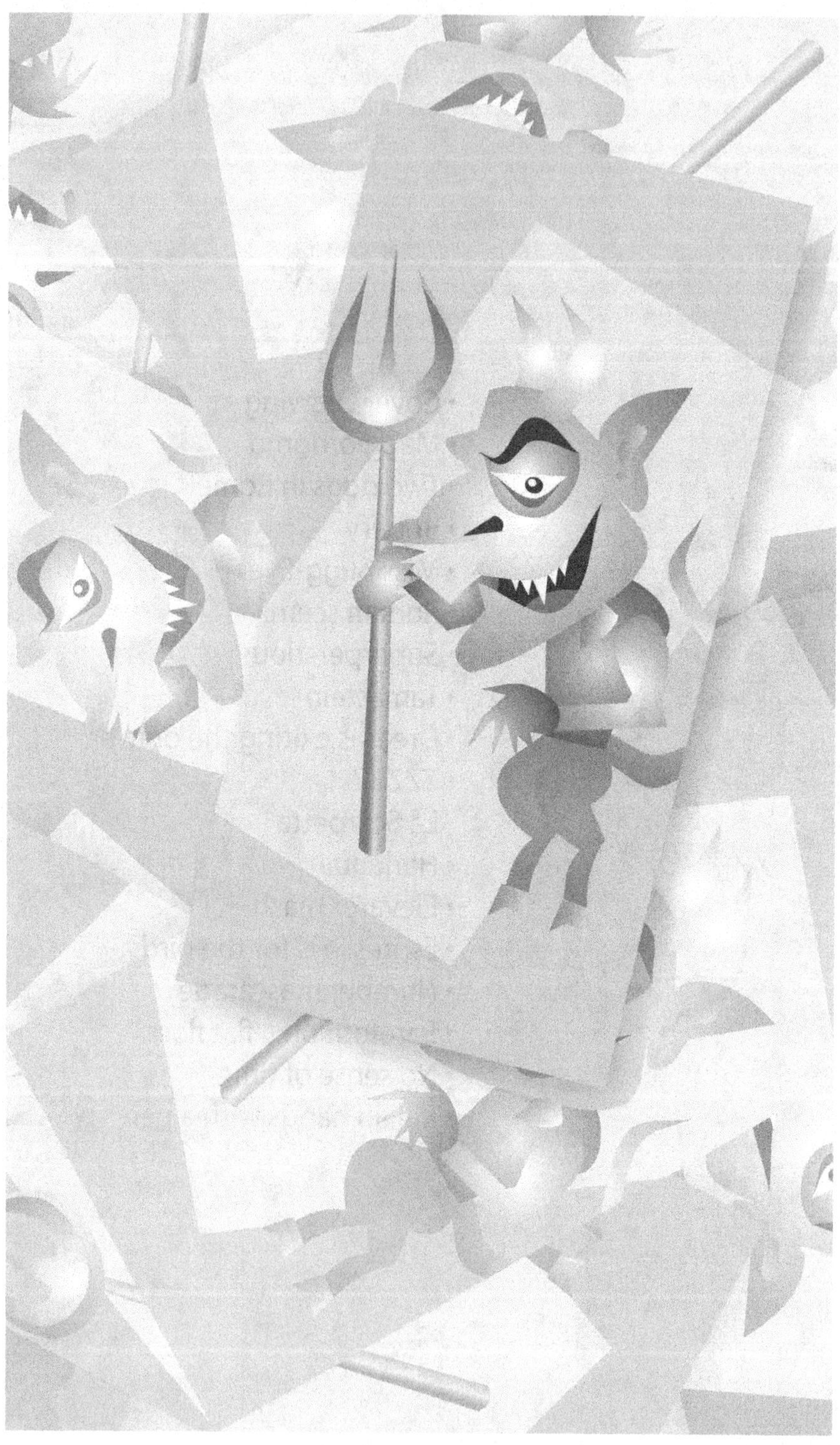

Dreams Rusting in Drawers and Collecting Dust

Dreams are a part of who we are; they are the blueprints of our soul. It is vital that we believe in ourselves and nurture our dreams until they produce. With desire and faith, we shall own our dreams and on that one fine day they will reveal themselves to us.

My desire became stronger the more I thought about it. I continued to nurture it until became a part of my feelings and emotions which turned into a burning desire.

This desire was to live among the Italian people, to learn and become a part of their culture and language.

Low and behold I found myself actually living that life within my own world, I was already there before I had arrived physically.

My days at work consisted of the work itself and the pampering of my dream. When I was free I would label everything in Italian with microscopic stick-its. And every now and then I peeked at one when no one was watching. I'd repeat cucitrice and specchio in my mind. I carried on regardless of doubtless looks and labelled all objects available until there was nothing left to label.

On my way to work I restricted myself, to Italian CD's only, and had entered the process of embedding Italian words into my head. It was quite an effective routine. With plenty of accumulated courage I had started to belt out words whose meanings I did not recognize.

At home I glued yellow post it's to wallpaper entire rooms. I then enrolled for classes at the local college, and even joined an Italo-American club where the members sat around the knight's round table to babble in Italian, an equivalent to Greek. But I was in the right place, with people who had similar dreams and desires. Those delicate seeds were tended to in a protective environment.

Did I realize I was doing the right thing? There's really no simple answer to that. In some way I knew it was the right thing, the desire filled my being and is what kept me fixated. Life leaves us to guess, imagine and hopefully risk, are we willing to risk though?

Whenever following a dream, time should never acknowledged. Time questions shouldn't be asked; how long will it take? Can I wait that long? Time doesn't exist in the dream-obtainment-world. Eyes should remain on a vision, faces moulded with a smile and energies used to trudge on. I sold everything and left for a country that was so upside down, so frightening and I did it alone. Someone somewhere had enlightened my way of thinking.

I wasted many years waiting for someone to come to Italy with me until I realized waiting on another person only wasted time, because no two people have the same dream detailed in their hearts.

It was when I realized I couldn't drag someone else into it, when I departed alone. I had learned a big lesson during my five years of waiting and during that time my desire heated up to boiling and outweighed my fears.

I met a nice woman who encouraged me to write these very pages. She asked me over and over to repeat my story. I had met her on a six month trip back to the United States after living abroad for three years in a music shop if I recall, around Christmas 2003. She told me I must go and tell people that they too can make their dreams come true. Inspire them, teach them she said. I never forgot this, only her name.

I lived within the borders of my dream comprised of my cat and chimney. I lived, breathed, and had awoken to the sounds of Italy. Church bells came to life, right there in Massachusetts. It was suddenly metamorphisizing.

As you know my home was garnished with those small yellow papers. Everything I looked at was in Italian. This obsession assisted my thriving, kept me believing and wanting. Funny thing is, I kept it to myself, as the suspicious have a sly way of talking one out of things.

Dreams have mysticism about them and they may be classified as 'false realities' by those who do not see, yet pose as the doorways one needs to step through in order to arrive. If we can't keep a commitment to the most important human being on this earth, how can we ever master commitment itself?

DREAMS IN THE DRAWER -
SOGNI NEL CASSETTO
People's dreams are kept in the bottom drawer,
the one that rarely creaks open.

Don't Do As Romans Do

Roman people nowadays have severed the ancient Roman umbilical cord. Once upon a time they were a people that conquerored, ruled, and charmed. This energy is lacking now amongst the Roman population of the 21st century.

May was a curious month, with birds chirping and cherry tree blooms thrusting their white flowers forth to cover meadows of trees. The hills became white caps and wilted flowers dotted yards and roads. The springtime brought paradise.

Bracigliano was my heart's destination. It is in a province of Salerno close to the Amalfi coast.

We rode down tight rubbled roads, and our seats became trampolines. It was the sign that caught my eye. I made the driver stop. I then rolled out of the car, standing looking with a quite baffled expression. In an utter stupor, the driver looked at this uneven girl. It was no illusion. A metal pole stood before me in white and blue; spelling; "Viale Springfield Massachusetts. " Why we were in the middle of nowhere, where did this street sign come from?

That day I had befriended a woman, who worked in the city hall of Bracigliano. She asked me where I was from straight away and was startled to hear the words Springfield, Massachusetts.

She explained to me, in her heavy Braciglianese accent, that she had relatives in Springfield, above all her sister that owned the biggest and most successful Italian Pizzeria called the "Red Rose Pizzeria" on Main Street. She said that half of Bracigliano had split some years ago to settle there. This explained why several of my friends had a mother, grandfather, or other relative from this place. Unbelievingly, I now had everything on a silver platter.

I grabbed the man coming out from the church for advice and he said to go to the Calvanese family, they were relatives of my relatives. I knocked at the door of a quaint old cottage attached to a factory. An older man opens it and says hello. The same magic again was'Springfield'. I found myself at the kitchen table and talking to these two strangers as if they were my parents. They showed me pictures of familiar streets and a group of youngsters who were posing in my neighbourhood for the shot. I recognized two people straight away. I somehow felt I knew this foreign family as familiar.

They offered me a job in their salami factory and then they asked me to stay the weekend. I was welcome to take as many of those wonderful super-ball-sized cherries that I could muster, and they sent me on my way with a heaping variety of salami's. We shared friends familiar things, and most of all, Springfield talks.

Sunday's were spent grazing at my grandparents. Their antique kitchen smelt of foreign vapours and the end tables were decorated with almond-shaped confections.

The crystal dish held large green sour and black wrinkled olives. Bowls overflowed with broth and tortellini's bobbing around specks of parsley. Gramp owned a little restaurant they named "Capri" on the corner of Main and Union.

My grandma took my elbow one day and lead me into the woods by the house. We ventured through the oaks and maples gathering up wild berries for pies. As a crafty seamstress she crafted us two coats of leopard and bear brown fur. We still have a photo in these coats sitting on my dad's red and white polka-dotted car, back in the early 70s. That summer was the greatest gift I had received from her. Shortly after this, she left us.

This book is dedicated to fellow travellers who've travelled and to those whom I've met and befriended. Most of all to my loving grandparents whose life dream was to travel back to Italy together and never made it. My grandfather lost the will after losing his love.

What gave me the big push to publish this book was that I had wished that such a book had existed. All of the incidents in this book are true and the stories were extracted from real fact, experience, Italian publishing's and documentaries. (Although real life may be mixed with fantasy.)

To my Grandma Rinaldi and Gramp, (big nose) my dearest friend.
To my father Richard Joseph who, without him, this passion could have never occurred.

Trauma: Romamor

Trauma only hits when you land. It hits when you've discovered that you are finally out of your own territory, and can understand very little of what is around you. It can be described as "culture shock". You have your presumptions, but with tired anxious eyes upon landing to earth, instead you crumble from jet lag before realizing that they were slightly off. Trauma leaves you only when it's squeezed out from overloaded excitement, but it returns to haunt you in every now and again.

You realize that nothing is as you suspected, nothing as you imagined it.

This all may slow you down, but despite these interruptions, you will start to master trauma by simply not paying attention to it. You may still panic when you get off at the wrong stop, darn it! you didn't understand the bus drivers lingo.

You may experience salt traumas, foods loaded with salt.

Overpriced item traumas will occur, your taxi ride should have been 30 not 150€.

Nevertheless, before you even realize how much of this trauma is lingering about you, you will have already conquered it with overwhelming feelings of being abroad.

Welcome to Rome!

The official version of the legendary times of Rome

Combining century upon century taking us back to the far distant times lost in the mists of legend is everlasting Rome. Virgil and Livy have established the official version of those legendary times. There is no guarantee of complete accuracy, but the poetic saga behind which we catch a better glimpse of reality always enchants our childish delight in stories. Beneath the green crown of the Farnese gardens in front of the Palatine, we can summon the ghosts of distinguished people who lived on familiar terms with the Gods.

There is Evander, a minor Roman deity who was believed to have introduced the Greek pantheon, laws, the alphabet, and other arts and skills in Rome; a shepherd king whom Hercules his host, in passage, rendered a noble service by ridding him of the presence of Cacus; originally a pre-Roman god of fire, who gradually became a fire-breathing demon. Cacus lived in a cave in the Aventine Hill from where he terrorized the countryside. These redoubtable bandits whose lair was dug in the hollow of the neighbouring Aventine. There is Aeneas fleeing from burning Troy after it had requested his aid. His aged father Anchises accompanied him and suffered great losses, why had Venus who had formerly granted her favours upon him, apparently abandoned his family? A hillside grotto shelters Lupercus; the Roman God of Agriculture and of the Shepard's.

It was there that a wicker cradle bearing two wailing infants was left at the foot of a fig tree, from the cavern nearby. Lupercus raised up a female wolf who stretched herself out beside them and offered her own milk, then Faustulus the herdsman, discovered them, took them home and brought them up as two strong Shepard boys. It was eventually discovered that these two orphans Romulus and Remus had an amazing lineage. They counted Aeneas, Venus, and Mars among their ancestors. Their great uncle Numitor King of Alba Longa had had them exposed to the current of the Tiber, to punish the Vestal Virgin Rhea Sylvia his niece, for letting herself be seduced by the warrior God one day when she was lingered at the fountain.

This was their divine origin, recognised herdsmen, though Romulus and Remus decided to become leaders of nations and to make the village where they grew up a real city. Romulus imposed the burden upon a pair consisting of a bull, and a calf, both attired in white. He harnessed them to a cart and marked out around the Palatine the sacred enclosure that no one would cross under penalty of death. To indicate the gates he raised his swords of steel.

Thus did"Roma Quadrata"come in to being one of the small hills dominating the swampland, thus did a bragging adventurer shape the tiny kingdom

which was to conquer the world, and insensibly we have left legend for history.

To make a court, other hills surrounding the new city were enclosed in what were from that time on, sacred district. In the muddy plain the herds were led out to graze. Sometimes bloody combats ensued for the possession of a head of cattle or a woman, the ravine which separated the Palatine from the capitol where Saturn had reigned, was the scene of one of these struggles. Romulus with a view to increasing the number of his subjects had made the city a place of refuge for robbers- in the oak forest which covered the neighbouring hill.

In one stroke he had increased his territory and his power. But it was essential for these new subjects to produce a family. The inhabitants of neighbouring villages were unwilling to give their daughters to these adventurers. A cunning trick was in store. The Romans invited the Sabines stationed on the Quirinal nearby to public games, and in the course of the festival they carried off the women of their guests- now a terrible war broke out. Tatius, king of the offended nation, soon took possession of the capitol by surprise owing to the reason of the vestal virgin Tarpeia. He made preparations to assault the Palatine and to engage in deadly combat on the site of the future forum when the victims of the rape intervened between their husbands and their brothers. Thus came about the realization that if the flowing of blood was so frightening to them, the women could scarcely be so ill contented with their new fate.

The two kings were reconciled on the spot and united their two peoples in one at the foot of the capitol. The place of this meeting"The Comitium"remained sacred, for the second time the power and the extent of Rome had grown. In traversing the scene of these events whose outcome was to be stupendous, one is struck by its scarcity. In this small triangle the roots of our civilization were to grow. Not far away a ten minutes walk, the Tiber encloses in one of its bends, the ancient Campo Marti, the Velabrum, where the rough legions that were to subdue the ancient world did their training, after having served their apprenticeship in the Roman country side for the possession of a shack or cornfield. Romulus disappeared; it is said, in a cloud. Actually, he must have perished at the hand of an assassin. But the momentum had been given. And Rome continued to grow.

THE END

Another Year Bites the Dust

Curtailing to beaches near and far
to mountainside cottages dreams of caviar

Leaving the tormenting furnaces of Rome in the mist
plummeting to cooler grounds somewhat of an animist

Italians desert Rome in August
another year bites the dust

Shops are morgues empty squares
even the pope escapes to his Castel Gandolfo solitaire

If you come in August you will find
quite an absence of all mankind

Accommodating hotel prices
and tourist mixtures in allspices

Alone in a cauldron to adjust
another year bites the dust

Susan Wheeler and the

Friends of Roman Cats (FORC) is guided by the desire to help homeless cats through international cooperation and educational initiatives. A few words about Italy's involvement with cats: Cats go way back in history on the Italian peninsula at least to the 9th century B.C. Throughout history, they have been appreciated as companions and for their ability to keep down rodent populations. As many of you know, in 1991 Italy passed a groundbreaking law saying that healthy stray cats cannot be killed. The Friends of Roman Cats organization was formed in large part to support the spaying and neutering of Italian street cats.

www.friendsofromancats. org

ROME'S CATS GET A NEW LOOK!

For the homeless street cats of Rome, tipped ears are becoming all the rage! A tipped ear means that the free-ranging cat has been spayed or neutered. As we know, this means less fighting and roaming, fewer cancers, fewer sickly kittens and, most important, a stabilization and eventual reduction of the homeless cat population.

For the last two and 1/2 years, Friends of Roman Cats has been helping bring about this new look. We have had a very successful partnership with Torre Argentina Cat Sanctuary, providing money for a voucher program by which poor cat caretakers all over Rome cat bring their cats to an approved veterinarian to be spayed or neutered at little or no cost. We have also been supplying Torre Argentina as well as other cat refuges with humane cat traps that people can borrow to catch their cats to get them sterilized.

"Italy is very different than the United States in dealing with its stray cat population. Since 1991 Italy has had a law that bans killing healthy stray cats and dogs. Stray cats live quite openly and are fed by numerous"Gattare"; others are cared for in sanctuaries. We will visit some of these sanctuaries and see how a different culture deals with its free-ranging cats. *"(Susan Wheeler)*

WE BELIEVE that the feral cat communities of the United States and Italy have much to learn from each other. Each country has areas of strength. We would like to act as a conduit to pass each county's strengths on to the other. We believe there can be great mutual benefit in this exchange for cats and their caretakers in both countries.

EVERY CAT whether owned or not should have the right to life and whatever care we can help it to find. We wish to help change the common view here that the life of a feral cat is not worth living. Torre Argentina not only cares for a large colony of homeless cats, it is trying to create a safety net for all of Roman cats.

For information contact Susan:

Friends of Roman Cats, PO Box 12571
San Francisco Ca 94112
415-334-8036/rappwheel@aol.com or
Mary Kennedy at marezie@appleisp. net

Some Rome Cat Sanctuaries:

- Largo Torre Argentina
- Protestant Cemetery
- Piramide Sanctuary
- Markets of Trojan
- Parco Celimontana
- Via Sacra

Bringing your cat back to the US:

- Call your airline carrier to see if they will fly an animal in the cabin, under your seat
- Ask them for the size dimensions of the cage, choose the largest available!
- Reserve a spot for your cat, there are only 2 animals allowed per flight
- There are no quarantines to take a cat back to the US
- Cats just require a certificate of good health and, a current proof of vaccination. FORC can provide this for you, as most all their cats have these requirements already

The sanctuaries are entirely supported by people like you, tourists in general.

DR. MMDIT guides are donated to the Cat Sanctuary to help the cats, with each purchase you automatically give to the animals.

News on Italy, Lazio and Rome

Rome's transportation system is simple to use and reliable half the time. Beware of strikes, drivers without a clue, breakdowns and clueless mishaps that take place 50% of the time. The system connects you to most Italian cities.

Rome's principle railway station is Termini station. Termini has two intersecting lines, lines A and B. Line A is represented by the colour orange and B with blue. Both lines intersect at Termini.

Aviation services include two main airports: International Leonardo da Vinci (30km from Rome's City Centre-southwest), otherwise known as Fiumicino, and the national airport Ciampino (15km from Rome's centre southeast).

Rome is the most important centre of aviation services in Italy.

ABOUT ITALY

Italy is divided into 20 regions like states, and then broken down into provinces, each taking on the name of the most important city in that region. Lazio-state, Rome-province, Frascaticommune or district. Each little town has its own city hall or municipio.

Lazio ranks ninth among all regions in size as it is 17,203 square kilometres/6,642 square miles, that's 4,250,954 acres!

LAZIO AND WINE

Lazio, Rome's state, largely focuses on the cultivation of grapes and this supports their agricultural economy. White wine accounts for an overwhelming share of the region's production 90-95%. White grapes: Malvasia, Trebbiano red grapes:

Cabernet Sauvignon, Merlot, San Giovese, Montepulciano, and Cesanese.

Vineyards cover 65,600 hectares/162,100 acres.

There annual wine production turns out 5,000,000 hecto-litres/500,000,000 litres. Vineyards are highly concentrated in the Roman Castle area. Classic restaurants serve wine directly from the bangs. Even if tourism is mild in these parts, wine from the Roman Castles continues to be the most consumed in the world.

"ROMA CAPUT MUNDI... ROME CAPITOL OF THE WORLD ROMA CITTÁ ETERNA .... THE ETERNAL CITY"
• Rome is located in southern Europe, on the same latitude with New York.
• Rome is in the Region of Lazio.
• Rome is 28km from the Seaside.
• Rome houses the independent Vatican State.
• Rome became Italy's capital city in 1870.
• Rome's area code is 06.
• Rome's dialect is Romanesco.

- *Lazio's important production industries include oil, fish, sugars, paper and pharmaceutics.*
- *The vast variety of cheeses coming from Italy left France's 400 varieties behind!*
- *Oil production is only merely behind Spain.*
- *Italy is the 2nd largest European producer of citrus fruits 90% coming from Sicily.*

With Rome's powerful influence over the world, it has sustained many important assets, including the world's largest amphitheatre in history: the Coliseum.

Rome is magical, creative and artistic, excitement never ceases, and some celebration will always be carrying on.

It's packed with art shows, festivals, and antique shows. There's the Cinema Festival and endless entertainment, painters and artisans. You may find that the mimes or street performers were once famous personage.

95% of Rome is Catholic, and it's not shy of demonstrating its endless selection of churches, even its exotic groups like Christian Science or Jehovah's Witnesses.

If we were to compare Rome to big cities like New York we could say Rome is a big place with its own mini Chinatown in the area of Vittorio Emanuele II, but it lacks the movement and agressiveness.

Authentic Roman cuisine you will find in the Castelli Romani, especially in Ariccia.

SENATUS POPULUSQUE ROMANUS SPQR: SENATE AND THE PEOPLE OF ROME

From 510 b.C., all public buildings and documents of the Republic had four letters on them engraved on them SPQR.

The Romans have their own designed lingo amongst them, and the length of a square block may alter the customs, dialects, and attitudes. Romans are the mantle, a blood continuation of the antique Romans. From what I gather original Romans were tall with glossy olive complexions. It shares strays and common streetwalkers and is quite safe. Italian police are more than merry on various street corner, and they'll fumble for words to help foreigners have a laugh or find their way back home.

Rome starts getting busy in early March continuing for months, especially July-October. A lunch pause freezes the frenzy. Romans go home for three hours, and eat and sleep. Rome by night is mysterious, classic, and romantic. The tiny vicolo-alleyways take one back in time to the classic-Italian film clips. Most of the city is a conglomerate of ancient Roman houses, ruins, baths, tombs, pillars, and bumpy cobblestone alleyways. 1/3 still hides underground.

Natural Hazards:

Regional risks include landslides, mudflows, avalanches, earthquakes, volcanic eruptions, flooding; land subsidence in Venice.

Graphic and Political Facts:

- Surface Area: 301.230km
- Inhabitants: 59,944,000
- Capital: Rome- more than 5 million inhabitants
- Ethnic Groups: Italians 92%, Others 8%
- Language: Italian (official) in some bordering countries German, French, Slovak
- Type of Government: Republic
- Confining Countries: West-France, North-Switzerland, and Austria; East-Slovenia
- Principle Mountains: Monte Bianco 4.812 m
- Religion: Catholic 80%
- Currency: Euro
- Natural resources: mercury, potash, marble, sulphur, dwindling natural gas and crude oil reserves, fish, coal
- Principle Rivers: Po River 652km, Adige River 410km, Tevere River (Tiber) 405km
- Principle Lakes: Lake Garda 370km, Lake Maggiore 170km (Italian part, total 212km), Lake Como 146km, Lago (Lake) Trasimeno 128km
- Principle Islands: Sicily 25.426km, Sardegna 23.813km, Isola d'Elba 223.5km
- Climate: Mediterranean-Continental-Alpine

As you may have imagined Italy forms the shape of a boot, one with a stylish heel. From heel to toe Italy's sandy beaches extend along its eastern coast lining the Adriatic Sea. In its north-western Riviera, the Ligurian Sea splashes brilliantly, glazing up the western side of the Tyrrhenian Sea.

The stylish heel can be described as low coastal areas, but the country is abundantly mountainous. The Appennini's Form a spine down Italy's peninsula, and the northern border is blessed with the Italian Alps and the Dolomiti Mountains.

Rome founded in 753 b.C., was named the city of Seven Hills and the Eternal City.

Because it is located in the region of Lazio, is it prized as the most historical region in Italy.

Not just years of civilization, but thousands of years of civilizations, resulted in making Roma the immense mantle it is in history. Each inch of Lazio, hides important historical remains.

Proudly grounded directly in the centre of the Roman Empire, Lazio is laced with imperial villas half stretched into the sea, sculptures, cobblestone roads, aqueducts, bridges, castles and beautiful fountains. After centuries of excavations, miraculous ceramics, paintings, frescoes, architectural structures, statues, and objects of gold have been uncovered, just a mere fleck of what's still lying underneath.

The Etruscans are the original peoples of Rome, just as the Indians are in the U.S.A., and the Aborigines in Australia.

OSTIA - forget not the famous Ostia Antica. Ostia is a city that's been entirely preserved, and located between Ostia and Roma. Founded by the 4th king of Rome Anco Marcio in VII century a.C.. Ostia's birth is connected to extraordinary salt deposits that formed at the mouth of the Tevere (Tiber) river. It was the area from which to patrol low vallies of the river that were under Etruscan influence. Streets, palaces, buildings, shops, stadiums, temples, and statues remain. You can even muster up glimpses of the Laurentum ruins close to the forest of Castelporziano, in a southern direction. Laurentum was the first capital of Lazio as well as the kingdom of the mythical King Latino.

THE ROMAN CASTLES - I CASTELLI ROMANI

A volcanic hill zone south-east of Rome's centre which awaits with woods bountiful in porcini and chiodi mushrooms, wild berries, nuts and herbs. It is a plentiful countryside with varieties of olive orchards and vineyards.

When in Italy try tartuffo (truffles), a speciality. These fungus have a distinguishing taste. They are found underground only in certain seasons, hard to come by, and expensive. You can find tartuffo in jars, accompanying risotto (rice dish), or nestled into pasta dishes. The Castelli towns are what make Rome famous for its wine and its authentic Roman food!

ROMAN EMPERORS 27-217 A.D.

DYNASTY GUILIO-CLAUDIA

1st Augusto-Ottaviano (Augustus-Octavian) 27 A.C. (A.C.) - 14 A.D.
2nd Tiberio (TIberio-Claudio) (Tiberius) 14-37 A.D.
3rd Caligola (Germanico) (Gaius-Caligula) 37-41 A.D.
4th Claudio (Druso-Nerone) (Claudius) 41-54 A.D.
5th Nero (Lucio Domizio) (Nerone Domiziano) 54-68 A.D.
'69 WAS THE YEAR OF THE FOUR EMPERORS
6th Galba 68-69 A.D.
7th Otone 69 A.D.
8th Vitellio (Vitellius) 69 A.D.

THE DYNASTY FLAVIA

9th Vespasiano (Tito Flavio) (Vespasian) 69-79 A.D.
10th Tito (Tito Flavio) (Titus) 79 A.D. -81 A.D.
11th Domiziano (Tito Flavio) (Domitian) 81-96 A.D.

THE DYNASTY ANTONINI

During this period, the city of Rome was in its maximum splendour

12th Nerva (Marco Cocceio) 96-98 A.D.
13th Traiano (Marco Ulpio) (Trojan) 98-117A.D.
14th Adriano (Publio Elio) (Hadrian) 117-138 A.D.
15th Antonino Pio (Tito Aurelio) 138-161 A.D.
16th Marco Aurelio (Marco Annio)161-180 A.D.
17th Lucio Vero (Lucio Ceionio) 161-169 A.D.
18th Commodo (Marco Aurelio) (Antonino) 177-192 A.D.

THE DYNASTY SEVERI

19th Elvio Pertinace (Publio Elio) 192-193 A.D.
20th Didio Giuliano (Marco Didio) (Severo Giuliano) 193 A.D.
21rd Settimio Severo 193-211 A.D.
22nd Caracalla 211-217 A.D.

IN TIMES OF MUSSOLINI

Mussolini Invented the term "Fascism".

> **"Fascism, which was not afraid to call itself reactionary... does not hesitate to call itself illiberal and anti-liberal. "**
> Benito Mussolini

Fascism is"... private economic enterprise under centralized government control.... "

The individual has"not rights but only duties... the common interest before self-interest... .... destroy economic liberty, free enterprise, and individualism .... private property and private enterprise are permitted, but are heavily controlled and regulated by government.

Rome Fascist Report Card 1932-33

ORIGINS OF THE TERM FASCISM

Fasces is from the Latin word FASCIS meaning "bundle used in symbolism to depict power and"strength through unity."

The traditional Roman fasces consisted of a bundle of birch rods tied together with a red ribbon as a cylinder. One interpretation of the symbolism suggests that despite the fragility of each independent single rod, as a bundle they exhibit strength. Wartime symbolism added an axe amongst the rods.

Numerous governments and other authorities have used the image of the fasces as a symbol of power since the end of the Roman Empire.

With the help of Giovanni Gentile in 1932, Mussolini wrote the entry for the Italian Encyclopedia on the definition of "Fascism".

A short stout guy from Predappio, which is near Forli in Romagna, Italy he was born on July 29, 1883. Mussolini was a powerful leader and founder of the Fascist party; he crazily tried to build an Italian empire, in alliance with Hitler and Germany.

When Italian armies were defeated in WWII, Mussolini's dream stopped in its mist. Then, on April, 1945, they caught them before they could ever get to Switzerland, shot Mussolini in the neck, chest and stomach; he wasn't even fully dressed. His mistress was seemingly shot fully dressed from the front and the back in the chest area. Mussolini was badly beaten, then hung upside down besides his lover in public. His window from where he shouted "Italians..." at the beginnings of a speech can be seen in the main plaza. It's the building you see when facing the white Vittorio Emanuele building, on your right.

IN TIMES OF JULIUS CAESAR

Roman Dictator: Julius Caesar-Giulio Cesare. Everyone admitted that Caesar was addicted to women and he was a convincing seducer, extravagant in his intrigues. Loving married women, he slept with the wife of a Roman Knight and he even had love affairs with many queens. His favourite was Cleopatra with whom he often partied with until daybreak.

He called her to Rome, and didn't let her leave until he garnished her with rich gifts, and he allowed her to give his name to their child. According to Greek writers the child was very much like him, in looks. He had an evil reputation for adultery and homosexuality. He was called "Every woman's man and every man's woman." He loved a woman named Servilia beyond all others, for whom he bought a special pearl costing him 6 million Sesterces ($246,000). Caesar was said to be tall, fair of complexion, with shapely limbs, a somewhat full face, with keen black eyes. He was prone to fainting and nightmares.

Caesar's death was foretold to him by many unmistakable signs, he had dreams about it the night before, and so did his wife. A note was handed to him on the way to the senate about the plot, and grabbing it with his left hand, stuffed it away with other notes, intending to read it, but never did. Taken by surprise, he was daggered twenty-three times, but only one was diagnosed as a mortal wound by the physician. Interesting enough, hardly any of his assassins survived him for more than three years, not a one died a natural death.

Many of them died either in battle, or took their own lives with the dagger that bludgeoned Caesar.

IN TIMES OF NERONE

Emperor Nerone (Nero) was born Lucio Domizio on December 15th, '37. A fiesty Sagittarius, one could compare him to Hitler, they say. He was known by his bronze coloured hair which brushed his shoulders, his distinct nose, and was average in height.

It is said that in 66 A.D. Nerone, in a fit of grief and guilt, cremated his wife on a year's supply of cinnamon sticks.

He murdered not only his wife, but also his mother and brother, and then launched himself onto a dagger in a fit of desperation. He planned to dispose of his mother after an invitation to dinner. He planned to make her trip home a very miserable one. Instead he killed her in her home saying she attempted to kill him first, and he had to defend himself against her. His mother married Emperor Claudio for a reason, and after Claudio was declared dead she slipped Nerone into his position.

After some time, Nero adopted Greek ideals in his mannerisms, dress, and his tastes contradicted Roman tradition. For an emperor to be consistently mocked for his preferences, paved way for unpleasantness, and political danger.

Nero was more enthralled by the theatre, music and sports then with his political duties. Was he responsible for the great onflagration that devastated Rome? It was believed he did it to persecute the Christians.

Before the fire that took Rome in 63 A.D., homes were built with from a certain wood which went extinct and easily took to fire. Soonafter, he ordered all homes to be constructed with cement only or to have a water compartment that held water installed, close

at hand in case of fire. Many cursed him and blamed him for the whole fiasco, when in reality he housed the most precious pieces of art and frescoes of unknown value. So why should he start a fire that would also ruin his own house of treasures?

AROUND THE ARENA WITH CHARIOTS

Circo Massimo Circus Maximus was a racecourse that could hold 250,000 spectators. The two-chariot or four-chariot races sped under a spotlight. A white sheet was dropped and the gates were released and chariots entered the game board. They all scurried to hit the central spot or spina. They needed to conquer a full seven rounds, and if one was injured or fell off he'd lose regardless if he crossed the finish line or not. Prizes were awarded of a palm and purse of gold. It is a mystery as to how much gold was in the purse and to how much it would be worth today.

BESIDES THE GREAT WALL OF CHINA AND TAJ MAHAL, ROME HOLDS ONE OF THE SEVEN WONDERS OF THE WORLD:
THE COLISEUM

GLADIATOR BATTLES ARE READY TO ENTERTAIN YOU

Gladiators battled to the death using daggers, swords, forks and nets. Judgement started the moment a gladiator was wounded. The gladiator would then get down on his knees, wait, and now the crowd decided his destiny. I saw a live acting show in Albano; it seemed real so very intense. With a thumb up and screams of Vivo! Vivo! he walked away, with thumbs down and a followed scream of Morto! Morto! He was exterminated. We took part in the decision making as once the crowd did!

Out crept a black demon, an official dressed in a morose cloak, to check the body. It was then dragged out of the arena. ARS Dimicandi at the amphitheatre in Albano puts you back 3,000 years, as the audience takes part in a life-like reproduction of Roman game fights. The audience chooses the loser's destiny and the actors are phenomenal.

AQUEDUCTS, WHO KNEW THAT THE ROMANS WERE WATER MASTERMINDS?

Romans were considered the most ingenious aqueduct builders in the ancient world. Most acquaducts are still standing above ground and below are in perfect functioning condition. Romans were smart, they knew that water had the capability of carrying and spreading diseases so they invested lots of money in the creation of their own water supply system. The system carried water across the valleys which poured out into baths, fountains and some homes of the wealthy. The business had its employees, soldiers, slaves to not only construct the aqueducts but to also maintain this genius network.

Red roses were cultivated in ancient Rome and the red rose of Province (rosa-gialla) was of Roman origin...

FASHION EXPLODES WITH ROMAN TREND WEAR

They wore sandals called Caligae; the women wore white instead of brown like the mens'. Women's house sandals bore bright colours decorated with jewels. The Romans also had their own equivalent of the modern-day bra (how ingenious). It was no other than a band of cloth or leather which tied over or under the breasts for support (depending on the size) which were referred to as a *strophium or mamillare.*

MEN'S TUNICS - were made from linen in the summer and wool in the winter months. Resembling a long t-shirt was more practical then the togas, which were a wrap of nine yards, wrapped all around the body. Your style or stilo depended on what class you were in. The commoners, slaves and cattlemen, wore dark materialed semi-short tunics. Tunics made from white linen or wool were worn by patricians, senators wore tunics with broad stripes and military wore tunics shorter than the civilians. Beards were clean-shaven, and hands bore 15 rings at a time.

THE BELLE DONNE - the women wore knee-length tunica's with long stolas draped around it (white grey or brown unless a bright colour vegetable dye was used). They loved to wear jewellery like earrings, pins, necklaces, bracelets, and pearls. They chose clothes that were multi-coloured, and wore make-up to hide her imperfections. They adored red lip tints and blonde, black or strawberry blonde hair dyes. Often their hair was worn up held by jewelled hair pins. Hair pieces were worn to make their hair seem longer or thicker, admiring themselves in highly polished metals.

COSMETICS AND BEAUTY

True and actual dyes existed; favourites were red, black and blonde.

THE FACE - incense and honeycombs were used to clean the face; it being the most cared for
EYEBROWS - carbon or lead (probably no FDCA)
TEETH WHITENING - cumin and wild melon
ASTRINGENT - poppies
SOOTHING - bulbs of narcissus
ACNE - butter, yes butter
PERFUME AND AGING - ointments and essences
FOUNDATION - biacca, waxy substances mixed with honey and fats with additional colorants added to the compound for rosiness or for brightening the skin
BLUSH - reddish dirt, sulino red
LIPS - cinnabar, a colourful mineral widely used in cosmetics today, minio
EYES - antimonio
EXFOLIATING - salt or baking soda (I do this myself)
TOOTHPASTE - powdered animal horns (maybe they added a little mint too)

Many Italian women nowadays overly partake in sun-worshipping covering up their imperfections with makeup, instead of taking good care of their skin. Unlike the ancient Roman women, there is a great lack of red lipsticks and bright red toes. It seems they are more partial to French manicures and nude feet.

Legends

The Madam and her Head on the Castel Sant'Angelo Bridge on Sept 11, Beatrice Cenci walks holding her head with one arm.

The Legend of the Brick Window in Piazza Mattei square of the turtle fountain, a noble family's daughter fell in love with a measly and broke musician instead of the lord her father wanted for her. She was then banned to leave the house and was kept on a short leash. She then began meeting him by her window each night, and soon after found it bricked up.

The Fake Window Legend when looking at the Trevi fountain to the building up above it, in the far right corner there is a window that seems real but is a fake. The legend says a young woman once jumped out of it and shortly after, the window was sealed up forever.

True Story of the American Soldiers and the Fountain Turtle

Towards the end of the war, when soldiers were returning home one decided to saw off a turtle in Piazza Mattei and conceal it somewhere on the ship.

The Italian police discovered the missing piece soon enough and stopped the departure of that navy. They had everyone's luggage searched until the turtle was found. And the Italian fountain turtle was returned to its proper place upon the fountain.

Via della Gatta

In a small corner of Palazzo Grazioli, their is a marble cat with a natural grandeur discovered near the temple of Iside.

There are two legends about this cat.

1. It's says its dedicated to a cat that meows"miagolò"to warn the mother of a child that was climbing on a ornamental contour of the building, to be able to be saved before falling.

2. Under the cat statue, there may be a buried treasure, though no one has ever been able to find it. It's proved quite impossible too, since it's down in between foundations of the buildings.

TOWER OF THE MONKEY

The legend of Monkey tower or Torre Frangipane is cute. Coming from Piazza del Popolo and into Via dei Portoghesi, to Via della Scrofa-which is called Scrofa because on the wall of ex-convent Agostiniani, there is an antique bas-relief representing a female pig or una scorfa. This is in front of the 16th century church of Sant'Antonio dei Portoghesi where Palazzo Scapucci has incorporated a 14th century tower called the Frangipane or the Monkey Tower. According to legend, a lantern always glows in front of the Virgin Mary representing gratitude of the owners for the salvation of their baby daughter who was carried to the top of the tower by a monkey and saved from disaster.

	B.C.
1184 B.C.	Legendary arrival of Aeneas in Italy
753 B.C.	21 April Rome was founded
578-534	Rome was divided in 4 regions closed in by the Serviane Walls
510	Establishment of Republic- S. P. Q. R. letters introduced (Till Caesar)
509	Inauguration on Campidoglio
312-311	Realization of the Circo Massimo-Maximus Circus
312	First Aqueduct built "Aqua Appia"
312 B.C.	The Via Appia Antica was constructed –censor Appio Claudio Cieco
272	City's second aqueduct built "Anio Vetus"
281-272	Tarentine –Pyrrhic Wars
270-266	War with Etruscans, Rome Supreme in Italy
268	First Silver coins made
264-241	First Punic War
221	Flaminio Circus built
215	First Macedonian War
200-196	Second Macedonian War
191-189	Syrian War
171-167	Third Macedonian War
142	First stone bridge "Ponte Rotto" is completed
125	Two new Aqueducts "Aqua Marcia" & "Aqua Tepula"
111-105	Jugurthine (African) War
80	Roma's population 400,000
73-71	Slave revolt under Spartacus
70-19	Virgil Latin poet
65-8	Horace, Latin poet
62 & 46	Agrippa had two bridges put up on the Tevere River and Tiburina Island "Ponte Fabricio and Ponte Cestio
59	Caesar's first consulship
49-46	Civil War Caesar vs. Pompey
44	Assassination of Caesar
43	Ovid, Latin poet
31	Battle of Actium; Octavian defeats Anthony and Cleopatra
27 B.C.	14 A.D. Augustus
15 B.C. - 50 A.D.	Phaedrus, Roman Fabulist

A. D. ANNO DOMINI (THE YEAR OF GOD)	
4 - 65	Seneca, Latin philosopher and dramatist
23-79	Elder Pliny, Latin encyclopedist
37-41	Caligula
54-68	Nero
55-120	Tactus, Roman Historian
64	Burning of Rome, Persecutions of Christians
69-79 A.D.	Emperor Vespasiano has the Coliseum built
79-81	Titus
80	Titus opened the amphitheatre-coliseum
81-96	Domitian
96-98	Nerva
98-117	Trojan
118	population of Roma - more than 1 million
118	Hadrian undertakes the reconstruction of the Pantheon
100-175	Appian, Greek historian of Rome
101-106	Dacian Wars
123	Beginning of the building of the Castel Sant'Angelo
117-138	Hadrian
161-180	Marcus Aurelius
211-217	Terme di Caracalla - Open to public
230-233	Persian War
249-251	Decius; persecution of Christians
270-275	Aurelian - Dacia abandoned; walls built around Rome
395	Empire Divided- Honorius (west) Arcadius (east)
410, 455	Vandals sack Rome
474-476	Julius Nepos and Romulus Augustulus – last to be recognized as colleague of eastern Empire
476	Fall of the Western Roman Empire...
476-493	Odovacar King in Italy
609	Transformation of the Pantheon into a Christian church
727	Foundation of the first hospital S. Spirito in Sassia
727	Rome population reduced to around 35,000

1200	First Tourist Guides of Rome-"Mirabilia Urbis"
1300	Beginning of transference of the Jews to the S. Angelo Area across from Fabricio Bridge
1425	Population 20,000
1473	The Sisto bridge is the only bridge reaching the Tevere River
1481-83	First decorations painted of the Sistine Chapel by Botticelli, Pinturicchio and others
1500	The Vatican "Pietà" first works of Michel Angelo in Rome
1508-1512	Second painting on Sistine Chapel by Michel-Angelo
1509	Decorations painted by Raffaello in the Vatican Rooms
1526	Population 55,000
1555	Jews were restricted to a walled in area of Rome
1574	Quirinale Palace was built, Italy's white house 1600 Giordano Bruno statue erected in Campo de' Fiori
1726	Spanish steps were connected to Pincio by the great staircase
1732	The glorious Argentina theatre is born
1771	Beginning the transformation of the Vatican buildings into museums
1800	Population Roma 150,000
1801... Leon....	Rome is made a part of the French Empire under Napo
1802-1804	Carlo Fea completes the first excavations in the Ostia Antica Area
1809-1814	French occupation in Rome (Napoleon)
1856	Inauguration of the railway Rome-Frascati
1871	King Vittorio Emanuele II is Italian governor
1874	Opening of the Termini zone, the new railway station
1876-1900	Opening of the Lungotevere (road along the river)
1879	Harriet Good hue improved an invention in the process of making artificial marble - in Rome
1881	Population Roma 273, 952
1885	First Monument to Vittorio Emanuele II – the Vittoriano
1889	Inauguration of the "Terme of Diocleziano"
1901	Population Roma 422, 411
1911	Population Roma 518, 917
1915	Italy joins allies in WWI...
1922	Mussolini's march on Rome...

1929	The Vatican was granted its liberty from Italy, becoming its own country
1929	Largo Torre Argentina has been a Roman Cat Sanctuary
1931	Population Roma 930, 926
1937-1939	Inauguration of the most modern equipped movie studio in Europe: Cinecittà
1938-1938	The area of "EUR" was developed
1939	Via Cristoforo Colombo was constructed further connecting the area of Ostia to Rome
1940	Italy joins Germany in World War II...
1943	19th of July American Airplanes Bombard the area of San Lorenzo
1943 many	16th of October the Jewish community is deported to Ger
1944	4th of June allied troops enter - Rome is liberated...
1944	King Vittorio Emanuele III renounces
1951	Population Roma 1,651,754
1960	For the Olympics the sport building of EUR was built and the Flaminio Stadium
1960	The Airport Leonardo da Vinci in service
1961	Opening of the "GRA" highway loop around Rome
1961	Population Roma 2,188,160
1980	Line A of the Roma subway in service
1981	Population Roma 2,840,259
1988	The region of Lazio approved the building of the regional park of the Appia Antica
1990	Subway Line B in Service
1990	Inauguration of the railway connection to Fiumicino (Leonardo da Vinci Airport)
1990	Rebuilding of the world championship Soccer Stadium
2000	Rome celebration 2,000 years of Christianity.... (In festival section)
2002	March the Italian lire left Italy forever and the Euro took its place
2004	29th of October signed the new European constitution at Campidoglio
2005	April Italy and the world loses the most special pope, John Paul II after 26 years of Papacy
2005	January Italy passed the non-smoking in public places law

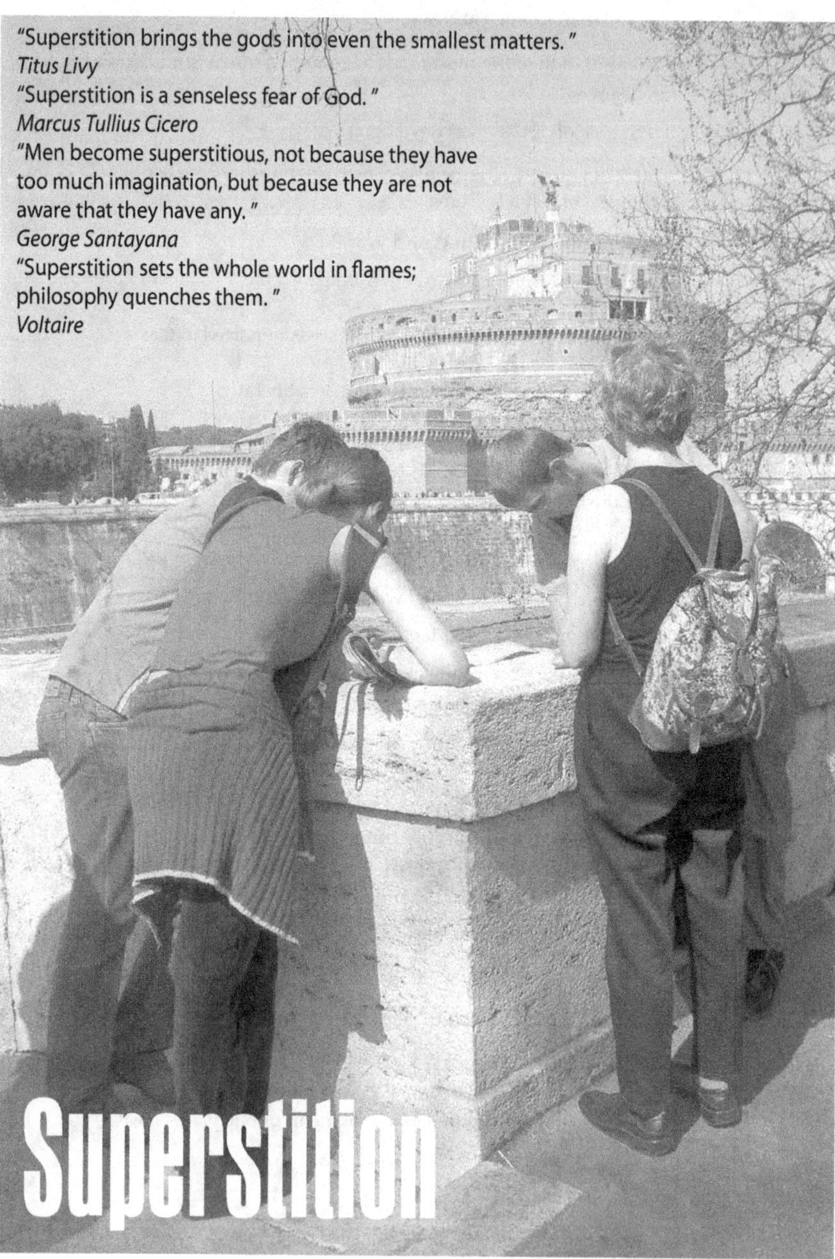
"Superstition brings the gods into even the smallest matters."
Titus Livy
"Superstition is a senseless fear of God."
Marcus Tullius Cicero
"Men become superstitious, not because they have too much imagination, but because they are not aware that they have any."
George Santayana
"Superstition sets the whole world in flames; philosophy quenches them."
Voltaire
Superstition

AN APPARITION IN CASTEL SANT'ANGELO

In and around Castel Sant'Angelo ancient mysteries linger. It is a great five level mansion with a safety passage. This passage appears somewhat of a bridge built over land or water when the gullies were filled. The inside is composed of two different levels, the top where the guards passed over, and the lower level which was dark and underground, but a brilliant corridor where the popes scrambled about trying to arrive to the castle from the Vatican for protection. It allowed people to escape from Vatican City into a strong protective fortress.

Be it the amazement of the three distinct layers that make up the castle itself, or the beautiful colour portrait of some handsome man that had the air of being human some hundreds of years ago, its inside where the strange happenings take place.

The lunar cycle plays a major roll in spirit activity and the full/new moon generates large geomagnetic fields as do magnetic storms. Ghosts are more vivid under certain circumstances, and when we see them it is usually under these circumstances. It is believed by many that ghosts are a form of energy and those sightings or encounters increase both in strength and clarity under certain atmospheric conditions that help conduce that energy. It's also believed by many that the whole winter season itself is an active time of the year for paranormal activity. The cold, dry air creates an ambience of static electricity. It's thought that when these static electrical conditions are present, the more ghost encounters take place because of that energy in the atmosphere.

Domenico the castle's night guard told me his story and showed me the photo of a ghost who dwells in Castel Sant'Angelo along with numerous apparitions.

The ghost head was visible; it was almost portrait-like, transparent and colourful. It looked large about 3ft in height and 2ft in width. He seemed to have been from centuries past rather like those of the 17th century. The apparition's hair was wavy, dark, and semi-long with an obvious obstruction of a huge nose that crept over his lips. He reminded me of the English films with Oliver Twist or Scrooge.

The Castle was the fortress of the great Emperor Hadrian, a prison, a torture chamber, housing for the popes, witness to prostitute visitors and thousands of marble cannon balls which are still present. The doorway to the underground prison is almost hidden in the far corner of one of the castle's courtyards. The steps are not so steep, but downwards the tunnel was dark and tinged with shivers. Just as I thought we had arrived, there was another tunnel or walkway to pass through. It is usually closed to the public. The next passage was brief but black, and then we ducked into a hallway of prison cells. I courageously ducked into two of them alone as the others were outside looking around. The air was limited and each cell so small with high walls, one window allowed air to come in from the ceiling. It gave off such a claustrophobic feeling and was usually stuffed with people.

As I sat overhead the prison listening to a medieval music, I couldn't help feel sullen for the people once prisoners under my feet, who maybe groped at the sides of the walls to ease their hunger pains. In evil amusement they were tossed crusts, bones and scraps from the Roman glutens above who projected them down through the sewer-like channels in the floor.

*Watch your steps, some of the stairways inside the castle were made for horses not humans.

The Castel Sant'Angelo bridge is one with many a story. It is safe-guarded by Saints Peter and Paul, whom lead at the head of its entrance, followed by rows of angels on either side.

Many of the bridges in Rome can tell a ghost story including the Cestio Bridge that leads onto the Tiberina Island in the river from Trastevere.

Black Cats and Seventeen

Italy is the proprietor country of superstitions involving black cats and the number seventeen.

For many, the poor black cat still cringes their spine as they ponder on misfortune.

A lady departing for work was suddenly shocked and she glared at the elegant strider that strode in front of her car. The scene upset her, and she went back home to call in sick. That's the power of the mind, of superstition.

For others it's the number 13 the number that jinxes and punishes those with painted strokes of bad luck.

Sadly for the number 13, astrological signs had to be stripped down to 12. For Lupercalia - a fertility celebration - originally on the 13th of February was transformed to the 14th which is now Valentine's Day.

The genuine story behind the number 17's glare of bad vibes was this; written in Roman numerals 17 is as so: XVII.

Mixing up these figures, they transform into a word; VIXI. In Latin, this is a verb meaning Live the first person singular, but past tense. Therefore it means, I lived, that is, I do not live anymore.

This represented nothing than death itself. This may explain Roman grief towards the number 17, for them it calls for great misfortune. If anyone happens to be stuck in Rome on Friday the 17th, it may seem everyone is quite disoriented, especially if the moon is full.

All in seven

THE SEVEN CONSULAR ROADS OF ROME

1. VIA APPIA ANTICA - Roma-Brindisi, Terracina, Santa Maria (365m/530km) open in 312A. D. , it begins outside Porta S. Sebatiano and is parallel to Via Appia Nuova. It is closed to traffic and stocked with catacombs, tombs, grottos, temples, a cistern, and a basilica.

2. VIA AURELIA - Roma to Pisa, Genoa (796m/1,178km) open in 241 A.D., it starts at the mouth of Doria Pamphilj and ends in Fregene.
ALONG VIA AURELIA: Villa Doria Pamphilj, Basilica di San Pancrazio, Aquaduct Paolo

3. VIA CASSIA (Statale 2/Route 2) - Roma to Bolsena, Lucca, Florence (219-272m/324-402km) it was finished in 117-107 A.D..
Via Cassia begins at piazzale di Ponte Milivio and ends at Santa Maria di Galleria Church.
ALONG VIA CASSIA: the Tomb of Nerone, Isola Farnese or Farnese Castle, Veio (important Etruscan ruins, and Apollo's Temple).

4. VIA FLAMINIA (Statale 3/Route 3) - Rome-Rinmini (191-223m/283-330km) finished between 223-219 A.D.. Via Flaminia begins right before Piazza della Marina.
ALONG VIA FLAMINIA: Viale belle Arti, Via villa Giulia, (Villa Guilia Museum), Olympic Stadium, Santa Andrea Church (Via Chiaradia), Flaminio Cemetary, house of Malborghetto.

5. VIA PRENESTINA- 338 A.D.. "Praeneste"or Palestrina
ALONG VIA PRENESTINA: Basilica di Porta Maggiore

6. VIA SALARIA (Statale 4/Route 4)"Salaria Vetus"
Beginning at Villa Albani, it runs to the Moschea Military Area (Fort Antenne) and is one of the most antique connections from Roma to the outer lands.
ALONG VIA SALARIA: Villa Albani Tel 06 686 1044, Mausolem of Lucillo Peto, Hotel Jolly, Catacombs of Priscilla (Villa Ada) Tel 06 862 06272, Villa Ada

7. VIA TIBURTINA - finished in 307 A.D.. "Tibur"or Tivoli-for thousands of years it was a direct route from the Abruzzo to the open plains.
ALONG VIA TIBURTINA: Verano Cemetery, San Lorenzo Area (Artsy college area), Universities, Museum of Classic Art Tel 06 499 13955, Museum of Antique Etruscan Tel 06 499 13315, Museum of the Originals (Prehistoric Culture) Tel 06 49913924, San Lorenzo Basilica, Catacombs of Ciriaca
VIA LATINA - Rome-Frosinone, Cassino (146m/216km)

THE SEVEN HILLS OF ROME

*L'AVENTINO HILL - the most southern and lowest of the hills
*CAPITOLINO HILL - is located behind the Vittorio Emanuele building and to the right of the Marcello theatre
*CELIO HILL - (Monte delle Querce) In Roman times this part of the city was very populated and had a bad reputation. It was full of stinky tramps and the people believed that invisible witches flew around and drank the blood of children. So a temple was built on the Celio of"Nymph Carna"that the people called upon to ward off vampires.
*ESQUILINO HILL - 75 meters high is located to the Northeast of the Coliseum.
*GIANICOLO HILL - located between Trastevere and Saint Peter's. Every day at noon the canon blasts reminders of battle victory.
*PALATINO HILL - Located between Circo Massimo (to its south), the Coliseum (to the east), the Roman Forum (on its head) and Campidoglio (to its Northwest).
*QUIRINALE HILL - in the past, the Quirinale building was the holiday residence of a papal society and from 1946, it became the residence of Italian presidents of the republican government. Flag up and the president is in, flag down and he's out.

THE SEVEN ROOMS - THE SETTE SALE

Refers to the reservoirs and pools of what remains of Tito's (Titus's) Spa

---

THE SEVEN KINGS OF ROME

The Etruscan Monarchy

In the first two hundred years Rome alternated seven kings...

1. Romolo 753-716 B.C..
2. Numa Pompilio 715-672 B.C., educated the Romans on religion and virtue.
3. Tullio Ostilio 672-640 B.C., engaged the city in many battles, one with the ancient city of Alba Longa.
4. Tarquinio Prisco was king for 40 years. He conquested all of Lazio region, had the Roman Forum enlarged, and Circo Massimo built.
5. Severio Tullio was responsible for a grand social reform.
6. Anco Marzio continued from Tullio's reign and developed the motto: "If you want peace, prepare for war "He was responsible for the formation of the"Door to Ostia".
7. Tarquinio the Superbo was thrown out in 509.

THE SEVEN GREAT CHURCHES

1. San Pietro - St. Peter's
2. San Giovanni in Laterano - St. John in Lateran
3. Santa Maria Maggiore - St. Mary Major
4. San Paolo - St. Paul's
5. San Sebastiano - St. Sebastian
6. Santa Croce in Gerusalemme - Holy Cross at Jerusalem
7. San Lorenzo

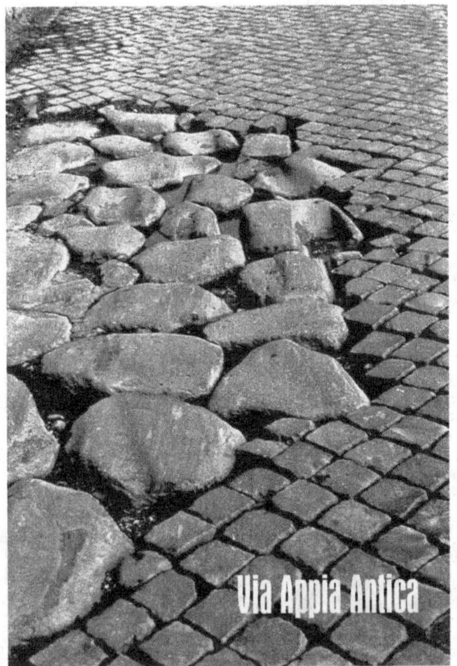

It was an antique road that spread out for miles patterned with ancient stones. Quiet emerges here leaving the fluttering of wings and delicate song of native birds to their naturistic business. 3,000 years ago, carriages hurried along the left side as the cars do in England. This was an advantage for right-handed swordsmen as they could draw to attack enemies passing on the right. Nowadays, the road is in the middle of nowhere and a well deserted path except for the occasional tour bus or cyclist.

We imagine it was very beautiful when the road was first paved with Roman stone-pastes and concoctions which painted a scene among the pine trees and daffodils. With use of tiny pebbles, they constructed the road, adding medium-sized stones then subsequentially large flat slates were shoved on top. To cement it all together, a magical Roman mixture of calcium, sand, water and a reddish dirt was spread on, the Roman recipe for tar. The roads were exceptionally well-designed for drainage. Strada means street in Italian whose underlying meaning is layers. The Romans layered their roads and this road was the Queen of Streets or Regina di Strade.

Imagine a vehicle approaching with metal-framed wheels cracking at the stone like an old truck. Rather, its a Roman cart with round wheels of extinct wood and quite the limosine of today. Such long trips without shocks promised bumpy rides and sore bottoms.

The Roman carriage passes and we see a leg hanging out of it, a bronzed leg, thin with velvety skin. It is the leg of a woman. The leg is kept smooth with olive oil, beeswax and honey. Its ankle dangles with jewels and the foot's leather sandal is a bit covered by a sheer material which teases the wind.

Now something else grabs our attention, a misty image covered by a haze. It could be a hill, it tricks us into having the desire to climb it and teases using its odd curvature. It's a lop-sided heap that's shaped all wrong.

Then we notice many more hills just like it. Several made of different shapes and sizes. Some are labelled Tomba di Famiglia. Roman family tombs were created for the noble, the superb, the intelligent. And we go inside to see beautifully decorated walls frescoed so colourfully and brilliant. Were these really tombs? The Romans would stop along Appia's roadside to rest, eat lunch and have a nap in the happy gravehouse. They were rest areas. Death was, as we see, obviously viewed with positivism and this road as we conclude, was somewhat of a mystic vein.

WHO WAS APPIO?

He was the Roman who donated his name to this road leaving the most interesting parts to lie between the Ceclia Metella's tomb and Casal Rotondo.

On a walk, this photo emerged as Italian workers were busy way down in a ditch. I saw a little hill that I couldn't climb as they were watching, with open gates of leaf green and iron. Through them in a distance, I could see the microscopic shapes of maybe old Roman walls or arches. After asking of its true nature, I continued to admire the ruins of an old Roman aqueduct which you see is pasted in this book.

VIA APPIA ANTICA CAMEOS

- The fantastic film Quo Vadis is a love story depicting Princess Barbara
- *Spartacus,* the gladiator of 73 A.D., battled against the Romans and thousands of slaves in order to grant liberty
- The film Titus by J. Taylor featured Villa Adriana in Tivoli and the grassy meadows of the Appia Antica

Taxi information

TAXIS ON THE STREET AND WHERE TO FIND THEM

ZONE 1: HISTORICAL CENTER
Piazza Barberini
Tel 06 4814447
Piazza Colonna Off Via del Corso
Tel 06 3217764
Piazza Repubblica
Tel 06 4817976
Piazza Venezia
Largo Torre Argentina
The taxi strip is on street in front of the Feltrinelli bookshop

ZONE 3: TRASTEVERE
Piazza S. Soninno

ZONE 5: PRATI
Piazza del Risorgimento
Tel 06 39723702
(Saint Peter's area)

TAXI QUICK CALL

Radio Taxis
06 3570
06 8822
06 5551

Pronto Taxis
06 6645

THE TWO TAXI CASES
A couple took a cab for a few streets and paid 150€ and should have paid no more then 15€. This made the young woman resort to tears.
A businessman from Long Island New York took a cab from Fiumicino airport to Via dei Balbiuno near Piazza di Spagna. The fare should have been 40-60€ and he paid 250€. He knew it was an outrageous amount and felt to consult a police officer but decided not to. Why?
Please do not feel intimidated.

TIPS

- Calling for taxi: meter is on when they receive the call
- Ask for many drivers before settling on a rate, they will vary greatly-bargain
- Agree on a price before entering and arriving or he may charge you whatever he wishes
- Tipping the driver is optional as the tip is added in
- Avoid taking taxis during peak hours unless you have to, and don't forget you pay by distance and time
- Before getting in write down the name and number of the taxi which is on the exterior. For example: Torino 25, Milano 13
- Do know you have the right to refuse to pay if they charge you an extraordinarily high fair? I advise discussing it and if they are not fair, say Carabinieri Cah-rab-bin-yair-ree/Police
- Ask another driver if one tells you he's never heard of the place requested, sometimes they are just lazy

ILEGAL TAXIS AROUND

- The cars do not have a TAXI notice, documented regulations, or rules
- They may not be yellow or white like the others
- They do not have a meter on the dashboard
- They probably do not have the validated fares visible on the back seat Le Tariffe
- They will rip you off if you are naive

TAXI FARE EXAMPLES

- Termini station to Vatican City is around 15-17€ for a 10-12 minute ride
- Termini station to the centre of Rome (Coliseum, Roman Forum, etc.) is approximately 7-15€ for a 5 minute ride traffic willing.
- Rome to Fiumicino (Leonardo Da Vinci Airport) is 35-45€ for a round 30 minutes
- Taxi fares Le Tariffe are clearly visible on the inside of the taxi and written in seven languages.

METER RATE EXAMPLES

- Night Rate 4.91€ (Starting Rate) from 10pm-7am
- Day Rate 3.36€ from 7am-10pm
- Extra charges procure after 10pm Sundays & Holidays 2.33€ 7am-10pm

FIXED FARES

Fiumicino airport to anywhere in the center of Rome inside Aurelian Walls/the whole centre of Rome is 40€.

Ciampino airport to anywhere in the center of Rome inside Aurelian Walls is 30€.

These new tariffs apply to all taxis licensed by the Local Administration in Rome. This means almost all taxis are available at both airports. There are only 37 taxis licensed by Fiumicino Local Administration. There are other fixed prices traveling to Rome for 60€. Make sure you board the most convienient, and check the outside of the car for the Roman Local Administration decal.

USEFUL PHRASES	
Take me to....	Portami a....
How much would it cost to get to....	Quanto costerebbe di andare a...
This is too expensive!	È troppo caro!
I won't pay that much.	Non pago così tanto.
Thanks, you've been quite nice.	Grazie, sei stato molto gentile.

Plane Info

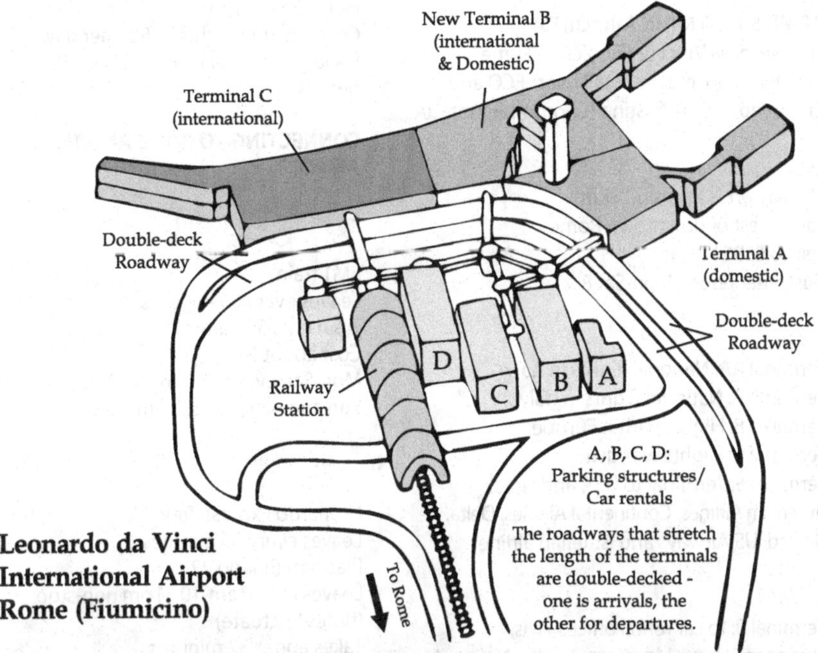

Leonardo da Vinci International Airport Rome (Fiumicino)

MAJOR AIRLINES TOLL-FREE IN ITALY		
Air France	848 884 466	
Air Portugal	848 888 910	
Al'Italia	848 8656 42	
British Airways	848 812 266	
Cyprus Airways	848 883 300	
Delta Airlines	800 477 999	
Finnair	840 0547 47	
Japan Airlines	848 874 700	
KLM	800 877 318	9-5, Monday-Friday
LOT (Polish Airlines)	848 8593 00	
Swiss Air	848 868 120	
US Airways	848 813 177	
Virgin Express	848 390 109	9-7, Monday-Friday; 9-6, Saturday; 10-4, Sunday
Volare Airlines/Air Europe	800 454 000	
Qantas	848 350010	Toll-free in Italy

Rome Airports

ROME'S TWO MAIN AIRPORTS:
Leonardo Da Vinci or Fiumicino (Fume-me-cheen-no, means small river)-FCO and Ciampino or G. B. Pastine (Chomp-peeno)-CIA

LEONARDO DA VINCI AIRPORT OR FIUMICINO
The airport is located 28km
southwest of downtown Rome
Tel: 06 65951
Customer hours: Mon-Sat 8-2

FIUMICINO TERMINALS:
Terminal AA: National flights in Italy
Terminal A: National flights in Italy
Terminal B: Flights within Europe
Terminal C: Flights worldwide
Terminal 5: Terminal to USA and Israel: American Airlines, Continental Airlines, Delta, United, US Airways and Israelian airlines.

FIUMICINO TERMINAL WALKWAYS:
Terminal B: to car rental offices-Avis, Europecar, Hertz, Maggiore, Thrifty, National
Terminal C: to train station

LEVELS
Ground Level: Arrivals and Baggage Storage
1st floor: Departures
2nd floor: Parking Garage, Hilton Hotel, Shops

Alitalia

Leonardo da Vinci Airport (Fiumicino)
Domestic: 06 656 34590
International: 06 656 34951/2
Termini Station
06 656 282 46 Binario 2
6:30am-9pm
General toll free number: 848-865-643
(In Italy)
24 Hours - Toll-free
Domestic 848-865-641
International 848-865-642
Special Assistance 848-865-649 (Saturdays, Sundays and holidays)

BAGGAGE STORAGE
Location: Lower level/Arrivals
Hours 7am-11pm
Costs: 2€ up to 7 hrs/3. 50€ per day.
For larger, heavier luggage about 6€ per day

CONNECTING TO ROME AND THE AIRPORT

ROME'S TIBURTINA STATION TO FIUMICINO AIRPORT
FM1 train
Leaves every 15 minutes
Train runs 5:36am-10:36pm
Cost about 5€
Mon-Sat, every 30 minutes
Sun and holidays 5:06am-10:36pm

ROME'S TERMINI STATION TO FIUMICINO AIRPORT
Leonardo Express Train
Leaves every 30 minutes
Platform Binario 22
Leaves at 5:51am-10:51pm non-stop (times fluctuate)
Takes about 32 minutes

FIUMICINO AIRPORT TO ROME'S TERMINI STATION
Airport to Termini Station
Leonardo Express Train FS
The train leaves every 30 minutes.
Everyday
Binario 22
About 11€
Takes 32 minutes
Runs from 6:37am-10:37pm

TICKETS
You may purchase your tickets at ticket booths Atrio Stazione Ferroviaria, newsstands Edicole, cigarette shops Tabacchi, or at self service machines or travel agencies.

BUYING TRAIN TICKETS
At vending machines at Termini and Fiumicino
Al'Italia office near track 22 at Termini (6:30-9:00pm)
Ticket window by the platform at Fiumicino

Shuttles and Taxis

AGREEMENT WITH TAXI ASSOCIATIONS - FIXED FARES

Taxi's from Fiumicino airport to anywhere in the center of Rome is 40€
Taxi's from Ciampino airport to anywhere in the center of Rome is 30€
These new tariffs apply to all 37 taxi's licensed by the local administration in Rome.
This means almost all taxis are available at both airports.
*You may encounter other fixed prices, airport to the centre of Rome, for 60€ or more.
Save money and check the side of the car to see if it has the *Roman Local Administration Symbol.*

Taxi Tip:
There is also an extra charge levied for every item of luggage

SCHIAFFINI TRAVEL SHUTTLE www.schiaffini.com

SHUTTLES:

FIUMICINO AIRPORT TO ROME TERMINI
A shuttle departs in front of national and international arrivals
Daily departures: 4:25 and 5:00

ROME TERMINI TO FIUMICINO AIRPORT
The shuttle leaves Termini Station in Rome on Via Marsala in front of the Royal Santina Hotel
Daily departures: 1:20 and 1:55

You many purchase tickets at tickets booths in the station or directly aboard

DRIVING TO ROME ON YOUR OWN:

AVIS	199100133
EUROPCAR	06 65010879
HERTZ	06 65954143
MAGGIORE	06 65010678
TARGA RENT	06 6529336
AUTO EUROPA	06 65017450
SIXT	06 65953547
ITALY BY CAR	06 6529133

DRIVING TO ROME WITH A DRIVER (CON AUTISTA)

Airport (Terminal A) Tel 800 017387 - toll-free in Italy
C. T. P. (Terminal B) Tel 06 659538651
Concora (Terminal C) Tel 06 65953932

CALLS FROM ITALY	
Aerolineas Argentinas	06 652 9257/ 650 11400
American Airlines	06 660 53169
Austrian Airlines	06 656 840 18
Air Berlin	06 650 11333
Air Canada	06 650 11462/ 650 10190
Air China	06 474 5045
Air Europa	06 421 231
Air Malta	06 488 4685
Al'Italia	06 65641/3
British Airlines	06 524 92800
Cathay Pacific	06 659 53692 Fax 06 474 1297
Cubana	06 650 17455
Czech Airlines	06 657 6111
Delta Airlines	06 420 10340
Egyptair	06 474 2641
Iran Air	06 474 1141
Israel	06 474 2301
KLM	06 650 11441
Lufthansa	06 656 840 04
Royal Air Morocco	06 478 233 36
Singapore Airlines	06 478 551
Thai Airways	06 478 1330 1
Turkish Airlines	06 487 3368
Qantas Airways	06 524 92579 Fax 06 524 92566

GOING BY BUS

Travelling to Termini station from Tiburtina Station
Tiburtina: Metro B (Tiburtina) or bus 649, 492 and departures between 11:30pm and 5am.
It also stops at Termini station
Departures every hour
Inexpensive

From Fiumicino: 12 mid - 5am
From Tiburtina Tea-bur-teen-nah: 1am - 4am

**Bus 40N connects Tiburtina and Termini during the night, validate tickets in the station machines before entering the train*

Taxi information/*Airport-Rome*

A 45 minute ride
Average costs:
Taxi 40-53€
Van taxi up to 6 persons 71€
Mini van over 6 persons 80€

LOST LUGGAGE

Alitalia Tel 06 65631
Ciampino CIA Tel 06 79494225
Fiumicino FCO Tel 06 65956777

AIRPORT PARKING INFO

P1: Car Rental and government organizations
P2: Airport Personnel
P3: Public (fee)
P4: Public (fee)
P5: Public (free)
P6: Public (free)
P7: Public (free)
P8: Public (free)

AIRPORT PARKING FEES

Up to 1 hr	1.30€
1-4 hrs	2.30€
4-12 hrs	3.60€
12-24 hrs	6.20€
Over 24 hrs	6.20€

Fees may change

G. B. Pastine in Ciampino

AIRPORT CIA
CIAMPINO NATIONAL AIRPORT (CIA)

Ciampino Airport, G-B Pastine-Ciampino
Via Appia Nuova
Rome Ciampino, Italy
Tel 06 79348521 or 06 79494234
Located about 15km outside Rome (9 miles)
15 minutes from the Castelli Romani

There are two ways to arrive to Rome from Ciampino;
By Taxi (30 min) cost about 35€ + tip and extra baggage
By Bus Cotral Arrives at Anagnina in 10-15 minutes, now take metro line A for the center of Rome
About a 25-30 minute ride

* Buses connecting Ciampino airport with the center of Rome stop running at 11pm, so the only way to get into town late at night is by taxi.

SHUTTLES AT CIAMPINO

TERRAVISION SHUTTLE

Connects you to Termini station for 8€ or 14€ for two-way ticket

SHUTTLES AT CIAMPINO

TERRAVISION SHUTTLE

Connects you to Termini station for 8€ or 14€ for two-way ticket
Tickets available at the number 356 ticket window at Termini Station

SITSHUTTLE

A bus connecting you to Termini Station from Ciampino
Leaves every 30-45 minutes, about a 30 minute ride - cost 6€

COTRAL - SCHIAFFINI

Connects you to Termini on Via Giolitti in 45 minutes for 5€
Leaves from Via Giolitti for Ciampino Airport

*You may also pick up an Urban bus for 2€ that will connect to Anagnina station and line A of the subway-leading you to Rome's Termini station

FCO & CIA AIRPORTS

INFO 06 65951
www.adr.it
www.terravision.it
www.schiaffini.com

LOST LUGGAGE

Ciampino Tel 06 79494225

AREOTAXI (AIR TAXI'S)

No charter flights
Within Europe only
Main number in Italy Tel 06 79340502
Management Tel 06 79341576
These charters don't usually allow animals aboard.

UNIFLY

Tel 06 79340583/06 79340502
www.aeroitalia.it
24 hours

AIRONE EXE

Tel 06 79340666

AERORENT

Tel 06 79340261_
Aero-rent@tiscali.it
Fax 06 793 40447
24 hours

MISTRAL AIR

Tel 06 79340901
Viale Mameli 131

ICARO

Tel 06 79341014

AN INEXPENSIVE WAY TO FIUMICINO AIRPORT BELOW:

LINE A SUBWAY TO PUNTO LUNGO STOP.

Across the way you'l find the Tuscolano train station. Here a train will take you to the airport for a few euros.

USEFUL PHRASES		
Cargo	Merci	mair chee
Domestic	Nazionale	nats tion ahl lay
Reservations	Prenatazioni	pray nah tots sea own knee
International	Internazionale	een tear nats own ahl lay
Flight	Volo	voh low

ROME'S TWO MAIN SUBWAY LINES

- Line A (Orange) runs southeast and was open in 1980. It has 27 stations Overnight: 55N follows line A's course
- Line B (Blue) runs northeast and was open in 1990. It has 22 stations Overnight: 40N follows line B's course

REGULAR STATION HOURS

Sunday- Friday 5:30am-11:30pm
Saturdays 5:30am-12:30pm
Rush Hour: 9am-4pm, runs every 3-4 minutes
Mid-Day: 4pm-8pm, runs every 5-6 minutes
Late evenings and Sundays runs every 8-10 minutes

TERMINI STATION METRO:

- To get in and out of the train, look for the buttons on either sides of the subway doors
- Be aggressive
- Check the chart on the wall at the bottom of the escalator on bottom level where train runs. The chart indicates two directions. Wait on the side that lists your destination.
- You can buy tickets at any ticket booth, cigarette stand or station ticket machine
- Follow the red M signs inside to the subway
- The subway lines are on the bottom floors
- Make sure you check the two signs at the bottom of the stairs for which direction each train is headed
- The destinations in which the train will travel to are bolded
- The towns located on the top are the final destinations and direction its headed

Rome will soon have a metro line C. In the process of being built, the metro C line will have 30 stops, 21 of which are underground. The entire line takes 45 minutes to complete. Now everyone will be able to ride directly to Largo Torre Argentina, Piazza Venezia and many other locations which were only accessible by foot. The metro system has two lines A and B, in anticipation for lines C and D. A and B cross at termini station. Line A is a level below line B.

Remember to purchase and use your ticket-the fine is 101€ if you're caught without one or a non-validated ticket. *The same tickets are used for both buses and trams.

METRO LINE A

BUS 590 FOLLOWS METRO LINE A'S ROUTE AND THE 55N OVERNIGHT BUS

Battistini ♿
Cornelia ♿
Baldo Degli Ubaldi ♿
Valle Aurelia
Cipro ♿
Ottaviano/San Pietro/Musei Vaticani
Lepanto
Flaminio Piazza del Popolo
Spagna Spanish Steps
Barberini Trevi Fountain
Repubblica Teatro dell'Opera
Termini
Vittorio Emanuele
Manzoni Museo della Liberazione
San Giovanni
Re di Roma ♿ (meaning: King of Rome)
Ponte Lungo ♿
Furio Camillo ♿
Colli Albani Appia Antica Park
Arco di Travertino
Porta Furba Quadraro
Lucio Sestio
Guilio Agricola
Subaugusta ♿
Cinecittà Film Studios
Anagnina - Transit to the Roman Castles/ Castelli Romani

METRO LINE B

40N NIGHT BUS FOLLOWS LINE B'S ROUTE

Laurentina ♿
EUR Fermi ♿
EUR Palasport ♿
EUR Magliana ♿
Marconi ♿
Basilica San Paolo ♿
Garbetella ♿
Piramide ♿
Circo Massimo
Colosseo
Cavour
Termini
Castro Pretorio ♿
Policlinico ♿
Bologna ♿
Tiburtina ♿
Quintiliani ♿
Monti Tiburtini ♿
Pietralata ♿
S. Maria del Soccorso ♿
Ponte Mammolo ♿
Rebibbia ♿

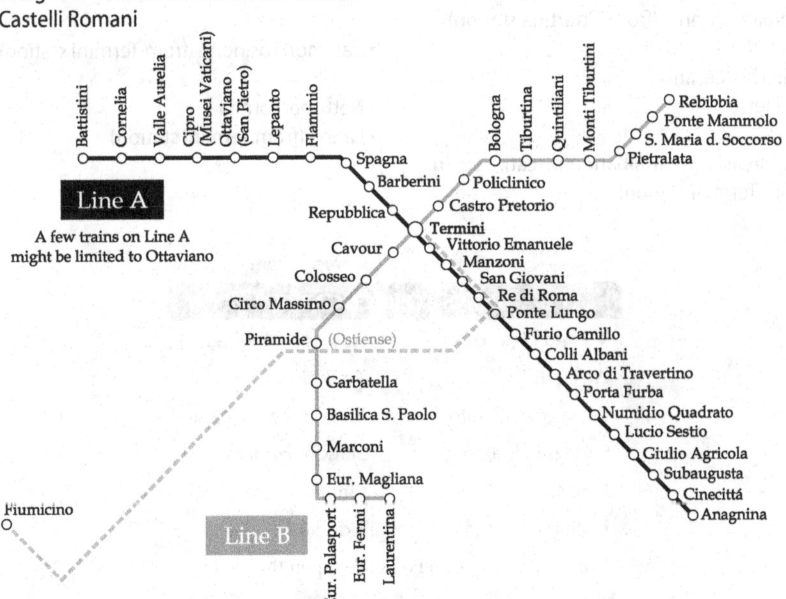

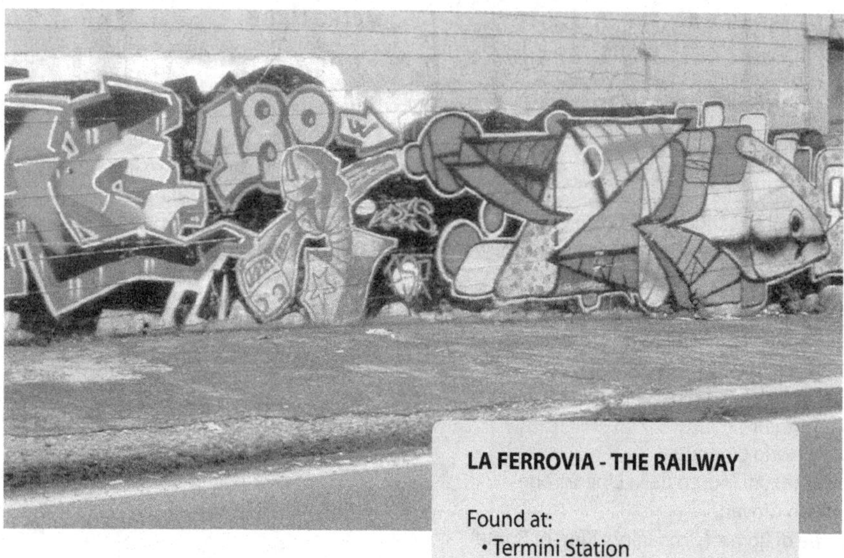

LA FERROVIA - THE RAILWAY

Found at:
- Termini Station
- St. Peter's Station
- Trastevere Station
- Tiburtina Station

TRAINS

FM1 CONNECTIONS:
- Orte/Fara Sabina
- Airport"Leonardo da Vinci"Fiumicino

FM2 CONNECTIONS:
- Tivoli/Guidonia (from Tiburtina station)

FM3 CONNECTIONS:
- Viterbo/Cesano
- S. Pietro

FM4 CONNECTIONS:
- I Castelli Romani-Albano, Frascati, Velletri (from Termini station)

FM5 CONNECTIONS:
- Civitavecchia
- Termini
- Trastevere

FM6 CONNECTIONS:
- Cassino/Frosinone (from Termini station)

FM7 CONNECTIONS:
- Nettuno/Formia
- Latina (from Termini station)

SIGNS TO RECOGNIZE	
Vietato L'Accesso	Access Prohibited
Ai Treni	To Trains
Passaggio Vietato	Entry Way Prohibited
Servizi in Stazione	Station Services
Linea	Line
Uscita	Exit
Pemere Per Aprire La Porta	To Open the Door

ATAC

Tram and buses are beginning to make tickets available directly on the buses with a price increase. Tickets will be marked with the word Scad, with a date and time. This is the time of your ticket's expiration.

Rome to the Castelli Romani towns is 2€

* Fortunately in 2006 they have been making many changes and improvements to the subway system and buses. The newer buses have a LCD display on the ceiling telling you at each stop fermata, so now you can get off knowing you're at the correct location.

BIT	PRICE 1,00€
BIG	PRICE 6,00 €
Three Day Ticket	PRICE 11.00€
CIS Weekly Ticket	PRICE 16,00 €
Monthly Personal Pass	PRICE 30,00 €
Non-Personal Pass	PRICE 46,00 €
Monthly Unemployed Pass	PRICE 16,00 €
Monthly Pass	PRICE 51,00 €
Annual Pass	PRICE 230,00 €

OUT OF ORDER TICKET MACHINES

Although it may appear to be so, the bus and metro system is not free. If you are caught without a validated ticket, the fine is 101€. Transit officials will remove you from the vehicle at the next stop and ask for your Id along with payment. If the stamping machine is out of order or malfunctioning, don't worry it's very common. In this case, simply write down the number of the bus, date, and time traveling on the ticket. If the bus is packed and you are not able to get to the ticket machine, you may use the same procedure.

You're considered to be without a ticket if:

- You have a ticket, but fail to stamp it as required
- You present the ticket or pass with visible signs of alteration
- If you use a ticket or pass with a fare lower than the one required
- If you use the ticket or pass beyond the time of validity
- If you use an ordinary ticket or pass on a special connection requiring a specific ticket

HOW TO GET ON AND OFF BUSES

- ENTER buses from the front or back doors
- EXIT buses from center doors
- Press the orange and black bell located on the wall or pole inside the bus and ring one stop before getting off

Free Public Transport for Senior Citizen Residents of Rome

The ATAC association of Rome has issued a free membership card to senior citizens 70 and over since January 11th, 2008. The senior citizen must be a resident of Rome and may obtain a card by calling 060606 or Atac at 06 57003.

They may travel for free around the city on public buses, trams, subway and on the trains ferrovie Rome-Lido, Rome-Pantano and Rome-Civitacastellana-Viterbo. Note the membership card is not valid for regional trains or the blue buses Cotral.

TICKET MACHINES

The orange ticket machines are almost exist having been replaced with the yellow and black machines.

LUGGAGE

Each passenger may transport free of charge one piece of luggage not exceeding cm 50x30x25cm/19x11x9 inches.

The transport of pets or luggage may be limited even refused at the discretion of company personnel.

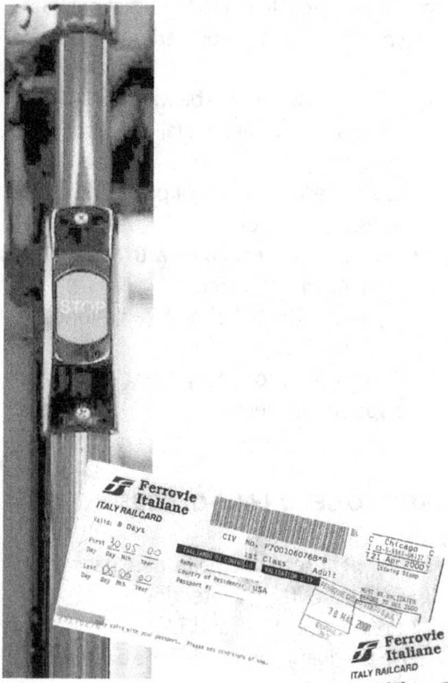

TOURIST LINES AVAILABLE

• Bus 110 the red open-air Londoner bus departs at Termini station from 9am-7:30pm everyday

13€ for a daily pass

Tel 06 46952252

• Archeobus tours all of Appia Antica and departs at Piazza Venezia everyday from 10am-5pm for 7.75€.

Tel 06 46952343

• Bus'n Boat runs every day. Tickets purchased on board. Ticket includes the "Open Bus Tour" and the regular navigation on the Tevere River. You can hop on and off at any of the 9 stops for the whole duration of your ticket.

Start to Finish:

- Via Ludovisi (close to Via Veneto)
- Piazza Barberini (corner of Barberini)
- Piazza Venezia (near Vittoriano museum)
- Via San Gregorio (100m from Coliseum)
- Circo Massimo
- Piazza Monte Savello (100m from Tiber Island)
- Via della Conciliazione (100m from San Pietro Basilica)
- Ponte S. Angelo
- Largo Augusto Imperatore (150m from Via del Corso)
- Via Ludovisi

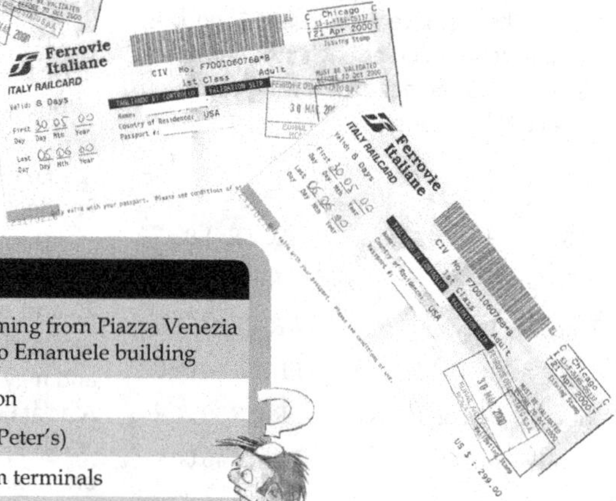

KEYS	
V	Signify buses running by or coming from Piazza Venezia Terminal, next to the Vittoriano Emanuele building
*	Buses starting at Termini Station
SP	Buses that pass San Pietro (St. Peter's)
T	Buses leaving and coming from terminals
**	Buses passing Tiburtina Station
TSV	Buses passing Trastevere

MOST USEFUL BUSLINES & TRAM

40EX Express: Termini (Viale Einaudi)-Via Nazionale-Piazza Venezia- Largo Argentina-Chiesa Nuova-Piazza Pia-Castel S. Angelo and St. Peter's

☺ Watch purse alert bus

64 Termini (Viale Einaudi)-Via Nazionale-Piazza Venezia-Largo Argentina-Corso Vittorio Emanuele-Stazione S. Pietro

Runs the same route as the 40 Express

☺ Watch purse alert bus

H Termini (Viale Einaudi)-Via Nazionale-Piazza Venezia-Largo Argentina-Ponte Garibaldi-Viale Trastevere-Trastevere station

☺ Watch purse alert bus

Tram 8 connects the historical centre with Trastevere. Largo Argentina-Ponte Garibaldi-Piazza G. G. Belli-Piazza Mastai-Piazza Ippolito Nievo-Stazione Trastevere-Monteverde-Casaletto

492 Stazione Tiburtina-San Lorenzo-Termini-Piazza Barberini-Piazza Venezia-Corso Rinascimento-Piazza Cavour-Piazza Risorgimento-Cipro station Vatican Museums

☺ Watch purse alert bus

23 Piazzale Clodio-Piazza Risorgimento Saint Peter's-Ponte Vittorio Emanuele II-Lungotevere-Ponte Garibaldi-Lungotevere-Via Mormorata-Piazzale Ostiense Roman Pyramid-Basilica di S. Paolo

170 Termini-Via Nazionale-Piazza Venezia-Via del Teatro di Marcello-Bocca della Verità-Testaccio-EUR-Piazzale dell'Agricoltura

714 Termini station-Piazza S. Maria Maggiore-Piazza S. Giovanni in Laterano-Viale delle Terme di Caracolla-EUR-Piazzale P. L. Nervi

660 Largo Colli Albani-Via Appia Nuova-Via Appia Antica near the Tomb of Cecilia Metella

7am-8:30pm

BUSES			
*/**	C	V	160
*/V/TSV	H	**	168
SP/V	23	* V/TSV	170
SP/*	40	* V	175
V	44, 46, 62	V	186
*SP/V	64	*/** V	204
* V	70	SP/V	271
**	71	**	490
*	75	*/**/SP/V	492
V/SP	81	V	571
V	84, 85	*	590
*	86	V	628, 63
V	87	*/**	649
*	90, 92	*	714
V	95	V	780, 81
* V	110	TSV	871
V	117, 119	*	910
		V	916
		SP	982

910 Termini-Piazza della Repubblica-Via Piemonte-Via Pinciana Villa Borghese-Piazza Euclide-Palazzetto dello Sport-Piazza Mancini

590 P. di Spagna-P. Barberini-Termini station-P. San Giovanni-Via Tuscolana- P. Cinecittà

6am-10:30pm

Runs the same route as Metro line A

Every 90 minutes

MA2 runs from Termini station and the bus stop is located close to the road on the slim sidewalk facing the main road. This bus stops at Anagnina station. From here you can take a blue Cotral bus from platforms 1-6 for the Castelli Romani.

BLUE BUSES - COTRAL

Cooperativa Trasporti Lazio/Lazio Region Transport

The blue buses travel to all points in the region of Lazio.

Travelling within the Castelli Romani towns tickets are 1-2€.

URBAN BUSLINES

The orange buses connect with many different zones and the express lines or directly to the city's centre.

SPECIAL BUSES

C BUS

Termini station-Piazzale Verano-Tiburtina station-V. Campi Sportivi-P. Mancini-Cemetary Flaminio

7am-5:50pm

H BUS

Termini station-Piazza Venezia-Piazza Sonino Trastevere-Trastevere station-San Camillo Hospital-Cataletto-Via Silvestri

9am-8pm

Watch purse alert bus

J BUS

Stops at Piazza San Silvestro. This one travels to most popular locations, is air conditioned, and not so crowded.

V BUS

Verano Cemetery runs on Saturday and Sunday.

06 BUS

To Ostia beach located on Via Cristoforo Colombo and Piazza del Cinghiale wild boar square.

ELECTRIC BUSES

Note: they do not run on Italian Holidays

These are the tiny buses that are practically noiseless. In order to minimize pollution in and around the tiny alleyways of old historic Rome, the city has provided several electric bus lines. They do not run on Sundays

116 Via Veneto-Piazza Barberini-Via Tritone-Piazza di Spagna-Corso Rinascimento Piazza Navona-Campo de' Fiori-Piazza Farnese-Via Monserrato-Via Giulia-Pantheon-Piazza Colonna

This bus makes a loop inside the Villa Borghese stopping near the Galleria Borghese before making its final stop at the top of Via Veneto. 8am-1:30pm

116T Via Nazionale-Piazza della Repubblica-Pincio Hill-Piazza Barberini-Piazza Navona-Pantheon-Granicolo Hill

117 Piazza S. Giovanni in Laterano-Piazza del Colosseo-Via dei Serpenti-Largo Tritone-Piazza di Spagna-Piazza del Popolo-Via del Corso-Piazza Venezia-Piazza del Colosseo-Via Labicana- Piazza S. Giovanni in Laterano 8am-9pm

118 P. le Ostiense-Viale Aventino-Terme di Caracalla-Porta S. Sebastiano-Via Appia Antica-Via Appia Pignatelli

119 Piazza del Popolo-Via del Corso-Largo Goldoni-Piazza Venezia-Via del Tritone-Piazza Barberini-Piazza di Spagna-Via del Babuino-Piazza del Popolo

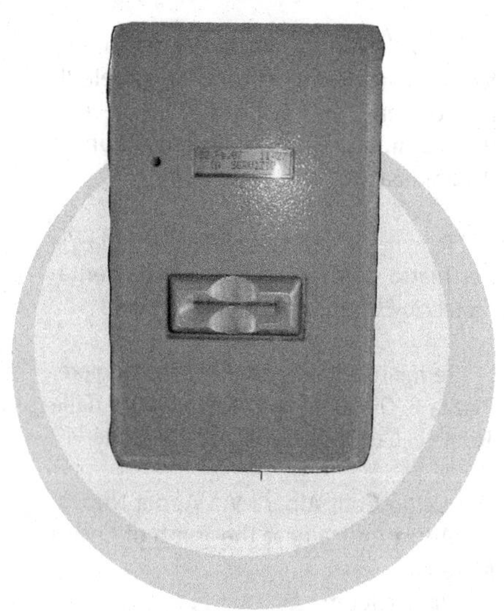

EXPRESS LINES

(Extra-long buses)

These bus lines cover more distance in a shorter amount time and make fewer stops.

Express buses 30 40 60 80 90 150

TRAMS (GROUND TRAINS) 2 3 5 8 14 19		
2	3	5
Piazziale Flaminio	Trastevere Station	Termini Station (Via Amendola)
Via Flaminia	Viale Trastevere	Via Gioberti
Viale Tiziano	Via Mamorata	Pza Vittorio
Viale Pinturicchio	P. le Ostiense	Via Principe Eugenio
Piazza A Mancini	Porta San Paolo	Porta Maggiore
	Via Aventino	Via Prenestina
	Colosseo	Centocelle
	Viale Manzoni	
	Porta San Giovanni V	
	Santa Croce in Gerusalemme	
	San Lorenzo	
	Verano	
	Viale R Margherita	
	Belle Arti	
	Valle Giulia	
8	14	19
Largo Torre Argentina	Via Amendola (Termini Zone)	Piazza Risorgimento (St. Peter's)
Via Arenula	Via Gioberti	Via Ottaviano
Piazza Soninno (Trastevere)	Pz Vittorio Emanuele	Viale D Milizie
Viale Trastevere	Porta Maggiore	Via Flaminia
Trastevere Station	Via Prenestina	Viale Belle Arti
Hospital San Camillo	Togliatti	P. le d Verano (Verano Cemetary)
Porta San Giovanni di Dio		San Lorenzo
Viale Colli Portuense		Porta Maggiore
Casaletto		Via Prenestina
		Piazza dei Gerani

Night lines

Hours 12 mid-5:30am

MOST USEFUL LINES

- 29N-Coliseum and San Pietro
- 40N-Termini station
- 55N-Termini station
- 78N-Termini and Piazza Venezia

BUS TABLE

These are some of the most popular stops.

☺ Be aware that timetables may flucuate

99N runs every 30 minutes
Via Trionfale
Viale Medaglie D'oro
Via delle Milizie
Piazza Cavour
Via del Corso
Piazza Colonna
Piazza Venezia
Timetable from Piazza Venezia:
12:04, 12:34, 1:04, 1:34, 2:04, 2:34
Every 30 minutes until 5:04am

98N runs every and 10 minutes
Via Gregorio VII
Ponte Vittorio Emmanuele II
Corso Vittorio Emmanuele II
Largo Torre Argentina
Piazza Venezia
Timetable from Piazza Venezia:
12:52, 2:02, 3:12, 4:27 last bus

96N runs every 1h and 10 minutes
Via Portuense
Circ. Gianicolense Trastevere
Viale Trastevere
Trastevere station
Piazza Sonnino Trastevere
Via Arenula Teatro Marcello
Largo Torre Argentina
Piazza Venezia
Timetable from Piazza Venezia:
12:55, 2:05, 3:15, 4:25 last bus

91N runs every 30 minutes
Via Ostiense
Piramide Club's
Porta San Paolo
V. Teatro Marcello near the Mouth of Truth
Piazza Venezia
Via Nazionale
Piazza della Repubblica
Termini station
Timetable from Termini station:
12; 30, 1pm, 1:30, 2pm and every 30 minutes until 5:15

78N runs every 30 minutes
Via Flaminia
Piazza Cavour
Corso Rinascimento Piazza Navona
Piazza Venezia
Via Nazionale
P. Repubblica
Termini station
Timetable from Termini station:
12:15, 12:30, 1pm, 1:30, 2pm and every 30 minutes until 5am

72N runs every 50 minutes
Via della Magliana
Viale Trastevere
Trastevere station
Piazza Venezia
Timetable from Piazza Venezia:
12:55, 1:45, 2:35, 3:25, 4:15, 5:05 last bus

60N runs every 20 minutes
Via Nomentana
Piazza Fiume
Porta Pia
Via V. Veneto
Piazza Barberini
Via del Tritone
Via del Corso
Piazza San Silvestro
Piazza Venezia
Timetable from Piazza Venezia:
12:15, 12:35, 12:55, 1:15, 1:35, 1:55, 2:15 every 20 minutes until 5:15

55N runs every 30 minutes
Piazzale Flaminio
Villa Borghese
Via V. Veneto
Via/Piazza Barberini
Termini station
Via Farini
Piazza Vittorio Emanuele
Piazza Porta San Giovanni
Appia Nuova
Cinecitta' film-making studio
Anagnina station
Timetable from Termini station:
12:55, 1:25, 1:55, 2:25, 3:25, 3:55
Every 30 minutes until 5:25am

50N runs every 45 minutes
Termini station
Via Amendola
Porta Maggiore
Via Casilina
Timetable:
12:30, 1:15, 2pm, 2:45, 3:30, 4:15, 5am

45N runs every 30 minutes until 5am
Via Torrevecchia
Via Aurelia
Corso Vittorio Emmanuele II
Largo Torre Argentina
Via del Corso
Via del Tritone
Piazza Barberini
Piazza della Repubblica
Termini station
Timetable from Termini station: 12mid, 12:30, 1pm, 1:30

44N runs every hour
Via Dandolo
Viale Trastevere
Piazza Venezia
Timetable from Piazza Venezia: 12:35, 1:35, 2:35, 3:35, 4:35 last bus

40N runs every 30 minutes
Line 40n follows line B metro
V. C. Colombo
Via Ostiense Piramide
Via Cavour
Termini station
Via Ravenna Piazza Bologna
Tiburtina station
Via Tiburtina
San Paolo Basilico
Timetable from Termini station:
12:30, 1pm, 1:30, 2pm
Every 30 minutes until 5am

29N runs every 30 minutes
Piazzale Ostiense
Piazza Risorgimento
Via Ottaviano
Via Belle Arti
Via Regina Margherita
Scalo San Lorenzo
Porta Maggiore
Porta S. Giovanni
Coliseum
Timetable from Piazza Risorgimento:
12:35, 1:05, 1:35, 2:05, 2:35, 3:05
Every 30 minutes until 5:05am

25N runs every 45 minutes
Via Cassia
Corso Francia
Via Flaminia
Via del Corso
Piazza Venezia
Timetable from Piazza Venezia:
12:15, 1am, 1:45, And 2:30, And 3:15, 4am, 4:45 last bus

12N runs every 30 minutes
Via Prenestina
P. Porta Maggiore
Piazza Vittorio Emanuele II
Via Gioberti
Termini station
Timetable from Termini station:
12:30, 1pm, 1:30, 2pm, 2:30
Every 30 minutes until 5am

6N runs every 30 minutes
Piazza Verbano Near Villa Alda
Piazza Bologna
Vl. del Policlinico Hospital
Piazzale Porta Pia
Via XX Settembre
Termini station
Timetable from Termini station:
12:30, 1pm, 1:30, 2pm
Every 30 minutes until 5am

MOST USEFUL LINES
- 29N: Coliseum and San Pietro
- 40N: Termini Station
- 55N: Termini Station
- 78N: Termini and Piazza Venezia

The main bus and train terminals

ZONE 2: ESQUILINO

STAZIONE TERMINI - TERMINI STATION

All transportation to and from Termini:

Bus C H 16 36 38 40 64 75 84 86 90 92 105 170 175 204 217 310 360 590 649 714 910

Metro lines A and B Trams 5 14

Trains 4 5 6 7

Termini station is the main and most familiar bus and train station in Rome. Two streets line Termini station,

on the west side Via G. Giolitti and along the east Via Marsala. Along the front entrance outside is Piazza del Cinquecento where the bus terminal is located. Termini and Tiburtina both take you to the airport.

REBIBBIA STATION

Bus 163 311 343 447 449
Metro line B Rebibba

ZONE H: TIBURTINA

TIBURTINA STATION

Piazzale della Stazione Tiburtina
Buses C 71 111 163 168 204 211 309 409 443 448 490 492 495 545 649
Metro line B Tiburtina FS
Trains FM1-2 Air terminal

ZONE 3: TRASTEVERE

TRASTEVERE STATION

Piazza Flavio Biondo
Bus 170 228 719 766 773 774 780 781 786 871
Tram 3 8 Train FM1-5

ZONE 5: PRATI

SAN PIETRO STATION

Bus 23 40EX 62 64
Metro Line A Ottaviano/San Pietro
Train FM3
Tram 19

USEFUL PHRASES		
Entrata	Entrance	Ain trah tah
Biglietto	Ticket	Bee lee yet toe
Uscita	Exit	Ooh she tah
Fermata	Bus stop	Fair mah tah
Capolinea	Bus Terminal	Cah poe lean yah
Machinetta	Ticket machine	Mah key ah net tah
Fermata Prenotata	Requested Stop	Fair mah tah Prey no tah tah
Dovè scendo per?	Where do I get off?	Doe vay shen doe pear
Scendi?	Are you getting off?	Shen-dee
Si, scendo	Yes, I'm getting off	Sea, shen-doe
Alla prossima	At the next stop	Ahl-lah pro-sea-mah

Rentals and driving

Getting in the car with an Italian behind the wheel is nerve-wrecking. Hands lift off to exclaim feelings of enthusiasm and excitement rather then steadying the car's direction. As my cheeks turn red I want to tell them, but the words don't come out, so I usually pray instead. Momentarily they are in a world of their own, an emotional world which makes them all who they are. Expressive little creatures we once coasted over the road almost ending up in the woods- car and all.

Driving horror stories are tall in Rome. Real streets once on maps are lost, closed up or transformed into inert objects. Bridges that say they are bridges turn into alleyways. Almost every street is a one way, so you must waste many hours trying to get somewhere. It's not so uncommon to find Romans themselves after twenty years, unfamiliar with this endless maze of Roman streets. As for the rules, there are no rules-only instincts. In the centre during the day, cars need a special pass to enter and on some days only cars with even or odd license targets will be permitted for the control of pollution.

A bit of truth some forty years ago:

National Geographic of 1969

Living through the traffic crisis in other cities such as Paris or New York will never surpass that of Rome's during rush hour. You will become familiar with words such as Cretino! Idiota! Scemo! Their hands ever ready on horns. Italian drivers are artists, more of abstractionists. Rome's clogged streets yield me to plug my ears to shut out the obscene racket and they collectively invite me to gag on exhaust fumes.

I surmise the only solution would be to wait until a colossal traffic jam, then bury the whole mess in wet concrete and let it harden. Then Rome could start all over again.

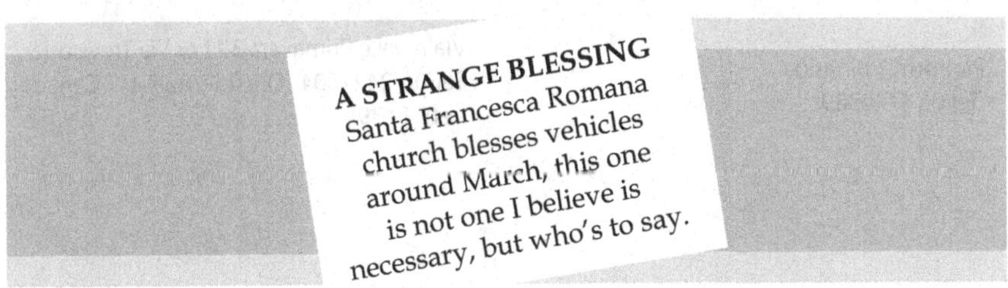

A STRANGE BLESSING
Santa Francesca Romana
church blesses vehicles
around March, this one
is not one I believe is
necessary, but who's to say.

Rental cars

ZONE 1: HISTORICAL CENTER

RENT-A-CAR

Via del Basilico 60

ZONE 2: ESQUILINO

HAPPY RENT

9am-7pm
Open 7 days a week
Via Farini 3
Tel 06 4818185
Fiat, Vespa, Alfa Romeo, Piaggio, BMW, Smart
Mini Van
Scooter price range 33-400€
10 hrs to one week
Motorcycle price range-70-844€
10 hrs to one week
Car price range-50-900€
10 hrs to one week
www.happyrent.com

TRENO E SCOOTER RENT

Piazza dei Cinquecento Rome's central railway station
Tel/Fax 06 48905823
9am-7:30pm Monday-Sunday
Located behind the taxi stand by Termini Station, go down the ramp.
Bicycle rents-per day 10€ Weekends 20€ One month 50€
Scooter price range-one day 37-80€
www.trenoescooter.com

ROMA-TERMINI STATION

Platform 1 Binario
Tel 06 4740389

Hertz

FIUMICINO

Via Dell'Aeroporto
Tel 06 65010256

ROMA CIAMPINO AIRPORT

Tel 06 79340616

ZONE 1: HISTORICAL CENTER

Via Giolitti Giovanni 34
Tel 06 4740389
Via Sardegna 35
Tel 06 3216886

ZONE 13: AURELIA

Via Gregorio Vii 207
Tel 06 39378807

ZONE 8: OSTIENSE

Via Pellegrino Matteucci 35a
Tel 06 5782420

ZONE J: SALARIA

Via Sacchetti Franco 15e
Tel 06 82097161

ZONE 7: PARIOLI

Viale Bruno Buozzi 103
Tel 06 3218095

ZONE H: TIBURTINA

Via del Casale Cavallari
Tel 06 41229938

Limousine services

ZONE G: PRENESTINO

MORIGGI LIMOUSINE SERVICE

Viale delle Primavera 323 or Via Treviso 15
Tel 06 2427504 (Outside Italy-US-Canada +011+39)

DRIVING INFO

AGE REQUIREMENT - for all car rentals is 18 years old. You also will need a license valid for at least one year.
YOUR LICENSE - a foreign license up to 6 months

TOWED CARS

For roadside assistance dial 115

TOW TRUCK ASSISTANCE/ CARROATTREZZI

Toll free 803116
Ask for an estimate over the phone
Service within Rome city limits (within the GRA Loop)
Tower will transport you to any address. If you don't have an address available they will transport the car to the city parking lot where you'll pay a fee of 5€ a day
Call the city hall main line to find your car 06 67691.
Ask to which location they transported your vehicle to
If they do not have the information handy, wait a while and try back again later.

HIGHWAY INFO

GRA Grande Raccordo Anullare - the highway loop around Rome
Legal Speed Limit- 130km/81.25 mph

TOLL BOOTHS

Yellow line lanes are for special passes
Blue line lanes pay by debit card or credit card (Diner's Club, MasterCard, Amex, and Visa)
No line lanes-pay by cash only,
where people wait forever.

EUROPA BY CAR - ROMA TO: (km/miles)

City	km	miles	City	km	miles
Amsterdam	1750	1094	Bologna	380	238
Barcelona	1410	881	Catania	826	516
Berlin	1560	975	Como	638	399
Bruxelles	1580	988	Florence	277	173
Budapest	1250	781	Genova	529	331
Dusseldorf	1610	1006	Milano	574	359
Frankfort	1410	881	Napoli	217	136
London	1920	1200	Padova	506	316
Madrid	2040	1275	Palermo	988	618
Marseille	930	581	Peruggia	176	110
Munchen	960	600	Siena	224	140
Paris	1500	938	Torino	715	447
Prague	1360	850	Trento	592	370
Warsaw	1870	1169	Trieste	686	429
Zurich	940	588	Venice	539	337

MPH	KM/H
10	16
20	32
30	48
40	64
50	80
60	96
70	112
80	128
90	144
100	160
110	176
120	188

Parking garages

You might need to be familiar with the parking rules in a city like Rome. They is an overabundance of them. They may be located in the strangest places as up on sidewalks, or horizontally in front of another car parked vertically. Parking spaces are defined as anywhere there seems to be a big enough space, yet every spot seems to be big enough. Everything seems legal, but is probably illegal.

Some cars park with half their rear-end on a curb with the other half out in the street blundering the oncoming traffic. Others squeeze into spots up on islands located in the middle of streets. There are blue, pink and yellow lines laid out all with a specific instruction, but they are often neglected and lose their colour only to become invisible and if you don't see the lines the Roman policeman will remind you of that invisible blue line that you should have seen that means no-parking.

Whenever someone wrongs you on the street, the Roman expression for it is"Cornuto!"or"C'hai le Cornata"meaning; your wife/husband is cheating on you.

ZONE 1: HISTORICAL CENTER

- Foro Traiano 60 spaces (Piazza Venezia)
- Via dei Fori Imperiali 30 spaces (Piazza Venezia)
- Piazza Di Monte Citorio 60 spaces (Via del Corso, Piazza Colonna)
- Piazza del Parlamento 60 spaces (Via del Corso)
- Piazza del Popolo 114 spaces (Popolo)
- Via Ludovisi 80 spaces (Barberini)
- Via Lombardia 60 spaces (Via Veneto)
- Via Barberini 20 spaces (Piazza Barberini)
- Largo di Susanna 37 spaces (Piazza Barberini)
- Piazza di S. Bernardo 50 spaces (Repubblica)
- Via Vittorio Emanuele Orlando 50 spaces (Repubblica)
- Via del S. Gregorio 70 spaces (Coliseum)
- Via dei Normanni 35 spaces (Coliseum)

USEFUL WORDS	
Acosta	Pull over
Da finestrino	Littering from a car
Casello autostradale	Toll Booth

ZONE 2: ESQUILINO

- Via Mazzarino 22 spaces (Santa Maria Maggiore)
- Piazza dell'Esquilino 180 spaces (Termini)
- Piazza dei Cinquecento 100 spaces (Termini)
- Via Giolitti Termini Station 4 Levels

ZONE 5: PRATI

PIAZZA CAVOUR
56 spaces (Castel Sant'Angelo)

CIPRO
Via Angelo Emo
277 spaces
Metro line A Cipro

SAN PIETRO STATION
Via Stazione San Pietro
141 spaces

ZONE 6: FLAMINIO

LA CELSA
Via Flaminia
120 spaces

LABARO
Via Flaminia
204 spaces

ZONE 8: OSTIENSE
Via Ostiense
153 spaces

OTHER PARKING GARAGES

ZONE B: CASSIA
La Storta
Via della Storta
478 spaces

ZONE I: NOMENTANO
Via Val D' Aosta
177 spaces

GAS TIPS

- There is no Super gas
- There is no Regular gas
- There aren't many gas stations in the center of Rome
- There is GPL, a transparent gas used in BMWs and other cars with the right apparatus
- The closest gas station to the center is on Viale Castro Pretorio behind Termini train station. Go down Via Marsala and make a U-turn at the end (baring left). It's parallel with Via Marsala

PROHIBITED ZONES

- Cars allowed in center of Rome only with special permit - called Zona Traffico Limitato (Zones that are limited to traffic) "ZTL" patrolled Monday-Friday 6am-6pm
- After 6pm all cars permitted.
- San Lorenzo Zone 10 Friday-Sunday night from 8pm-6am it's prohibited to enter the area by car.
- Gas stations - most are closed on Sundays or at 7:30pm Monday-Friday. Some self-services are open all night and you may pay by euro or credit card.

PARKING LINES

- Blue line parking is paid parking on the street
- Excludes: motorcycles, police, and those with permission stickers
- Pink line parking are spaces for pregnant women
- Yellow lines are free parking spaces

PETROL COMPANIES

- American-Shell
- Italian-IP
- Italian-AGIP
- Kuwait-Q8
- European-Esso

USEFUL WORDS		
Uscita	Exit	oo she tah
Gasolio	Diesel	gah so lee oh
Benzinaio	Gas Station	ben zee nai oh
Benzina	Gas	ben zee nah
Senza Piombo	Unleaded	sense ah pea ome boe
Piombo	Leaded	pea ome boe
Autostrada	Highway	ah oo toe strah dah
Corsia	Lane	core see ah
Parcheggio	Parking Garage/Lot	park edge oh
Gas (GPL)	Gas (vapor)	

PLACES OF INTEREST	BUSES	NIGHT BUSES	LANDMARKS
Campidoglio	H 30EX 64 70 84 75 170		Steep staircase behind the Vittoriano monument
Colosseo/Coliseum	60EX 75 85 110 117 175 186 271 571		
Pantheon	30EX 40EX 64 70	25N 60N 98N	
Fori Romani/Roman Forum	40EX 60EX 70 75 84 85 87 175		
Villa Borghese	95 110 217 910	55N	
Musei Vaticani/Vatican Museums	64		
San Pietro/St. Peter's	Bus 23 64 81 110 271 492 Tram 19	29N	
Piazza di Spagna/Spanish steps	590 116	55N 60N	French steps
Gianicolo	75 115		
Via del Corso	119 160 492		Vittoriano monument on one end, and Piazza del Popolo on the other
Piramide	75 271	91N 40N	Roman-Egyptian pyramid
Piazza Navona	30EX 40EX 64 70 87 110 116 492 571 628	45N 55N 78N 98N	Piazza San Pantaleo
Testaccio	170 175	91N	
Villa Torlonia	62		
Piazza Venezia	60EX 62 64 70 81 84 87 110 186 571	45N 78N	Vittoriano
Stazione Tiburtina/Tiburtina Station	70 168 204 492	40N	
Barberini/Via Veneto	52 53 62 80EX 95 110 116 175 204 492 590	45N 55N	Hard Rock Cafè
Via Nazionale	40EX 60EX 64 70 110 117 170	78N 91N	
Trastevere	H 170 780 Tram 3 8		Across the Garibaldi bridge
Largo Torre Argentina	30EX 40EX 63 64 81 110 492 571	45N 78N	Ruins in the middle with the Cat Sanctuary
Basilica San Paolo/St. Paul's Basilica	271 Metro line B Basilica S. Paolo		
Fontana di Trevi/Trevi Fountain	175	45N 60N	The bus stop across from Burger King on your right on *Largo Tritone*
Campo de' Fiori	30EX 40EX 64 70 116 116T 571	98N	Statue of cloaked Bruno Giordano in the middle of the square
Piazza del Popolo	110 117 119		Twin churches
Lido di Ostia Beach	Termini-metro line B Piramide Railway for Ostia Lido centro		
Capannelle	FM4 FM6 Termini trains	66N	
Villa Doria Pamphili	710		
Terme di Caracalla/Baths of Caracalla	118 160 628 714		
Castel Sant'Angelo	64 110 492		The castle and the bridge of
San Giovanni in Laterano/St. John in Latern	81 117 186 571 590 650 714	55N	
Bocca della Verità/Mouth of Truth	95 110 715		
Fori Imperiali/Imperial Forums	110 571		The Trojan column
Quirinale	110		
Circo Massimo/Circus Maximus	110 175 628		Ancient empty racetrack, an oval track for running
Cinecittà	590 650		Statue of man kneeling with torch
Stazione Termini/Termini station	C H 16 36 40EX 64 75 84 86 90EX 92 105 110 170 175 204 217 310 360 590 649 714 910	6N 12N 45N 50N 78N 91N	McDonald's is across from the entrance
Via Prenestina	Tram 5 14 19 Bus 81 105 412 810	12N	

Termini Station

Buses

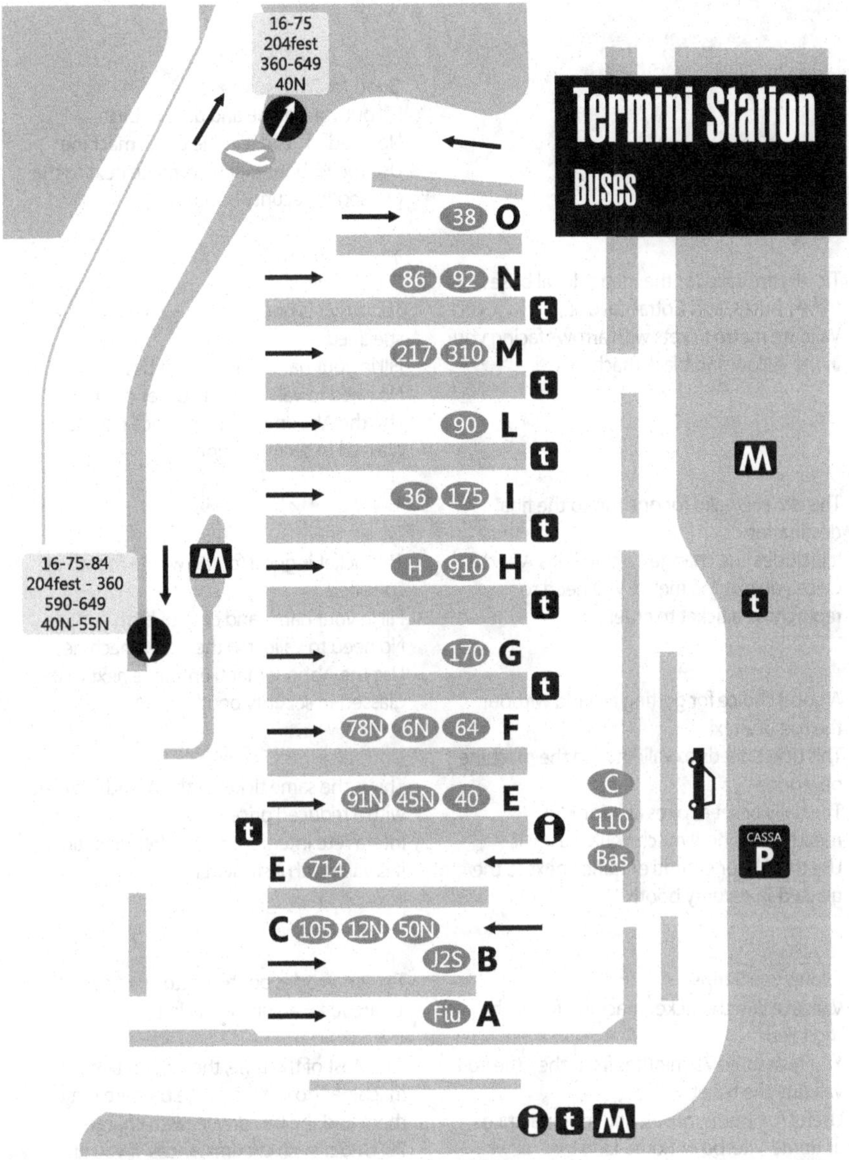

16-75
204fest
360-649
40N

38 O

86 92 N

217 310 M

90 L

36 175 I

H 910 H

16-75-84
204fest - 360
590-649
40N-55N

170 G

78N 6N 64 F

91N 45N 40 E

C
110
Bas

CASSA
P

E 714

C 105 12N 50N

J2S B

Fiu A

G Bus/Taxi Lane/Corsia

64 Capolinea Bus/Bus Terminal

12N Capolinea Bus Notturno/After Hours

110 Tourist Bus

Bas Lines to Basilicas

Fiu Bus Service for Fiuggi

Night Bus Service to Fiuminico FCO

J2S Terminal for bus 125

Bus Stop

M Metro-Subway-Underground-Tube

Taxi

Information

t Ticket/Biglietto

CASSA P Parking/Parcheggio

Tickets are valid for the metro, local buses, trolley buses, and Cotral coaches
Validate metro tickets with arrows facing you in the yellow and black machines

BIT Ticket-Intergrated Tourist ticket-11€

Metro-Bus Ticket 1€
This ticket is valid for one trip to the final destination
It includes line changes within lines A and B
Once you exit the metro, you need to repurchase a ticket to enter

Daily Ticket 4€
A good choice for getting around without the use of a taxi
This ticket needs to validated in the machine only once
The daily ticket expires at midnight regardless of how much you've used it
Use the Abbonementi entrance next to the glassed-in security booth

5 Bit MultiBit Ticket
Allows you 5 trips
Validate it in the ticket machine for each trip taken
You're assured 75 minutes from the time you validate the ticket
Useful for: trams, buses, and regional trains as Rome-Viterbo or Rome-Lido
You may save this ticket for another day if the five trip limit wasn't reached

Weekly Ticket 16€
Good for 7 days
Fill out your name and date of birth
No need to valid it in the ticket machine
Use the Abbonementi entrance next to the glassed-in security booth

Monthly Ticket/Ordinary Personal Pass for Rome Center 25-30€
This ticket is good for the whole month as specified
Fill in your name and date of birth
No need to valid it in the ticket machine
Use the Abbonementi entrance next to the glassed-in security booth

Monthly Ticket for Castelli Romani and Rome Center 50€
This ticket is good for the whole month as specified
Fill in your name and date of birth
No need to valid it in the ticket machine
Use the Abbonementi entrance next to the glassed-in security booth

Monthly Student Ticket 20-25€
This is the same ticket as the monthly ticket, with a reduced price
Intera rete integrato ridotto/reduced ticket
It is valid with a student ID

Yearly Pass 230€

Tip: 2 barcodes on the bottom = a used ticket
1 barcode = an unused ticket

Tip: Most of the time, the station ticket machines do not work, the bars are out of them and the bus drivers with charge you 7€. Under such circumstances, if you are desperate just take the bus.

Metro-Bus stations with customer service and ticket booths:

METRO A:
Anagnina
Termini
Lepanto
Ottaviano-San Pietro
Battastini
Flaminio

METRO B:
EUR Fermi
EUR Palasport
EUR-Magliana
Ponte Mammolo
Laurentina
Piramide

J- Urban Bus Ticket- 1-2€
This is an express bus that is usually less crowded that travels to the most common places. The bus is striped blue instead of orange and destinations flash across the front of the bus.

Regional Tickets/Tariffa Regionale Lazio
Depending where you go, the prices will vary. Purchase them in Tabacchi shops, asking for"a ticket to say Latina', and they will determine the correct one. Distances will be written inkm on the ticket. Use the platform trains inside Termini station and be very careful to read the schedules or ask at information booths for train verification.

Cotral Tickets/Rome Suburbs Tickets Blue Buses 1-1. 50€
These buses travel outside the immediate center of the city and to the Castelli Romani area.

TIPS your destination may or may not be labeled on the train schedule. It may note a train to 'Latina' yet the name of your destination may not be specified, this is because it's merely a stop along the way.

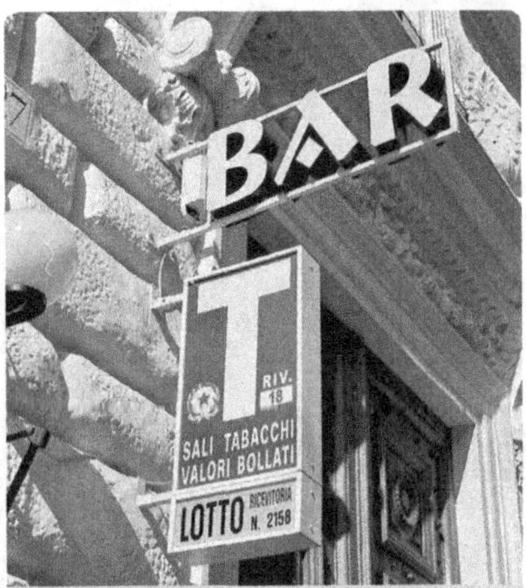

Tabacchi Shops - usually close at 8pm, though the one in Termini station is open until 11pm
Newsstands - are located inside train stations or outside on the streets. The one on the corner of Via Giolitti and Via Gioberti is open 24 hours across from Termini station

In this situation, you need to watch for signposts outside or ask the man in charge where to get off.

TRAIN AND BUS TICKETS
It may be comfortable to buy all your tickets in the American Express offices where there are English speakers in Piazza di Spagna.

*Automatic ticket machines are also available at Termini Station but do not give change for large bills
*The same ticket is valid for buses, metro-tube-subway, and trams alike except for J buses

TOURIST BUS INFORMATION
Tel 06 571 18666/Fax 06 571 18676
turistici@atac. roma.it

Hotel Book

Most of us are used to the modern-day glass speed boxes. These elevators fly you anywhere in a blink-a good way to travel if you don't suffer from vertigo. Roman elevators do not.
Most of them are ancient and make you weary, some never worked at all.

But Rome elevators have similar functions and here we hope to conquest the complexity of their operations.

Sometimes they have outside doors and inside doors.
The inside doors are usually made up of two smaller doors. First open the outside door by hand, then open the inside doors. Getting in-close the outside door, Next close the inside doors and voilà! And proceed. Some close by themselves if you're lucky.

Important: When you step out, don't forget to close the inside doors before you exit, then the outside door. If it doesn't close itself it will remain open and will not work for anyone waiting on other floors.

Another important point to consider, elevator dimensions...
they are similar to matchboxes, try getting in them and turning around-you may not be able to. If you have a family and a few backpacks or large luggage, prepare to load and reload several times-until all of your luggage and family are in one place. You now may be thinking about reserving a room on the ground floor or even taking the stairs and I don't blame you.

ZONE 1: HISTORICAL CENTER

Bettoja Atlantico
Via Cavour 23
Tel 06 485951

Pensione Arenula
In the Jewish Ghetto, pensione Arenula is inexpensive and lovely. It is surrounded by all the wonderful Jewish bakeries and restaurants and near Trastevere, the Tevere River and Largo Torre Argentina.
Via Santa Maria de' Calderari 47
Tel 06 687 9454
Fax 06 689 6188
Metro line B Colosseo
Bus 64 70
www.hotelarenula.com

The BeeHive
Via Marghera 8
Tel. 06 447 04553
Vegetarian Cuisine-Organic-Yoga-meditation, Shiatsu, Swedish massage, aromatherapy
Bathrooms are stocked with homemade soaps, shampoo's and gels.
info@the-beehive.com

Rinascimento
Via del Pellegrino 122
Tel 06 687 4813
Campo de' Fiori area

Oxford
Via Boncompagni 89
Tel. 06 428 28952
Metro line A Barberini
Near Villa Borghese, P. di Spagna and Via Veneto
info@hoteloxford.com
www.hoteloxford.it

Domus Aurea
Via Volturno 30-34
Tel 06 478 26012

Albergo del Sole
Piazza della Rotonda 63 (Pantheon)
Tel 06 678 0441
Fax 06 699 40689
www.hotelsolealpantheon.com

Quirinale
Via Nazionale 7
Tel 06 4707
Fax 06 4820099
Metro line A Repubblica
info@hotelquirinale.it
www.hotelquirinalerome.com

Savoy
Via Ludovisi 15
Tel 06 421 551
Fax 06 421 55555
Metro line A Barberini
info@savoy.it
www.savoy.it

Raphael
Largo Febo 2
Tel 06 682 831
Fax 06 687 8993
Bus 70 81 87
Piazza Navona area
www.raphaelhotel.com

Regina-Carlton
Via V. Veneto 72
Tel 06 476 851
Metro line A Barberini

Della Nazioni
Via Poli 7
Tel 06 679 2441
Trevi Fountain Area
www.nycerome.com

Memphis
Via degli Avignonesi 36
Tel 06 485 849
Fax 06 482 86290
Metro line A Barberini
www.hotelmemphisrome.com

La Residenza
Via Emilia 22-24
Tel 06 488 0789
Fax 06 485 721
Metro line A Barberini

Imperiale
Via V. Veneto 24
Tel 06 482 6351
Metro line A Barberini

Nazionale Monte Citorio Hotel
P. Monte Citorio 131
Tel 06 695 001
Via del Corso Area

Jolly-Vittorio Veneto
Corso Italia 1
Tel 06 8495
Fax 06 8841104
Metro line A Barberini
roma_vittorioveneto@jollyhotels.it
www.jollyhotels.it

Bernini-Bristol
Piazza Barberini 23
Tel 06 488 3051
Metro line A Barberini

Grand Hotel Plaza
Via del Corso 126
Tel 06 699 21111
Fax 06 699 41575
Metro line A Spagna
www.grandhotelplaza.com

Majestic
Via V. Veneto 50
Tel 06 486 841
Metro line A Barberini

Eden
Via Ludovisi 49
Tel 06 478 121
800 225 5843 (in USA)
Fax 06 482 1584
Metro line A Barberini

Excelsior
Via V. Veneto 125
Tel 06 470 81
Metro line A Barberini

Grand Hotel
Via V. E. Orlando 3
Tel 06 47091
Metro line A Repubblica

Hassler
P. Trinità de' Monti
Tel 06 699340
800 223 6800 (in USA)
Fax 06 678 9991
Metro line A Spagna
www.hotelhasslerroma.com

Hotel Minerve
Piazza della Minerva 69
06 695201
www.grandhoteldelaminerve.it

De le Ville
Via Sistina 67-69
Tel 06 67331
Fax 06 678 4213
800 327 0200 (in US and Canada)
Metro line A Spagna or Barberini
www.interconti.com

GoldenTulipMecenatePalace
Via Carlo Alberto 3
Tel 06 44702024
Fax 06 4461354
Near Santa Maria Maggiore church
A walk from Termini station
Metro Line A or B Termini
Email: info@mecenatepalace.com
www.mecenatepalace.com

ZONE 2: ESQUILINO

Atlantico
Via Cavour 23
06 485 951
Line A or B Termini

Corot
Via Marghera 15-17
Tel 06 447 00900
Fax 06 447 00905
Metro Line A or B Termini
www.hotelcorot.it

Archimede
Via dei Mille 19
Tel 06 445 4600

Amalfi
Via Merulana 278
Tel 06 474 4313
Metro Line A or B Termini

Accademia
Piazza Accademia di S. Luca 74-75
Tel 06 699 22607
Metro line A Spagna

Palatino
Via Cavour 213
Tel 06 481 4927
Metro Line A or B Termini

Marriott Rome Flora
Via V. Veneto 191
Tel 06 489 929
Fax 39 06 4820359
Metro line A Barberini
info@grandhotelflora.net

Ariston
Via FilippoTurati 16
Tel 06 446 5399
Fax 06 446 5396
Metro Line A or B Termini
hotelariston@hotelariston.it
www.hotelariston.it

Napoleon
P. V. Emanuele II 105
Tel 06 446 7264
www.napoleon.it
Metro line A Vittorio Emanuele

Massimo D'Azeglio
Via Cavour 18
Tel 06 488 0646

Mediterraneo
Via Cavour 15
Tel 06 488 4051
Metro Line A or B Termini

Barocco
Via della Purificazione 4
Tel 06 487 2001
Metro line A Barberini

Holiday- Inn
Crown Plaza Minerva
Piazza della Minerva 69
Tel 06 695 201
Pantheon Area

ZONE 4: SAN GIOVANNI

President
Via Emanuele Filiberto 173
Tel 06 770 121
Metro line A San Giovanni

ZONE 5: PRATI-ST. PETER'S

Adriatic
Via Vitelleschi 25
Tel 06 686 9668
Castel Sant' Angelo area

Columbus
Via della Conciliazione 33
Tel 06 686 5435
Metro line A Vaticani

Cicerone
Via Cicerone 55
Tel 06 3576
Castel Sant'Angelo Area

Michelangelo
Via della Stazione di San Pietro 14
Tel 06 393 66861
Metro line A San Pietro

ZONE 7: PARIOLI

Executive
Via Aniene 3
Tel 06 855 2030
Villa Borghese area

Beverly Hills
Largo B. Marcello 220
Tel 06 854 2141

Borromini
Via Lisbona 7
Tel 06 884 1321

Regency
Via Romagna 42
Tel 06 481 9281

Aldrovandi
Via U. Aldrovandi 15
Tel 06 322 3993

Ritz
Piazza Euclide
Tel 06 808 3751

Polo
Piazza B. Gastaldi 4
Tel 06 322 1041

ZONE 12: EUR

Cristoforo Colombo
Via Cristoforo Colombo 710
Tel 06 592 1315

Shangri-Là
Viale Algeria 141
Tel 06 591 6441
Metro line B EUR

Sheraton-Roma
Viale del Pattinaggio
Tel 06 5453
Metro line B EUR

Hostels

ZONE 2: ESQUILINO

Y. W. C. A
Via Cesare Balbo 4
Tel 06 4880460/06 4883917
Fax 06 4871028
Young Women's Christian Association - U.C.D.G.
foyer. roma@ywca-ucdg.it

Yellow Hostel
Via Palestro
(Walking out of Termini station on the east side, not the McDonald's side) head onto Via Marsala and take a right turn onto Via Vicenza. The 4th street will be Via Palestro.
Two streets line Termini station-along the west side Via G. Giolitti and along the east Via Marsala.

Included:

- Laundry facilities
- Linens included
- Security lockers
- Luggage storage
- Guest kitchen
- 24 Hour reception
- Travel desk/travel Info
- Common room
- No Curfew
- Free internet access
- Breakfast

ZONE 5: PRATI-ST. PETER'S

BellaRoma
Via Accinni 63
Mixed dorms - from 18-25 €
International staff
Free Internet access
Free luggage storage
Small Kitchen
Laundry machines
No Curfew

Lido di Ostia by the Beach..................

Litus
Tel 06 5697275
Lungomare Paolo Toscanelli 186
Entrance on Via Cozza 7
Your Hostel by the Roman Sea.
This is the first hostel by the sea in Rome. It is close to Ostia Antica (the ancient Roman city that was buried underground). The building holds the Elsa Morante library one of the most prestigious in the city-with the Lido cinema theatre available to guests at Litus and not far from the Fiumicino Airport.
Directions; Metro to line B for Piramide. From Piramide take train for Ostia centro-bus 01 and get off after 5 stops. Walk to your right and take the first road on the left which will be Via Cozza-it's number 7.
info@litusroma.com
www.litusroma.com

The Passport controversy

Let us not be alarmed when the check-in moment approaches. The hotel will take your passport until you visitors are properly registered. This information is then sent to the polizia, as this is way it works in Italy. In the early 80s, there was a big problem with terrorism and for security purposes people who stay in hotels or rent rooms, have their information sent to the authorities.

Most pensions or hotels with less stars do not like the idea of handling credit cards, be it the taxes or the tediousness. It's real luck if you find a hotel to suit all of your needs if its stars are low. This book does not share opinions on this as different people have loved and hated the same places. Some people love the tiny spaces offered by Roman hotels when others will look at you striken with claustaphobia.

Particular Suites and Inns

ZONE 1: HISTORICAL CENTER

Gianicolo Inn
Set on one of the highest and most panoramic points in Rome, it is in one of the most elegant spots in the entire city, outside the city's noise but inside and near to all the best Rome has to offer.
Operated by well-established individuals and warm Romans.
info@gianicoloinn.com
www.gianicoloinn.com

Victoria
Via Campania 41
Tel 06 473 931
Between Via Veneto and Villa Borghese
In an 18th century building, elegant and welcoming
www.hotelvictoriaroma.com

Casa Howard Guest House
Capo le Case 18
Tel 06 69924555
Charming! 100m to Piazza di Spagna
www.casahoward.it

Hotel Teatropace
Via del Teatro Pace 33
Tel 06 6879075
1500's Cardinal building
www.hotelteatropace.com

ZONE 2: ESQUILINO

Hotel Alpi
Via Castelfidardo 84
Tel 06 4441235
Termini Station Area
Baths with hydro massage
www.hotelalpi.com

ZONE 5: PRATI

*Caput Mundi Suite**
Via Tacito 7
Tel 06 3244376
Four rooms on the fourth floor of an Umbertino Building area of prati near Castel SAnt'Angelo
www.caputmundisuite.it

ZONE 8: OSTIENSE

*Sant'Anselmo**
Piazza Sant'Anselmo 2
Tel 06 570057
Next to the Benedettino convent, in an ancient villa
www.aventinohotels.com

ZONE 12: EUR

*Aris Garden**
Via Aristofane 101
Tel 06 52362443
Located between EUR and the airport, well connected,
Especially for conferences, conventions, with gym and health centre
www.arishotel.it

*Le Clarisse**
Piazza Merry del Val 20
Tel 06 58334437
Ex-convent with rooms named after flowers that face the internal garden
www.leclarisse.com

ZONE H: TIBURTINO

*Hotel Turner**
Via Nomentana 29
Tel 06 44250077
A charming place and elegant atmosphere with pieces of antique furniture.
Baths in marble with Jacuzzi
www.hotelturner.com

The Ancient castles await you...

Hotel Castello della Castelluccia
Via Carlo Cavina
Tel 06 30207041
www.hotelcastellucciarome.com

The Castle Hotel Castello della Castelluccia is snuggled within Lazio's luxuriant countryside. Arise to views of rolling woodlands and scents of floral. The Castelluccia's landscape is a colourful nest-egg for aspiring artists who are drawn here to hone their artistic talents.

Share your presence with the spirits that reside therein. Tales told of haunted castles are tall; sometimes without concrete truth however there are those that foretell true tales! At the Castle Castelluccia there are three ghosts said to be present.

Swimming-Hotel Castelluccia has opened one of Rome's largest hotel pools running 25 meters/82 feet, which is located below the hotel's courtyard and immersed in a Roman forest. Open June to September. Horseback Riding-The Hotel Relais la Castelluccia was one of the most famous stables in Italy; whom produced numerous fine thoroughbreds. Horse breeding was the principal source of income for owners of the Castelluccia for a good part of the last century.

Mountain Biking and Cycling-Tracks around the castle are rough and bumpy, but you may go free-willingly.

Golf-the"Olgiata"is one of the oldest and most prestigious golf clubs in Italy which welcomes their guest and residents to the green landscape of the Italian golf countryside.

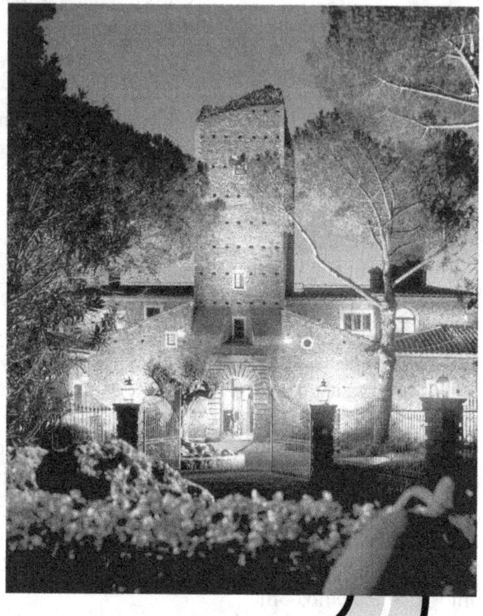

TRANSPORTATION SERVICES

Taxi service, car for hire or the castle's shuttle bus service (on the premises).

By car
Take exit 3 from the GRA (Grande Raccordo-Rome's city loop) and follow Via Cassia in the direction of Viterbo. Turn off at"La Giustiniana"
If arriving from the centre of Rome take Via Trionfale and Via Cassia.

Hotel Scandeluzza
Via Scandeluzza 11
Tel 06 61561840
Fax 06 61565397
info@castleofrome.com
Boccea district
Only 3 miles from the Vatican
12 miles from Fiumicino Airport
15 miles from Ciampino Airport
Autobus 904
Metro line A Cornelia
www.castleofrome.com

Experience an unusual air, sleep in a spacious castle. Enjoy a light breakfast served in the"Botti"near a crackling fire or in your room. Meals are served on the finest porcelain and golden glasses that belong to the noble family Pellegrini. Guests are assigned a waitress to be at their disposal during the entire stay. Excellent wines stored in the Princes wine cellar are to be shared.

For spiritual access visit the small garden where the sacred church sits ("Madonna of the Deposition"), or peek inside at the 15th century Christ in wood sculpted by the Duccio School from Boninsegno. All castle guests are welcome to the SS Mass and special banquet held once a month.

PLUSES

- Security guards
- Medical Assistance
- Billards
- Piano
- Fireplaces
- Castle private car services from the airport to the castle, available - must be pre-booked.

Castello Orsini

Via Aldo Bigelli
Nerola
Tel.: 07 74 683272
Fax: 07 74 683107
Reservations: prenotazioni@castelloorsini.it
www.castelloorsini.it

Orsini Castle built in 1235, became a prestigious hotel situated among gardens, woods and tight alleyways in an old village in a place called Nerola. The imagination festers mysteries and old stories of a manor which bore witness to battles, lovers and crimes. Here you will find a beauty farm for relaxation and internal/external cleansing. Situated in a greenery of the Tiber Valley near Rome, its charm does not end with enormous rooms, long hallways (decorated in ancient frescoes) and luxurious restaurant.

BY CAR

Follow the signs for the Rome G.R.A. (Raccordo Anulare-Rome's city loop). Head to the A1 (Rome-Florence) and exit at Roma Nord-Fiano Romano. From that exit follow indications for: Rieti-Salaria. On the Salaria, you then head towards Rieti and turn right after the sign to NEROLA.

BY TRAIN

Underground FM1 from Fiumicino Railway Station to Fara Sabina Railway Station (place: Passo Corese). From Fara Sabina to the Station in Nerola, is only by reserved car. From Rome Tiburtina Railway Station: Take the FM1 train from to Fara Sabina-Passo Corese. From Fara Sabina station travel to Nerola (only by car or taxi).

Rome Real Estate

STUDIO DE SETA
Tel 06 3220500
Fax 06 3226974
deseta@homesinitaly.com
www.homesinitaly.com

ROME PROPERTY NETWORK
Tel 06 3212341
Fax 06 3215087
"Serving the International Community. "Long/short-term rentals
Sale assistance; vacation rentals. American-managed firm
romeproperty@yahoo.it
www.romeproperty.com

ROME SWEET ROME
Tel/Fax 06 69924833
info@romesweethome.it
www.romesweethome.it

MP INTERNATIONAL HOUSE
Tel 06 6892624
Fax 06 6892415
At home in the heart of Rome. Fully equipped apartments of various sizes for daily, weekly or monthly rentals.
info@mpinternationalhouse.com
www.mpinternationalhouse.com

NELSON INTERNATIONAL REAL ESTATE
Tel/Fax 06 3337162
Cell 337 747493
nelsoninternational@libero.it

HOMELAND ITALIA
Tel 06 6892148/335 7012232
All you need is Home.
Rent and buy; contract assistance. English, French, Swedish, Finnish spoken
lena. w@tiscalinet.it

KLEMM AGENCY
Tel 06 39739559
www.klemm.it

EDWARDS REAL ESTATE AGENCY
Tel 06 8611262
Fax 06 8610871
Established since 1965. A vast selection of exclusive apartments and villas. Furnished or unfurnished, for rent or sale. English, French, and Spanish spoken.

EUROCENTER
Tel 06 52205391/2
Fax 06 52205389
eurocenter. srl@tin.it

AT HOME ITALY
Tel 06 32120102
Fax 06 3215489
info@at-home-italy.com
www.at-home-italy.com

CITY APARTMENTS
Tel 06 76983140
Apartments for short/medium term lets, photos, prices and bookings.
www.cityapartments.it

An Italian home/villa purchase service that includes the facility to buy holiday, retirement and investment homes throughout Italy.
www.holiday-villa-italy.com

www.realestateinrome.com
www.rome. angloinfo.com
www.romeloft.com

Barefoot on flat floors

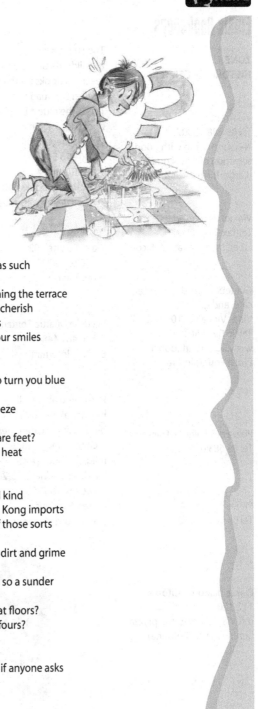

Don't go running all about
In bare feet throughout
Thrown to you will be a chill
Who's no stranger for a shrill

Nude skin taps the floor
As one hurries down the corridor
Looped wool that makes a rug
Is softness that feet long to hug
All of this disappears from touch
Why in Italy there's not so much as such

With loving terracotta for garnishing the terrace
There are mosaics stairs for us to cherish
As driveways are of flowered tiles
Coldness marches in to eat up your smiles

It goes up an extremity or two
The freezing is mighty enough to turn you blue
Falling cold upon your knees
Helplessly you squeeze out a sneeze

Walking on tile or marble with bare feet?
God save us from absence of the heat

In Italy you will find
Materials of the rare and unusual kind
Not including non-organic Hong Kong imports
Italians do not produce things of those sorts
Erase from the mind
Hard to vacuum carpets holding dirt and grime
For many of us still wonder
What makes cool tiles put germs so a sunder

Will you walk barefoot on cold flat floors?
Would you crawl on them on all fours?

Italians are fine with those tasks
Italy doesn't design wall to walls if anyone asks

Ethnic Bookshops

ZONE 1: HISTORICAL CENTER

Il Librario
Via Arenula 24
Tel 06 688 08897
Nice bookshop with good selection of travel guides
(Largo Torre Argentina)

Liber. men TÈ Books & Tea
Via del Pellegrino 94
Tel/fax 06 686 1279
Liber. mente@katamail.com

Mondatori
Guidebooks, Cd's, internet, café, and gifts
Via S. Vincenzo 10
Tel 06 697 6501
www.librimondadori.it
(Trevi Fountain Area)

FRENCH
La Librairie Francaise di Roma
La Procure
Piazza di S. Luigi dei Francesi 23
Tel 06 683 07598

SPANISH
Libreria Spagnola Sorgente
Piazza Navona 90
Tel 06 688 06950

GERMAN
Herder International Book Center
Piazza di Monte Citorio 117-120
(off Via del Corso the piazza behind Piazza Colonna)

ENGLISH
The Lion Bookshop & Café
They have a wide selection of children's books and teaching books for the English Language.
This is the oldest English bookshop in Rome.
Via dei Greci 33-36
Tel 06 326 54007
10-7:30pm
www.thelionbookshop.com
(Piazza del Popolo Area)

Angelo-American Bookshop
Via della Vite 102
Tel 06 679 5222
mbox@aab.it

Libreria 4 Fontane
Via delle Quattro Fontane 204
Tel 06 481 4484
English/International

IL Museo del Louvre
Books and above all, individual photos in black'n'white categories; architectural, politics, religious, and sports
Via della Reginella 26-28
Tel 06 688 07725
Closed Sundays
(Largo Torre Argentina Area)

ZONE 3: TRASTEVERE

Open Door Bookshop
Via della Lungaretta 23
Tel 06 589 6478

Almost Corner Bookshop
Via del Moro 45
Tel 06 583 6942

Librerie del Cinema
Via dei Fienaroli 31/d
Tel 06 581 7724
Closed Mondays
A place for those in love with film
Foreign books
DVD's Books Accessories
Bar and restaurant open from 5pm
Saturday and Sunday brunch 12-3

ZONE 8: OSTIENSE

Motamot
Via Giulio Rocco 37/39
Tel 06 573 00082
Foreign literature, courses, concerts and cinemagraphic
Closed Mondays and Friday mornings

GIAMPIERO POGGI BELLE ARTI dal 1825
Via del Gesù 74/75
Tel 06 6784477
Hrs 9am-1pm/4pm-7:30pm Thurs,
non stop hours
Closed on Sunday
www.poggi1825.it
(Pantheon Area-Piazza della Rotonda)

POGGI Trastevere Location
Merry del Val 18/19 (Piazza Mastai)
Tel 06 5812531
Fax 06 5895936
Hrs 9am-1pm/4pm-7:30pm
Closed Sundays
Ditta G. Poggi is a specialized art-supply emporium. Folded in between fashion boutiques, was the first to begin as a spice shop, and has sold canvases to famous faces. Poggi carries Kolinsky sable brushes, mahogany easels, and other artistic products.

VERTECCHI
Stationery
Via delle Croce 70
Great selection of paper, portfolios, pens, art supplies, cards, wrapping paper, boxes, mailing tubes, decorative paper plates and napkins, and briefcases.
(Spanish Steps Area)

PHOTO AND FILM ITEMS

DE BENARDIS
Piazza della Cancelleria 63
Tel 06 704 74923
Film, lens, and other photo related accessories
For excellent prices shop here. There is a photo shop around the corner where film costs 10€ for one roll. At Benardis you'll pay 4-5€.
(off Via Vittorio Emanuele II,
and across from Piazza di S. Pantaleo)

HOTEL PHOTO EXPRESS SERVICES
Tel 06 372 4405 or 329 4317686
(Private; let hotel reception call)
Roll of 24 13€
Roll of 36 15€
Leave your rolls of film with the hotel reception before 8pm, and they will be returned in a few hours
Free photo album with every roll of film

Spatola	Pallette knife	spah-toe-lah
Penneli	Brushes	pain-nail-lee
Acrilico	Acrylic	ah-cree-lee-coh
Smalto	Enamel	smahl-toe
Vernice	Paint	vair-knee-chay
Cavalletti	Easels	cah-vahl-lay-tea
Solventi	Solvents	sole-vain-tea

Business Needs

LIBRERIE PROFESSIONALE-PROFESSIONAL BOOKSTORE

LIBRERIA BUZZOLI
Via Merulana 97-98
Tel 06 704 95516
Buzzoli@tin.it

BUFFETTI
Large Italian chain for office supplies as office depot.

Locations:

L'Ufficio Moderno di R Montesi
Viale Beethoven18
Take metro B exiting at Eur Palasport
(EUR Area)

La Risorgente
Via G.G Belli
(near Castel Sant'Angelo and Piazza Cavour)

Cichi SRL
Viale Pinturicchio 32
(At the end of Via Flaminia going towards the Tevere-Tiber river)

Many edicole newspaper stands by Piazza Chigi and Via del Corso supply magazines such as; Business Week, the Economist, The Wall Street Journal, Focus, the New York Post, Financial Times and the Herald Tribune.

GREEN PEACE- ITALY

Viale Manlio Gelsomini 28
Metro line B Piramide stop
Off Via Avertino
(Piramide Area)

VITTORIO LA BARBERA-OPTICAL

Piazza Barberini/Galleria Alberto Sordi
Via Condotti 23/Via del Corso 160

Contact lens solutions from 3€
Sunglasses
A little English spoken
Metro line A exiting Spagna or bus 175
(Piazza di Spagna Area)

Contacts	Lenti a contatto	laint-tea ah cone-tah-tow
Lens Solution	Salina	sahl-lean-nah
All in One	Soluzione Unica	soul-lou-ts-own-nay oon-knee-cah

HARD TO FIND ITEMS

Index cards
Coiled Notebooks with more than 70 pages
Little cap erasers for pencils

OFFICE SUPPLY WORDS

Portamine tecnico	Design pencil (Automatic)	
Carta Velina	Tracing Paper	car-tah vay-lay-nah
Gomma	Eraser	go-mah
Penna	Pen	pain-nah
Matita	Pencil	mah-tee-tah
Temperamatite	Pencil sharpener	tame-pair-rah mah-tea-tah
Cucitrice	Stapler	coo-chee-tree-chae-
Graffette	Paperclips	grah-fay-tay or attash ah-tah-sh
Carta	Paper	cartah
Evidenziatore	Highlighter	"a"-"v"-dense-ah-tore-ray
Cd Rom	Cd Rom	chee-dee rome
Masterizzatore	Cd writer	mah-stare-reetz-ah-tore-ray
Computer	Computer	computer
Dischetto	Disk	dee-skay-toe
Posta elettronica	E-mail	poe-stah ay-late-trone-knee-cah
Floppy	Floppy	flow-pea
Palmari	Handhelds	pahl-mahr-ree
Disco rigido/Fisso	Hard Drive	dee-skoh ree-gee-doe
Cartuccia	Ink Cartidge	car-two-cha
Tasto	Key	tah-stow
Tastiere	Keyboard	tah-stee-yeah-rey
Portatile	Laptop	pore-tah-tee-lay
Memoria-Ram	Memory-Ram	memoria-rahm
Modem	Modem	modem
Schermo	Monitor	scare-mow
Scheda Madre	Motherboard	mah-drey-skay-dah
Mouse	Mouse	mouse
Rete	Network	ray-tay
Alimentatore	Power Supply	ahl-lee-main-tah-tore-ray
Stampante	Printer	stahm-pahn-tay
Scanner	Scanner	skahn-nair

Raindrops and Umbrellas

Dark-faces come out of stones and up from subway tunnels each time it drizzles. Suddenly entire bags are filled with umbrellas for sale; they knew it was going to rain.

On these occasions, Rome visitors and residents alike find themselves surrounded by two, three and four people holding bushels of multi-coloured canopies. They will test your patience. They can be reasonable. Negotiating works and since the umbrellas were acquired in a local shop for 3€ it makes you want to ask them where they made their purchases. They are nothing but disposable umbrellas that will eventually fold up under any gust of wind. You will now be stuck with nothing more than aluminium and a distorted canvas.

For good quality umbrellas, see the"Specialty Shop Section"
Valigeria Ferrari

Tax Free Shopping

Global Refund is committed to customer satisfaction for the traveler.

As a visitor to a foreign country and a non-EU resident you are entitled to claim back the tax you pay on purchases when you take them home.

SAVE MONEY! Go Extra Early to Airport to Collect Your Money-Don't Stand in Lines!

"Each time you shop, ask retailers for tax-free shopping forms!"

Global Refund Italia Srl.
Phone (011 from US and Canada)
+ 39 0331 283 555
Http://www.globalrefund.com

THE IVA TAX IS 16. 67% of the purchase price of nearly everything sold in Italy. Non-European residents shopping in Italy can claim a refund of IVA on each purchase that exceeds about 150 euro otherwise the only refund options are by credit card or by bank check. Bank check refunds should be avoided, as fees to cash them in the USA can be very expensive. As with all exports, purchases must be declared at the Custom Office upon departure from Italy or the European Union (EU) and a validation stamp must be obtained. Validation stamps can be obtained at the Customs Office of an Italian airport only if purchased goods are shown first to the Custom Officer and then inserted immediately into the luggage to be checked in for final destination outside of the EU.

Exchanging Your Money- Better Rates!

It's a better idea to exchange your money in a bank or at a Thomas Cook or American Express location, instead of a shop or hotel. Some shops charge up to 20% commission!

REGULAR BANK HOURS

8:45am-1:30/2:45-4pm M-F
Their commissions are 3-5€

Thomas Cooks

ZONE 1: HISTORICAL CENTER

Piazza Barberini 21
Metro Line A exiting Barberini
Open Mon-Sat 9am-8pm Sun 12:30-5pm

Via del Corso 23 (Piazza del Popolo)
Mon- Sat 9am-8pm Sun 9:30-5pm

ZONE 5: PRATI

Via della Conciliazione 23
Bus 40ex 62 64
Mon- Sat 8:30-7:30pm Sun 9:30-5pm
(St Peter's Area)

ZONE 1: HISTORICAL CENTER

AMERICAN EXPRESS

Piazza Di Spagna 38
Metro Line A exiting Spagna
(Take a left out of the metro station passing the steps on the left)
Tel 06 72282 (24hrs)
800 914 912 toll free number (Italy)
Hrs Mon-Friday 9am-5:30pm
Sat 9am-12:30pm
Closed Holidays (Check Italian Holidays)

CANCELED STOLEN OR LOST CREDIT CARDS

Tel 06 72900347 (7am-1pm everyday)
For a new card, you need to make a police report with your social security number, home phone number, and issuing office.

Money = Soldi
Cambio = Change

THE EURO

The world's biggest changeover concerning money has affected millions. The Euro has been brought forth into existence since 2002, but was in the making way before. The Europeans were looking to increase their prosperity economies-- making it their goal to do so, even way back in 1957. One chief role was to form a more intimate union among the European people. Through the Single European Act in 1986, the Euro was further developed.

The Euro was accepted by eleven European countries, and on January 1st 2002, this currency was official.

Rome underwent difficult times during the slow phasing out of the Lire. People rejected it, despised it. People fought over it. It made the news almost every night of the week for a long time. Notes range from 5-10-20-50-200 and 500. Windows and stars conglomerate both sides of the bills, representing the open coop with other European nations. Bills were striped of beloved faces such as; Caravaggio, Bernini and Marconi. These were replaced with European monuments with a low identity. The only lasting representations of adored Italians were left on the insignificant metal coins with Leonardo Da Vicini's drawing on the 1 Euro coin, Dante Alighieri on the 2 Euro, and Botticelli's imprint of Venus left only on a mere 10 cent piece. It seemed suddenly that 1,000 was equal to 1 Euro, when it was in fact 1,936 almost 2,000 Lire. This is what caused such an uproar in stores, because they had to spend double the amount.

TIPS

Choose using ATM's and not travellers cheques, you'll find trouble trying to cash them, ATM's are must more convenient. Cards with the Cirrus symbol are accepted almost everywhere.

Special Shops

ZONE 1: HISTORICAL CENTER

Violavà Lab
Tel 06 683 08895
Violavà lab on skype
lab@violava.com
Showroom and laboratory found on Vicolo Cellini 29 (Corso Vittorio Emanuele-Via del Pellegrino)
Handmade cloth purses, stoles, slippers, and tops-for artistic personalities

ZONE 3: TRASTEVERE

Rivendita di Cioccolata & Vino
Vicolo del Cinque 11A
Tel 06 583 01868
www.cioccolataevino.com
Closed Mondays
Chocolates, wine and books-an artist little place
Trastevere (Across the river)

La Bottega del Cioccolato
Chocolates shaped into everything imaginable
Via Leonina 82
Tel 06 4821473
Bus 70 71

ZONE 2: ESQUILINO

Trimani. . Wine! Trimani
Best wine selection-the largest Enoteca in Rome
Via Gioto 20
Tel 06 446 9661
Fax 06 446 8351
www.trimani.com
info@trimani.com
A walk from Termini Station

ZONE 2: ESQUILINO

Panella
L'Arte del Pane -
The Art of Bread-Making
Via Merulana 54/55
Largo Leopardi 2/10
Tel 06 4872344
Fine pastries, breads and gelati

ZONE 8: OSTIENSE

Volpetti
Via Marmorata 47
Gourmet shop
Tel 06 574 2352
Area: Piramide

ZONE 9: TESTACCIO

Volpetti Location 2
Via Alessandro Volta 8
Self- service restaurant
Tel 06 574 4305
Bus 30 75 719 23 280
Subway-metro exiting Piramide
www.volpetti.com

ZONE 5: PRATI

Castroni- International Grocer
Via Ottaviano 55-59
Via Cola di Rienzo 196
This is the place you need when you feel nostalgia
Metro line A exiting Ottaviano
Roasted coffee on the premises
Confectionery
Grocery
Chocolates and Candies
Crafted Pasta's
Grains and Flours
Teas and cereals
www.castronigroup.it

Pasticcerie/ Pastry Shops

ZONE 1: HISTORICAL CENTER

Dolce Roma
Via del Portico d'Ottavia 20
Tel 06 689 2196
Jewish-Austrian couple
Delightful Strudel! Sinful cheesecake! Criminal Sacher!
It's the best chocolate cake between heaven, hell and earth.
Area: Jewish Ghetto

Limentani
Another of the Jewish Ghetto's marvels.
Found on Via del Portico d'Ottavia 1
Tel 06 687 8637
Specialities-Marzipan that is not sickening sweet.
Marzipan cakes
Macaroons that are out of this world, even people I know that don't even like macaroons love these.

ZONE 11: APPIO

Frediani
Via Appia Nuova 481
On the corner of Via Turno 2/4
Tel 06 786217
Closed Mondays

This treasure has a small espresso bar snuggled into the corner, which serves espresso's, juices, sandwiches, pizzette (finger pizzas), arancini (rice balls filled with cheese and tomato sauce) and brioche
A counter along the back serves fresh Italian cookies and sweets.
The magical part of this particular place is that they produce cookies, cakes, strudel and gelato without sugar, and without animal fats, fantastic. They use organic flours, and some products are even made without milk or eggs, it's dandy if you're a vegetarian or diabetic.
www.senzazucchero.com

They carry jams called"Solo Frutta"only fruit are make homemade in 9 varieties-no preservatives, no sugar.
The chocolate comes from the best quality cocoa and made without sugar, maltitolo is added.
Sold in 100g bars; milk chocolate latte, bitter chocolate, white chocolate cioccolata bianca
Assorted chocolates; milk chocolate latte, bitter chocolate fondente, and filled chocolates ripieni
There is still more in this little place...

Specialities: mousse, pangiallo a Roman traditional cake, birthday cakes
Colombe Pasquali Easter cakes-without sugar or candied fruits, and without milk or animal fats
Panettone (Italian holiday sweet breads) served at Christmas, classic white or chocolate, with or without; sugar, animal fats, eggs and or milk.
Confetti-the many coloured candy coated almonds-the traditional Italian ceremonial candies.

ZONE 1: HISTORICAL CENTER

Krechel
Via Frattina 134
Tel 06 6780946
Austrian pastry and ice cream
Area: Piazza di Spagna

La Bella Napoli
Corso Vittorio Emanuele 246
Tel 06 6877048
Neopolitan pastry shop
Pasticceria
Area: Piazza Navona

Jeff Blynn's
Via Zanardelli 12
Tel 06 6861990
Caffetteria
American pastry
Area: Piazza Navona

A Charming Caffè....

Antico Caffè Greco
Via Condotti 86
Tel 06 679100
Coffee Bar
You may purchase Italian or American coffee
Mark Twain spent a good amount of his time here, and so did Buffalo Bill- portraits of them adorn the walls of Caffè Greco.
Area: Piazza di Spagna

Bartolucci's
Via dei Pastini 98
Tel 06 69190894
info@bartlucci.com
www.bartolucci.com
Specialty Shop hand-crafted woodworks
Pine creations are patiently crafted by Francesco, Matteo, Anna and Chiara Bartolucci
Area: Pantheon

ZONE 7: PARIOLI

Harley Davidson Shop Roma
Via Piciana
Across the street from Villa Borghese
Bus 52 53

Tattoo Shops

ZONE 4: SAN GIOVANNI

Gladston Tattoo Studio
Tel 06 772 50175
Via Illiria 1
Bus 218 360 665
Open until 8pm

Sun Vibrations
Tel 06 702 7376
Piazza Camerino 4
Metro Line A stop
Bus 16 81 810

ZONE 9: TESTACCIO

Max Art Tattoo
Tel 06 575 6761
Via L. Vanvitelli 25/23
Bus 23 30 75 280 716

Shoes!

ZONE 3: TRASTEVERE

Joesph Debach
The most unusually artistic shoes you'll ever see....
Via Vicolo de Cinque 19
Largo Torre Argentina-get off right over the bridge and you're in Trastevere. Head to your right down the alleyways.
350-450 €

Trinket Shops!

ZONE 1: HISTORICAL CENTER

Il Fico Fiorone
Piazza del Fico 23/24
Tel 06 68210995
Little quaint shop in the Piazza del Fico, right around the block from Piazza Navona.
A wonderful gift spot, especially if looking for unique items. Lamps, slippers, and everything under the sun.

Terracotta & Ceramics

Artigiani Style

Il Giardino di Domenico Persiani
Via Torino 92
Tel 06 488 3886
Try and bargain discounts can be very generous
They carry artisan quality terracotta and ceramics for garden and home
Vases, busts, masks, and other Roman-type objects
Area: Piazza della Repubblica-between via Nazionale and Via XX Settembre
www.anticamanifatturaroma.com

Luggages, Leather Products

Valigeria Ferrari
Piazza Vittorio 102
Tel 06 446 1670/446 4670
Luggage and hand-crafted leather bags, briefcases, luggage, umbrellas, purses, and gifts-extraordinary prices for the optimum quality.

ZONE K: CASTELLI ROMANI

Yaqui
Artigiani's
Giulio Agro is the artisan whose last name does not coincide with his honeyed personality-Ágro means bitter or sour.
Do pass by Guilio's little shop if you are hunting for hand-crafted leather bags, purses, or briefcases. Bring your own design and Giulio will create it for you. Prices are very reasonable for the quality.
Via Bezzecca 24
Frascati Castelli Romani
Tel +39 (out of the country) 06 9419937

Vetrate Artistiche of Massimo Cavaliere
One of the most inspiring stories I've heard.
The House of Varies Treasures-Massimo's love for his work was expressed throughout his being, expressing to me that, he'd gladly work just the same, even without any recognition, and that said a lot to me. He explained that the creation of iron laid stained glass is a very antique process, a beautiful expressive talent, very difficult, and you must have an inbreeded passion for it. He is the only one left in the Castelli Romani area, which still creates these pieces of art, and by far knows his will be the last in his family carry it on.
Today the younger generation has no interest in continuing the unique and true process of this art, he said.
He does astounding works, and each piece is the only of its kind, each original in its own particular way, he said he can't ever make two the same. So, if you pick something out and take it home, know that you've come across a special treasure.
Some items: clocks, wall decorations, tables, shelves, mirrors, jewelry boxes and more.

ZONE 1: HISTORICAL CENTER

Vertecchi Stationery
Via delle Croce 70
Tel 06 679 0155
They have a great selection of: paper, portfolios, pens, art supplies, cards, wrapping paper, boxes, mailing tubes, decorative paper plates and napkins, briefcases, mailing tubes for posters, wrapping paper, Italian birthday cards and Christmas cards.
Christmas decorations start early on in November.
From Piazza di Spagna turn onto Via delle Croce and walk towards Via del Corso.
The shop will be on your right.
Area: Piazza di Spagna
www.vertecchi.com

Ferdinando Codognotto wood Sculptures
Via dei Pianellari 14
Tel 06 687 7281
Ferdinando, the expressive artist, works with Cembro wood sculptures. He is well appreciated in Japan and the United States. His works adorn the Bank of Italy in New York and Rome. Admire the wooden street directionals placed on the building next to his shop.

La Contea del"Look"
The Eden of Accessories dress-making Laboratory
Prêt-A-Porter of high quality
Borgo Pio 31
Tel 06 68301514
A small wonderland of unique clothing, shoes of high quality and of Italian origin.
Purses of the soft textures and accessories of all sorts.
Ornella. Agostini@ fastwebnet.it
(San Pietro area)

Albero del Pane-The Bread Tree
Macrobiotics, herbal shop, natural cosmetics
Via S. Maria del Pianto 19/20
Tel 06 6865016
Off Via Arenula
They offer fresh yogurts, cheeses and organic produce.
Pastas, seeds, and a huge variety of tinctures and natural medicines, teas, and grains.
(Largo Torre Argentina)

La Fiorentina
The Marvels of Nature
Corso Vittorio Emanuele II 95/97 - Tel 06 686 5043
Italian-owned historical shop situated in the heart of Rome, with a vast selection of minerals and rare fossils to collect or simply appreciate. Shells for decoration, precious and semi-precious gemstones for mounting, necklaces and objects in hard stones. Everything for crystal therapies and more.

ZONE 12: EUR

Book City
Viale Marconi 92
Tel 06 45470871
9:30am-8pm everyday
One of the largest bookshops in Rome with a café corner
www.libreria-bookcity.it

Gli Artigiani/ Handicraftsmen
These men make anything from shoes to furniture by hand, but they are excellent and prodigious. Often you'll find them in small towns, or on islands. In the bigger cities they really don't exist anymore, and it's exactly what gave character and beauty to these places in the beginning.

You may find friends and acquaintances you haven't seen in months at the farmers markets, coffee bars, or simply in the main squares gabbing. Each little village in the Castelli Romani has a special day reserved for the farmer's market and the opportunity is optima because most vendors sell their own organic produce, freshly picked and very inexpensive. Farmer's market's in the center of Rome are wonderful too. Sundays are Bio days and you'll find numerous farmer's market with organic produce grown locally.

1 kilo = 2.2 lb
1 lb = 450 g

Market	Mercato	mair-cah-toe
Grocery store	Alimentari	ali-men-tar-ree
Discount	Uno Sconto	ooh-know scown-toe
Supermarket	Supermercato	sew-pear mair-cah-toe
Skim milk	Latte Parzialmente Scremato	lah-tay scray-mah-toe
Whole Milk	Latte Intero	lah-tay een-tay-air-no

Farmer's Markets/ Mercato delle Pulci

(Market of the Fleas)

ZONE 1: HISTORICAL CENTER

CAMPO DE ' FIORI
Piazza Campo de' Fiori
7am-1:30pm Monday-Saturday
Bus 40EX 64 116
It's one of the most picturesque markets in the city. It's also easy to loose yourself between the ruffles of cabbage and curls of red lettuce.
Fresh fish, meats, vegetables, fruits of all kind, nuts, and fresh cut flowers
Try the pizza on the corner shop

NUOVO MERCATO ESQUILINO
Via Principe Amedeo188
8:30-2pm
A huge open/indoor market...
with fresh cuts of meats, fish, fruits/dried fruits, vegetables, cheeses, breads, dried beans, flours, spices, oriental foods, and more.
A ten minute walk from Termini station.

ZONE 2: ESQUILINO

PIAZZA VITTORIO
Piazza Vittorio Emanuele
Metro line A Vittorio Emanuele
Bus 70 71105 516 517 Tram 11 14
Opens at 6am
Closed Sunday
One of the cheapest and best stocked food markets
Excellent regional cheeses and fish

ZONE 3: TRASTEVERE

PIAZZA SAN COSIMATO
Piazza San Cosimato
Bus 13 44 75 710 718 719 280
6am-1:30pm
Closed Sunday
Quality farmer's market for food and flowers

ZONE 9: TESTACCIO

PIAZZA DI TESTACCIO
Bus 13 23 57 95 716
6am-1:30pm
Closed Sunday
Rich and lively market, mostly food

Supermarkets

ZONE 1: HISTORICAL CENTER

DESPAR
Via Nazionale 211 or Via Pozzetto124
Bottles of water from. 20-70
Monday-Saturday 8am-9pm
Sunday 9am-9pm

SUPER MERCATO DIMEGLIO
Via Giustiniani 20
Every day 9am-10pm
Off of the Pantheon square, it's street to the left of McDonald's

GS
Via Monte di Farina
Monday-Saturday 9am-8pm
Bus 40EX 64 62 or 492 to Largo Argentina
Between Campo de' Fiori and Largo Argentina

ZONE 2: ESQUILINO

CTS MARKETS
Via Merulana 33a-c
Via Marsala 52/54
Via Gioberti 30e-g
8:15am-1:30pm/4:30pm-8:30pm

SUPERMERCATO STANDA est. 2003
Supermarkets on the bottom floor of department stores
Piazza Santa Maria Maggiore 5A
Next to Upim department store

To Shop or not to Shop?

The classic Italian-style has vanished among the general public.

A couple years ago nose-rings were everywhere in Rome and this would tell anyone that Rome's become modern. For the most part, fashion seems to be universal these days.

Below are some of the main streets of Rome where people shop, areas of designer clothing, fashion outlets and department stores.

EASIEST SHOPPING STREETS

- Via del Corso-main street running between Vittorio Emanuele Building-Piazza del Popolo
- Via Nazionale-a walk from Termini, Piazza Venezia, Coliseum
- Via Cola di Rienzo-runs off of Piazza Risorgimento
- Via del Governo Vecchio-near Piazza Navona
- Viale Giulio Cesare-metro Line A exit Ottaviano
- Via Tritone metro line A exit Barberini
- Via Sistina-metro Line A exit Barberini (off the square)
- Via Crispi-metro Line A exit Barberini
- Via Appia Nuova-metro Line A exit Furio Camillo, Punto Lungo
- Via Tuscolana-Metro Line A exit Numidio Quadraro or Cinecittà
- Trastevere Area-bus H from Termini station-first stop over bridge
- Via Giulia

PIAZZA DI SPAGNA AREA

VIA DEI CONDOTTI
Designers:
Battistoni
Giorgio Armani
Valentino
Prada
Gucci

VIA DEL BABUINO
Emporio Armani
Valentino

VIA BORGOGNONA
Gianni Versace
Versus Uomo
GianFranco Ferrare
Fendi'

VIA FRATTINA
Versace Jeans Couture

PIAZZA DI SPAGNA
Dolce & Gabana

VIA DEL CORSO
Benneton

MY CUP OF TEA
Via del Babiuno 147
Tel 06 32651061
Good selection of clothing, accessories and bijoux
Closed Saturday and Sunday

NIA
Via Vittoria 48
Tel 06 6795198
Stylish and classy women's shoes and accessories
Closed Sunday and Monday morning

ATELIER RITZ
Via Frescobaldi 5
Out of fashion treasures...
This misfit market is where various strangers unload designer clothing not yet in fashion in other countries.
Twice a month clothing is dumped here and discounted and most items are like new.
North-western end of Villa Borghese
(Hotel Parco dei Principi)
Bus 52 53 910

FOR MEN

BRIONI
Classic suits for men

ERMENEGILDO ZEGNA
Via Seminario 93
Tel 06 69942199
Mastermind tailor
Casual to tux
La cravatta su misura/custom-made ties in days
Buses 64 70 75

NAVIGATORE
The clothing name just for men
Clothes that last forever ...

FOR MEN AND WOMEN

ETRO men and women
Silk, cashmere
Via del Babuino 102
Tel 06 6788257
Closed Sunday mornings

CARLOTT RIO
Custom made shoes
Via dell'Arco della Ciambella 8
Tel 06 6872308
Bus 64 70 75

ZONE 3: TRASTEVERE

JACCHE
Via Vicolo del Cinque 24b
9am-12noon/3:30pm-12midnight
20-40€
Tram 8 from Largo T Argentina
Bus H from Termini
Or a nice walk over the Tevere bridge

IN THE JEWISH GHETTO
L'AMORE SCEGLIE SEMPRE L'AMORE
Via Arenula just past piazza towards river on left- little classy shop, owner with unique taste

DON'T FORGET!!
SAVE 20% MORE!

TAKE ADVANTAGE OF Tax Free Shopping (CENTAX)
Don't pay the taxes on Purchases!
Look for the tax free logo, and then ask for a form

GOLD AND LEATHER
Isn't that what you think of when you think of Italy?
Gold you'll find will only be in 18K or 24K. and you might not find 14K but isn't that great?
For gold and gold crosses Via Ottaviano (San Pietro area)

Try the Jewish quarters in Rome for diamonds and gold.

Pelle Nappa is a soft type of leather
True leather made by hand is labelled by law as follows; Vera Pelle
Made in Italy
Lavorazione Artigianale means: products are hand-crafted
The law: A norma de legge 883 del 26-11-73

BULGARI Tiffany's
Via Condotti 10
Tel 06 6793876
The biggest name in Rome jewellery
Metro line A Spagna

YAQUI
Via Bezzecca 24
Tel +39 06 9419337
Hand-crafted leather products
Purses, briefcases, bags, wallets, rings, belts and other items.
Frascati Castelli Romani

QUESTIONS - DOMANDE	
Can I try them on?	Do you have this in a smaller/larger size?
Posso provarli	Questo, l'avete più piccola/grande?
poe-so pro-vahr-lee	qway-stow lah-vay-tay p-u pea-co-lah
Style	Do you have it in other colours?
Stilo	C'è l'ha altri colori?
stee-low	chay-lah ahl- tree coal-lore-ree?

LADY'S SHOES							
Italian	35	36	37	38	39	40	41
British	4	4. 5	5	6	6. 5	7. 5	8. 5
American	5	5 1/2 - 6	6 1/2 - 7	7 - 7 1/2	7 1/2 - 8	8 1/2 - 9	9 1/2 - 10
Japanese	21	22	22. 5	23. 5	24. 5	25	25. 5

WOMEN'S SIZE CHART	Italy	UK	USA	Japan
X-Small (2-4)	36-38	4	2-4	5-7
Small (4-6)	38-40	6-8	4-6	7-9
Medium (8-10)	42-44	10-12	8-10	11-13
Large (12-14)	46-48	14-16	12-14	15-17
X-Large	48-50	16-18	14-16	17-19
1x	50-52	18-20	16-18	19-21
2x	52-54	20-22	18-20	21-23

SHOPPING MALLS

LA ROMANINA/Centro Commerciale
Shopping center
Tel 06 7233583
By car GRA Roma loop exit Napoli/La Romanina

CENTRO COMMERCIALE CINECITTA
There are more than 90 stores in this mall. Remember, the Romans constructed the Trojan markets nearly 2,500 years ago...
Metro line A Cinecittà

OUTLET SHOPS
30-70% discount scale

VALMONTONE
Outlets multi-coloured pastel buildings you can see from the highway
Tel 06 9599491
Winter hours from Oct 1st
Monday-Friday 10am-8pm
Saturday-Sunday 10am-9pm

NAME BRANDS
AVAILABLE AT VALMONTONE
Rocco Barocco Laura Biagotti Gianfranco Ferrè Roberto Cavalli Cacharel Pierre Carden Fornarina Lancetti Shoes Fellini Modesto Bertotto Idea Bassetti Popi Villane Carpisa

BY CAR OR TAXI
Get onto the GRA Rome Loop, then onto highway A1 in direction for Napoli- get off at the Valmontone exit and turn right off the highway, then right off the rotary and you'll then see the fashion district sign.
Just 17miles from Rome
inforoma@fashiondistrict.it

CASTEL ROMANO OUTLETS
90 shops
30-70% off
Phone Info 06 505-0050
Directions Via Pontina - (SS 48) get off exit "Castel Romano"
Via Ponte di Piscina Cupa
www.mcarthurglen.it

Lose everything you owned?

RESTOCK EVERYTHING IN ROME'S DEPARTMENT STORES:

COIN
Piazziale Appio 7
Tel 708-0020/708-0091

RINASCENTE
Largo Chigi 20/21
Tel 06 6797691

UPIM
- Via del Tritone
- Viale Trastevere

USEFUL WORDS		
Fabric	Tessuto	tay-sue-toe
Sales	Saldi	saldi sahl- dee
Discount	Uno Sconto	oo-no scone-toe
Size	Taglia	tahl-yah
One Size Only	Unica	oo-knee-cah
Outfit	Abito	a-bee-toe
Top	Maglietta	mah-ye-tah
Sweater	Maglione	mal-lee-own-nay
Blouse/Dress Shirt	Camicia	cahm-me-chah
Sandles	Sandoli	sahn-doe-lee
Shoes	Scarpe	scar-pay
Jacket	Giubino	jew-bee-no
Coat	Giubbotto	jew-bow-toe
Long Jacket	Capotto	cah-po-toe
Dress Jacket	Giacca	gee-ah-cah
Underwear	Mutande	moo-than-day
Skirt	Gonna	go-nah
Pants	Panteloni	pahn-tay-loan-knee
Shorts	Pantoloncini	pahn-tel-loan-chee-knee

Theatre & Shows

Rome as you would have guessed, is very much endowed with theatres that perform everything under the sun. Here you have opera's, music concerts, ballet's, gladiator shows, plays and musicals. From June to August all theatre's are closed. With the exceptions of the open-air theatres that are set up on the premises of grand villa's, on the Ostia Antica ruins and Gianicolo hill. Caracalla baths hold opera's and ballet's all summer too.

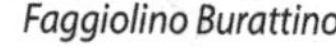

Faggiolino Burattino

ZONE 1: HISTORICAL CENTER

ROSSINI THEATRE
Piazza S. Chiara 14
Tel 06 687 5579/0668136390
TICKET OFFICE
Mon-Fri 9:30am-2pm,
Sat 4pm-8pm
Sun 3pm-8pm
bus 30ex 40 46 62-64 70 80 81 87 492 628 640
Call for reservations
inforossini@
gisapromotion.191.it

ARGENTINA/THEATRE OF ROME
Largo Argentina 52
Tel 06 6875445
The Barber of Seville debuted here.
Tram 8 Bus 44 46 56 60 62 64 70 81 87 170 492
www.teatrodiroma.net
www.romaeuropa.net

CASA DI GOETHE
Via del Corso 18
Tel 06 32650412
10am-6pm
Closed Monday
Bus 52 53 60 61 62 63 175 204 492
www.casadigoethe.it
info@casadigoethe.it

TEATRO DELL'OPERA
Via Firenze 72
Tel. 06 481601/06 48160255 for tickets
Rome ballet performances are held at Teatro Olimpico and Teatro dell'Opera and in the summer in one of Rome's night air open arena's.
Ticket office online ufficio.
biglietteria@opera. roma.it
www.opera. roma.it

GALLERIA DELLA TARTARUGA TURTLE GALLERY
Via Sistina 85A
Tel 06 6788956
Closed Sunday and Monday morning
10am-1pm/5pm-8pm
Bus 52 53 56 58 60 62 95
Metro line A Barberini
www.galleriadellatartaruga.com

SISTINA
Via Sistina 129
Italian broadway adaptions
English language musicals
Metro line A Barberini
Bus 52 53 56 58 60 61 95
www.helloticket.com
www.ticktone.it
www.ilsistins.com
info@ilsistina.com

ELISEO
In Italian only!
Via Nazionale 183 (near Termini and Repubblica)
Tel 06 48808311
(toll free in Italy) 800-907-080
reservations online:
botteghino@teatroeliseo.it
Bus 60 64 70 71 170 117 116
Metro line A Repubblica
www.teatroeliseo.it
www.helloticket.com

ZONE 7: PARIOLI

GALLERIA NAZIONALE DI ARTE MODERNA/NATIONAL GALLERY OF MODERN ART
Viale Belle Arti 131
Tel 06 32298221
Closed Monday
8:30am-7:30pm
Bus 30 52 926 Trams 3 19
www.gnam. arti. beniculturali. it/gnam

More theatres

ZONE 2: ESQUILINO

BRANCACCIO
Via Merulana 244
Tel 06 47824893
Fax 06 47824190
Artistic Director:
Gigi Proietti (actor)
Monday-Saturday
11am-7pm Sun 11-6pm

ZONE 3: TRASTEVERE

TEATRO BELLI
Piazza Sant'Apollonia 11/a
Tel 06 5894875
Fax 06 5897094
Near: Via della Lugaretta, Via della Scala, Vicolo de' Cinque Valle
Teatro Belli is one of the most antique Roman theatres, with a ghost story in its history.
For Tickets;
Mon-Sat 10-2pm or 3pm - 6:30pm
Sunday 3pm-6:30pm
Show Hours
Mon- Sat at 9pm
Closed Tues
Tickets about 15€
botteghino@teatrobelli.it

MIRACLE PLAYERS ENGLISH THEATRE IN ROME

The Miracle Players are an English speaking theatre troupe based in Rome. They perform original texts and comic adaptations of classics in various historical locations. Every summer the Miracle Players perform comic theatre in English at the Roman Forum.

The smaller theatres

DEI SERVI
Via del Mortaro 22
Tel 06 6795130

SATIRI
Via di Grotta Pinta
Tel 06 6561311

Variety

ZONE 3: TRASTEVERE

IL PUFF (In Italian)
Restaurant and Theatre
Via G. Zanazzo 4
www.ilpuff.it
ilpuff@ilpuff.it
You can have dinner at 8, then enjoy the show at 10:30.
Reservations 06 5810721, 06 5800989, 06 5813710
Tram 8
Bus H 23 710 780

ZONE 1: HISTORICAL CENTER

SALONE MARGHERITA/ DAISY LOUNGE
Restaurant & Theatre
Via Due Macelli, 75
Tel 06 6791439/06 6798269
Metro A line Spagna
Bus 95 116 117 175
www.salonemargherita.com

SILVANO TOTI GLOBE THEATRE
Tel 06 82059127
Born as an intuition of actor Gigi Proietti-was the original theatre Elisabettiano
Largo Aqua Felix (Piazza di Siena-Siena Square/in Villa Borghese)
Guided visits available with reservations
www.globetheatreroma.com

TEATRO STABILE DEI BURATTINI "SAN CARLINO"
Burattini Theatre
Tel 06 3335320
An outdoor theatre where the big and small, short and tall can enjoy ever-changing shows all in the same place.
Open every Saturday and Sunday -
and during the week in September-December and February-July
Viale dei Bambini (Pincio)
Reservations obligatory
www.sancarlino.it

Tickets for shows and events

ZONE 1: HISTORICAL CENTER

MESSAGGERI MUSICALI
Via del Corso 473
Tel 06 68192349
Fax 06 681 92338
mmpreno@libero.it

RICORDI MEDIASTORE
Via del Corso 506
Tel 06 320 2790
Via Giulio Cesare 88

TEATRO DE' SERVI
Via del Mortaro 22
Tel 06 679 5130
Fax 06 697 89897
(From via del Tritone to Via del Corso
and it's across the street from Piazza S. Claudio)
www.teatroservi.it
www.labilancia.it

ZONE 2: ESQUILINO

HELLO TICKET
Via Giolitti 16
Tel 06 478 25710
Toll-free 800-907080

ORBIS
P. Esquilino 37
Tel 06 681 92338
Fax 06 4744776

ZONE 3: TRASTEVERE

INTERCLUB
Piazza Ippolito Nievo 5
Tel 065895431
www.interclubservice.com interclubservice@tiscalinet.it

ZONE 4: SAN GIOVANNI

TARIFFA RIDOTTA PER I TEATRI-DISCOUNT THEATRE TICKETS
Via Foscolo 11
Tel 06 772 03770
Fax 06 1782715464
assocard@tiscali.it
Head towards San Giovanni from Termini, and it's off of Piazza Dante

ZONE I: NOMENTANO

IL SOGNO
Viale Regina Margherita 192
Tel 06 85301758
Fax 06 85301756

ZONE J: SALARIO

GENTI E PAESI
Via Adda 111
Tel 06 853 01755
Fax 06 853 01757
Trams 3 19
Bus 63 86 92 630
gentiepaesi@romeguide.it
www.gentiepaesi.it
www.dolcisogni.it

CAMOMILLA
Via A. Olivieri 70
Ostia (towards Fiumicino Airport)
Tel 06 568 3712
Fax 06 568 3653
BoxOstia@tiscali.it

STADIUMS FLAMINIO & OLIMPICO-SPORTS EVENTS AND CONCERTS

FLAMINIO
Via Flaminia
Tel 06 368-57832

MINOR CITY SPORTS
Olimpico 1960 Olympics
Home of the Lazio and Roma soccer teams

STADIO OLIMPICO
Via Foro Italico
Metro line A (direction Battistini)
to end of line
In Piazza della Farnesia (square) take bus 32
www.asroma. listicket.it

Films in English

ZONE 1: HISTORICAL CENTER

QUIRINETTA
Via Minghetti 4
Tel 06 679 0012
Always in English
(Trevi fountain area)

AUGUSTUS
Corso Vittorio Emanuele II 203
In English Tuesday
Tel 06 6875455
Bus 40EX 46 62 64 571 916

MAJESTIC
Via S. S. Apostoli
In English on Mondays
Tel 06 6794908
Bus 40EX 46 62 64 571 916
(Piazza Venezia area)

ZONE 2: ESQUILINO

CINECLUB DETOUR
Via Urbana 47
Tel 06 4872368
Original language when available
From Termini station take Via Cavour, the main street directly across from the station. The first square will be Piazza Esquilino, and then take a right and Via Urbana is up just a little ways.
www.cinedetour.it

ZONE 3: TRASTEVERE

FILMSTUDIO est. 1967
Via degli Orti d'Alibert 1c
Tel 06 45439775
From Corso Vittorio Emanuele II, take a left on Via Acciaoli towards the end of Vittorio Emanuele
Go over the Ponte Principe Amedeo and finally take a left onto Lungotevere/Along the Tiber
It's on your right
www.filmstudioroma.com
www.ilfilmstudio.com

NUOVO SACHER
Largo Ascianghi 1
In English Monday and Tuesday
Tel 06 5818116
Bus 23 44 75 280

PASQUINO MULTISCREEN
Piazza Egidio 10
Always in English
Tel 06 5803622
Bus H 23
Tram 3 8
www.multisalapasquino.com

ALCAZAR
Via Merry Del Val 14
In English on Mondays
Tel 06 5880099
Bus 780 Tram 8

USEFUL WORDS		
Theatre	Sala	sahl lah
Movie	Film	feel m
Tickets	Biglietti	beel yet tea
Popcorn	Popcorn	pope corn
The End	Fine	feen nay
Please	Per Favore	pear fa vo ray
Two tickets	Due Biglietti	dew ay bee lee yet tea
Usher	Maschera	mah scare rah
Intermission	Intervallo	een tear va low

Blockbuster Italia Est 1994

ZONE 1: HISTORICAL CENTER

Piazza di Spagna/Barberini Blockbuster
Via Barberini 3
Tel 06 4871666

ZONE 5: PRATI

Vatican Blockbuster
Circonvallazione Trionfale 114
Tel 06 39738107
Metro line A Cipro

ZONE 3: TRASTEVERE

Trastevere Blockbuster
Viale Trastevere 253
Tel 06 58335449

ZONE G: PRENESTINO

Prenestina Blockbuster
Viale D. Serenissima/Via Prenestina
Via Collatina 73/79
Tel 06 2153455

ZONE 13: AURELIO

Villa Pamphilj Blockbuster
Via Satolli 35
Tel 06 39366441

ZONE 7: PARIOLI

Parioli Blockbuster
Corso Trieste 27
Corso Francia 259
Tel 06 3296689

ZONE 8: OSTIENSE

San Paolo Basilica Blockbuster
Viale Giustiniano Imperatore 88
Tel 06 5412564

ZONE F: TUSCOLANO

Tuscolana Blockbuster
Via Tuscolana 1048/1058
Tel 06 79610355
Metro line A Arco di Travertino

Cinecittà Blockbuster
Via Antonio Ciamarra 250
Metro line A Cinecittà

ZONE 11: APPIO

Appio Blockbuster
Via Siria 1
Tel 06 78348761
Metro line A Punto Lungo

Blockbuster has an original language section, a small one, but you may find many films in English. Video machines available for rent. Use your Blockbuster international card.

HOURS OF OPERATION:
11am-11pm weekdays
11am-midnight on weekends

Rome Summers

IPPODROMO DELLE CAPANNELLE
Via Appia Nuova 1245
Tel 06 716771
Concerts in the beautiful outdoors
A spacious park open during the summer June-September that has Latino-Americano dancing and several dance clubs, shops with unique clothing and accessories, great restaurants and grills, and finally concerts and Brazilian shows.
Entrance fee €5-20 depending on what concerts you are attending.
Termini station trains FM4
Metro line A Cinecittà, and bus 654 direction Via delle Capannelle
Metro line A Colli Albani and bus 664
Night bus 66N
From the Rome GRA highway loop, take exit 23 to Appio San Giovanni Via Appia Nuova, direction Roma
www.capannelleippodromo.it

Fontana delle Api
Il Nasone

VILLA CELIMONTANA Jazz
Piazza della Navicella
Tel 06 5897807
Entrance fee 5-25€
June-September
Brazilian artists, funk, and famous names
Bus 75 81 671 714 175 60EX 628 85 87
Metro line B Colosseo or Circo Massimo
www.villacelimontanajazz.com

JAZZ & IMAGE FESTIVAL
Tel 06 4742286
An ancient amphitheatre lights up with classics in the Villa Celimontana
RomaEuropa festival-performing arts festival, one of Italy's most famous.
July-August/September-November
Jazz films and dance
www.romaeuropa.net

TEATRO ROMANA DI OSTIA ANTICA
Comedies and classics performed on ancient grounds and ruins
Via dei Romagnoli 717 - Tel 06 688 04601
Everyday in July and August 10am-2pm/3-6pm
Box office hours

Some Coffee Some Cream - Some Pasta Steam

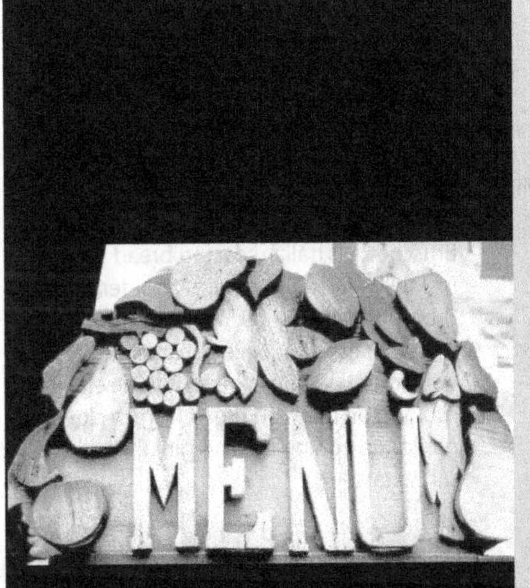

Alfredo di Lelio

The Origins of Alfredo's Sauce

An inspired cook opened a Roman Restaurant in 1914 his name was Alfredo di Lelio. He was a rather extravagant character, and liked to form paper thin fettuccine to be eaten with golden forks. He was the man who started what is known as Fettuccine Alfredo. The sauce was so simple that it wasn't believable and the recipe turned into a variety of cream sauces with spices, nutmeg and garlic in other countries. But the true sauce was made of aged Parmigiano cheese and butter. The al burro preparation is so simply Roman, it might not be called a recipe at all.

Alfredo All'Augusteo's restaurant is found in Piazza Augusto Imperatore 31.

THE PLEASURES OF ROMAN CUISINE

Drinking wine for lunch is as normal as tying your shoes and Italians drink it as a sheer compliment to a meal (the smaller glass holds the wine, as the larger is for water).

Restaurant salespersons work to get customers to come in and sit down and Italians label them: the butta dentro or the people who fling you inside. They also label the opposite fact; the butta fuori which are Italians who fling you out, like bouncers.

Buttare is the verb meaning throw away or throw. Fuori means out or outside and dentro means inside.

A distinguished Italian gentleman kindly explained to me why Italians eat dinner between 8-10pm. He said 'if we ate at 5 or 6pm, we'd become hungry at 11pm and have to make dinner all over again'. This is simply a European habit.

LA ROMANELLA
Romanella is a spumante red or white, drink them chilled. It is typical of the Castelli Romani area.

COPPA SOTT'OLIO (Cope-pah sote oh-lee-oh)
La Coppa is cured pork found in the Castelli Romani that depicts a patchwork quilt knitted with: salami, olives, garlic, hot pepper, fresh parsley, yellow or red bell peppers and capers.
La Coppa can be a smoked ham affumicato, a cooked ham prosciutto cotto, or an air-dried salt-cured and lightly smoked ham prosciutto crudo.

SALUMI (Saul-loom-me)
Salumi consists of all types of dried cured meats such as Lonza pig thigh and capocollo. Lonza is a dried meat that is dark in color and hard in texture. Capocollo means head and neck. It is spicy salami flavored with fennel seeds, black pepper and garlic.

CAPRESE (Cop-praise-say)
Caprese is a tomato salad made with ripe tomatoes, fresh basil, extra virgin olive oil, mozzarella di bufala-mozzarella made from buffalo's milk-salt, lemon juice or a dash of white vinegar.

BRUSCHETTA (Brew-sket-tah)
Bruschetta is Italian toasted bread that is slowly grilled until slightly golden and thoroughly hardened. It is then smothered with tomatoes, an olive pâté or other condiments. You can make it yourself by rubbing on the hard bread, a fresh clove of garlic and adding extra virgin olive oil and salt to taste.

BRUSCHETTA DI POMODORINI small cherry tomatoes
Cherry tomatoes, olive oil, basil, and salt

Italians seem to be speedy eaters especially with pasta dishes vacuuming it in while it's still hot.
To make them flee, serve them up a cold plate of yesterday's pasta.

There are two common dishes in Rome: rabbit coniglio and wild hare lepre and cinghiale. Papperdelle al cinghiale is a specialty in the Castelli Romani towns just outside Rome's centre. It is made with wide egg pasta and smothered in wild boar sauce, it's very rich.

A CAUTION TO VEGETARIANS:	THIS DISHES ARE NOT FOR YOU!
Coda alla Vaccinara	A Dish of oxtail – braised tail in tomato sauce
Pagliata (Italian) Paiata (Romano)	A Dish of unweaned calf intestines
Animelli	A Dish of pancreas – lingua or tongue
Cervello	A Dish of brains
Prosciutto Crudo	Raw cured ham
Carpaccio	Thin slices of raw meat in lemon juice

Roman Cuisine

ZONE 1: HISTORICAL CENTER

MOVING RESTAURANT RESTO TRAM
Reservations 06 46952252/ 06 46954695
View Rome and enjoy wonderful Italian cuisine.

A CRUISE WITH DINNER
Tel 06 69294147
Call for reservations
Departs at Ponte Sant'Angelo
Every night at 7:30pm board 15 minutes before departure time
A two hour and fifteen minute ride
Bus 492
www.battellidiroma.it

TAD CAFÈ
Via del Babuino 155
Tel 06 32695123
Unique women's fashions and exotic house décor, lunch, brunch and cocktails
Summer
June-September Monday 12-8pm Tuesday-Saturday 10:30-8pm
Winter
October-May Tuesday-Friday 10:30am-7:30pm Saturday 10:30-8pm
Sunday and Monday 12-8pm
Closed Sunday
The staff is extremely friendly, the atmosphere modern. Sun roofs and fountains mix with ancient Rome, contemporary and Asian
www.taditaly.com

LUCIANO'S
Via Amendola
A tiny family-owned restaurant that you'll need to squash yourself into. They serve homemade Roman dishes that are very inexpensive and delicious. They serve pasta carbonara, buccatini all'amatriciana, pasta al' ragù, veal plates, chicken, liver, steaks, broccoletti broccoli rabe sautéed in garlic and olive oil, chicory, minestrone, antipasti* and fresh breads. Every thing is fantastic, and if there is a line, it's worth waiting in.
A three minute walk from Termini station. Open until 9pm.
Sundays closed
Bus 70 71 75 Tram 5 14

RISTORANTE DER PALLARO
Largo del Pallaro 15
Tel 06 688 01488
Closed Mondays
Closes at 12:30am
An authentic Roman trattoria offering an array of Roman dishes and a preplanned menu. Don't be intimidated by the snippy old lady, she means well. They serve house wine with lentils, prosciutto, fried eggplant, olives, and tomatoes as antipasti.1st course is pasta with classic tomato sauce and Parmigiano. 2nd course roasted veal or other meats. The menu changes according to what's in season. Between 8pm-11pm the lines are long.

TRE PUPAZZI RISTORANTE
The Three Puppets
PIZZERIA ROMANA
A typical tavern of the 1500's
Borgo Pio 183
Via dei Tre Pupazzi 1
Tel 06 6868371
Closed on Sundays
(San Pietro area)

CUL DE SAC
Piazza Pasquino 73
Tel 06 68801094
(Piazza Navona Area)

ZONE 2: ESQUILINO

GRAN CAFFE STREGA Grand Witch's Café
Roman Cuisine
Piazza Viminale 27/31
Tel 06 9485670

GEMMA ALLA LUPA
The Wolf's Gem
Via Marghera 39
Tel 06 491230
Tripe, oxtail stew, and classic Roman dishes
Closes at 11pm

ZONE 3: TRASTEVERE

ANTICA PESA
Via Garibaldi 18
Tel 06 5809236
Closed on Sundays at 11:30pm
Only for dinner
Preplanned menu

GLASS HOSTARIA
Pasta fatta in casa/ homemade pasta
Via del Cinque 58
Tel 06 58335903

ZONE 4: SAN GIOVANNI

MAUD
Via Capo D'Africa 6
Tel 06 77590809
Classic Roman food, creative
Kitchen closes at midnight
Only for dinner
Closed Mondays

ZONE 5: PRATI

OSTERIA DELL'ANGELO
Via G. Bettolo 24
Reservations 06 3729470
Open to 11pm
Closed on Sundays
Everything is alla carte.
A preplanned menu for 25€ includes such dishes as: spaghetti alla gricia bacon, onion, white wine, olive oil, Romano cheese, salt and pepper and a second course of roasted baby lamb.

TAVERNA ANGELICA
Piazza Capponi 6
Tel 06 6874514
Only for dinner
Closes at midnight
Raw fish and stringozzi short pastas made with flour and water.
All desserts are made by hand on the premises.
www.tavernaangelica.it

ZONE 7: PARIOLI

CAFFE DELLE ARTI
Via Antonio Gramsci 73
Tel 06 32651236
Kitchen closes at 11pm
Caffè delle Arti sits on the terrace of the National Modern Art Gallery
Sunday brunch, lunch and dinner
Closed Monday evenings
www.caffedelleartiroma.it

ZONE 8: OSTIENSE

AL BIONDO TEVERE
Via Ostiense 178
Tel 06 5741172
Kitchen closes at midnight
A patio terrace overlooking the Tevere River
Pizza, meat and fish

ZONE 9: TESTACCIO

CHECCHINO Roman Cuisine
Est. 1887
Via Monte Testaccio 30
Tel 06 5746318

DA"FELICE"
Via Mastro Giorgio 29
Tel 06 5746800
A place frequented by famous faces because it's fantastic.
Kitchen closes at 11:30pm

Il TALISMANO DELLA FELICITÀ COOKBOOK 1929
It is composed of a tale of recipes collected by Ana Boni from 1915, quite the first cookbook written in the Italian language. It still sells heavily today in the springtime, close to wedding season.

ZONE A: MONTE SACRO

Olivio's
HOSTARIA MAMUTONES
Piazza Monte Gennaro 29
Tel 06 8185237/
06 87193264
Full of fun as the waiters become showmen and ask audience participation. The food is delivered In courses, automatically-goes on a preplanned menu.
Closed Monday

LO ZODIACO in Monte Mario
Caffè Tea Room/Restaurant
Via del Parco Mellini
88/90/92
Reservations 06
35496640/06 35496744
A classy place set on a hill with an outside patio bordering an exuberating view. At night you can sit by the windows and see the city lights of Rome.
They have a good selection of Sicilian ice cream
Piano music
Casual to classy
Taxi

AL RISTORO DEGLI ANGELI
Authentic Roman Food
Via Luigi Orlando 2
Reservations 06 51436020
Recommended to me by two Roman residents of the Monte Verde area
In front of the Palladium theatre
Closed on Sundays
Metro line A Garbatella
www.ristorodegliangeli.it

> "*Fortune sides with him who dares*"
> Virgil

ZONE K: CASTELLI ROMANI/THE ROMAN CASTLES

Town of Rocca di Papa
DA"PEPETTO"
Via Ariccia 4
Tel 06 9498888
Sensational grilled meats: abbachio baby lamb, beef, pecora sheep, pork and fresh antipasti. Delicious desserts are made from scratch.

TOWN OF ROCCA PRIORA

SORA ROSA
Via dei Castelli Romani 38
Tel 06 9470799
Unique vegetables baked perfectly, homemade breads, pastas, grilled meats, and prime desserts

**L'ANTICO ROMANO*
Restaurant, pizzeria, and mini-hotel
Via Roma 37
Tel 06 9470526
Grilled meat and fish
Specialty seafood salad
www.lanticoromano.com

TOWN OF MARINO

LA MADRE PANZA
Via Maronchelli
Elegant Medieval-style atmosphere.
Scrumptious antipasti and meat dishes

TOWN OF ARICCIA

LA LOCANDA DEL BRIGANTE GASPERONE
Via Borgo Rocco 7
Tel 06 9333100
Good roasted pork, prosciutto, salami, wine
Roman-style pastas, roasted sheep, steaks, sausage

DA COIOLI AL GROTTINO
Next to La Locanda del Brigante Gasperone
Homemade pasta's, great antipasti, roasted pork, and house wine
Order inside then seat yourself outside

CHIOSCO "LA SELVOTTA"
Via della Selvotta
Lampioncino
Between Ariccia and Albano in Chigi Park
Pasta all'Amatriciana, sandwiches, Casereccio bread, homemade wine, espresso and gelato
Reservations necessary on Saturday and Sunday
Roman-style atmosphere-picnic tables set up in the back yard

ZONE 1: HISTORICAL CENTER

JAPANESE CUISINE

RICCIOLI CAFE-SUSHI BAR
Via delle Coppelle 13
Tel 06 68210313
(Pantheon area)

MIDDLE-EASTERN CUISINE

ZONE B: CASSIA

RISTORANTE PERSIANO KABAB Persian
Via di Grottarossa 52
Tel 06 30310231

SCIAM
Via del Pellegrino
Fantastic Middle-Eastern cuisine, enjoyable atmosphere. Smoke a Hookah a tobacco water pipe, for relaxation or try their jasmine tea. Their little shop sells unique Turkish items: lamps, coloured glass objects
Bus 30EX 40EX 62 64 70 81 116
(Campo de'Fiori Area)

HEBREW/ROMAN CUISINE-IN THE JEWISH GHETTO

DA GIGGETO AL PORTICO D'OTTAVIA
Via del Portico D'Ottavia 21
Tel 06 6861105
Closed Monday

CHINESE CUISINE

ZONE G: PRENESTINO

CITTA ALLEGRA
Via Bellegra 44/48
Tel 06 2155156
Wonderful Chinese cuisine with excellent service. Family-owned and run by Giulia and Michele.
Tram 14 from Via Gioberti near Termini station or Piazza Vittorio Emanuele

MARGUTTA RISTORANTE-VEGETARIANO est. 1979
Vegetarian restaurant on the famous artist's lane Via Margutta 118 runs parallel to Via Babuino
Tel 06 32650577
Kitchen closes at 11:30pm
www.ilmargutta.it
Metro line A Spagna or Flaminio

**All public places were smoke free as of January 10, 2005*

PIZZA

FRONTONI
Via S. F. a Ripa 129
Tel 06 58334 265
Trastevere
Oldest pizzeria in Rome off Via Nazionale

IL BUCHETTO
Via Flaminia 119
Tel 06 3201707
Saturday and Sunday for lunch 11:30am
Try and get there before 8pm-it gets busy
Closed Tuesday evenings
Mozzarella di Bufala, thick pungent prosciutto, roasted seasoned pork, homemade bread, Romanella wine, pasta all'Amatriciana and more.

Deruta ceramics

La Scarpetta

"La Scar-pet-tah." In reality this might as well be a small shoe or a short boot—scarpa means shoe, when adding "etta" you have a smaller one.

The tiny shoe that isn't a shoe
It is a slip of bread to soak up goo
To be dipped in oil
To be meant to soil
And if missed at the table it could spoil
A dinner so graced in pleasure
But in the end, with nothing to measure
Up to the satisfaction awaited for this moment
To soak up remainders at the bottom of a bowl
To make all happy as a whole
To do this scarpetta don't worry no fretta
For this tiny shoe is made of bread
And in its absence creates those to dread
So don't forget to have it with you
And clean up your dishes
Now all is well
And many wishes

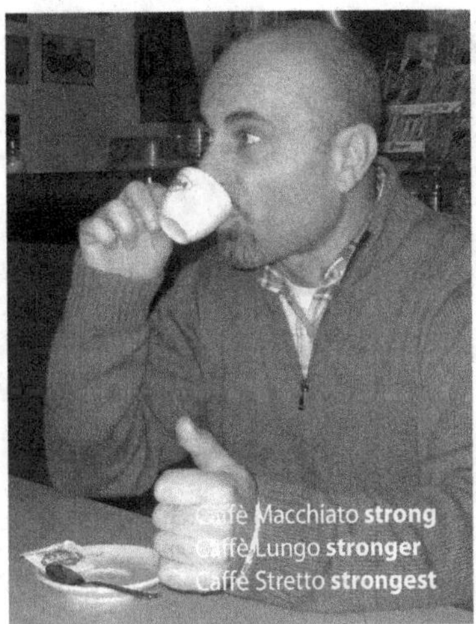

Caffè Macchiato **strong**
Caffè Lungo **stronger**
Caffè Stretto **strongest**

Caffe-Espresso

If you are crazy for espresso seek no further, Rome has good options. Try the delicious traditional espresso native to the Campania region of Italy, a hazelnut espresso famous in Salerno and Napoli. (See"Caffè et Café)

ITALIAN-STYLE: CHINOTTO

Chinotto is a type of dark brown soda made from a variety of herbs including: rhubarb, gentian, china, and citrus fruit of chinotto, sweet orange, bitter orange, tamarind, and thyme. The original brand is called Chin8neri. The soda is slightly bitter but a bit sweet and refreshing.

WHAT CAN YOU EXPECT IN A COFFEE BAR?

Chiaro - less espresso than a regular cappuccino, lighter in colour
Cappuccino - one shot of espresso with milk
Cappuccino scuro - cappuccino with extra espresso
Latte macchiato - a shot of coffee in warmed milk
Caffè latte - mostly milk, with a shot of espresso
Caffè lungo - weaker than regular espresso, more water is allowed to enter the espresso
Caffè - one shot of espresso
Caffè hag - they pronounce it"ahg", this is decaffeinated espresso
Caffè ristretto - less water, thicker, stronger
Caffè doppia - double shot of espresso
Caffè corretto - shot of espresso with a dash of liquor
Caffè macchiato - one shot of espresso with a dash of hot or cold milk
Caffè americano - a very watered down espresso
Caffè in vetro - one shot of espresso in a shot glass they swear it tastes different served in glass
Caffè d'orzo - coffee made with toasted ground barley, good for children and no caffeine. Some bars have an orzo cappuccino machine and they'll ask if you want it in a large mug or a small one piccolo o grande? that's just a preference.
Caffè freddo - sweetened espresso made up in the morning, no milk added
**Caffè shackerato* - fresh espresso made on the spot, shaken up with ice
**Cioccolata calda/hot chocolate* - a pudding of hot chocolate with whipped cream
Cioccolata americana - hot chocolate Italian Style with milk added
Cioccolata bianca calda - hot white chocolate
Tè caldo - hot tea
Spremuta - freshly squeezed oranges and lemons or just blood oranges
Latte - milk
Tè freddo - iced tea
Corbello - sorbet
Granita di caffè con panna - shaved ice with sweetened espresso and heavy cream, a must try!
Cornetto or brioche - breakfast croissant
Aperitivo/Aperitif - red, orange or white bubbly appetite stimulant, enjoyed in coffee bars before lunch or dinner. The reds are alcoholic: campari soda and aperol.
Tramezzino - triangular sandwich sponge-like wonder bread without a crust usually made with tuna and tomato or ham and cheese.
Panino - a sandwich with focaccia or pizza bread

**Cappuccino is served warm, not scalding hot which dulls the taste.*

Roma for expresso (caffe)

Rome is seeping with coffee shops, as you will see, but it's easiest to select from my fondest list of five.

ZONE 12: EUR

BAR PALOMBINI
Via Cristoforo Colombo
Piazza dell'Obelisco
Close to Luna Park
EUR area near the man-made lake constructed by Mussolini

ZONE 1: HISTORICAL CENTER

LA TAZZA D'ORO
Via Degli Orfani 84
Tel 06 6789792
Gelateria-caffetteria-Pantheon Area - the street is right off the piazza

BAR SANT'EUSTACHIO
Piazza Sant'Eustachio
Close to Piazza Navona

ZONE G: PRENESTINO

CAFÉ et CAFFE A
Charming coffee shop....
Originally from Salerno,
the staff creates espresso like the ones in Naples and Salerno.
Noccolino or hazelnut espresso

ANTICO CAFFÈ GRECO
Via Condotti 86
Tel 06 679100
You may purchase Italian or American coffees at the Caffè Greco.
Mark Twain spent a good amount of his time here, as well as Buffalo Bill-portraits of them décor the walls in Caffè Greco.
Specialità: granita di caffè con doppia panna/coffee shaved ice with double cream.
(Piazza di Spagna area)

CAFÉ ET CAFÉ ESPRESSO MENU

- Caffè et Café (espresso, crema di cafè, and hazelnut cream)
- Caffè et Nocciola Amore (espresso, cocoa and crème di caffè)
- Caffè Viennese (espresso, cream and cocoa)
- Mont Blanc (espresso, cream and Baileys)
- Cappuccino alla Nocciola (hazelnut cappuccino)
- Caffè alla Nocciola con Panna (hazelnut espresso, cream)
- Caffè Freddo Shekerato (cold sweetened espresso and shaken with ice)

The Cappuccino is an invention of Vienna, Austria

ORDERING AT THE COFFEE BAR:

- Find the menu and decide what you'd like
- Go to the cashier and say Buon giorno or good morning, then order and pay.
- Take your receipt to the bartender and tell him what you've ordered.

ESPRESSO BRAND NAMES

You may recognize some of these Italian brands at home.

AVAILABLE IN MARKETS:

Hag (decaffeinated)
LaVazza
Illy
Passalacqua
Kimbo
Granaroma
Caffè Trombetta (Roman espresso est. 1890)
Carpino
Chicco Rosso

ACQUA - WATER
Acqua Minerale Naturale: non-carbonated water with minerals
Acqua Frizzante/Gassata: carbonated water
Acqua Normale: tap water
Acqua Vite: italian brandy
Analcolico: non alcoholic
Acqua Naturale: regular spring water

Italians drink water or wine with meals never a coffee or cappuccino, not until the end with desserts and liquors

Marcello's bar, Rocca Priora

USED PROFESSIONALLY IN COFFEE BARS:

Caffè Danesi
Jolly Caffè
Caffè Fantini
Gran Brasil
Caffè Sciubba
Caffè Circi
Caffè Ciamei
Caffè Pacetti
Caffè Morganti
Gran Caffè Santos
Caffè Miani
BonCaffè Montorsi
Profili Caffè
Caffè Negresco
Caffè Perù
Peri Caffe
Caffè Viola

"Torrefazione" bars ground and roast espresso on the premises.

Have a cup of tea!
I must squeeze in a teahouse in the mist of all this espresso...

The Russian Tea Room
Via Dei Falegnami 7
www.russtearoom.com
9am-midnight

Bar Sinario

Cashier: *Prego?/May I help you?*
Guest: *Si, un cappuccino e un caffè*
Cashier: *Basta?/Is that it?*
Guest: *Si, Grazie/Yes, thank you*
At this point the guest moves over to the bar and hands or sets down his paid receipt. If asked he replys:
Bartender: *Prego?/May I help you?*
Guest: *Un cappuccino e un caffè/one cappucino and one espresso*

Sitting endlessly for an espresso

She had a nest of black hair, birds and all. She lacked everything including a personality but her neck because it folded into the plump rolls that were her chin. She served espressos day in and day out, day beginning and day ending besides running her mouth to everyone but customers. Her English vocabulary, was well, that's how it was and not very good. She came wiggling over with spiked heels pinning into the pavement and birdsong whistling from the top of her head.

"Main-you?"

We looked simultaneously at each other and were amazed at the bundle of hair she had. Her plump rump jiggled and she wiggled back to the bar with the hairpins holding the contraption on her scalp bending like a storm hit them.

"Zucchero?"she said then itched her head.

"What?"we both said at the same time again.

"Eh, sue-gar?"it was much better this time.

"Yes"we replied.

Our choice was zucchero, zucchero di canna, or a sugar substitute made by Barnaby's laboratory if I could remember. We worried about her mop, at least about what was about to fall on us.

The espressos were finished voilà. We were ready to quick order another two. Quick? The cafeteria signorina came back once then vanished.

Looking out the corner of our eye, we witnessed just what was happening behind us. She was yapping away, flirting and contorting with the coffee barman. Her big-lips fluttered her rump jiggling around. Our day called for a long rest and this was the perfect harmless Roman café or was it? She had to come back to see if we were still breathing, but when?

Finally she came back, took our tiny mugs without looking at us and left. Wait....

We did want to order something else. But back to the barman. This means another half hour. From noon till past five she had come to see us three times and in the meantime, she married the barman, divorced him and managed to knit ten pairs of mittens in her rocking chair on the porch.

Gelato

The first ice cream cone was produced in 1896 by Italo Marchioni. Marchioni emigrated from Italy in the late 1800s, inventing his ice cream cone in New Jersey. He was granted a patent in December 1903.

Italo Marchioni arrived in Hoboken from Italy in 1895 and sold ice cream and lemon ice from a pushcart on New York's Wall Street. He initially used liquor glasses to serve his confections to stockbrokers and Wall Street runners. But the glasses smashed and broke or were stolen besides having to be washed after each serving. Marchioni devised a better way to serve ice cream-the edible cup we know today as the ice cream cone. Marchioni baked waffles and while still warm folded them into the shape of a cup stuffing it with ice cream. The customers relished the cups which proved convenient, sanitary and tasty. The waffle cup made Marchioni the most popular vendor on Wall Street and soon afterwards, he had a chain of 45 carts operated by men he hired.

Along the slopes of the Trinità dei Monti church and the Villa Medici, there's a park called Pincio. In the 1950's, this area dominated the city because in the evenings terraces filled with people there to take sherbets without leaving their cars to do so. Trays were hooks onto car doors oddly shaped trays made to fit in just right. Maybe you remember the car hops?

**FASSI*

Via Principe Eugenio 65-67
Tel 06 4464740
Fassi is the largest and most antique ice cream parlour in Italy. It all started in the year 1880 as trial and error, in the beginning they sold Italian ices mixed with beer. Giacomo founded this ice cream dynasty, and with his first tiny shop near piazza Barberini, he signed to the beginnings of four generations. Fassi was granted a gold metal for fidelity and economic progress.
10 min. walk from Termini Station
Fassi is Rome's antique gelateria ice cream parlour, and considered one of the best.

LO ZODIACO

Viale Parco Mellini 90 Via Trionfale
Tel 06 35496744
By taxi is the best way to get there
Overlooks Rome, is romantic and relaxing
Mint gelato, Sicilian espresso ice cream and many other varieties.
Closed on Tuesdays

LAGO ARTIFICIALE

Mussolini's work of man-made art. It's a modern area of Rome. The lake of EUR was intended to be part of the 3rd Rome, which Mussolini had intended to create.
Metro line B EUR-Fermi
Nice place for a stroll
Sundays & weekend nights is the favorite among Italians.

**OLD BRIDGE GELATERIA*

Via dei Bastoni di Michelangelo 5
Tel 06 397 23026
It's a little cove always covered with a crowd of waiting people and bulging cones. They will not only be generous with the amount of ice cream they plop onto your cone, they will greet you with a smile. The ice cream is made fresh every day. It's worth the wait. You'll find it around the corner from Piazza Risorgimento. Walk towards the high brick wall that winds around the corner. Antonio is across from that wall. He is the tall kind one with the puffed hat and sparkling eyes.

The ice creams of San Crispino

Giuseppe, Pasquale Alongi and Paola Nesci

Quality comes first regardless of material costs. San Crispino ice creams are sincerely produced with passion and devotion. A miraculous team, they are full of inspiration and creativity and we thank you Giuseppe, Paola and Pasquale Alongi.

The trio produces natural ice creams (emulsifiers are nothing but egg yolks) which are handled carefully and perhaps result in the best ice cream in Italy. Flavors fluctuate within the seasons. (You shouldn't find strawberry ice cream in the dead of winter). Each piece of fruit, nut, and spice are gathered by hand from the habitat in which they dwell and flourish, picked during peak seasons so the ice cream flavors are prime. Mysteriously, they store them at lower temperatures then usual, which as they say quality to endure. The coffee ice-cream is made from Blue Mountain Jamaican single-bean coffee grounds.

All San Crispino ice creams are free of artificial preservatives, chemical emulsifiers, frozen foods and sundry mixes. Ice cream and sorbets are served in cups only as cones are loaded with five different types of colourings and may change the flavour of the ice cream.

SOME FLAVORS OF SAN CRISPINO

- Cannella and zenzero/cinnamon and ginger
- Licorizia/licorice root
- Meringe di nocciola/hazelnut meringhe
- Cacao al Rhum/cocoa and rum
- Castagne and rhum/chestnut and rum
- Walnut and fig
- San Crispino/Sardinian wild honey
- Whisky malpighi
- Passito Pantelleria/a sweet Sicilian dessert wine made into ice cream
- Nocciola/hazelnut
- Crema/cream
- Armagnac
- Pistacchio (pea-stah-key-oh)
- Zabaione/Marsala ice cream, a 30-year-old reserve produced by De Bartoli
- Meringe di nocciola/hazelnut meringhe
- Meringe di ciocolato/chocolate and meringhe
- Bergamot citrus
- Camomille

SORBETS

- Limone di Amalfitana/Almalfi lemon
- *Pompelmo/grapefruit
- Isabella grape
- Seville orange
- Clementine
- Antofagasta grape
- Melone/cantaloupe
- Pera/pear
- Limo/lime

SAN CRISPINO LOCATIONS:

Via Panetteria 42
Near the Trevi fountain
It's a little tricky to find, we always tend to walk right by it
Via Acaia 56
Via Bevagna 90
Towards Via Flaminia and Corso Francia

GIOLITTI

Ice cream parlour-Coffee bar-Pastry shop
Quite the oldest ice cream shop in Rome
est.1900
*Open all week all year around from 7am to 2am
It's absolutely divine. The ingredients are nothing but the freshest.
www.giolitti.it

Giolitti locations:

ZONE 1: HISTORICAL CENTER

Via Uffici del Vicario 40
Tel 06 6991243
This location is at the fork of Via del Corso, Largo Chigi and Piazza Colonna
Bus 116

ZONE 12: EUR

Viale Oceania 90
This location is by a man-made lake- nice for a romantic evening stroll
Metro line B Eur Fermi

P. S. The tartufo at the Tre Scalini in Piazza Navona...is lovely.

You will be given a choice of 2-3 different flavours of ice cream and asked "Con la panna?"
Panna is an unsweetened fresh whipped cream.

GRATTACHECCHE/ITALIAN ICE

Italian ice along the river...

These stubby stands are usually found along the roadside running along the river on both sides. They operate through the warm summer seasons. The Italian ice is produced from large slabs of ice that is shaved and syruped.
Some flavors included: Coco (coconut), Limone (lemon), Fragole (strawberry), Ananas (pineapple), Pesca (peach)

They will ask if you would like yours piled with fresh fruit con la frutta.

GRATTACHECCHE

Piazza Ponte Umberto/Lungotevere Marzio

SORA MIRELLA est.1915

It's along the Lungotevere, the street lining the river.
Cross the Ponte Cestio bridge and turn to your right, it's a little past the corner of Lungotevere degli Anguillara/Ponte Cestio.
Look for the little stand outside.

ZONE 3: TRASTEVERE

FONTE D'ORO

Piazza G. G. Belli
Ponte Garibaldi/Garibaldi bridge
10am-2pm

USEFUL WORDS AND PHRASES		
Cono	Cone	cohn no
Coppa	Cup	cope pah
I Gusti	Flavors	ee goo stee
Che gusto?	What flavor?	k goo stow?
Panna	Heavy whipped cream	pahn nah
Basta così?	That's all?	bah stah coe zee
Colla frutta?	With fruit?	cone lah froo tah

Tours

ZONE 1: HISTORICAL CENTER

TEMPLAR TOUR

S. BONIFACIO
San Alessio
Alberico di Spoleto, a frank desc
once transformed a building int
monastery on the Aventino hill i
The internal church was dedicated to the mystic Greek San Basilio.

Underneath SANTA PRISCA there is a mitreo with an affresco of souvetaurilla the sacrificing of a ram, bull and wild boar.

SANTA SABINA The Keyhole
This is an antique church like
a pagan temple.
Piazza Pietro D'Illiria 1
Tel 06 57941

MONASTERY CELLA NUOVA
Santa Saba
This church was granted by Lucio II Caccianemici to the Cluniacs in 1144.
Piazza Gian Lorenzo Bernini 20
Tel 06 5743352

ZONE K: I CASTELLI ROMANI

CASTLE TOURS
SOVRANA VIAGGI
Via Guelfo Civinini 26/34
Tel 06 82003119
www.castles.it

SUBTERRANEAN TOURS
Tel 347 3811874
www.romasotterranea.com

ABBEY OF THE FERRATTA CRYPT
L'Abbazia di Crypta Ferrata
in Grottaferrata

PALAZZO ALBERICO
The Church of Santa Maria/Santa Basilio
Corso del Popolo 128
Tel 06 9459309
Grottaferrata
This church was assigned to the knights of Rodi and to the knights of Malta in 1522. Even though the Templars existed in Rome, their memory had vanished for centuries, but then an article turned up in 2006. It was published in a Roman magazine called the Controluce. "Its says the hill of the Aventino where Remo founder of Rome's tomb is for the Templars, a representation of the imagine of Jerusalem. A perfect place to construct a Templar organization. In 1138, Innocenzo II Papareschi took possession of Rome assigning, what was known as Sancta Maria de Aventino to the Order of the Knights Templars of Jerusalem. From the tower of the building, today you can see the surrounding hills, the Sublicio bridge and Porta Portese. The Templars who settled in Rome, were among the first Templar organizations in Italy.

SANTA BALBINA
Piazza di Santa Balbina
Tel 06 578 0207
This church wasn't mentioned in the article, but it's on the Aventino, maybe worth a visit.

TOURS WITH AUTORIZED GUIDES

Many tours unauthorized tour guides do not give exact information. They usually watch out for the police, and are busy breaking the law.
It's better to use a well spoken guide with a good reputation, and who will announce their license upon request.
Rome's professional tour guides have studied long and hard to earn their license, and are proud to show it.

ODYSSEY TOURS
www.odyssey-tours.com

Odyssey was founded in 2001 by a Dutch/ Australian woman who understood the need for English tours of a different nature. Odyssey guides are native English speakers and have degrees in Renaissance Art or World History.

**Odyssey specializes in private tours and custom tours of Rome and all over Italy.*

Odyssey is happy to offer Devils of Rome readers a 5€ discount for booking more than one tour with them.

WALKS INSIDE ROME
PRIVATE and SEMIPRIVATE tours of Rome, the Vatican and the outskirts of the city
E-mail: info@walksinsiderome.com
Marilena Cell +39 335 8193359
Salvatore Cell +39 335 282615

JEWISH ROMA WALKING TOURS
"Your Roman holiday would not be complete without a visit to the Jewish Ghetto with someone that can take you through with knowledge, anecdotes, legends and humour.
I am that person, and I would be glad to share all that with you."
Micaela Pavoncello
info@jewishroma.com

THE ETERNAL TOURIST
Tel 06 5817571/348 3360850
rometours@eternaltourist.com

OPEN TOUR WITH BUS 110
These red buses depart at Termini station every 15 minutes
In the two hours you will see:

Quirinale Rome's White House
The Coliseum
The Mouth of Truth
Piazza Venezia
Santa Maria of the Angels Church
The tour bus runs from 8:30am-8:30pm
It's 13€ for a daily pass
Tel 06 46952252

THE STOP N GO CHRISTIAN ROME BUS TOUR
The open-topped yellow buses depart from Termini station with 16 stops to some of the most sacred basilicas including:

St. Mary Major
St. Peter's
Santa Maria in Cosmedin

ARCHEOBUS TOUR
The green buses tour all of Appia Antica
The depart from Termini station everyday from 9am-4pm
Leaves every 40 minutes 8€
Tel 06 46952343
If you've purchased the Roma Pass, there is a ticket discount*

COMBINATION TICKETS

1. L'Archeobus and the 110 Open Bus Tour 20€
2. L'Archeobus and the Polo Museale 16€ giving you admission to the most important museums of the capitol.
3. L'Archeobus, 110 Open, and the Polo Museale 25€

*All valid for two days-5 days for museums
Tel 06 6840901
Toll free 800 281281
www.trambusopen.com

The World's Smallest State

It is the territory of the Knights of Malta. It resides on a minute 3 acres.
A sign hangs on the inside gate as so; you have stepped across the frontier, and now you are no longer in the state of Italy. Palazzo Malta, the 13th century villa, resides on the Aventine Hill. This Roman Catholic order is recognized in more than 30 countries and maintains full diplomatic relations with them. Today thousands of Knights of Malta carry on the tradition of being the Hospitallers the name of persons that band together to give aid to the poor and sick.

The Via Veneto Est. 1889

Kirk Douglas and Gregory Peck walked up this prestigious road causing American's and others to dream. In the 50's and 60's a good majority of films were staged in Europe and created with a series of romantic prose.

Since given the Dolce Vita symbol, local establishments on this street have made use of it. Some say this film turned the street into an ordinary one, as the aftermaths of fame forced people to be something they were not. These pressures turned the Dolce Vita sour and eventually it all fell down.

Glass gazebos hide people in jacket and tie like fish in aquariums who look out onto the perfect street one possessing the only one of two dog fountains in all of Europe.

We must look back to classic films and relive the life the Veneto experienced a one point in time.

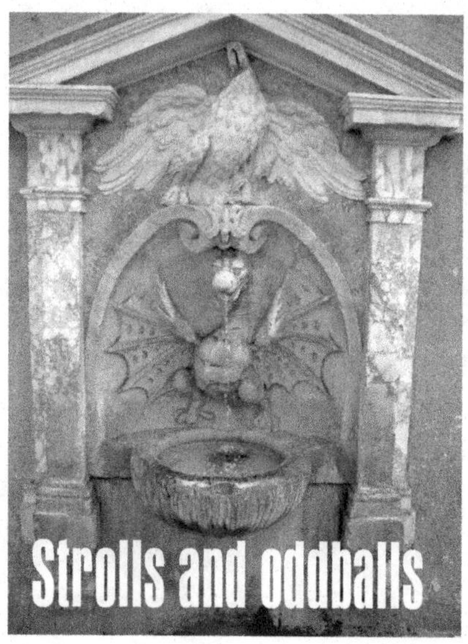

STROLLS AND ODDBALLS may be encountered in the very hidden and unknown areas of Rome. Yet some people say"I did Rome already". You did? But what does that mean exactly? Maybe tourists come with magic recipes in their pockets. How did they dig into a hidden world of ancient treasure centuries old in a week or two? It is truly mystical. Maybe someone should write a book series called the Roman magic pocket recipes. What's left you ask? Plenty.

QUIET STROLLS AND HILLS THAT ROLL

LAKE EUR

This spot may not be the quietest spot depending on the time of day or night and weekend nights are busy.
Metro line B Eur Fermi and a minutes walk.

GIANICOLO HILL

Will you attempt to climb the hill? The winding maze leading you up to one of the Seven Hills of Rome? You will be rewarded. Lights glare from the Fountanone, or huge fountain at the top of the hill, illuminating the main street on stark nights. See marvellous panoramas of Rome and the lip-lockers zone, where romantic couples congregate all along the stone wall which overlooks the incredulous Roman city.
Bus 116 from Via Veneto, Piazza San Silvestro or Corso Vittorio Emanuele II. Or you may take 116T from Piazza di Spagna.

BUS & BOAT

How about a boat ride tour? Join the others at the port of the Battelli di Roma right on the walkway of the Tevere Tiber River. Take your dog or bike aboard, and it's there you can buy your tickets.

ISOLA TIBURINA

The island is sealed off from the rest of the city above. Silence is Rome's gold little island set in the Tevere River. Many people visit in the summer to read along the side of the falls, or to tan their white bodies. Many walk, bike, or jog along the paved paths. The traffic above seems to come to a mute, which gives more of a peaceful state and serenity. There are many staircase entrances leading to off of the Lungotevere main road, and Ponte Fabricio leads you to the sunny side in the middle of the island. Go over the bridge and past the tiny piazza and go down the stairs on the right.

During August the boardwalk turns into the Paris Plage and there are restaurants, pubs, live music stages, beaches and gyms. People are out till late hours and the falls roar under the Roman moon.

TRASTEVERE

"It's the place for rustic colours and dangling clothes".
Largo Torre Argentina will send you to Via Arenula which ends near the Garibaldi Bridge, then sends you over the Tevere Tiber River and there you are.
All the windy old-fashioned alley ways that you love and see in films are here, it's kept that old-fashioned Rome alive. This is the artsy section of Rome which has many fantastic shops owned by local artists. It is filled with vegetarian spots, wine bars, jazz clubs and show persons filling the squares. You may sit outside and have dinner beside the sounds of music.

Quiet strolls

CEMETARY VERANO
Tel 06 49236330
A true taste of heaven. A quiet world all its own, for miles and miles it continues on. A place for reflection, meditation and enchantment. A place deserving solace and respect. You'll find the tombs of famous people who've had the privilege to rest here: Marcello Mastroianni, Vittorio de Sica, Alberto Sordi, Aldo Fabrizi, Roberto Rossellini, Vittorio Gassman, Maria Montessori and Natalia Ginzburg among many others.
Monday-Friday 8:30am-12:30pm
Tuesday and Thursday also 3pm-5pm
Saturday 8:30am-11:30am

VIA APPIA ANTICA
This old road was once a young thriving popular and often busy racetrack. It brought people to and from faraway lands and back to Rome again. Now in its last quarter of life, barren and voiceless, it shares nature with hideaway homes and maybe a daily cyclist. Visit with the peaceful sounds and rustling Roman spirits.

VILLA BORGHESE
The premise of the villa is certainly vast enough to find a quiet place to rest. Towards the centre of the estate there is a pleasant lake where swans and other little creatures stretch their wings. Entering from Via Washington by metro line A Flamino, continue to Piazza Flaminio and onto Via Esculapio.

Options for arriving at Villa Borghese:
• Walk up the Spanish steps from Piazza di Spagna and bare left at the top. It's down the road on the right
• Take metro line A and inside carefully follow the directions for Villa Borghese where there is a walkway with signs
• Exit metro line A at Barberini and walk all the way up Via Veneto and Villa Borghese will be in front of you across the intersection.
• Take the 53 or 53 bus both found on Via Veneto and exit on Via G. Puccini or Via Pinciana which run along the park.

Villa Medici-metro A Spagna
Galleria Borghese- bus 52 53
The Zoo-trams 3 19
Bus 110 goes right through Villa Borghese from Termini station

Strolling among the gardens

THE SACRED WOOD/PARK OF MONSTERS
PARCO DEI MOSTRI
Tel 07 61924029

In Bomarzo, a tiny town near Viterbo, bizarre testimonies of fantastic yet horrid tastes were created by Vicino Orsini in the middle 1600's was evident. But after his death, no one took interest in this bizarre ensemble. It was only till centuries later, that the Bettini family purchased it.
Numerous inscriptions keep you company along the paths in the woods.
Upon beginning your monster tour, you will be abruptly welcomed by the first statue on your map. Stunned at first you may not realize that you are looking at a man peering between a woman's open legs.
Up on a high hill subdued to the panoramic outstanding view, you'll fall upon statues built to resemble peculiar monsters only the prince could create in his head.
The map describes a delfino dolphin who sits to the left of Neptune, though it resembles an alligator or a prehistoric frog. You can walk through the tongue of the open-mouthed monster that isn't shy to expose its teeth. The teeth serve for chairs and the tongue as stairs. The prince was insane, but what prince wasn't? At some point you must pass by the sloping house la Casa Pendente and what a shake it is to the brain. Upon entering the nest level of the garden, you shall see an entrance to the right. The little house has two rooms on the upper level, crooked rooms.
Its rush affects the entire head and body, as you feel that"something just isn't right. "Makes you gasp for air, and unable to control the queasy feeling and sensations to purge. This leaning house had a magical recipe that produced intentional results. Made to perfection by an architect, friend of the prince, it counteracted his failures in seducing women due to his unpleasant looks.

**You may purchase souvenirs here and they sell all types of marmalades and honeys made by the monks in a small village close by. All products are organic.*

Oddballs

THE MAGIC MYSTERY OF VIA PICCOLOMINI

Piccolomini road can be seen while strolling or driving. It is better to drive as results are much quicker.

There is a point in the Via Piccolomini that is a grand illusion. It's a short street next to the crossing of Via Aurelia Antica and Via Leone XIII. It runs off Largo Cardinal Ferrata and is close to Villa Pamphilj. At the end of the street you'll see you have a clear view of the St. Peter's cupola and that's when the adventure begins.

The Illusion:

Fix your eyes on the Cupola of St Peter's. Go up and down the street and you'll realize that something abnormal is happening. As you get closer to the cupola, you'll see it transform into a smaller image, as you move farther away it will become larger before your eyes. Shouldn't that be the other way around?

It's too incredible for the sane imagination and a true trick of nature.

It left me without words.

PALAZZO SPADA

Within the gallery courtyard Palazzo Spada another incomprehensible brain boggler lurks. Borromini's optical illusion is this; as a spectator witnesses a person entering into the courtyard, he grows into a literal giant. Or it may seem that the courtyard is shrinking before your eyes.

THE QUADRIVIUM DELLE QUATTRO FONTANE

Yet another. The Quadrivium delle Quattro Fontane is found at the intersection of Via XX Settembre and Via delle Quattro Fontane. At this intersection from the bottom of the street you can see three obelisks at the same time: Trinità dei Monti, Quirinale and Santa Maria Maggiore.

*see Garden of Oranges page 123

Unique

ZONE 1: HISTORICAL CENTER

L'OLFATTORIO Est. '02

Via di Ripetta 34
Tel 06 3612325
Tuesday-Saturday 3:30pm-7:30pm
Closed in August
Walk-in's welcome

Discover a new way of testing fragrances. You create them.

Glass vials line the walls labelled with various scents. The fragrance bar frees one to mix and create the fragrance of her choice. Learn about fragrances too and chat with the charismatic staff. You will then be given a list of shops that carry your newly invented perfume. No Fee. Nothing for sale. Only for enlightenment.

Ask to see the DVD perfume encyclopedia. You may research any brand of perfume and read the history behind it.

Metro Flaminio line A
www.olfattorio.it

THE ROME RIVERBOATS/BATTELLI DI ROMA

Call for reservations 06 69294147
Departures at Ponte Sant'Angelo and Isola Tiberina Tiber Island every day
Tiber departures: 8am, 8:50, 9:55, 10:55, 11:50, 12:50, 4pm, 4:50, 5:55 6:45
Sant'Angelo bridge departures: 8:25am, 9:15, 10:20, 11:20, 12:15, 1:15, 4:25, 5:15, 6:20 and 7:10pm
Boarding 10 minutes before departure
A 1 hour and 15 minute ride
Tickets:
1€ one way
2. 30€ all day
30€ monthly pass
www.battellidiroma.it

THE TIME ELEVATOR
Via dei S. S. Apostoli 20
Via del Corso/Piazza Venezia
Tel 06 6990053/06 97746243
An unforgettable show that takes you back 3,000 years. You can relive the days the Romans roamed the earth. See the superstitious story of Remo and Romolo, the she-wolf that raised infants and the stories of Jullus Caesar and Michelangelo. Involves 45 minutes of pure story and culture.
info@Time-elevator.it

THE ROMAN HOUSES
Tel 06 70454544
Houses lying beneath the 5th century Basilica of Saint Paul and Saint John. They are located behind the Coliseum on the Colle del Celio Caelian Hill. It will lead you into the several rooms of ancient roman houses. Many are tastefully decorated in frescoes.
10am-1pm/3pm-6pm
Closed Tuesday and Wednesday
Tours upon request 15-25 person maximum
www.spazioliberocoop.it
www.caseromane.it

ZONE 3: TRASTEVERE

GIANICOLO/JANICULUM
The Greatest View of Rome
www.gianicoloinn.com
In Piazzale Garibaldi, it's Rome's highest and most scenic hill, counted as one of Rome's seven hills. A brutal battle took place here in a fight for independence 1848. It was Garibaldi who led this fierce battle against the French. Piazzale Garibaldi is northwest of Trastevere and just above the Botanical gardens. It is up the hill a "Passeggiata del Gianicolo," the Gianicolo walk. Every noon the cannon blasts the afternoon air in remembrance of the battle won. The view is impeccable.
Bus 115 870

ZONE 4: SAN GIOVANNI

SANTA CROCE IN GERUSALEMME
Piazza di Santa Croce in Gerusalemme 12
12:30-3:30pm
This church holds relics of the cross on which Jesus was crucified. It contains the crossbar from the cross of the good thief who was crucified next to him. In the upper sanctuary is the finger of St. Thomas which reached into the wound of Jesus. And behind a bullet-proof glass one of the nails that held Jesus' hand to the cross is displayed.
Besides all this, two of the thorns from the crown of thorns are preserved here.
Metro line A San Giovanni

THE HOLY STAIRS
Opposite the Basilica of San Giovanni in Laterano St. John Lateran, are the Holy Stairs. There is reason to believe they were the stairs outside the government building of Pontius Pilate, and the ones Jesus walked up before his crucifixion. They are now 28 preserved marble stairs in which people climb up on their knees.
The stairs are across the street from the Basilica of San Giovanni in Laterano, close to San Giovanni
Within walking distance from the Coliseum.
Bus 85 87 850 117

SANTA MARIA DELLA CONCEZIONE
Via Veneto 27
Closed from 12pm-3:45pm
4,000 monks donated their bones as raw material for the macabre decorations. They are gruesome indeed, but astonishing bone designs.
Metro line A Barberini
A donation is expected
Bus 52 53 490 495

ZONE 6: FLAMINIO

PINCIO

Just above Piazza del Popolo, Pincio can be relaxing for a stroll. Bordering Villa Borghese, you can now pedal around the park in a tandem, though it's a four wheeled contraption for two.

ZONE 8: OSTIENSE

PIRAMIDE DI CAIO CESTIO
PYRAMID OF CAIUS CESTIUS
Piazza di Porta San Paolo

Even though the Romans stole this pyramid invention from the Egyptians, it's worth a look inside the tomb of a wealthy Roman that died in 12 B.C..
You must stoop into the tiny doorway that sends you into a tunnel.
During the reign of Augustus and after the Roman conquest on Egypt 30 B.C. the Romans stole the idea the conquested city. Many wall decorations in the pyramid disappeared, and an inscription states that the pyramid was built in 330 days. It's cousin to the Roman cat sanctuary in Largo Argentina.
Bus 60 75 95 175 715 716
Metro line B Piramide
Tram 3 Trains FM1 FM3 FM5

IL GIARDINO degli ARANCI
THE KEYHOLE
The Garden of Oranges
An optical effect brings you close to heaven on the Aventino hill.
It is a beautiful illusion created by Piranesi. Giovanni Battista Piranesi also went by Giambattista October 4th, 1720-November 9th, 1778, born in Mogliano Veneto. He was an architect, engraver, etcher and stenographer.

Focus through the large ornate keyhole and see a row of green bushes lining a heavenly walkway. It will lead out into a far distance right onto the clouds, a stairway to heaven. You can also see the white top of St. Peter's cupola in the background.
From Circo Massimo Circus Maximus find your way to Via Valle Murcia, which is off of Via Circo Massimo, Piazzale Ugo La Malfa Walk past the rose garden and along Via di Santa Sabina to Piazza Sant'Alessio. The street then becomes a dead-end. The dark green gate with the large key hole is in Piazza dei Cavalieri di Malta.
Metro line B Circo Massimo

ZONE J: SALARIO

CITY FLY
Via Salaria 825
Tel 06 88333
Why don't you fly over the city?
You'll then be 1476ft/450m above sea level.
www.cityfly.com

ZONE K: THE CASTELLI ROMANI

PET CEMETARY
Rocca Priora Strada Provinciale
Rocca Priora 72
It's the only pet cemetery in the Lazio Region.

Two
dogs are walked

They are parallel, Siamese, clones, intertwining and identical.

Dogs walking in Rome suggest the likeness of two. Pedigrees, mutts all of them come up from the woodwork mysteriously in pairs.

Is there a dire necessity to walk two dogs instead of one? One dog will not satisfy the Roman 'A Spasso' and beware along narrowing sidewalks, hop-scotch may be the game to play.

Doggy bags are insulting when foreigners ask for them as no one in Italy brings anything home in a plastic or paper bag. Smaller are the quantities, but not the qualities.

June the last weekend in June

INFIORATA FLOWER FESTIVAL
GENZANO, CASTELLI ROMANI

A street carpeted with flowers an old tradition started in 1778, in honour of the procession of Corpus Domini. Each year the scenes change but handbooks are provided with each design in the series.

This street is on an incline and scenes are aligned vertically up the steps to the church on the hill.

they use different types of herbs and flowers for the designs: sand, barks some including; wild fennel leaves medium green, clove petals light yellow, acacia flowers white, white rice, fresh and dried olive flowers, yellow grapes, white and red rose petals, ground pine bark dark red-brown, chestnuts infiroescenze staminifere brown, ground coffee beans fondi dark brown, pine seeds tabacco brown, olives black-brown, dried and toasted grapes black, daisies disco del capriolo yellow, Veccia pelosa blu-violet, galega officinalis-blue

---

See roses that are roses that don't seem like roses from a normal garden.

ROSETO COMUNALE

Rome's famous rose garden

Via di Valle Murcia on the Aventino Hill
The most beautiful garden in the world, say experts.

They all paint the roses red each year in May in the Roseto Comunale, the Roman rose garden est. 1933.
Ornate roses flown in from world, they become the Jekyll and Hyde of roses as new creations are formulated. At least ten nations participate which brings more than 100 varieties of roses.
Roseto Comunale is the most beautiful garden in the world, say experts.
They look for the star of the year, a new type of rose to introduce into the flower market.

You will find Trellises with roses climbing about from different continents. The garden across the way is where the most fragranted roses are. All roses in the garden are marked with a classification and the year in which the rose species was first introduced to Rome. In 2006, I declared the rarest and most exotique roses were New Zealand's which plants grew roses the color of terracotta. Many species came from France, fewer from China and Japan. They were brought over from England and the United States and from Germany who's rose bushes were so odd, a single bush flaunted a bouquet of roses, but each in a different color.
The few Italian roses that were displayed were all very unique and beautiful, and quite similar to the French types.
Tel 06 5746810

Jazz & Image Festival
Ancient Amphitheater lights up with classics
Roma Europa festival
One of Italy's most famous performing arts festivals
June-July and September-November
Tel 06 4742286
www.romaeuropa. net

Book trades and antiques

ZONE 1: HISTORICAL CENTER

FIERA DEL LIBRO
Book show
Weekdays from 9am to 7pm
Via delle Terme di Diocleziano
Metro line A Repubbica
A short walk from Termini station and off Piazza della Repubblica

FONTANELLA BORGHESE
Antique book trade
Antique engraving, magazines, postcards.
Largo della Fontanella di Borghese
Metro line A Spagna
Take Via Condotti off Piazza di Spagna. Pass Largo Goldoni square, proceeding to Fontana Borghese.

LA SOFFITTA SOTTO I PORTICI
Piazza Augusto Imperatore
Every 1st and 3rd Sunday of the month (Excluding August)
10am till sunset
More than 100 exhibitors
Collector's items and antiques to fairly new items
Metro Spagna exit to the right and hit Via Babuino briefly, swing a sharp left onto Via della Croce til you come upon Largo Lombardo go straight ahead onto Tribuna di S. Carlo and at the end you will find Piazza Augusto

ZONE 8: OSTIENSE

LA SOFFITTA IN GARAGE
The first Sunday of the month
Exchanging of collectables and antique trade
Underground car park of Piazzale dei Partigiani, Ostiense station (Park-Si)
10am to 7pm
Metro line B Ostiense

ZONE 12: EUR

TUTTI IN PIAZZA
Antique exhibition
Viale America-Laghetto
Tel 338 4060223

ZONE I: NOMENTANO

PASSATO-PRESENTE
Via del Casale di San Basilio
Tel 06 298304
This is a enormous antique exhibition
Music, literature
Saturday and Sunday
8am-8pm

Flea markets

ZONE 3: TRASTEVERE

PORTA PORTESE
Via Portuense/Piazza di Porta Portese
This is the famous flea market written in many books Every Sunday from dawn to 1pm the Porta Portese is set up along Via Portuense and adjacent areas. There are used, stolen and new items available. Leather shoes can be economical and good quality if you look thouroughly. Find everything from music albums and cd's to clothes and household items, make-up, antiques, jewelery, toys, plants, hardware items, jackets, to rugs and tapestry and bedding. It's a good place for replacing lost items if you don't want to spend of money.
A man confessed that his car was completely stripped one afternoon.
They took everything down to the inside upholstery. The next morning, he went to the Portese Portese market and it was the booth selling miscellaneous items that interested him. And it was exactly there where he found the seats to his car, but not being able to prove they were his, he had to purchase them back.
This is not a fluke, people have found the items at this market had been the results of burglaries, and every now and again the law cleans it up.

From Largo Torre Argentina take Tram °8 and get off right at the 2nd stop, Porta Portese is within walking distance from there. Go down Via Portuense and it's on your left.
Bus 75 from Termini station or bus 44 from Piazza Venezia
Tram 3

ZONE G: PRENESTINO

PORTA PORTESE 2
This one is a cousin to the original Porta Portese. It's open on Sunday from dawn to 1pm in the Prenestino quarter in front of Nuovo Mattatoio/Piazza Pino Pascali. Displays include a variety of items new or second-hand. Peak hours start at 12 noon, so do pickpockets.
Tram 5, 14 from Termini

Tutti in Piazza
Antique exhibition
Viale America-Laghetto (EUR) Zone 12
Tel 338 406 0223

ITALIAN HOLIDAYS	
January 1st	Capodanno-New Year's Day
January 6th	Befana/Epifana-Epiphany
January 7th	Flag Day
February 8th	Il Carnevale-street celebrations Sunday to Tuesday each year before Lent
March 8th	Festa della Donna-a holiday for ladies
March 19th	Festa del Papa, Father's Day
March 27th	Pasqua di Resurrezione-the resurrection
March 28th	Lunedì dell'Angelo-the day after the resurrection
April 1st	Primo Aprile-April Fools Day
April 20th	Pasqua-Easter
April 21st	Lunedì dell'Angelo-Easter Monday
April 25th	Festa della Liberazione-Liberation Day
May 1st	Festa del Lavoro-May Day
May 9th	Festa della Mamma, Mother's Day
June 2nd	Festa della Repubblica-Republic holiday
August 15th	Ferragosto August Vacation/Assunzione the Assumption
November 1st	Tutti I Santi-All Saints/Day of the Dead
December 8th	Concessione Immacolato/Immaculate Conception
December 15th	Holiday for the Carabinieri military police
December 24th	Vigilia di Natale/Christmas Eve
December 25th	Natale-Christmas
December 31st	Capodanno-New Year's

The Holidays explained...

January 6th EPIFANA

The name Epifana was derived from the Greek term meaning apparition or manifestation. The story goes back to the pagan pre-Christian world.

In medieval times, the figure of Befana was similar to that of a witch and she brought gifts to children on the night of Epifana, January 6th. During the Medieval epoch, an important emphasis was placed on this period from Christmas to the 6th of January. These days were named The Twelve Nights or Dodici Notte.

During those twelve nights the people of the country thought Goddess Diana was really flying above their seeded fields. Diana is known as the Goddess of fertility.

In Antique Rome she was the Goddess of fertility and the moon. Because people believed it always remained a tale. Diana and the girls were considered nothing but harmless, but after the Christian church took control this was no longer a reality. The church condemned them for paganism and to emphasize this, declared them daughters of Satan.

This tradition is also celebrated throughout Europe, not just in Italy.

If you pass by Piazza Navona during this time, you'll find a wonderland of gifts and toys for children. Everything is creatively transformed into a magical Befana toyland. In the old days most people were quite poor, and when chocolates and candies would cause them to starve for a week, they couldn't justify the purchase.

Simple stockings were hung up over fireplaces and the next morning kids found chocolates and candies bulging from the big socks. The naughty children received a piece of candy disguised as coal and I'm sure it wasn't very attractive, but it was still edible.

January 7th FLAG DAY

The Italian flag was raised in Reggio Emilia over 2oo years ago and a celebration is held for this symbol of unity and freedom. It is the flag of the 5 days of Milan, Garibaldi's mission, and the wars for independence. It represents the soldiers who died in the two World Wars.

March 8th FESTA DELLE DONNE-A lady's holiday

Italian women vouch to free themselves for twenty four hours during the lady's holiday. One of the most popular gifts received are Mimosa flower bouquets bought or picked from lovely yellow-beaded trees. The small fuzzy buttons project a powerfully satisfying perfume. If you're ever out, order a Torta Mimosa for dessert. The cake itself resembles a fuzzed yellow button only larger made with rum, orange and lemon zest, toasted almonds and fresh cream.

April 1ST PRIMO APRILE

In Italy on April 1st people play pranks on each other then shout Pesce di Aprile! which doesn't translate very nicely, so I'll tell you that it simply means April fool's. They even play pranks on people they don't know. Kids go around the beaches dumping buckets of water on strangers.

Emperor Constantine handed this day and the entire Roman Empire to King Kugel the jester. Kugel decreed it would be an entire day filled with absurdity.

April 21st PASQUA/EASTER

Holy (Easter) Week

Catholics from around the world make pilgrimages to Rome's various basilicas or to hear the Pope give his sermon at the Vatican.

Easter Sunday: Papal blessing at St. Peter's. Domenica delle Palme/Palm Sunday is traditionally celebrated by the Pope who gives mass in St. Peter's square.

August 15th FERRAGOSTO/THE ASSUMPTION

This holiday was created by Emperor Augustus. There was free food, drink and shows for all as a sort of hiding from the Roman heat. This day always marked the beginning of the August holiday for Italians and numerous of Europeans in general. Starting on this day, everyone heads to the mountains or the sea for the entire month. This means the city is desolate except for tourists and hot abandoned city streets.

IL CARNEVALE (February or March)

Street celebrations happen and children dress up like it's Halloween from Sunday to Tuesday each year before lent.

December 8th CONCESSIONE IMMACOLATO/ IMMACULATE CONCEPTION

During this holiday a Christmas tree from Austria (the largest found in the Austrian forest) is transported to the premises of San Pietro St. Peter's in remembrance of a gift given to the Pope by the Austrians.

December 25th NATALE/CHRISTMAS

Midnight Mass is on December 24 in most churches.
Christmas Day in St. Peter's Square Blessings by the pope

Natale is very much a family holiday in Rome. There are no public celebrations other than solemn religious rituals beginning on Christmas Eve. They are especially beautiful in the city's older churches and in St. Peter's Basilica where the pope officiates both at midnight mass and during the late morning mass on Christmas Day before imparting his blessing in the square. Rome has more churches per square foot than any other city in the world.

Dec. 31st-January 1st CAPODANNO/ NEW YEAR'S

The 1st of the year morning there is a concert in the Sala Nervi in the Vatican. A special architecture produced this room and it has been studied by architect Pier Luigi Nervi, to produce the most beautiful acoustic sounds known to man. The Vatican invites the most famous orchestra's and conductors in the world.

L'ONOMASTICO/HOLIDAYS FOR NAMES

In Italy, each day of the year a particular saint is celebrated. In the past people extracted names for their children by the saints. The boys were never named after their fathers but their grandfathers and for anyone attempting to give their child something other than a saintly name was considered uncatholic so the child would be refused by the local priest and to baptized in the Catholic Church.

Today, Italians celebrate a friend or family member when that person's name falls on the day of their saint; it's somewhat like a second birthday.

Bycicles and boats for rent in Villa Borghese

Noleggio Biciclette/Bicycle Rents in Villa Borghese
Piazzale M. Cervantes
Viale Dell' Uccelliera
Viale J. W. Goethe
Viale delle Belle Arti
Viale Medici Pincio
Viale Dell'Orologio Pincio

Noleggio Barche/Boats for Rent in Villa Borghese
Giardino del Lago
Every day including holidays
9:30am till sunset

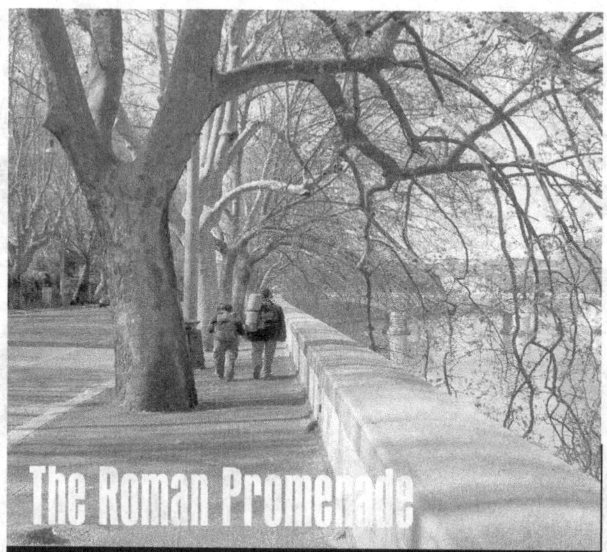

The Roman Promenade

Sidewalks sway, snicker and play
Tickled by roots come what may

Roman and foreign shoes are collected within holes
The slates, the cobblestones, and the knolls
'Cover that hole' she says to him
It's dark, it's treacherous as Roman grim

The feminine fanny reluctant to jiggle
Perhaps with no time to fuss or be niggle
Was licked by the alleyways, streets, and via's
Oh such a mess it made of Sophia

His top hat rotated as a machine
This wavered Professor Quillman
He strode up and down ancient cobblestones
Proceeding at his own risk as planned

The floor slates and stones bustled
His firm walk turned uncertain
And upon an obscured and rotting abyss
He slowly halted before the curtain

For shame such unruliness and utter glitch
His thoughts fell into an ancient glow
He watched his footing unravel unhitch
Out at the heels the entire sole

Wearily he gathered forlorn frays of silk
A prize from the ancient McNeil
Left was such uneveness in Quillman and Sophia

Oh
The places you'll go!

Italians are sociable creatures that love and are forever faithful to their friends. They are dramatic and fast with expression, and many a time boastful.
Some of the men place the facts on the table even if the mirror of amour propre proves unconvincing; they will try and conquer the most beautiful women nevertheless. Unknown laws drawn from weary rulebooks prove the Italian mentality is unique: "I'd love to date a girl of your stature, though I realize I am just too ugly for you."
Inviting a woman for an 'espresso' is metaphor for "let's have a date".

STREETS TO CONSIDER ON YOUR NIGHT OUT:

• Via Veneto-high class, cocktail bars, restaurants, hard rock café
• Testaccio Via Monte - discothèques
• Piazza Del Fico fig tree square - near Piazza Navona, laid back, wine bars, trattorie
• Campo de' Fiori - square filled with pubs and bars and young crowds
• San Lorenzo - young crowds, pubs, university students
• Trastevere - pubs, cocktail bars, restaurants, artsy mixed crowds and shops

NOTE: try not to head out earlier than 11pm because before this time you'll find yourself the only one in the club world. Do dress nice.

Mind the Eyes

The eyes may forsake thee in this faraway land. Femine Italian eyes drift downwards from all public men.
Glancing must be authorized and closely monitored.... .
One stare, the mistake, could give a man 'the go' to advance, to prance, to think impossible is fable.
European women protect themselves by using such mechanisms.
From a deeper part of their being, Italian men don't mean any harm just play, tease and charm.

P. S. stereo-typing Italian men as rear-pinchers is a cliché. Don't be under the notion that you'll be pinched in the fanny every where you go, it's just not so.
It's an out-dated phenomenon.... unless the ancient ones are still in circulation.

Pubs and live music

ZONE 1: HISTORICAL CENTER

ANTICA BIRRERIA PERONI
Via San Marcello 19
Tel 06 6795310
12pm-12am
Closed Sunday
www.anticabirreriaperoni.com/en/index.php

LITTLE BARDI GHONEIM
Via Gregoriana 54
Tel 06 6796386
Metro line A Spagna

VICTORIA HOUSE BAR
Piazza di Spagna
Via Gesù e Maria 18
Tel 06 3201698
Close to Piazza del Popolo intersecting with Via del Corso.
One of the first English pubs in Rome.
Wide range of beers and a dim relaxing atmosphere.
Metro line A Spagna

ANTICO CAFFÈ DELLA PACE
Via della Pace 5
Tel 06 6861216
Literati hang out, known to all as bar della pace peace bar, a turn-of-the-20th-century-style café near Piazza Navona.
The atmosphere ranges from relaxed to electric; it's a cult coffeehouse with an upscale pizzeria.
Bus 40EX 46 62 64 571 916

CINECAFFÉ CASINA DELLE ROSE
Largo M. Mastroianni 1
Tel 42016224
9am-12midnight
Everyday
A restaurant cocktail bar, outdoor theatre in the green park of Villa Borghese.
www.casadelcinema.it

ZONE 3: TRASTEVERE

FIDDLER'S ELBOW BAR
Via dell'Olmata 43
Santa Maria Maggiore
Tel 06 4872110
The fiddler's elbow is the oldest Irish pub in Rome
Metro line A or B Termini
www.thefiddlerselbow.com

ROCK CASTLE CAFÉ
Via Beatrice Cenci 8
Souly rock music, a foreign student's hangout.
Tel 06 68807999
9pm-3am
Bus 63 271 630 780 Tram 8
From Largo Torre Argentina, take Via Arenula (street where tram runs) and walk almost to the end- taking a left onto Via Cenci

LE BON BOCK CAFE
Circ. Gianicolese 249-251
Tel 06 5376806
6pm-late evening
Scottish whiskey bar
Music, sandwiches
www.lebonbock.com

ZONE 8: OSTIENSE

IRISH VILLIAGE PUB
Via Ostiense 182
The biggest Irish pub in Rome. Located at the corner of Via Ostiense and Lungotevere di San Paolo.
Metro line B Piramide then take bus 769 down Ostiense - it's on the right

THE DRUID'S DEN PUB
Via San Martino ai Monti 28
Tel 06 48904781
5pm-2am every day
The third oldest Irish pub in Rome
Monday evenings;
traditional Irish music night
Follow Via Giolitti (Termini station) up to a big church called Santa Maria Maggiore and then turn left down Via Merulana. Follow Via Merulana and take the second on the right, that's San Martino ai Monti. The Druid's Den is on the right.
www.druidspubrome.com

ZONE 10: SAN LORENZO

CIRCOLO VIZIOSO
Via dei Reti 25
Tel 347 8146544
9pm-2am
Tuesday-Sunday
Bus 492

ZONE 13: AURELIO

HARTIGAN'S IRISH PUB/PIZZERIA
Via Giovanni Tamassia 28-30
Tel 06 6621819

ZONE K: CASTELLI ROMANI

COLORADO PUB
Restaurant-Steakhouse
Via Fontana Candida 48
Tel 06 97602069
Off Via Casilina SS6

Night clubs

ZONE 1: HISTORICAL CENTER

LE BAIN ART GALLERY
Piazza Venezia
Via delle Botteghe Oscure 32A
Tel 06 6865673
Le Bain Art Gallery is a highly refined cocktail bar, the restaurant is inside a 16th-century palazzo

JACKIE O'
Italian Dance Club
Via Boncompagni 11
Tel 06 42885457
Closed Sunday and Monday
Comprised of a restaurant, piano bar and disco, dressy.
Bus 52 53 63 80EX 630
Metro line A Barberini

ZONE 2: ESQUILINO

PERCHÈ NO
Via XX Settembre 88a
Tel 06 45441217
9pm-2am
Closed Sunday
Eat according to what the cook fantasizes
Jazz, soul and 60s

ZONE 3: TRASTEVERE

SUITE Dance Club
Via degli Orti di Trastevere 1
Tel 06 5861888
Suite is an amazing reproduction of a futuristic hotel suite
Sushi is available in the private lounge
Bus H 780

ZONE 7: PARIOLI

BELLA BLU
Dance Club
Via Luigi Luciani 21
Tel 06 3230490
Glitter haunts with face masks from various worlds of politics. Bella Blu. A supper club with disco dancing and piano bar.
Bus 52 926

Dance clubs - Discotheques

ZONE 7: PARIOLI

PIPER CLUB the Roman Disco
Via Tagliamento 9
Tel 06 8555398
11pm-4am
Tuesday-Sunday
Established in the 1970s by
famous Italian Singer Patty Pravo
Bus 2363 86 92 271 769 Piazzale Ostiense

SUMMERTIME May-August
Via Maremmana
Tel 07 74326538
Piper relocates by the seaside at the
Acqua Piper di Guidonia

ZONE 8: OSTIENSE

ALPHEUS DISCO
Via del Commercio 36
Tel 06 5747826
10pm-4:30am
Young crowd
Metro line B Piramide
Bus 75

CLASSICO VILLAGE
Via Libetta 3
Tel 06 5743364
9:30-3am
Blues, jazz, and pop in collaboration
with Rome's University of Music
Restaurant
www.classico.it

ZONE 12: EUR

DOWNTOWN LAKESIDE CLUB
Piazza Umberto Elia Terracini 10/14
Newyorkese style 70's
Metro line B EUR-Fermi

Jazz clubs

ZONE 3: TRASTEVERE

BIG MAMA Best Jazz in Rome
Vicolo San Francesco a Ripa 18
Tel 06 5812551
9pm-1:30am
Closed Monday
Bus 75 170
Radio Taxi 06 5551
www.bigmama.it

CASA DI JAZZ
Viale di Porta Ardeatina 55
Tel 06 704731
7pm-midnights
Dinner
Once the residence of band leader
Enrico Nicoletti. The house of jazz
is an auditorium, bookshop and
Mediterranean restaurant.
www.casajazz.it

Other

ZONE 8: OSTIENSE

LINUXCLUB ITALIA
Cultural Association
Via Libetta 15C
Tel 06 57250551
Linux offers its knowledge, and technological curiosity for improving the use of Informatics tools of communication.
www.linux-club. org
12noon-3am
Dinner

ZONE 5: PRATI

GARDEN GROVE/ART GALLERY BISTROT
Borgo Pio 42
Tel 348 7765365
12noon-3am
Closed Monday
Gardengrove.
artgallerybistrot@gmail.com
A simple bistro presenting musical talents, theatre and cultural events

ZONE 4: SAN GIOVANNI

GENDER
Via Faleria 9
Tel 06 70497638
11pm-3am
An open free expressionable world of taboo
Bus 85 87 360 650
Metro line A San Giovanni

Erotica

ZONE 1: HISTORICAL CENTER

BOITE PIGALLE
Via dell'Umiltà 77
Tel 06 6785475
10pm-5am
Closed Sunday
A club with a French twist of cultural style
Striptease 12-2am
Bus 62 63 81 85 95
(Trevi Fountain area)

ZONE 2: ESQUILINO

COLISEUM
Striptease
Via Pietro Verri 17
Tel 06 77591116
www.colosseumnightclub.it

ZONE 9: TESTACCIO

DEGRADO
Via Ignazio Danti 20
Tel 06 2753508
11pm-5am
Atmosphere resembling a Harem or Geisha.
Bus 105

LA GIOCONDA PRIVÈ E BENESSERE
Via dei Pescatori 495
Casalpalocco/Axa Rome
Adult Spa Club
Reservations 3388658935
www.lagiocondabenessere.com
20 minutes from Ostiense Piramide station. Take the train for Ostia and exit on Acilia. Go to bus 08 towards Piazza Antifane and get off at the Macchia Saponara and Via dei Pescatori intersection.

A side street off the Pantheon

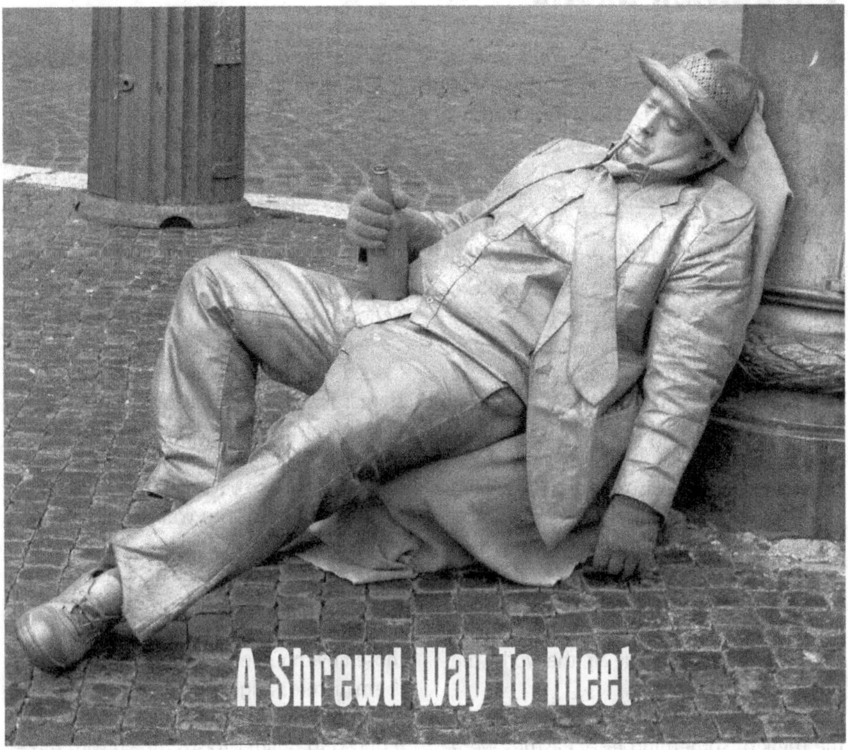

A Shrewd Way To Meet

This other world called Italy is a place where some think it's alright to push, nudge, stick, poke and slam others. To many though, a rough shoving wouldn't be misunderstood, but results in a bad reaction by foreigners. The shape, size, age and gender of these people are irrelevant. In my culture as in many, we wait. We wait in lines, we wait for our food, we wait for the mail, for the bathroom - we even wait for our turn and never complain - a good conditioning never hurt us.

On the contrary, these people tend not to notice that they've shoved anyone, it's natural. Crowds seem to be the perfect time for this, but anyone can be pushed, nudged, stuck, poked or slammed in other places too - like in lines or trying to board the train. Usually the subway is witness to this. This is a collective art and can be useful for certain types, like the gypsies who decide they want something another has. Not speaking the language is hard enough, so demonstrate an unhappy body language and don't let Europeans or any foreigners slam, poke, nudge nor squeeze in front of you, if it's not their turn. Don't mind anyone and stand up to the bullies, speak up in the coffee bar, otherwise the morninq coffee shall arrive upon Caesar's return.

The Jewish Ghetto

Behold the Jewish quarters. Which smears the word kosher among non-living objects. And yes, dozens of David's stars lurk on walls, clasp to necks and brighten the spirit. Windows, shining metals, and Hanukkah holders blind and people are smiling and waving and laughing.

Pressures grew, but for me it was self-satisfying to know that Jewish women evolved in gangs and sat on wooden benches. They were the décor for the 'L' shaped bench wrapping the corner. They gabbed and hissed as my position of foreigner pricked at my head.

Strangers are like spots on white shirts, in the ghetto. The Jewish people I knew were Orthodox and wore funny hats and long curls dangled at their ears. And the strangers they knew were people like me.

Rome was thrown away, it wasn't Rome now, and I knew that. The air, the world, the noise was all backwards.

Sounds were twisted in the air to make me think of something else. Pastries were gold and gold was hidden within the tiny street's pockets. Some worked their way to Largo Sixteen or the finest line of Via Porta D'Ottavia, which was it? You choose. But never forget to look under the rug edgings of Via Santa Maria del Pianto.

The moment wanted to throw me off further. Someone ornamented a church with multi-coloured vegetables. It was a Jewish handy-crafter who was mad, he was mad for sure and tittered while I looked. When that awful elf-shop noise stopped, the little hammer stared at me too. What did I do? I just thought of the Elves and the Shoemaker. But that face frightened me away. Why may I ask did he paint cactus, lemons, tomatoes, and tulips with stems a mile long? in blues, whites, pinks, rich reds and deep yellowish gold's? Anyone would love to purchase a madman's hard work, one with a frightening expression, one holding a hammer. Perhaps that was his reason for sprawling them all over the church of Catherine Virgin.

I was mad myself at this point, and back-tracked towards Via Arenula and Largo Torre Argentina, running straight into Palazzo Caetani. Some think it's a laugh but it wasn't indeed at all. It started when the milk white statues lining one entrance rose up smoking flecks of earl grey. Now it was exactly this place that spun my head. Everything was falling to rubbles. What else but towers of infinite stone heads cemented into walls of an outside courtyard; Palazzo Caetani. Looking wasn't enough, neither was spinning. One bust met the other and no bust was without a space and no space was alone without a bust. I'll tell you those tiny thousands of sculpted faces, eyed the miniature bridge of the perched eagle. The powerful bird overlooked taunting noblemen reduced to quarter torsos. Again with those expressions. Plaques with brims and stone bodies missing parts mixed with worn faces that grimaced; they grimace at you.

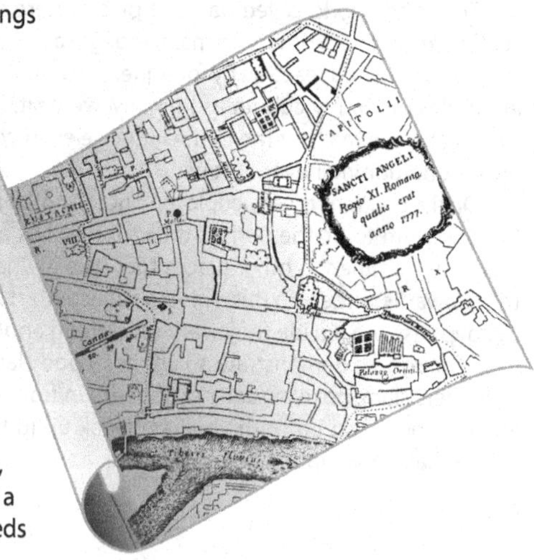

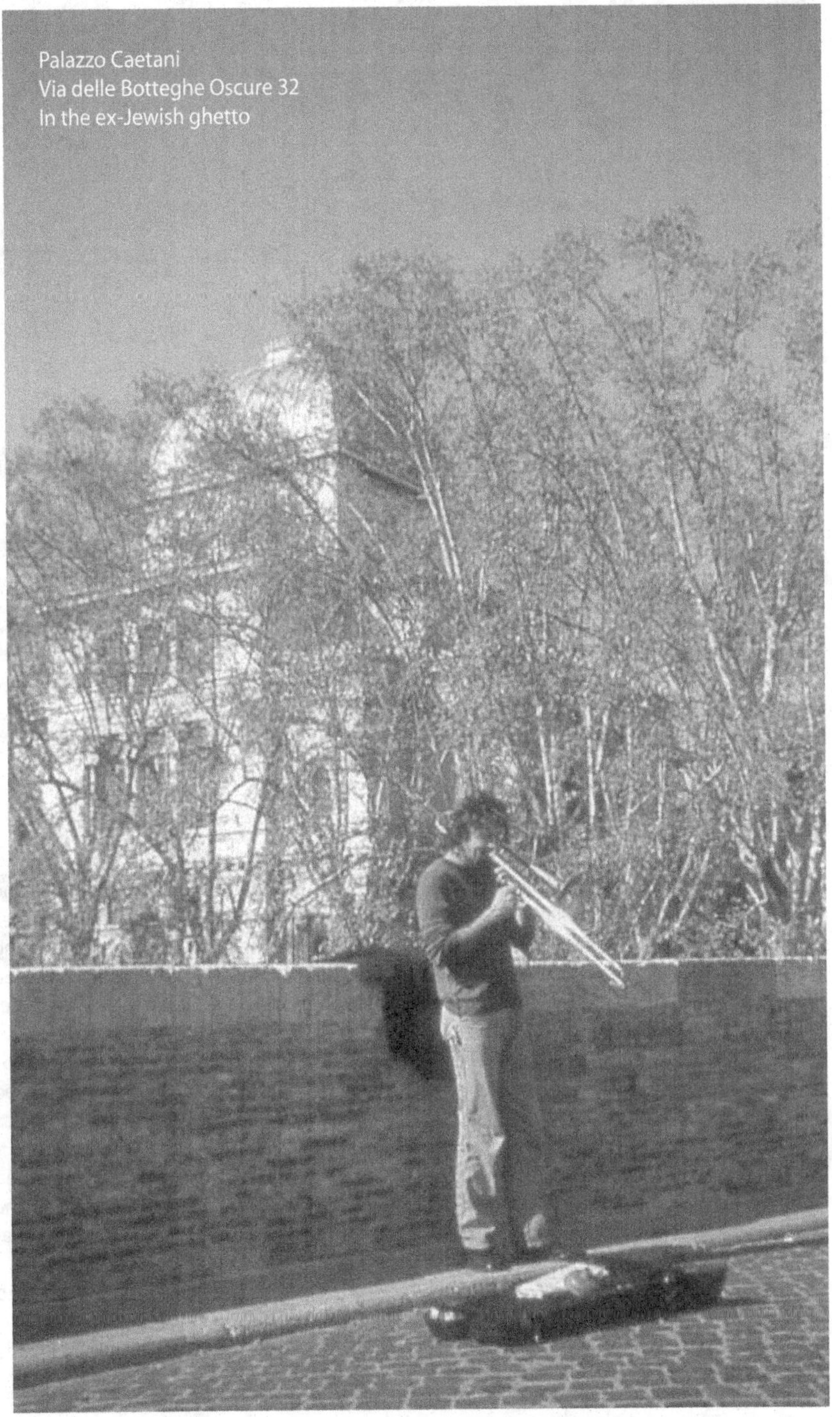

Palazzo Caetani
Via delle Botteghe Oscure 32
In the ex-Jewish ghetto

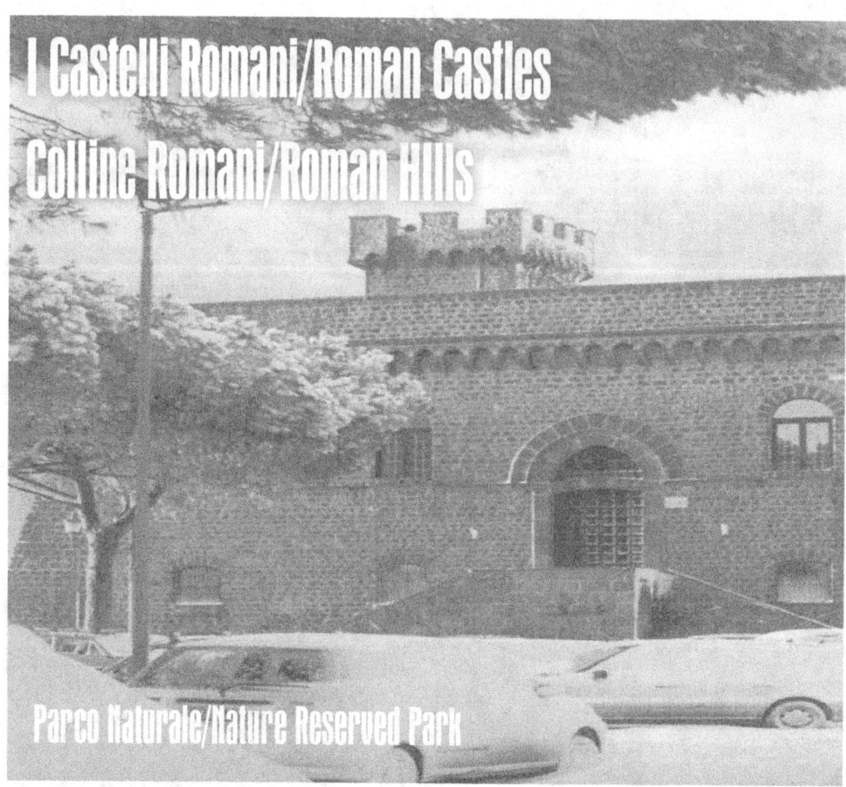

I Castelli Romani/Roman Castles
Colline Romani/Roman Hills
Parco Naturale/Nature Reserved Park

I CASTELLI ROMANI

Chestnut country

Intertwined in a mushroomed wood, are several volcanic towns called the Castelli Romani. All are nicely shaded by vast bunches of chestnut trees and overpopulated by rich vineyards.

15-25miles southeast from the centre of Rome, this area consists of unique panoramic villages making up a 60m circular pattern of the Regional Park or Parco Naturale.

Albano Laziale, Ariccia, Castel Gandolfo, Colonna, Frascati, Genzano, Grottaferrata, Lanuvio, Marino, Monte Compatri, Monte Porzio Catone, Nemi, Rocca di Papa, Rocca Priora, Velletri, Lanuvio and Lariano. The last two are geographically beautiful but are farther away and Velletri is wine making territory, but not so tempting.

Geologically speaking, the Castelli Romani belongs to a volcanic group named Volcano Laziale. They are the result of a complex volcanic phenomenon that took place during the Quaternario four eruptive periods when an enormous crater actually built an outer edge onto the group of towns.

During Roman times, these areas flourished with villas and lush gardens folded into a preserved forest once the birthplace of a Latin civilization.

Blessed with two mysterious and sacred lakes, Lake Albano and Lake Nemi, was the result of two extinguished volcanoes that filled with water over time.

The name Castelli Romani appeared without explanation in 1879, and the name Colli Albani or Albanian Hills seized to be its given name.

The wealthy were lured to these magical hill towns: renaissance princes, emperors, the mighty, medieval barons, poets, writers, and a long string of others. Treasuring the multitudes of dense forests, fresh air, and the high altitudes, they also offered astonishing views with intense blue-green lakes.

The Castelli Romani had been a theatre of inspiring battles and in 1944; a military post was built in the area which became an importance to Rome's freedom.

The most ideal way to explore the Castelli Romani is by car, although you may hop on one of the blue Cotral buses at Anagnina station.

A favorite vineyard:
VINEYARDS OF GRANDI VINI
Via Tende 67b
Tel 06 9539414
Palestrina another small village near the Castelli Romani
Romanella is sold by many different grocers for 2€ a bottle.

PALAZZOLO

Facing of the town of Albano, from across Lake Albano, lay the town of Palazzolo. It was thought the exact spot that occupied the Albalonga the original city of Roma which hung over the younger city of Ascanio. The was once the grand capital of the Latin Confederation that Romans had to destroy in order to conquest the world.

Albano Laziale

Population 35,320
Surface area 23. 8km/ 10.92 miles
Altitude 400m/1312ft
Distance from Rome City 25km/16miles

HIGHLIGHTS

Mercato Romano/The Roman market
June 12th
Gladiator battle show on Vita dei Legionari - June

Flea Market - Thursdays
February carnival and puppet show

Lake Albano, Cisternoni cisterns
Baths of Cellomaio others near S. Maria della Rotonda church

TYPICAL PRODUCTS
Broccoli, wine, ciambelli wine biscuits, baby lamb with artichokes and Vignarola

Castel Gandolfo and Ariccia border Albano Laziale and often Albano is called the Mother of Rome, as the Via Appia runs through it as a live vein, creating the principle street of this city. History has it that the name Albano is derived from the mythical city of Alba Longa, then possessing both Albano and Castel Gandolfo territories.
The Romans themselves called it Albanum since King Latinus ruled there, master to the sacred town of Alba, the parent city of Rome. The territory of Alba was always considered sacred and forbidden to build upon. The city consisted of with temples, shrines, places of worship and sacred woods.
The Middles Ages were the time of rule for the Savelli family who built a castle in Albano, a Baronial Palace. In the early 1900's, Albano became a place of cultural, tourist, and administrative interest by many including: D' Annunzio, Goethe and Stendhal.

THE LAKE
The Lake Albano or Lago Albano is one of the town's grand attractions. The lake once a volcano is not the result of the fusion of two craters. Its maximum depth is 170m. In the summer it's open for paddle boats, water-skiing, and swimming and sun-bathing.
I once bathed in the Lake Albano myself and because it was a lake, I expected to leave smelling like one. Lakes were full of green weed and sometimes an awful stench. But as I waded and swam I found there were no long brown weeds, nothing slimy. Back into the paddle-boat, to my astonishment I found my hair incredibly clean and fresh smelling. The Albano village dwellers are welcoming and kind, a refreshing change to city dwellers.

Ariccia

Population 18.510
Surface area 18.36km/7.08 miles
Altitude 412m/1352ft
Distance from Rome 27km/16miles

HIGHLIGHTS
- Maria S. S. dell'Assunta in Cielo Church, Opera of G. L. Bernini, Piazza di Corte, Palazzo Chigi Key-Gee
- Gallery and Ariccia Nuova a street built with small villas or houses
- Flea market - Mondays
- Artisan flea market - third week of the month
- September - sagra della porchetta pork festival
- Piglet race - 1st weekend

TYPICAL PRODUCTS
Roasted pork

LOCAL CUISINE
In Ariccia, many dishes consist of vegetables and pasta and various seasonings. They make tozzetti, a ring-shaped cake with wine. Albano and Genzano border Ariccia which is located halfway between Lake Albano and Lake Nemi

STORY
Ariccia is one of the Castelli Romani volcanic towns located on the Colli Albani hills. When we think of Ariccia we think of roasted pork and amazing food. It is one of the oldest towns in Lazio and its territory

was a federal sanctuary to the Latin league, consecrated to a goddess or huntress named Diana. Ariccia became Roman in 338 A.D. and then owned a city hall. In medieval times, the counts of Tuscolo and Savelli were in the picture; in 1661 the Chigi princes appeared. It extends along the Via Appia, one of the longest roads spread out between two big vallies. A grand bridge called the Ponte-Viadotto or the viaduct embeds various stories. It is also known as the suicide bridge by Italians. Just recently sturdy metal nets have been affixed along the sides of it, to prevent more disaster. In its principle square there is a splendid park, and the Chigi building which is still private and owned by the Chigi's.
The territory of Ariccia is made of vallies, craters, and much cultivation.
It is one of the best places for true traditional antique Roman cuisine.

ARRIVING
Highway A1/E45 heading southbound exit Monte Porzio Catone northbound at the Roma GRA take exit 23 Via Appia Nuova towards the Ciampino Airport/Albano Laziale.

Backroads S. S. 7 Via Appia Nuova to Via Nettunense S.S. 207 and finally S.S. 217 Via dei Laghi

ARICCIA DINING

OSTERIA DEL PARCO
Via dell'Uccelliera 28
Closed Wednesday
Tel 06 9330067

IL VECCHIO TORCHIO
Piazza D. Sabatini 18
Closed Monday
Tel 06 93392067

L'ARICCIAROLA
Via Borgo San Rocco
Closed Monday
Tel 06 933413

ARICCIA QUARTERS

MOTEL FONTANA DI PAPA
Cecchina 12
Tel 06 9340922

Castel Gandolfo

Population 8,539
Surface area 14.71km
Altitude 426 m/1,398 ft
Distance from Rome 24km

HIGHLIGHTS
- The peach festival/ La Sagra delle pesche (every last Sunday in July)
- The Vatican Observatory
- S. Tommaso da Villanova church in piazza della Libertà
- Villa Cybo
- Flea market-Fridays (antique flea market-the last Sunday of the month)

TYPICAL PRODUCTS
Peaches, lake fish and biscotti

STORY
The territory of Castel Gandolfo is cultivated with vineyards, vegetable gardens, and olive trees. The town was named after the Gandolfi family, who erected a 12th century castle inside an immense estate.
You may like to take a relaxing stroll, collect photos, and admire the peaceful lake. Enjoy the panoramic views from the restaurant terraces, and the offering of local cuisine.
Castel Gandolfo is the Pope's summer residence, a papal tradition dating back to Pope Urban VIII in 1623-1644. The 17th century palace was built upon the foundations of Emperor Domitian's summer residence. From pontifical villas to religious foundations, much of Castel Gandolfo is holy property.
In Piazza della Libertà Liberty square, the papal palace possesses hidden gardens and an astronomical observatory. The Pope's gardens are breathtaking and private with views of the valleys and sea.

THE VATICAN OBSERVATORY
Tel 06 698 85266
The Vatican Observatory is one of the oldest astronomical research institutions in the world. The headquarters is located in the papal summer residence, and its

dependent research centre is in Tucson, Arizona. It all started with Pope Gregory XIII and his group who studied scientific dates involving the reform of the calendar in 1582. From this point on, the papacy had manifested a supportive interest in astronomical research.
Generations of Romans were offered services by the Observatory telling the time of day, under Father Secchi. Father Secchi was fascinated by the study of the sun and after his death in 1878, his successor was removed from the observatory and its name changed to Regio Osservatorio al Collegio Romano, or the Royal Observatory at the Roman College. It was active until 1923 and was reopened in the 1930s.
The Vatican Observatory Foundation VOF is a tax-exempt corporation in the state of Arizona. It is the official astronomical observatory of the Vatican, Osservatorio Pontifici and in Rome Father Angelo Secchi relocated it in the Church of St Ignatius in Rome.

ARRIVING
From Rome Termini station or Anagnina station

CASTEL GANDOLFO DINING

L'ANGOLO VERDE RISTORO
The Green Corner
Via Spiaggia del Lago 28A
Tel 06 9386914
Specially crafted pizzas
Everything made fresh delicious lasagne, pastas especially grilled meats Lamb, veal, and homemade wine
The tables outside face Lake Albano and make a very pleasant spring or summer atmosphere. There is a long boardwalk along the lake.

CASTELVECCHIO
Via Pio XI 23
Tel 06 9360139

SOR CAPANNA
Corso della Repubblica 12
Closed Monday
Tel 06 9361259

CASTEL GANDOLFO QUARTERS

PAGNANELLI LUCIA
Via Gramsci 2
Tel 06 9361422

Frascati

Home of the Noble Mansions Ville Tuscolane, to science, to emperors, and to national and international events
Population 19,882
Surface Area 22.4km/8.65 sq miles
Altitude 327m/1,073 ft
Distance from Rome 21km/13 miles

INFORMATION POINT
Tuesday-Sunday
10am-7pm
Tel 06 94015378
frascatipoint@libero.it

HIGHLIGHTS
Villa Aldobrandini
Villa Torlonia
Villa Falconieri

The Festival of the Tusculum Villas
June-August every year visitors are able to enter the many mansions that are otherwise closed. Ask for information at Frascati point.

Villa Aldobrandini
Piazza Roma
A place of mervigilia ... built by Giacomo della Porta towards the end of the 16th century. The land was given to Cardinal Pietro Aldobrandi by his uncle Pope Clement VIII.
Villa Torlonia-1563 - great scholar Annibal Caro.
The villa was completely destroyed in WWII, but the lovely gardens survived and are now a public park.
Villa Falconieri - 1st half of the 16th century, it was the first villa in Frascati bought by the Falconieri family in the 17th century originally called Villa Rufina. It now belongs to the Italian state and holds the European centre for education.
Giochi di Acqua e di Verde-all of June
Live the ancient splendours of nobility. The Ville Tuscolane Tuscolo villa's that are always kept private and secret are open to the public in June, and you can step on the inside of the noble world. Enter the noble historical residences

of Villa Falconieri, Villa Aldobrandini, Villa Torlonia, Villa Lancellotti and Villa Sora.
There are characters dressed in era costumes. There are clowns, shows and delicious dishes from the very best of the region, Colline Romane.

Flea market-Wednesdays
June 23rd-festival di San Giovanni and Lumacata or the festival of witches
October-last weekend-festa di Cortesia festival of thanks for vineyard owners and workers
December-2nd and 3rd weekend Una Fojetta a Frascati
The tasting of Vino Novello

TYPCAL PRODUCTS
Flour, honey, spices

LOCAL SPECIALITIES
Baby lamb, ox tail, fettuccine with chicken giblets, Roman tripe, pagliata calf intestines with potatoes
Frascati is a major centre for scientific research; it holds the National Institute of Nuclear physics the ESA, ESRIN European space agency, and the Astrophysics Institute.
First Sunday of every month in Piazza Marconi they hold an antiques show and market

ARRIVING TO FRASCATI
Taking a train is very convenient

GENIUS POINT
Frascati internet point
Via di Villa Borghese 11
Tel 06 94017086
www.geniuspoint.it

Very clean, great service, and about 2€ an hour. You will need an ID and he'll give you a card with a password and ID. They also carry stationary, gift items, computer accessories, and provide photocopying services.
From the main Piazza in Frascati which is Piazza Roma there is a street with Gran Caffè bar on the right of it, the bank on the left corner of it, it's Via C. Battisti, pass the church on your right go straight down Via Matteotti, it's about the second street on the right. Via Villa Borghese, it's half way down, and the shop is on your right.

DINING IN FRASCATI

LA VOLPE ALL'UVA
Via Nino Bixio 2
Closed Sunday night and Monday
Tel 329 0233450

CACCIANI
Via Armando Diaz 13
Closed Monday
Tel 06 9420378

FRASCATI QUARTERS

POGGIO REGILLO
Via Pietra Porzia 26
Tel 06 94015235

VILLA PINA
Via Carlo Lucidi 2
Tel 06 9421063
Fax 06 9417711

VILLA TUSCOLANA
Via del Tuscolokm 1, 500
Tel 06 942 900
www.villatuscolana.com

THE TUSCULUM

The Tusculum is an ancient area whose wealth is comprised of famous villas. It sits as a treasure box inside of five Castelli Romani towns: Frascati, Grottaferrata, Monte Porzio Catone, Monte Compatri and Rocca Priora. Poetic tradition calls it the antique grounds. The son of Ulysses of Circe, said they founded the city, which historically rose in the 9th century B.C.. It was known to be the powerful sacred alliance of Albana before falling under Roman dominance.
Along the grounds of the Tusculum villa ruins were left by many refined personage; Asinio Pollione, Quintili, Passieno Crispo, Matidia, Augusta Cicerone, and Tiberio.
On the highest point there is a water reserve which supplied water to the Tusculo garden fountains and privately owned homes. It was populated with ninfe and tritoni. An amphitheatre remains along an inclination which is a well-preserved and gracious theatre of

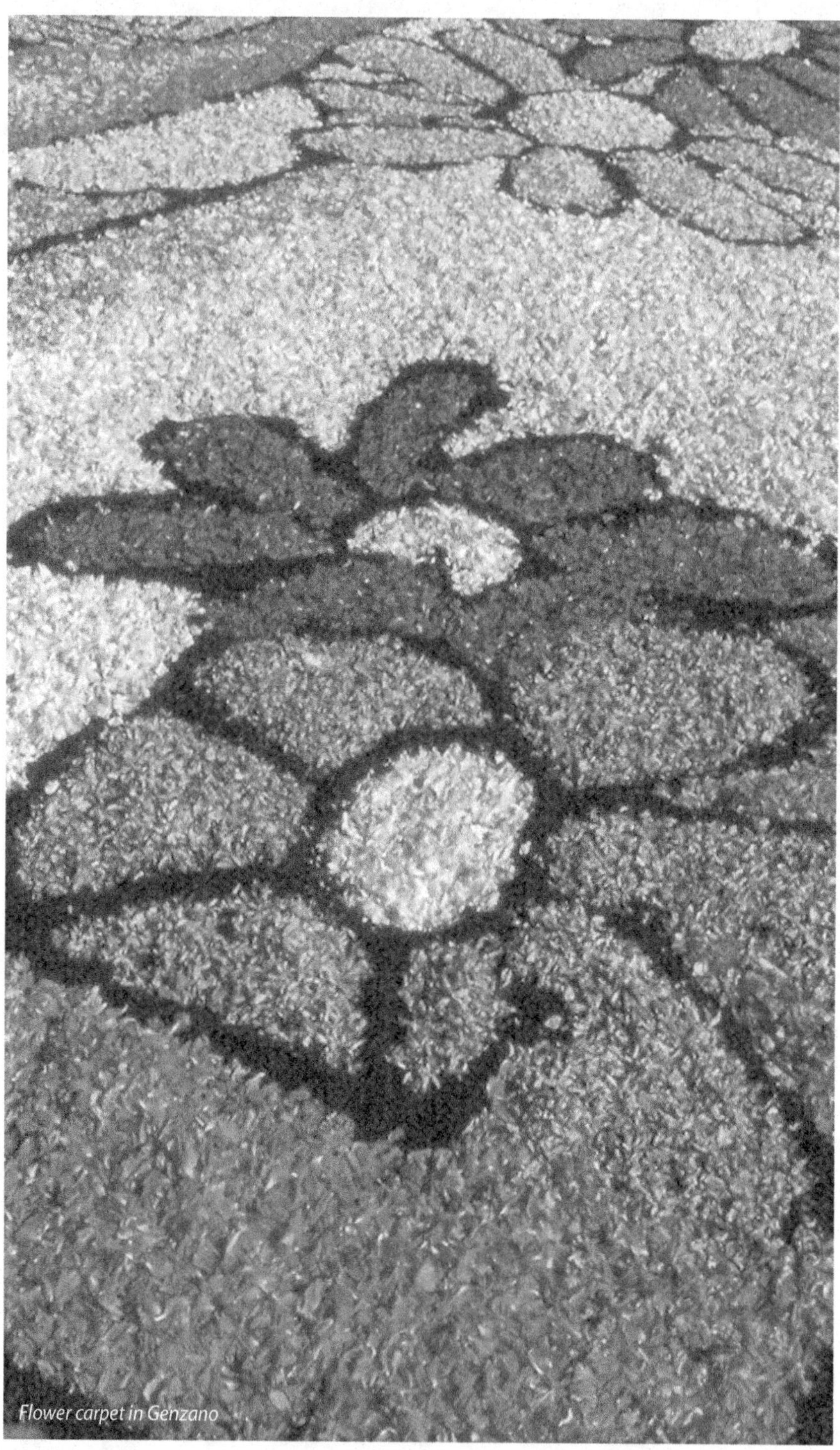
Flower carpet in Genzano

the 1st century B.C.. The Praetorium building hides in the woods decorated with Greek flare. Foreign popes were attracted to the Tusculum.
The desire for its independence from Rome led to the destruction of the Tusculum's fortress, at sunrise of 17 April, 1191. It called for the end of Tuscolo but not for a powerful family of the Tusculum counts from the Colonna family who still existed. In Piazza Marconi, the main square in Frascati, you can see the area of the Tusculum from up the street that runs to the left of the Aldobrandini mansion. You must pass Via Cardinal Massaia and proceed about four kilometres. The Tusculum villas: the Rufinella, Falconieri, Torlonia, and Aldobrandi which can be visited for free in the month of June.

Genzano

Population 22.577
Surface Area
18.15km/7.01miles
Altitude 435m/1,427ft
29km 18miles from Rome
Flea Market-Tuesdays

TYPICAL PRODUCTS
Casareccio bread famous

LOCAL SPECIALITIES
Roasted baby lamb, wild hare pappardelle, rigatoni pasta with Pajata intestines

STORY
Genzano rises on the outer slope of Nemi's crater.

HIGHLIGHTS
Palazzo Sforza Cesarini
Villa Antonimi
The Tridenti
Festa del Pane the bread festival
September 20-21

Genzano is called Bread City. Genzano bread is the only bread in Italy to be geographically protected by the European Union. It's considered one of the best breads in Italy and is. The world's largest bruschetta 1,200m is presented during the festival.

L'Infiorata or flower festival attracts people from all over the world.
Since June 1778, in celebration of Corpus Domini, one whole incline leading to a church above is carpeted designed according to sacred scenes. The carpet consists of flower petals, herbs, sand, coffee, rice, and tree bark. It a magnificent aroma of fragrance.
Genzano is below Ariccia and near Lake Nemi in the town of Nemi.

April festival of violets
May strawberry festival
June grappolo d'oro, the wine festival

DINING IN GENZANO

LA CASINA DELLE ROSE
Via Piave 2
Closed Monday
Tel 06 9330115

LA SCUDERIA
Piazza S. Cesarini 1
Closed Mondays
Open only for dinner at 7:30-8pm
Tel 06 9390521

GENZANO QUARTERS

AGROPOLIS
Via San Gennaro 2
Tel 06 9370335

Grottaferrata

Population 19,004
Surface Area 18,15km/ 7,01 miles
Altitude 329 meters/ 1,079 feet
Distance from Rome 29km/18 miles
Grottaferrata is located between Marino and Frascati

TYPICAL PRODUCTS
D. O R. C. wine and roasted pig

Flea market-Mondays
Early mornings to 1pm

HIGHLIGHTS
Villa Grazioli, Villa Muti, Abbazia di Grottaferrata

Villa Muti 1579
was built by Ludovico Cerasoli over ancient Roman ruins. It xchanged hands then returned to the Muti family in the 20th century until the end of World War II.

Villa Grazioli 1580
was built by Cardinal Antonio Carafa and passed down to Cardinal Ottavio Acquaviva, his relative. In the 17th century, Agostino Ciampelli decorated it with some of the areas most beautiful frescoes and in 1987, it was purchased and transformed into a hotel.

San Nilo
A Catholic church used for Greek masses and weddings

Abbazia di Grottaferrata of Saint Nilo
Il Monastero di Monaci Basiliani or monk's monastery
Tel 06 9459309
The abbey was also built on the ruins of a Roman villa and protected by the popes. And the bronze statue of Saint Nilo still resides in the courtyard.

Festival of the Tuscolane Villa's
June-Aug

Festival of San Nilo in the Greek Orthodox tradition
September 26th

Na Votta C'era - the ancient fair in the Abbey

DINING IN GROTTAFERRATA

IL FICO VECCHIO The Old Figtree
Via Anagnina 257
Closed Tuesday
Tel 06 94315940
Taxi may be a good way to arrive

L'OLIVETO
Via Tuscolana 196
Closed Monday
Tel 06 9456219
Taxi may be a good way to arrive

GROTTAFERRATA QUARTERS

IL CASTAGNETTO
Via Tuscolana 27
Tel 06 9406292

SQUARCIARELLI
Via Ventiquattro Maggio 2
Tel 06 9410882

HOTEL VERDE BORGO 3
Via Anagnina 10
Tel 06 945404
Fax 06 94546193
www.hotelverdeborgo.it

Marino

Population 36,708
Surface area 26.10km/10.08 miles
Altitude 360m/1,181ft
Distance from Rome 24km/15 miles

TYPICAL PRODUCTS
Bean soup and Casareccio bread

LOCAL CUISINE
Bruschetta, fettuccine with ragù meat sauce and fish guts, panzanella stale bread topped with onion, tomato, cucumbers, and olive oil, roasted pork, pasta and chick pea soup

Flea market-Wednesdays

HIGHLIGHTS
The festival of San Giovanni and Lumacata
June 17th
Sagra dell'uva/grape festival and the Sagra delle ciambelle/biscuit festival
2nd Sunday in October
Piazza Matteotti square was decorated by Sergio Venturi's Fontana dei Mori from the 1600's, and it became Marino's emblem as it is connected to the annual grape festival

THE MITREO
is one of most evocative sites in the town. The ancient Roman religion considered God Mitra the defender of the well and patron of the empire venerating it with special sacrificial ceremonies in the underground temple

Mitrei. The temple was excavated in 1962 in Marino and consisted of a 25 meters long arcade that is brimming with frescoes.

Festa del vino/
The wine festival
First weekend in October
Tel 06 9385681
Marino has been famous for its white wine for hundreds of years. The fountain in Marino gushes wine instead of water, for all to drink.

CIVIC MUSEUM
Prehistoric, Roman, and Medieval epoch, with fragments of frescoes.

Marino is just north of lake Albano and below Grottaferrata.

DINING IN MARINO

PARADISO TERRESTRE
Via Salvatore Quasimodo 4
Closed Tuesday
Tel 06 9388212

AL QUATTRO MORI
Piazza Lepanto 2
Closed Monday
Tel 06 9386178

MARINO QUARTERS

IN VILLA
Via delle Barrozze 79
Tel 06 9496472

VIGNA DEL SOLE
Via Vivaldi 9
Tel 06 9384342

Monte Porzio Catone

Population 8,372
Surface Area
936km/361 sq miles
Altitude 451m/1,480ft
25km/16 miles from Rome

HIGHLIGHTS
Osservatorio Astronomico
The Astrolab
Located on Via dell'Osservatorio 2
Sits way up on a hill, and is painted in an attractive shade of yellow cream. You can clearly see the Astro-Dome towards the centre on the top. Tel 06 9428641, 06 9448315, 06 9447371
Villa Vecchia
Villa Mondragone 1572-Cardinal Altemps constructed it. This villa belonged Borghese family until the late 19th century
Villa Parisi

Museo Difuso del Vino-Museum of wine
Via Emanuele II 22, 32, 46
Tel 06 94341027

FESTA DELLE Fraschette - March
FLOWER FESTIVAL-May-June

Flea market-Thursdays

TYPICAL PRODUCTS
Olive oil and fruit

LOCAL CUISINE
Bruschetta, Fettuccine pasta

Monte Porzio is the most northern town of the Castelli with Frascati on its left, and Montecompatri on its right. This little town was named in the honour of Roman writer and politician Marcus Porcius Cato who was born there.

ARRIVING
The easiest way is to hop on the subway
Line A to Anagnina
Exit the subway into the lobby and go left; you will then come to a hall of numbered staircases take staircase 6.

ANGELETTI SERGIO taxi services
Telefax 06 9448520

TOUCH AND GO touring services
Via Roma 31
Monte Porzio Catone
Tel. 06 9449444
Fax 06 9449440
www.touchandgoviaggi.it

DINING MONTE PORZIO CATONE

FONTANA CANDIDA
Via di Fontana Candida 5
Closed Thursday
Tel 06 9449030

CANTINA ROMOLETTO
Via Verdi 25
Closed Monday
Tel 06 9449495

MONTE PORZIO CATONE QUARTERS

VILLA SCIARPA 3
Via Montecompatri 30d
Tel 06 9449272
Fax 06 94341136
www.hotelvillasciarra.it

HOTEL DEI GIOVANNELLA
Piazza Trieste 1
Tel 06 9447433

Nemi 10th Century B.C

Population 1,816
Surface Area
7.36km/2.84 miles
Altitude 521m/1,709ft
Distance from Roma
40km/25 miles
Tel 06 9365011
Little town of Nemi, is to the southeast of lake Albano and nearby Genzano

TYPICAL PRODUCTS

Strawberries, flowers, honey and mushrooms

STORY

Nemi has an awkward story that reflects upon the lake, and the Mirror of Diana.
On the banks of the lake is where the Temple of Diana was built.
Nemi's main square possesses a castle castello which was erected by the Tuscolo family.

Handmade sign of Nemi strawberries

HIGHLIGHTS

Wild Strawberry Cup

Tel 06 9368001
June every first Sunday of the month
Celebrations involve the tiny wild strawberries that are cultivated around Nemi's naturistic land.
The strawberries fragole are displayed in a huge 8-10ft transparent cup and covered in a rosy spumante called fragolino. It is free strawberries to everyone, if they can squeeze into the pack of people.
They fly the big strawberry filled with balloons for the kids and at some point break it and the children go wild. All over town you'll find luscious strawberry desserts.
www.comunedinemi.it

Romitorio di S. Michele

Arcangelo 1255
A twenty minute walk from Piazza Dante, it was dug out of the rock and decorated with numerous frescoes.

Museum of the Roman Navy/Museo delle Navi Romane

Inaugurated in January '36 and destroyed June '44
Tel 06 9398040
They put up with Emperor Caligula's trips and built him imperial navy ships for parties and festivals which were dedicated to the Goddess Diana.
Museum ships of Nemi
Winter 9am to 2pm
Summer 9am to 7pm

The Temple of Diana

Above Lake Nemi, you will find the remains of a huge complex built upon a large artificial platform. The statues that once stood here are now scattered throughout European museums, including the Roman Navy Museum and the National Roman Museum in the centre of Rome.

Caesar's Villa

It may have been Caesar's villa and excavations tell that is was composed of: baths, cisterns, two streets leading to it, a great terrace overlooking the lake, and rooms decorated with mosaics and paintings. The villa was destroyed by an earthquake in the 3-4th century A.D.

The flower expo is a day before the Strawberry celebration.
Flowers are cultivated in the valleys surrounding Nemi lake and arranged by Italian artisans.
Plants are crafted using the tiny wild strawberries and colourful lake flowers.

DINING IN NEMI

LA ROSA
Corso V. Emanuele 41
Tel 06 9368348
Enzo is an exceptional person and he specializes in porcini mushrooms and freshly prepared pastas. The antipasti is perfect, the atmosphere warm decorated in reds oranges with nothing but pasta.
Try the lemoncello his wife makes it using honey, it's most delicious.

L'INCANTESIMO DEL LAGO
Corso Vittorio Emanuele 24
Closed Monday
Tel 06 9368461

ANTICHI SAPORI
Piazza Roma 22
Closed Wednesday
Tel 06 9368777

NEMI QUARTERS

LO SPECCHIO DI DIANA
Corso Vittorio Emanuele 13
Tel 06 9364206

IL CORTILE
Bed & Breakfast
Via Giulia 9
Tel 06 9368147
You have a view of Nemi lake and the sea from here. It is located on a corner dead end in the middle of a Medieval village in the centre of Nemi. The privacy is due to the greenery and its lonely position. It is very inexpensive, as you many stay one week for less than 500€ and there is a common kitchen.

INFORMATION POINT NEMI
Piazza Roma

Nemi's strawberry festival

Rocca di Papa

Population 13,242
Surface Area
40.18km/15.51miles
Altitude 680m/2,231ft
27km/17 miles from Rome

Flea market-Thursdays

TYPICAL PRODUCTS
Chestnuts and porcini mushrooms

HIGHLIGHTS
Antiques fair
The first Sunday every month

Festa delle Castagne/ Chestnut Festival
The third Sunday of October
Sagra del fagiolo/the bean festival September 4-5th
Vivi il Vivaro Equestrian show

There are many pastries made from chestnuts and roasted chestnuts are everywhere.

Also enjoy dishes like tripe, sausage and beans, polenta and sausage with wine and music.

DINING IN ROCCA DI PAPA

VILLA FIORITA
Via Frascati 254
Closed Tuesday
Tel 06 94749217

IL NOCE
Protoni del Vivaro
Closed Tuesday
Tel 06 94437019

ROCCA DI PAPA QUARTERS

ANGELETTO
Via del Tufo 32
Tel 06 949020

VILLA FRANCA
Via delle Ortesie 15
Tel 06 9495657

IL MOSAICO
Via Enrico Fermi 61
Tel 06 9498733

Rocca Priora

Population 10,764
Surface Area
28.07km/10.84 miles
Altitude 768m/2,520ft
31km/19miles from Rome

HIGHLIGHTS

Castello Savelli
Pet Cemetery
Festival of Snow-each year in August, they celebrate the lady Madonna of the snow, many varieties of music, a show for children and the fall of the artificial snow.

Farmer's market-Thursdays

TYPICAL PRODUCTS

Mushrooms founded in the Middle Ages

Rocca Priora is known for its daffodils and narcissus and is highest of the Castelli Romani. It is owned by the regional park of the Castelli Romani and also a protected area fertile and with vineyards, chestnut trees and olive groves.
It is lush with chestnut woods and home to many creatures such as the porcupine and squirrel. The centre of town is on the highest part of the mountain and like a maze of alleyway vicolo's. The Savelli castle is the most outstanding building, which sits across from the Santa Maria Assunta church, also built by the Savelli's.

Rocca Priora has splendid water known as the Acqua Regilla found at a depth of 86meters from the basin of Dognanella, located where Lake Regillo once was.
Its mysterious contents can be a magical remedy to lowering high blood pressure, in fact, if you have low blood pressure be careful.
Enjoy horse-back riding, jogging and parachuting all available at Rocca Priora

DINING IN ROCCA PRIORA

SORA ROSA

Via dei Castelli Romani 38
Tel 06 9470799
Tucked away around a windy road, honestly one of the best in town.

ROCCA PRIORA QUARTERS

BED & BREAKFAST MARCELLA

It's a small villa on a residential street
Via Vecchia della Fontana 55
Tel 06 947182/3281752942
marcellabeb@tiscali.it
Very inexpensive around 30-40€ a night

VILLA LA ROCCA HOTEL 4

Via dei Castelli Romani 18
Tel. 06 9471594
www.hotelvillalarocca.it

Wild flower and chestnut honey is produced in the villages of the Castelli Romani.

For wild flower honey, propolis, royal jelly and bee pollen contact:
Alessio Dandini
Vicolo Fontana Bella 11
Tel 06 9470824/3392751600

Rocca Priora

Castelli Romani trains and transport

From Rome, take metro line A to Anagnina and left outside the station all the way to the end where the numbered staircases lead you to the blue Cotral buses above.

BY CAR
A1 Firenze Napoli motorway
A2 Fiano-Roma-S. Cesareo motorway, Monteporzio, S. Cesareo exit
Via Tuscolana to Frascati

F. S. TRAINS FROM TERMINI STATION	
Tivoli	FM2
Albano	FM4
Frascati	FM4
Colonna	FM6
Latina	FM7
Nettuno	FM7

ANAGNINA STATION STAIRWAYS TO BUSES	
Ariccia	2
Castel Gandolfo	3 - 5 - 6 - 7
Colonna	8
Frascati	6
Genzano	2
Grottaferrata	5
Lanuvio	2
Marino	6
MonteCompatri	6
Monte Porzio Catone	6
Nemi	2
Rocca di Papa	5
Rocca Priora	6

Lazio and outside Rome

TIVOLI

20km from Rome

Tivoli was an ancient holiday resort for the Romans.
Emperor Hadrian possessed over 95 hectares of land there with Greek and Egyptian city reproductions, his dream property Villa Adriana. The immense town-sized villa is composed of baths, fountains, statutes and colourful mosaics.

Villa D'Este is the recreation of the Garden of Eden by Cardinal Ippolito D'Este. It's a magical kingdom with hundreds of water fountains mixed around Italian gardens.
Tiburtina station FM2 train

OSTIA ANTICA-HARBOR CITY

20 miles from Rome

Ostia beautifully preserved its ruins in the meadows between the Tevere River and the Tyrrhenian Sea.
Used as a military colony to guard the river mouth against seaborne invasions, has a history since the 4th century B.C.
The Marine Gate, which once stood by the harbour, is now more than a mile away from the sea.
By the 2nd century A.D., it started to flourish with shops, housing, taverns, butcher shops, schools, homes, fish markets, inns and they are still intact today.

HIGHLIGHTS

The Baths of Neptune are comprised of beautiful mosaics
Ostia's Amphitheatre 12 B.C., held up to 3,500 people
The Jewish Synagogue built by Jews
Castello di Giulia II

Metro line B Porta S. Paolo
Now take the train for Ostia and get off at Ostia Antica

By Car
Take Via del Mare/Via Ostiense and follow it for indications Scavi di Ostia Antica
By Bus
The Stop'n'Go bus is available at Termini station

LATINA (LT)

NINFA
The Gardens of Ninfa/Giardini di Ninfa
NINFA sounds like some kind of strange village set upon Mars, yet there is much life on Ninfa especially green plant and animal life. You'll see creeping plants winding over broken towers and walls, refuging in the lush damp moss.
Roses long for footholds in archway ruins, the frescoed church wall stands open to the weather. Roses, banana trees, maples and resident ducks thrive in the microclimate of Ninfa.
Ninfa was a substantial town in Roman times, but was then abandoned at the end of the 14th century for many reasons. During the Middle Ages squabbles took place and the village was ransacked but also plagued by malaria. The castle and town hall were all that survived.
Swirling Ninfa waters are operated by a dam from the 1200s. If you attempt to find Ninfa, you've found a well-kept secret.
Ninfa is usually visited by garden-lovers.

TICKETS FOR NINFA:

WWF offices Close to Galleria Borghese in Rome
Via Po 25c
Tel 06 84497206
Ninfa is opened to the public only from April-October

ARRIVING TO NINFA

The train to Latina 1/2 hour
The station (which is actually at Latina Scalo, 9km from Latina itself) is the closest to Ninfa.
Infrequent local bus services will take you a little nearer to Ninfa, but it's easiest to go by taxi or car.
Still in the Lazio region, Ninfa is 40 miles south-east of Rome

PIANA DELLE ORME/ PLAIN OF FOOTPRINTS

Museum dedicated to World War II- only Museum Park in Europe from 1997
Exposition of 14 Pavilions
Original photos during World War II
Deploys of planes, arms, tanks, clothing recovered
Restaurant Eucalipto genuine ingredients used from surrounding farms
Small market with antiques, war clothing, military boots

ANZIO

In Anzio true masterpieces of sculpture were found; Apollo del Belvedere in the Vatican Museum and the Fanciulla d'Anzio in the Museo Nazionale Romano.
Anzio is a port village on the seashore east of Rome. The original harbor was built by Emperor Nerone and was well-known till medieval times.
Legend pronounces that Anzio was founded by Antheus son of Ulysses and the sorceress Circe. It was conquered by the Romans, destroyed and rebuilt. Emperors Nero and Caligula were both born in Anzio and Nero had a grandiose villa built on a drop overlooking the sea. The ruins can be seen from the beach.

Anzio was connected to numerous events in history:
538 A.D., during the Gothic-Byzantine war, all sea traffic was directed here due to the occupation of Portus
1190, English King Richard Lion hart passed by on his way to Palestine

Today the harbor is frequented by pleasure boats and racing yachts and is where one takes the ferry boat for the Pontine Islands
Tel 06 9845083

ANZIO HIGHLIGHTS

Nero's port, Nero's Villa
International Sailing week - last week in March
The fish feast - 2nd and 3rd week in June
Gastronomic festivals - August
Concerts and Ballets - July and August

AMERICAN WAR CEMETARY/ CIMITERO DI GUERRA

Nettuno lies just below Anzio. It was named after the great Greek God Neptune himself.
Memorial Day, the last Sunday in May, is the commemoration of the American soldiers fallen during WWII.
Every morning at 5am, the American flag is raised and the pledge of allegiance said.

Trains from Termini for Pomezia, Anzio or Nettuno will take you here, as well as the Tiburtina railway stations.

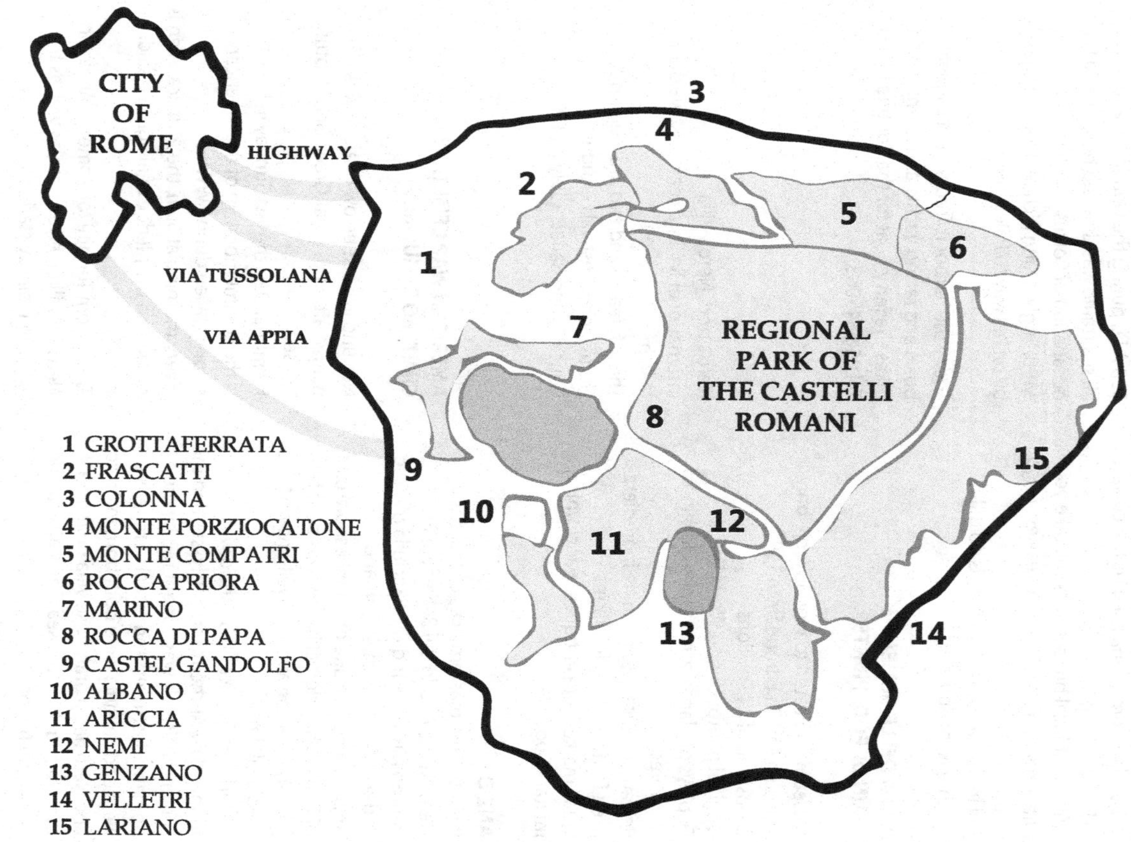

CITY OF ROME
HIGHWAY
VIA TUSSOLANA
VIA APPIA
REGIONAL PARK OF THE CASTELLI ROMANI
1 GROTTAFERRATA
2 FRASCATTI
3 COLONNA
4 MONTE PORZIOCATONE
5 MONTE COMPATRI
6 ROCCA PRIORA
7 MARINO
8 ROCCA DI PAPA
9 CASTEL GANDOLFO
10 ALBANO
11 ARICCIA
12 NEMI
13 GENZANO
14 VELLETRI
15 LARIANO

IL CALDARIUM is the Roman steam room that was heated by an exterior furnace called a Laconicum.

LE BOTTICELLE are the Roman coaches that are carried by Rome's city horses.

EDICOLLA'S are the tiny housings holding the Madonna or other figures which usually adorn corners of countless buildings.

BREAD AND CIRCUSES were open circuses filled with foods, drink and shows that lasted endless days.

Powerful Family Names

Albani, Aldobrandini, Altieri, Barberini, Barbo, Braschi, Boncompagni, Borghese, Carafa, Cappellari, Castagna, Castiglioni, Cervini Chiaramonti, Chigi, Ciocchi, Colonna, Conti, Corsini, Cybo, De Borja, Della Chiesa, Della Genga, De' Medici, Del Monte, Della Rovere, Facchinetti, Farnese, Florensz, Lambertini, Lucani, Ludovisi, Manganelli, Mastal Ferretti, Orsini, Ottoboni, Pamphilj, Parentucelli, Peretti, Piccolomini, Pignatelli, Ratti, Rezzonico, Roncalli, Sarto, Todeschini

The Hey-Days of Using Poisons

The heyday's of poisoning was the 17th century. One of Rome's leading chemists believed that the Acqua Tofana still existed a few decades ago. It was an odourless colourless substance; one drop given each week caused death within two years. This poison could be mixed in coffee and chocolate and still be effective. Wine though, neutralized it to some extent. These recipes are believed to have been lost.

Roman Film

Cinecitta Studios

AN IMPORTANT PART OF ROME AND THE WORLD

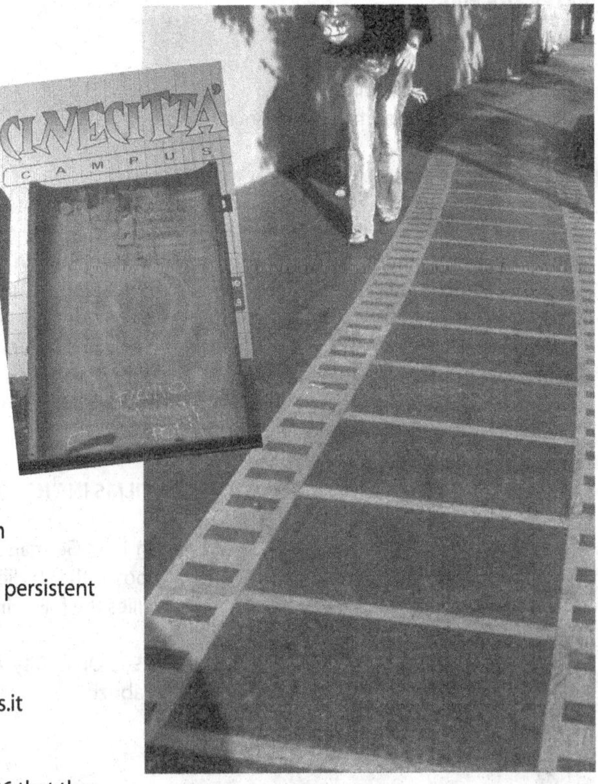

ZONE F: TUSCOLANO

Via Tuscolana 1055
Located only 5.6 miles from downtown Rome
Call to set up a tour and be persistent
Tel 06 722931/06 7221821
Fax 06 7222155
Metro line B Cinecittà
direzione@cinecittàstudios.it
info@cinecittaworld.com

It was on January, 29th 1936 that the largest film studio in Europe was being built. On April the 28th of the next year, Cinecittà was inaugurated housing sixteen theatres and pools for aquatic scenes, offices, and restaurants.
Cinecittà produced twenty films in its first year of life, and over 3,000 productions.
It's played a part in the biggest production communities in the world, only second to Hollywood.
Production services include; feature films, television, commercials, music videos and more.

The studios are open to the public on La Notte Bianca every first or third weekend in September, a weekend filled with shows and special events. 2006 was its first year and it featured the marvellous Roberto Begnini director and actor of the film Life is Beautiful.

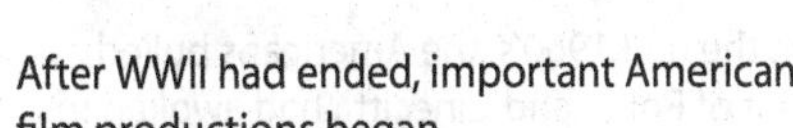

After WWII had ended, important American film productions began.
The first frenzies of cinema began during the years 1915-1929. Silent films were created with some of Italy's silent screen stars: Francesca Bertini, Lydia Borelli (Il Fior di Male, The Evil Flower 1915), Pina Menichelli (Tigre Reale, The Royal Tiger, 1916, La Storia di Una Donna, The Story of a Lady, 1920).
In the 1930's, Cinecittà worked continuously to pump out over fifty films in just two years 1937-1939 along with Italy's top directors and actors of the time: Alessandro Blasetti, Roberto Rossellini, and Alida Valli. On September 26th, 1935, Cinecittà was destroyed by a fire and they decided to rebuild the new 'Cinema City' almost as fast.

ITALY'S MAJOR DIRECTORS AFTER THE WAR:

Federico Fellini: Satyricon, Amarcord, Casanova, E la Nave Va, Ginger e Fred
Luchino Visconti: Bellissima, Notti Bianche, Ludwig.
Ettore Gianinni: Carosello Napoletano

By the mid 1950's, Cinecittà was swarming with famous international faces: Gregory Peck, Rock Hudson, Ava Gardner, Elizabeth Taylor, Kirk Douglas, and Audrey Hepburn. Their love affairs weren't only private news. The first director to show at Cinecittà from Hollywood was Henry King to shoot the 'Prince of Foxes' with Tyrone Powers and Orson Welles. Two years after that, Mervyn Leroy shot 'Quo Vadis'.

In the mid 1960's, the Americans pulled out of Rome and Cinecittà had awoken to a nightmare-a real cinema crisis. The studio then headed into the darkest period in all of its history.
Only sparse films were made during this time: the Damned and Ludwig by Luchino Visconti. Fellini came out with Satyricon in 1969. Cinecittà lived through these difficult years and the paralleled world film crisis.

Finally in 1983 cinema made a slow comeback, and Sergio Leone directed Once Upon a Time in America.
From the 1980's Cinecittà studios were sadly no longer filled with movie props and American actors as before but were instead replaced by television studios.

FILMS IN THE 1940'S

In 1943 German Troops smashed and looted the studios and it was bombed by allies the following year.

1945 Open City, Anna Magnani and Aldo Fabrizi

ROME IN FILMS 1950'S	
'50 September Affair	Joseph Cotton and Joan Fontaine
'53 Roman Holiday	Audrey Hepburn and Gregory Peck
'53 The Robe	Richard Burton and Jean Simmons
'53 Androcles and the Lion	Jean Simmons, Victor Mature, and Alan Young
'54 Three Coins in the Fountain	Clifton Webb, Dorothy McGuire, and Jean Peters
'56 War and Peace	Audrey Hepburn, Henry Fonda, Mel Ferrer and Vittorio Gassman
'59 La Dolce Vita	Marcello Mastroianni and Anita Ekberg
'59 Ben Hur	Charlton Heston

ROME IN FILMS 1960'S	
'60 Spartacus	Kirk Douglas
'60 Plein Soleil Purple Noon	Film adaptation of Patricia Highsmith's The Talented Mr. Ripley
'60 Come September	Rock Hudson, Gina Lollobrigida, Bobby Darin, and Sandra Dee
'60 Big Deal on Madonna Street	Marcello Mastroianni and Vittorio Gassman
'62 Rome Adventure	Suzanne Pleshette and Troy Donahue
'62 Two Weeks in Another Town	Kirk Douglas, Giancarlo Giannini filmed on Via Veneto
'63 Cleopatra	Elizabeth Taylor and Richard Burton
'64 Yesterday, Today and Tomorrow	Sophia Loren and Marcello Mastroianni
'68 The Shoes of the Fisherman	Anthony Quinn

ROME IN FILMS 1970'S	
'70 The Pizza Triangle	Giancarlo Giannini and Marcello Mastroianni
'70 Julius Caesar	Richard Chamberlain and Charlton Heston
'74 We all loved each other so much	Vittorio Gassman
'77 A Special Day	Sophia Loren and Marcello Mastroianni
'72 Fellini's Roma	Federico Fellini

TELEVISION TAX

Just owning a television set in Italy entitles you to receive a bill for the taxes on it. This is so politicians can frequent more golf courses in Siberia. A lady's son once received a threatening letter related to this tax; if she did not pay it, they would come and confiscate her car. She had been dead for over a year and never owned a car.

THE GREATEST ITALIAN-ROMAN ACTORS OF ALL TIME

ALBERTO SORDI FILMS	
A Taxi Driver in New York	*Lo Sceicco Bianco
Made in Italy	Finche cè Guerra cè Speranza
*Il Marchese di Grillo	Riusciranno I Nostri Eroi a Ritrovare L'Amico Scomparso in Africa?
I Know That You Know That I Know	*Bello Onesto Emigrato Australia Sposerebbe Paesana Illibata
Viva Italia!	Presidente del Borgoresso Football Club
Journey with Papa	*Professore Dott. Guido Tersilli
Il viaggio con papa	
It Happened in Rome	*Nell'Anno del Signore
An Italian in America	*I Complessi Dentone
I Complessi	*Il Vigile
The Miser L'Avaro	*Il Medico Della Mutua
Thank You Very Much	The Imaginary Invalid
Fumo di Londra	

ALDO FABRIZI FILMS	
Live in Peace	Vivere in Pace
Open City	Roma Città Aperta
The Angel Wore Red	La Sposa Bella
	Guardie e Ladri
	El Maestro
Life is for the Dogs	Vita da Cani

MEMORABILE ITALIAN FILMS	
Fantozzi	Paolo Villaggio
Così è La Vita	Aldo, Giovanni and Giacomo
Johnny Stecchino	Roberto Begnini
Questi Fantasmi	Eduardo di Felipe
Mediterraneo	Claudio Bisio Vana Barba
IL Ciclone	Leonardo Pieraccioni
Non Ci Resto che Piangiare	Roberto Begnini and Massimo Troisi
I Giorni della Civetta	Franco Nero
Boccaccio by Vittorio de Sica	Sophia Loren and Peppino de Filippo

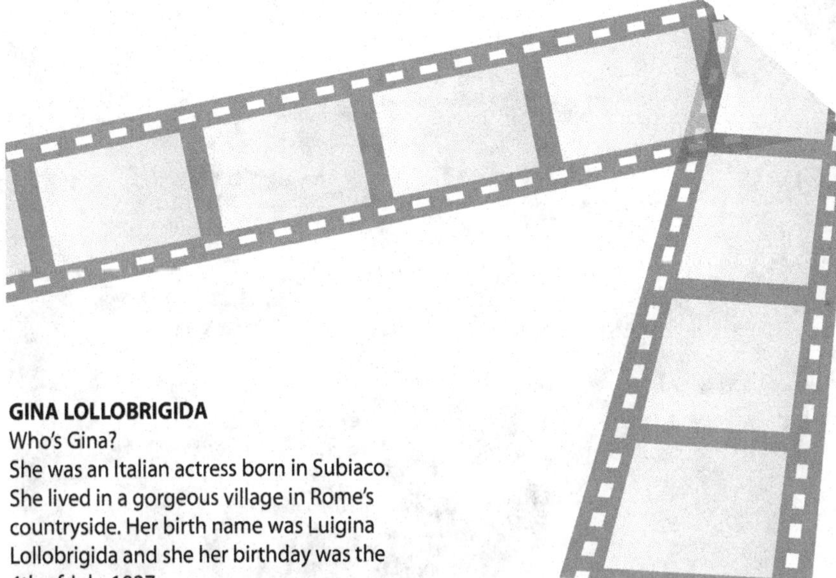

GINA LOLLOBRIGIDA

Who's Gina?

She was an Italian actress born in Subiaco. She lived in a gorgeous village in Rome's countryside. Her birth name was Luigina Lollobrigida and she her birthday was the 4th of July, 1927.

She was nicknamed The Mona Lisa of the Twentieth Century and she produced over sixty films during her career.

- *When Love Calls 1947*
- *A Man about the House 1947*
- *Mad about Opera 1948*
- *The Bride Can't Wait 1949*
- *A Dog's Life 1950*
- *Miss Italy 1950*
- *Children of Chance 1950*
- *A Tale of Five Cities 1951*
- *Fan Fan la Tulipe 1952*
- *Bread, Love and Dreams 1953*
- *Beat the Devil 1953,* her big Hollywood break film
- *Woman of Rome 1954*
- *The World's Most Beautiful Woman 1955,* her signature film
- *The Hunchback of Notre Dame 1956*
- *Anna of Brooklyn 1958*
- *Come September 1961,* the world's favorite film
- *Imperial Venus 1963*
- *The Dolls 1965*
- *Strange Bedfellows 1965*
- *Buona Sera Mrs. Campbell 1968*
- *That Splendid September 1969*

NINO MANFREDI

- *Pane e Ciocolato* - Bread and Chocolate
- *We All Loved Each Other So Much*
- *La Grande Guerra* - The Great War, Vittorio Gassman, directed by Mario Monicelli

MARCELLO MASTROIANNI

- *The Pizza Triangle*
- *A Special Day*
- *Big Deal on Madonna Street*
- *Yesterday, Today and Tomorrow*
- *La Dolce Vita*

LUCHINO VISCONTI

- *La Terra Trema*
- *Senso Livia*
- *The Panther,* Burt Lancaster
- *Rocco and his Brothers*
- *Ossessione the Postman Always Rings Twice,* based on James M. Cain's novel
- *Il Gattopardo* - the Leopard
- *Vaghe Stelle dell'Orsa Sandra of a Thousand Delights*
- *Le Streghe* - The Witches
- *Ludwig*

Piazza Venezia

Anzio

Roman streetwalkers

Trevi Fountain

Roman Forum

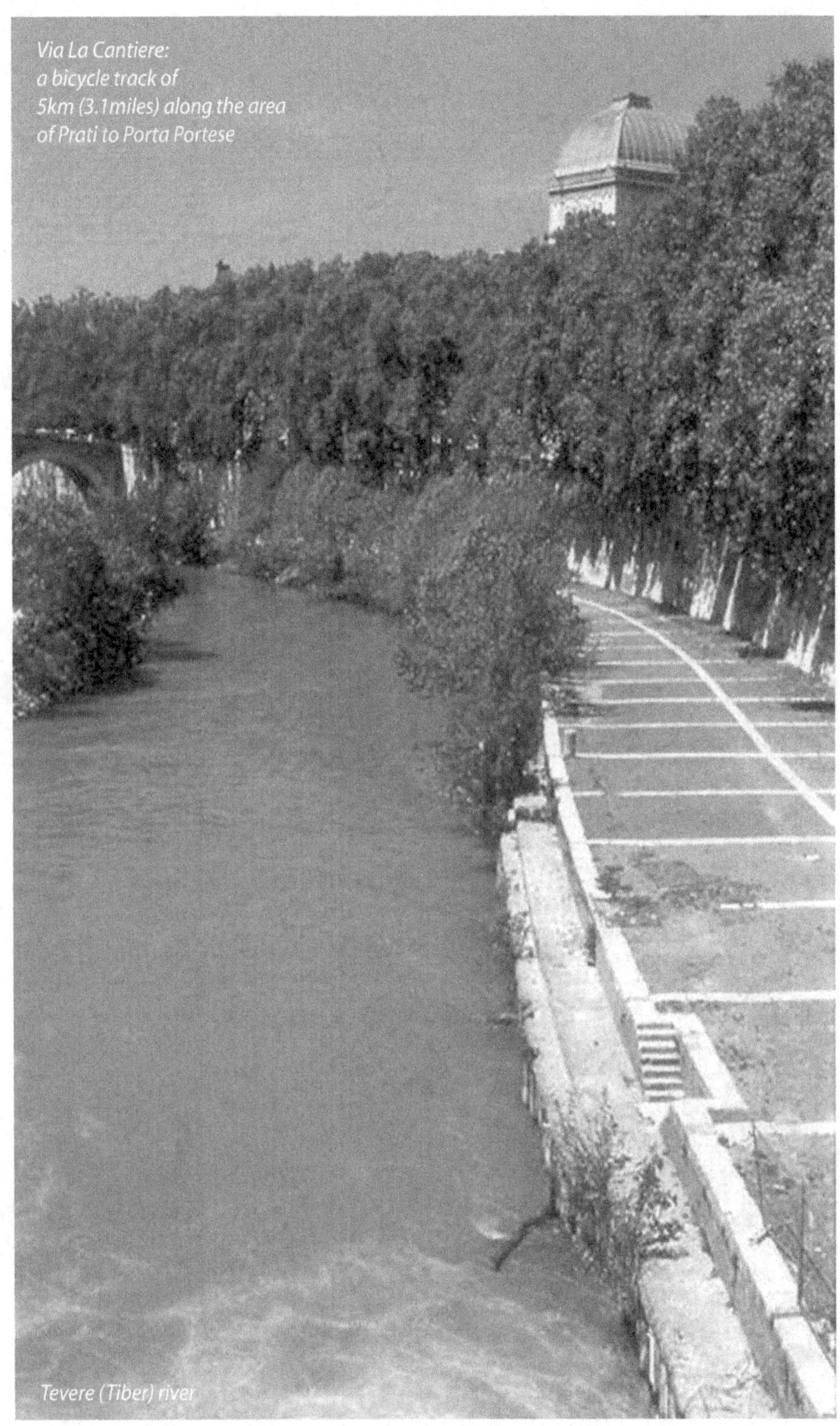

Via La Cantiere:
a bicycle track of
5km (3.1miles) along the area
of Prati to Porta Portese

Tevere (Tiber) river

Il Coliſeo.

cillimum direptioni molliſſimum plumbum, de ornatu mæn
referentur eſſe ſublata, quæ auctores ſuos ſæculis conſecrarunt.

Il primo, che habbia trouato hauer conceſſo li ſaſſi di queſ
edificiò fù Theodorico Rè de' Goti ad iſtanza del Popol
Romano, con queſte parole. *Saxa ergo, quæ ſuggeritis, de*
Amphiteatro longa vetuſtate collapſa, nec aliquid ornatui pu
blico iam prodeſſe niſi ſolas turpes ruinas oſtendere, licentiam
vobis eorum, in vſus dumtaxat publicos, damus vt in murorum
faciem ſurgat, quod non poteſt prodeſſe, niſi iacet. Ma Paol
II. tagliando quella parte, che riguarda SS. Gio: e Paolo
impiegò li trauertini nel palazzo di ſan Marco, e ſeguendo
il Cardinal Raffaelle Riario, ne fabricò con i medeſimi il pa
lazzo della Cancellaria a S. Lorenzo in Damaſo, & il Cardi
nal Farneſe (che fù Paolo III.) il ſuo palazzo a Campo d
Fiore tutti edificij delli più nobili, ch'habbia Roma. In que

ſto·

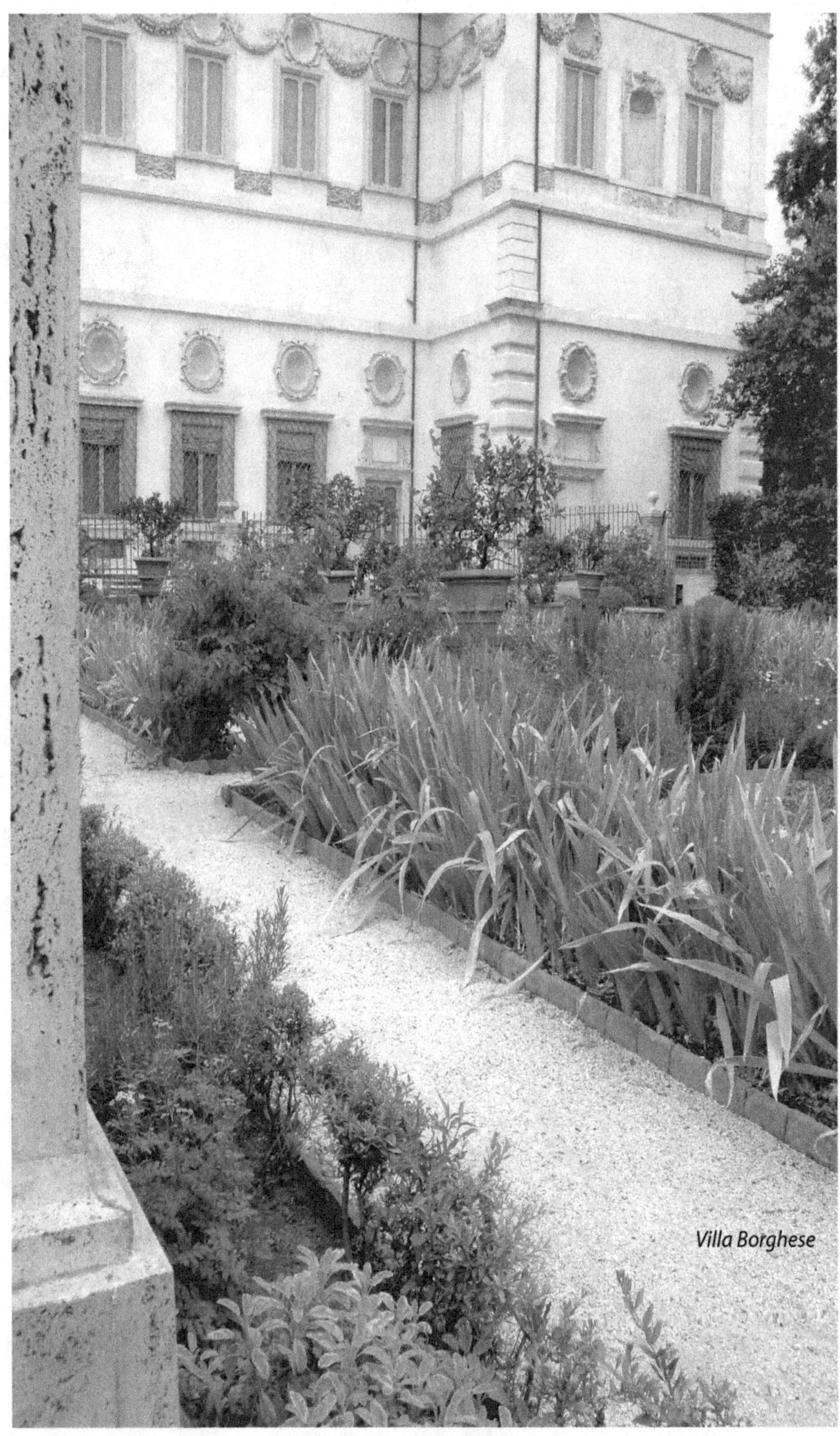

Villa Borghese

Mouth of Truth

Top of Spanish steps

Pantheon

Roman Forum

Rome Classics

Classic: classes of the Roman people especially to the highest class; hence superior, an excellence of its kind, a famous traditional or typical event.

Below you will find a list of the Roman classics to visit. All of them chosen for a specific category according to their location in Rome, and some may be combined as follows:

Sections 6 & 8
Sections 3 & 5
Sections 2 & 1
Sections 2 & 3
Sections 10 & 2

Withholding from the use of cliché, most descriptions come from the author's point of view.

Section 1

VENEZIA SQUARE

Piazza Venezia

The name of this square was derived from the Venetian palace. Mussolini's terrace is located in the centre of it where crowds used to gather to hear his speeches. Below his terrace flowers form two gardens. The square was rearranged during the works of the Vittoriano monument and the Venezia Palace was moved. In front they built a new one, called the"Assicurazioni Generali di Venezia"palace.
A step across the street and you are at the Monument of Vittorio Emanuele.

THE VITTORIANO/VITTORIO EMANUELE

Tomb of the Unknown Soldier

Piazza Venezia, Via dei Fori Imperiali
The monument of a thousand names, it's called a wedding cake or a typewriter, where this all started is a mystery.
The correct name is the monument of (entitled to Vittorio Emanuele II of Savoia, first king of Italy) Vittorio Emanuele II, and that is what it is known as among the Italians. If you're curious to know when it was built, it was started by G. Sacconi in the year of 1885 and finished in 1935.

In the centre there is an altar where an eternal flame burns non-stop. Two carabinieri guards stand in turns guarding this altar dedicated to men lost in war, the unknown men that died in WWI. The altar in Italian is called the Altare della Patira and was opened in 1925.
An unknown warrior is buried somewhere inside justifying this building's existence.

The style of Vittoriano follows Greeks and Latin criteria. At the head of Piazza Venezia, its bright white with torches always alive to symbolize life.
Bus H 30 40 44 46 60 62 63 64 70 81 84 85 87 95 117 119 160 170 175 492 571 60 715 780 810 850 916
If you are on the steps looking at the Vittorio monument, the Campidoglio is down a ways on the left hand side of the road.

CAMPO D'OLIO/CAMPIDOGLIO

The Oil Field

PIAZZA DEL CAMPIDOGLIO
Campidoglio Hill (Rocca Capitolina) is the Sacred Hill of Rome. Here, sores the first temple of the newborn city, called the Temple of Giove that stood on the hill at 900m. Mamertino Prison was carved out of the Campidoglio's rock, and Servio Tullio ordered another one to be built, The Tullianum. To enter into the Mamertime prison of Saints Peter, Simon and Paul, you must enter through the church of San Giuseppe. It's a cell that's 20ft long and 16ft wide. The Doglio's city hall is the place to go if you want to marry in 15 minutes.

The most interesting fact is if you've already read the official story of Rome in this book, you'd be familiar with Romolo and Remo and the she-wolf. Up in till twenty years ago, a real wolf was kept there in a cage representing Rome. This fact was revealed by a dear Roman friend named Tama.

Located quickly right after the Vittoriano, there's Via Teatro di Marcello, and taking the second set of stairs (the first is to Santa Maria in Aracoeli) you'll find the plaza at the top. The steps take your breath away their inclination is of 124°. The original name of this staircase is"Le Scalinate delle Gemonie"but today they are simply known as Le Scalinate del Campidoglio/ The Campidoglio Stairway. It's called the Cordonata, the elegant elongated style of Michelangelo.

From here, you look to your right, you'll see a structure similar to the Coliseum and that is the Marcello theatre - or Teatro Marcello. After you climb the stairs you'll see a wonderful statue on your left of a boy and his horse. In the back is Palazzo Senatorio which holds the office of the city's mayor. The centre statue is one Marcus Aurelia of 161-180 A.D. which stands in the spot where Romolo and Remo's statue once stood which is now in the museum. Behind Marco Aurelio and against the Palazzo Senatorio there is a fountain with statues. The woman in the middle is the Goddess of Rome or the Dei. To the right another statue of the famous she-wolf with Remo and Romolo. The Capitolini museums are located on both sides of the plaza. Palazzo Nuovo and Palazzo dei Conservatori. They contain the classical busts and Renaissance paintings. This all sits on the Capitoline Hill, the smallest of the Seven Hills of Rome. It's a very serene location with a spectacular view from above especially in the dark.
Bus 44 46 64 70 81 110
You can literally see the Marcello theatre from the Campidoglio, it's right across the street.

TEATRO MARCELLO

Theater of Marcellus

Via del Teatro Marcello
Tel 06 4814800
Begun by Caesar and dedicated thereafter by Augustus to the memory of his nephew and son-in-law Marcellus, this was one of greatest theatres in ancient Rome. It could hold around 15,000 spectators. It was used as a source of building materials, then as a medieval fort belonging to the Pierleoni family. It was then transformed by Peruzzi the architect, into a sumptuous renaissance palazzo for the noble Savelli family Open for summer concerts
Bus 23 81 95 160 780
If you follow your way down Via del Teatro and straight onto Via Petroselli, in the end on the corner you will find the Mouth of Truth.

1 Vittorio Emanuele II Monument
2 To the Forum, Trajan's Markets Excavations, and Coliseum
3 To Santa Maria in Aracoeli, Teatro Marcellus, and Campidoglio areas
4 San Marco
5 Palazzo Venezia
6 Gesu
7 Post Office
8 Acra Sacra
9 Teatro Argentina
10 Biblioteca del Burcardo
11 Palazzo Altieri
12 Palazzo Doria Pamphilj
13 San Marcello al Corso
14 Fontanella del Facchino
15 Palazzo del Collegio Romano
16 Pie'di Marmo
17 Santa Maria sopra Minerva
18 Post Office
19 Sant'Ignazio di Loyole
20 Pantheon
21 Sant'Eustachio
22 Sant'Ivo alla Sapienza
23 Palazzo Madama
24 Di Rienzo's Restaurant (Piazza della Rotonda, 8-9)
25 San Luigi dei Francesi
26 Fragola e Limone by Alessandro Gelateria
27 McDonald's
28 La Maddalena
28 Palazzo Capranica
30 Tempio di Adriano
31 Column of Marcus Aurelius
32 Palazzo di Montecitorio
34 Caffe Giolitti
35 Palazzo Baldassini
36 Santa Maria in Campo Marzio
37 Diesel Clothing Store
38 Autogrill Ristorante
39 Post Office
40 San Lorenzo in Lucina
41 Palazzo Borghese
42 To Piazza del Popolo

N

Pantheon Quick Map

BOCCA DELLA VERITA

The Mouth of Truth

Piazza della Bocca della Verità
A short walk from Piazza Venezia
Tel 06 68300230
Closed 1-2:30pm

Once a large sewer cover, now it's known as a lie detector. If you have never heard of the Mouth of Truth (Bocca della Verità), it looks like a large medallion with a crack running down its right side. This medallion has the face of some kind of lion, two holes for eyes, and its mouth wide-open for hands to be slid into. It is a marble mask with a cute fairy-tale attached to it. The mask is situated in the atrium of St. Mary's in Cosmedin Church. Facing the church at your back is the round temple of Vesta. According to popular belief it was said that any one putting his hand in this mouth and swearing falsely, could not withdraw it.

From the Mouth of Truth across the way you will find the Via dei Cerchi and here you cannot miss Circo Massimo.

CIRCO MASSIMO

Circus Maxiumus

This baron desolate oval space represents the ancient setting of the chariot races, an arena along Via dei Cerchi road. They played famous Roman games called the Circenses as fighting sports, track, horse and ferocious beast hunts and held various exhibitions where 400,000 people could watch.

Bus 81 175 628
Metro line B Circo Massimo

Moving on to the Baths of Caracalla, means to follow Via dei Cerchi to the end, to find yourself in Piazza Porta Capena which is next to Largo Vittime del Terrorismo. Viale Terme di Caracalla runs off of this plaza and the baths are on your right hand side.

TERME DI CARACALLA

Terme di Caracalla

Tel 06 39967700
Summer 9am-7:15pm Winter 9am-4:30
Closed Mondays, Christmas and New Year's

It's a beautiful site at night... the Baths of Caracalla or the Antoninian baths were created by Septimius Severus in 206 and inaugurated in 217 by Caracalla. Caracalla's life is a havoc story, he arranged the murder of his brother Geta and five years later was murdered himself; the typical sequence for power struggle.

The baths were sixteen hundred made of marble where people could bathe all together. One would enter into the dressing room Apoditerio, then into the cold baths frigidarium. The warm baths Tepidarium or Bagno Tiepido were almost basins large enough for you to swim in and were made of basalt, granite, and alabaster. The great round room was where one could relax in the steaming vapours of the caldarium. The baths were staffed with anointers, perfume makers, massage therapists, aestheticians, and personnel for hydrotherapies or for the treatment of disease using water. The ceilings are splendour; there are porticoes and pillared halls, gymnasiums with the most colossal columns, and the finest statues ever seen. Hercules L'ercole, Farnese, Venus La Venere Callipigia, La Flora, the bust of Belvedere, il Toro Farnese are all masterpieces extracted from the 16th century from these ruins.

On foot from the Coliseum, walk past the Arch of Constantine down to Via di San Gregorio and you'll arrive in Piazza di Porta Capena, in which Viale delle Terme di Caracalla, is on the right.

Bus 81 85 87 117 186 590 714 810 850

Section 2

DOMUS AUREA

Nero's House of Gold

Via della Domus Aurea 1
Tel 06 39967700
9am-6:40pm
Closed Tuesday

Domus Aurea is one of Emperor Nerone's homes built for him after the fire in 64 that destroyed the Domus Transitoria, his previous home. It extends right on the slope of Celio and the Palatino.

His home blessed its guests. It was an environment of sound example for luxury in which his banquet hall ceiling was made of moving and pierced raw plugs, so flowers and perfumes could be spread on guests. Up the Celian hill on Via Claudia, you will find Nero's Sanctuary of Nymphs Ninfeo di Nerone by the ruins of his Domus residence.

Domus Aurea was actually a group of buildings decorated in gold, ivory and mother of pearl connected by long colonnades and surrounded by vast gardens, parks, ponds, and forests which were fully stocked with animals brought in from the far corners of the Empire.

The Nero's largest pond was like a sea only to be filled in later by the Emperor Vespasiano. He also demolished Nero's property and built an enormous stadium in its place called the Coliseum. Nero's bronze statue was hauled from his residence by twenty four elephants to the amphitheatre and left there. Notorious orgies were held in the huge theatre and the slaughter of luckless Christians.

The Domus lasted 36 years after Nero's suicide.

Bus 75 81 85 87 175 186 204 810 850

Metro Line B exiting Colosseo and turn left down the sidewalk as you come to the intersection, there will be Via Labicana ahead but right on the corner is a black iron gate and some curved stairs go up, that is your Via della Domus Aurea

COLOSSEO

Coliseum

Piazza del Colosseo
Tel 06 39967700
Summer 8:30am-7:15pm Winter 8:30-4:30pm

The Roman kingdom's largest amphitheatre was a terrible circus indeed, where a tent was placed over the top to protect the players from the sun. Around 700,000 were killed in the Coliseum including condemned men, women, and children who were forced into the ring to play with animals and gladiators to the death. Gladiators were first publicly exhibited in Rome by the two Bruti brothers. In medieval times, the theatre was named after the emperors of the Flavian Dynasty; Anfiteatro Flavio. It was an enormous ring of 56m (184ft) and divided up into four floors that was capable of holding 87.000 people. In ancient times, it was the location for animal hunts Venationes, where men were armed having to confront different types of beasts; lions, tigers, bears, and crocodiles when it was filled it with water. There were gladiator fights Munera and Navy-Battles Naumachie.

Approaching the year 523, the Coliseum was beginning to deteriorate and was abandoned. It became useful only as a quarry for materials for constructing other compositions like: San Giovanni in Laterano, San Pietro, and Piazza Venezia. The Coliseum's name in Latin would be Colosseus, meaning gigantic or colossal. The modernized name complemented the 114ft colossal bronze statue of Emperor Nerone.

The Coliseum sits in the spot where an artificial lake once glistened. Nero's lake. Construction of the gigantic theatre began with Emperor Vespasiano and was completed by his son Tito, who's arch Arco di Tito is up Via Sacra which is the bumpy road running across from the Coliseum that leads to the Roman Forum. Arches were gifts to emperors from the Senate and the Roman People (SPQR). Instead of sculpturing new arch's for each different emperor the Romans just chiselled off the heads and replaced them with heads of the current characters. The Romans were splendid recyclers.

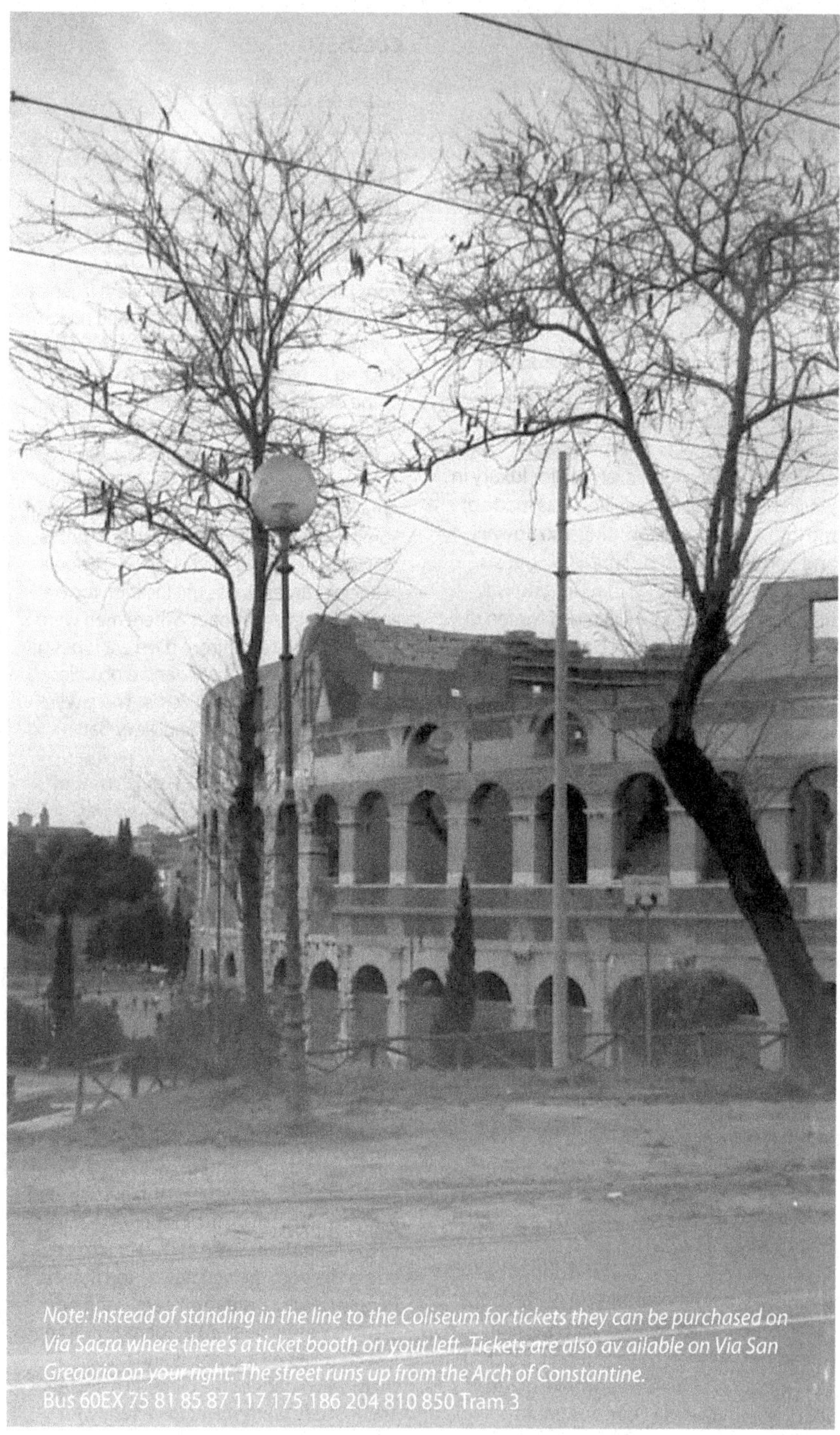

Note: Instead of standing in the line to the Coliseum for tickets they can be purchased on Via Sacra where there's a ticket booth on your left. Tickets are also av ailable on Via San Gregorio on your right. The street runs up from the Arch of Constantine.

Bus 60EX 75 81 85 87 117 175 186 204 810 850 Tram 3

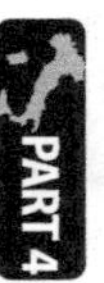

Colosseo good luck map

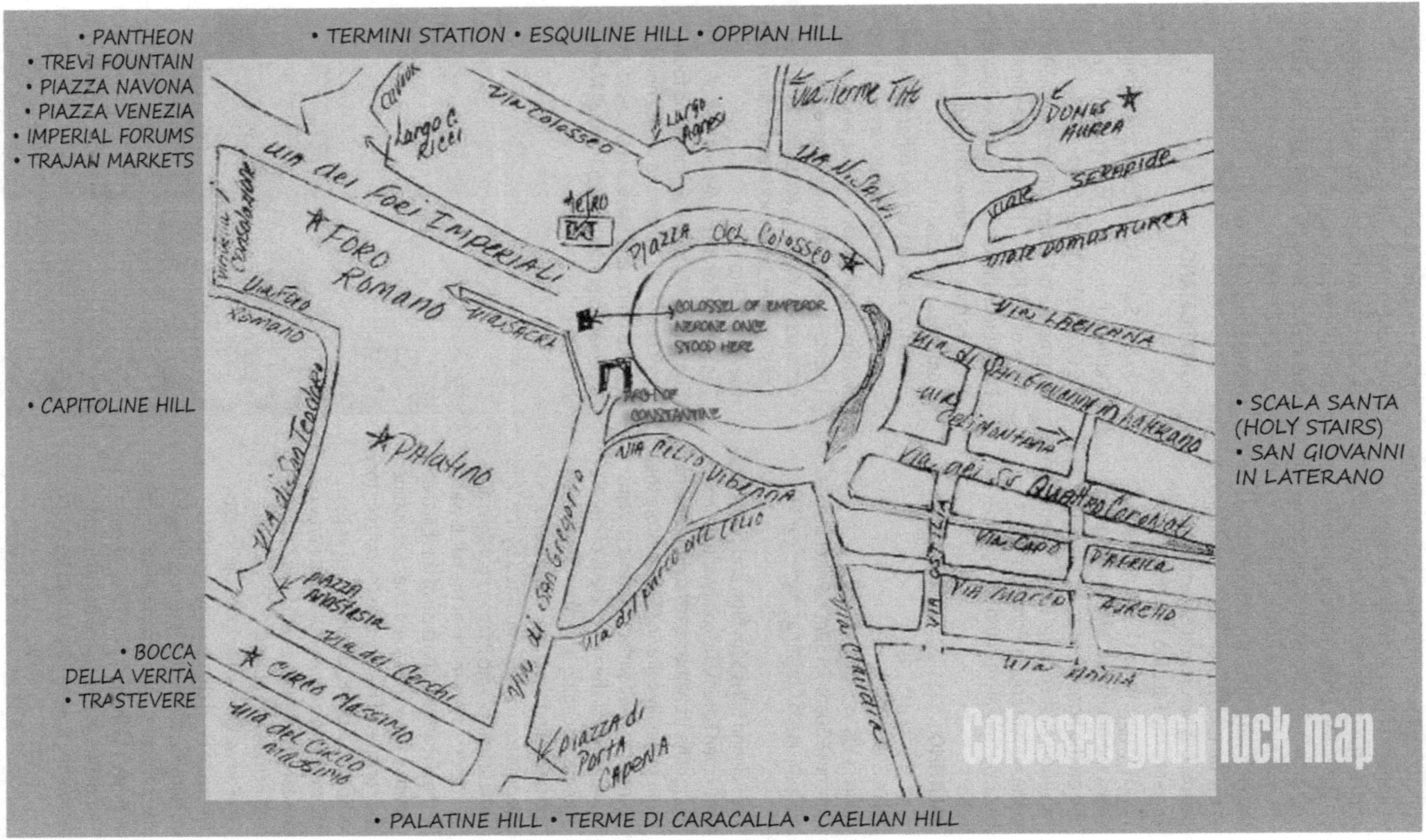

• PANTHEON
• TREVI FOUNTAIN
• PIAZZA NAVONA
• PIAZZA VENEZIA
• IMPERIAL FORUMS
• TRAJAN MARKETS
• TERMINI STATION • ESQUILINE HILL • OPPIAN HILL
• CAPITOLINE HILL
• SCALA SANTA
(HOLY STAIRS)
• SAN GIOVANNI
IN LATERANO
• BOCCA
DELLA VERITÀ
• TRASTEVERE
• PALATINE HILL • TERME DI CARACALLA • CAELIAN HILL
Via Colosseo
Largo C. Ricci
Via dei Fori Imperiali
Foro Romano
Via Sacra
Metro
Piazza del Colosseo
Colossel of Emperor Nerone once stood here
Arch of Constantine
Palatino
Via di San Teodoro
Piazza Anastasia
Via dei Cerchi
Circo Massimo
Via del Circo Massimo
Via di San Gregorio
Piazza di Porta Capena
Via Celio Vibenna
Via Claudia
Via Labicana
Via di San Giovanni in Laterano
Via dei SS. Quattro Coronati
Via Capo d'Africa
Via Marco Aurelio
Domus Aurea
Via N. Salvi
Via Terme Tito
Largo Agnesi
Viale Serapide
Viale Domus Aurea

A victory present for Emperor Constantine in honour of his 10th year as emperor and for the remembrance of his victory on the Milvio Bridge three years previous. This arch is the largest and best preserved antique monument Rome. The figures on the arch tell stories about the people living at the time. They were hard-working tired people but heroic and determined.
To get to the Palatino from Piazza dell Colosseo pass the arch and go half way down the main road 'Via San Gregorio' and on the right there an entrance for the Palatino/Palatine. There is also an entrance in the Roman Fourm/Foro Romano because they are located side by side.

PALATINO

The Palatine Hill

Tel 06 39967700
Address Via V. S. Gregorio 30
Summer 8:30am-7:15pm - Winter 8:30am-4:30pm closed Christmas, New Year's Day

The Palatino hill is 52m high and overlooks the Roman Forum, Tuscolani and Albani mountains. Its name seems to indicate that it was originally a grazing land pastore that maintained itself with numerous streams of water. It was the first nucleus of city life in Rome managing a number of palaces and becoming thereafter the Imperial Headquarters. It is surmounted by the Villa Farnese which, with its many gardens and staircases, covers much of the hill. It was in the dirt around the base of this hill that Romulus drew the sacred line that outlined the confines of his city. See the official story of Rome on page 16. It is known as the Monte Aristocratico or Dio/God Pan, and the cavern of the she-wolf where Romolo and Remo were nursed.
Dio Pan was known to roam the forests where he lived chasing tiny nymphs to terrorize them, and he forced these natural deities (in forms of beautiful young maidens) to flee.
Famous faces during the Republic era before the Roman Empire had built upon this area until the Cesari slowly confiscated every one of them. Tiberius's famous residence was propped up on the southern point of the Palatino hill.
Bus 40EX 60EX 63 70 75 81 84 85 87 160 175 186 628 810 850
Metro line B Colosseo

FORO ROMANO

The Roman Forum

Piazza di Santa Maria Nova/Largo Romolo and Remo
Tel 06 6990110/06 3996770
Summer 9am-7:30pm Winter 9am-4:30pm
Think of the Roman Forum as the ruins lining the main road Via Fori Imperiali, all on the right if walking towards the Coliseum from Piazza Venezia.
Along the sidewalk on the other side green statues depict famous emperors who keep watch; Caesar, Traiano, Nerva, and Augusto.
To enter the Roman Forum there's an entrance on Via Sacra accessible from the Coliseum, the small rocky road ending with the Arch of Tito.
The Roman Forum makes on think of Commercial-Politics-Religion or the focal point of the city, where the senate house, records office, and basilica were. Across the way was an outdoor shopping mall Markets of Traiano.

Eventually most of the area became abandoned and deteriorated just as the Coliseum. A minute few architectural objects survived, what nobility possessed, and a few temples. The Roman Forum is located between the Capitol, the Imperial Forums, the Coliseum and the Palatino.
Bus 40EX 60EX 63 70 75 81 84 85 87 160 175 186 628 810 850
Metro line B Colosseo

From here, and going on to the Imperial Forum, if you find your way back out onto the main drag of Via dei Fori Imperiali, you'd find part of the Imperal forum located on the same side of the Roman forum and the other part across the street. You see, the main road destroyed some of it, cutting it through the middle. The bigger part is on Via Alessandrina which is quite a tiny street that almost doesn't seems like a street at all.

FORI IMPERIALI
Imperial Forum
Via IV Novembre 94
Tel 06 6797702
Open 9:30am-7:30pm
Closed Monday

This area was built to deal with the Roman population boom. On August 1931, Benito Mussolini, dictator of Italy, was waiting for a visit from his friend Adolph Hitler. He wished to impress his friend to see the Coliseum from his office window in Piazza Venezia, but obstructions blocked this panoramic paradise. So how could this problem be solved to suit his needs?
The Coliseum was well buried beyond a whirl of Renaissance churches, palaces and medieval houses, and along this jungle of treasures he ran a paved road called the Via Fori Imperiali (850x30 yards) straight through it.
The serious historical damages were irreparable and changed history forever, as this road divided the Imperial forums of Trojan, Augustus, Nerva and Vespasian that are on the side of the Trojan Markets. It really halved Caesar's forum, the other fraction of it now belonged to the Roman Forum, but the view through that window was a day's impression.

A good landmark for locating the Imperial Forum is the Trojan Column. The forum overlooks the brick coloured markets Mercati di Traiano lined with windows. Various types and colours of marble sit right out in the sun: oranges, blacks, yellows, pinks, and greens that produced beautiful floor patterns. Some sections of flooring include circular and square patterns of white and pink and beyond broken columns of marble lay in pieces of green, grey, peach, tan and white. Some of the exotic marbles were brought in from other countries and floorings were glued together using the multi-coloured pebble mixtures once a cement-like paste. Evidence of how the Romans welt together the huge columns using melted iron is apparent in the marks left where the iron was melted and poured in. It's a good thing the slaves did all that work.
Bus H 40EX 60EX 63 64 70 75 84 87 117 170 175 186 810

From the part of the Imperial Forum located on Via Alessandrina, the Trojan Column stands between it and the main street, in the piece of land in the middle.

COLONNA TRAIANA
The Trojan Column
Tel 06 6790048
Summer 9am-7pm winter 9am-6pm
Closed Mon
Located in the Fori Imperiali, the column is across from the Vittoriano Emanuele II monument.
The column is a 660ft. tall spiral band detailed with accounts of the Trojan's wars-Traiano against the DACI. The reliefs are

fascinating especially early in the morning under the rising sun. There are 26,000 brightly coloured figures easily visible from the library rooftops.
In 1588, Sixtus V replaced the bronze statue of Emperor Traiano with one of St. Peter. Inside a spiral staircase runs up the column to the top from where Coliseum watching was popular.
Bus 40EX 60EX 64 70 117 170

I MERCATI DI TRAIANO
Trojan's Markets and the Forum of Trojan
Designed by B.C. Apollodoro
Piazza Madonna di Loreto
Tel 06 82059127
Summer 9am-7 Winter 9-6pm
The remains of an ancient Roman strip mall, not a modern-day invention. After 3,000 years one hundred and fifty shops still see the light of day.
The semicircle rose on six floors on the Quirinal hill overlooking the Roman Forum. The shops gave out free grain in the corridor on the ground floor level and sold fruits, vegetables, wine, oils, and a myriad of other commodities. Via Biberatica, 3d floor: taverns and muffled the noises of Senators and other important people from the Forum. 4th floor: peppers and exotic spices, 5th floor: public assistance, 6th floor: ponds with live fish and a running aqueduct supplying fresh water with another supplying sea water from Ostia.

The most important part of the markets is the hall; the building covered with six cross vaults considered the first covered trade centre in history. Notice the stairs are still engraved with dates in Roman numerals.
Bus 40EX 60EX 64 70 117 170

Section 3

LARGO TORRE ARGENTINA
This holy area was a cat-filled sanctuary since 1929. Largo Argentina shows its remains as ruins of four temples dating back to the IV century to II century A. D. Nowadays, the organization Friends of Roman Cats inhabits it. On the far corner there is a staircase and you are welcome to go down. This was the so-called location where Caesar was murdered and where his grave marker can be photographed.

From Argentina, you can pick up tram 8 to Trastevere or wander the streets of the Jewish Ghetto. Head down Via Arenula (tram track follows it) then cut over onto San Maria Pianto, go on straight ahead and Via Portico D'Ottavia is there in the heart of little Israel.
Bus 30EX 40EX 46 62 63 64 70 81 87 492 630 780 - Tram 8

Moving on to the turtle Fountain, you must walk a slight bit down Via di Torre Argentina, the road leads from the main square and past the Argentina theatre whose entrance faces the tram tracks. Here you will find Largo Arenula and the beginning of Via Arenula- now bare left onto Falegnami which leads you right into Piazza Mattei.

FONTANA DELLE TARTARUGHE
Fountain of Turtles
Piazza Mattei

A hop away from Little Israel/Jewish Ghetto, this fountain was designed by Giacomo della Porta with a little touch of turtle magic by Bernini. Quite charming, this fountain is known for its fresh water and is rarely passed up for bottling spring water.

Moving on to the Portico D'Ottavia, go down Via Reginella or S. Ambrogio from Piazza Mattei and Via Portico D'Ottavia will be found.

IL PORTICO D'OTTAVIA

The Door of D'Ottavia

Via del Portico D'Ottavia

This Ancient temple is in the heart of the Jewish Ghetto. The Ghetto is situated south of Largo Torre Argentina and runs off to the left of Via Arenula and extends to the Tevere River facing Isola Tiberina or Tiber Island.

Via Portico D'Ottavia is the boundary marking the Jewish quarters in Rome and is still the centre of Jewish life. The Jews lost rights and were segregated in 1555 where a curfew affixed on them kept them within a walled-in area. They were pressed to live clustered together on only 3 hectares/ 7.41 acres. In this miniature neighbourhood they found high walls and only one gate for accessing the outside world. Their hats were adorned with yellow tags for three hundred years marking them as Jews.
The hostile dream of Roman bishops was to convert the Jews into a faith in which they did not believe. Roman guards would physically force them into Catholic masses and to be baptized.
Jews were obligated to dance around shoeless in cold February during Carnevale to amuse harlequin crowds.
Orti Degli Ebrei is the name of the Jewish cemetery located in the old Circo Massimo. The main gate was guarded and financed by the Jews. In1847, Pope Pio IX had the Jewish Ghetto walls demolished. Although freed to do as they pleased now, the society persisted to live in small quarters just like their ancestors did.

Jewish money-making secrets were acquired with force by nobles and princes who were in debt and lacked the money-making smarts. They used their newly confiscated knowledge to suck the Christians dry. They stole the smarts of the Jews to rob from the Christians.

The Jewish Ghetto is a moment's walk from Largo Torre Argentina and from the Tevere Tiber River. Walking down Via Arenula from Largo Torre Argentina where tram 8 runs, there's a street called San Maria Pianto on the left. This runs into Via Portico D'Ottavia, where the Temple of Portico D'Ottavia and the Jewish Synagogue are found.
The Jewish bakeries on Via Portico D'Ottavia are scrumptious, in particular the Jewish macaroons.

This street joins the streets that run along the Tevere River. Lungotevere de' Cenci runs on the right if you'd like to see the Jewish museum.

MUSEO EBRAICO

Hebrew Museum of Rome

Lungotevere de'Cenci
Tel 06 68400661
Filled with photos of the entire Jewish ghetto story to WWII.
April-September 9am-7:30pm Monday-Thursday
9am-1:30pm Friday and Sunday
Oct-Mar 9am-4:30pm Monday-Thursday
9am-1:30pm Friday
9am-12:30pm Sunday
Closed on Saturday
Bus H 23 63 280 630 780
Tram 8

ISOLA TIBERINA

Tiber Island/Bartolomeo Island

Bridge to Tiberina Island:
Piazza Monte Savello Ponte Fabricio/ Fabricio bridge
Largo Tevere degli Anguillara Ponte Cestio/ Cestio Bridge

At one time people destroyed a field owned by tyrants and threw grains out into the Tevere. These bundles eventually became clogged up in the middle. The result was a nucleus of land that developed over time into the consistency of an island. In 461, the image of Esculapio under the form of a snake was brought to Rome to help stop the plague that hit the city of Quiriti. There at the south point of the island, the sick and diseased disembarked where a temple

was built in its memory. Later a wall was constructed to represent the stern of an ancient warship in memory of the boat that had transported them. At one time peoples of Egypt, Greece and Turkey journeyed to Rome thus travelled up the Tevere River when two snakes jumped in the water side by side off the river bank. The snakes slithered to the other side and into the holy temple which coaxed the people to build a hospital right there. The Greek symbol of medicine represents two serpents on a staff as venom was used as medicine.
The word farmacia in Italian is farmachi in Greek meaning poison in English.
When the famous temple of Esculapius the Greek god of medicine was gone, the St. Bartholomew church was erected in its place.

A popular place for summer sun-bathers and the ideal place to relax. Some areas in the summer are still isolated and muffle the city's traffic above.
Bus 63 Tram 8 from Largo Torre Argentina

Section 4

CASTEL SANT'ANGELO

Castle Sant'Angelo

Mole Adriana II/Mausoleo di Adriano
Lungotevere Castello 50
Tel 06 6819111/06 39967600
Tuesday-Sunday 9am-8pm
Closed Monday

I could write a book alone on this castle, from outside it doesn't prove much, but the inside takes one into an elegant medieval kingdom. Emperor Hadrian's fortress still has that special room with nothing in it but an enormous trunk looking 8ft x10ft in size. You wonder how much money and golden treasures one could store in it? You also wonder why they tell common people that being poor is a virtue? Saint Clements's bath is a hidden frescoed marvel of oranges and greens found up a set of tightly narrowed stairs.
The five-floor castle was a prison and torture chamber while under Papal control.
A huge stone angel on the attic terrace overlooks the entire city with a clear view of San Pietro by night. You will also see part of the Coliseum, Piazza Venezia and of course the fantastic Tevere River passing by with its Roman reflections. The castle is topped with a metal bell rung whenever someone was put to death.
In 1277, a 400m outer corridor built of brick was erected, an escape route from the Vatican to the Castle. For a few euros anyone may pass through it. When the doors to the Tevere were opened, the land below swelled with water, impeding to enemy advances.
The castle's chapel is worth a visit too.
Bus 23 34 49 62 64 80EX 87 492 926 990

From the castle it is easy to arrive at St. Peter's. Just follow the street along the river on the same side as the castle heading to your left if you are looking at the castle, as long as you find Via della Conciliazione you will run into St. Peter's.

SAN PIETRO

Saint Peter's

Piazza San Pietro
Tel 06 69883462
San Pietro was the first location of Christian persecutions. And during that time, it was a deserted infamous place called the vaticinio or primitive church. The idea for the San Pietro Basilica grew from Saint Peter the Apostle's grave and in the 2nd century a monument was placed over it. His tomb is still present in San Pietro under the altar. Peter was crucified on these grounds in the end of the 60's, and buried there.

Constantine came to Rome in 312 A.D. and ended most of the worst Christian persecutions. Constantine protected them and gave them their own land. He later gave orders to erect a church over Peter's grave around 324-329.

2,000 years ago the site was occupied by a Circus or Arena. Young Emperor Nerone inherited it from his relative Caligola. It was located inside an immense villa belonging to Agrippina the mother of 3rd Emperor Caligola; it was a private arena and was rarely open to the public.

In 1377, the Vatican became the official residency to the Pope. But Rome went downhill during the medieval period and barbarians and vandals declined the city. St Peter's was headed for ruin until the big projects started with the renaissance period. Projects by Leon Battista Alberti and Bernardo Rossellino were involved in the restorations. By monuments, bridges, basilicas and aqueducts were all being restored.
Works in St. Peter's were created by the biggest architectural geniuses of the Baroque and Renaissance periods.

Michelangelo's Pietà
Bernini's Papal Altar
Bernini's Throne of San Pietro
Canova's Monument to the Stuarts
Bernini's The Piazza circular colonel arms

The Swiss Guards are the little men with funny red and yellow striped and puffed outfits. They pose as guardians for the Vatican State and especially to the Pope. They were once Helvetian soldiers sent to Rome by Pope Julius II in 1506 to form a protecting Vatican Army.

The 266th Pope Benedetto Joseph Ratzinger from Germany was just elected in April 2005.

Basilica Nov-Mar 7am-6pm Apr-Oct 7am-7pm
San Peter's Basilica is situated in Città del Vaticano, the residence of Popes since 1377, is the most important church in the world
Cupola Winter 8am-4:45pm summer 8am-5:45pm
Sacre Grotte Vaticane Oct-March 8am- 5pm April-Sept 8am-6pm
Museo Del Tesoro Treasure Museum Winter 9am-5:30 Summer 9am- 6:30

**There are separate fees for each different part of San Pietro*

METRO SUBWAY TUBE FOR SAN PIETRO
Line A San Pietro or line A Ottaviano
Exit the metro towards Via Ottaviano and go straight down Via Ottaviano where San Pietro will be on towards the far side of the square.
Bus 23 32 34 46 49 62 64 81 492 913 990
Tram 19

Section 5

SANTA MARIA IN TRASTEVERE

Saint Mary in Trastevere
Piazza di Santa Maria in Trastevere
Tel 06 5897332
Everyday 7am-9pm
The present day basilica was built under Pope Innocentius II 1138-1148 out of materials plundered from the Baths of Caracalla. The first church on this site dates back to Pope Julius I to the middle of the 4th century A.D.. Beautiful marble and sculptures can be admired in the portico, and inscriptions which originate from the basilica and catacombs. This is the oldest church in Rome.
Bus H 23 44 75 116 280 Trams 3 8

A minute's walk from Termini Station
To get to San Pietro in Montorio from here you'll need to exit the piazza and head towards Piazza S. Egidio and Largo Fumasoni Biondi not towards Via Lungaretta. Go straight passing the two squares, and head to Via Paglia then take a right on Frusta. There'll be a main road here but right across the way is the entrance to San Pietro in Montorio.

SAN PIETRO IN MONTORIO *

Piazza S. Pietro in Montorio

A characteristic gothic rosette decorates the façade of the church and although this church was perhaps founded in the ninth century, its style is that of the fifteenth century. Inside paintings are signed by Vasari and Gian Lorenzo Bernini amongst others. At the centre of the cloisters temple of Bramante rises, erected on the spot which is purported to be the final resting place of the cross of St. Peter.
Off of Via Garibaldi Granicolo
(Janiculum Area)

Section 6

MAUSOLEO DI AUGUSTO

Mausoleum of Augustus

Piazza Augusto Imperatore
Built in 27 B.C., the Mausoleum was pillaged as a source of building materials and later became the place of a variety: a vineyard, a hanging garden, an amphitheatre, a theatre, and an auditorium. It was originally 44m high and formed like an Etruscan tumulus burial ground was surrounded by cypresses and crowned with a bronze statue. It was spacious enough for the remains of Augustus. Around the central pillar, graves of the distinguished members of the Giulio-Claudia noble families were placed.

From Piazza di Spagna take Via Babuino and a left on Via della Croce. Joining Largo Lonbardi at the end, the mausoleum is straight ahead past Tribuna di S. Carlo. From here you can reach the Spanish Steps taking Via Grottino from Piazza Augusto Imperatore. You will hit Largo Goldoni and take Via Condotti from there which will bring you to the steps.

PIAZZA DEL POPOLO

This square opens from the classic walkways of Via del Corso, Via del Babuino and Via Ripetta. It's a square that also performed public executions. The twin churches at the far end of the piazza are known as S. Maria dei Miracoli 1675-1679 and Monte Santo 1662-1675.
Carlo Rainaldi began the constructions and GianLorenzo Bernini finished them with the help of Carlo Fontana.
The Flaminio Obelisk stands in the centre at 79ft high 1200's.

Towards the other side of the square there's the church of S. Maria del Popolo or Saint Mary of the people housing Caravaggio paintings including the Crucifixion of Saint Peter and the Conversion of St. Paul.
Metro line A Flaminio
Bus 81 95 117 204

Pincio stands just above Piazza del Popolo and you can adjoin it through Viale D'Annunzio off the square and by walking up the hill (Viale D'Annunzio turns into Viale Trinità dei Monti-which heads back to the Spanish Steps)

PINCIO

Beautiful views of Rome and a photographer's heaven. Have a walk to Viale Orologio/Clock Street.

Pincio is located above Piazza del Popolo, a seven minute walk from Piazza di Spagna.
Bus 95 117 204
Metro Flaminio

TRINITA DEI MONTI

Trinity of the Mountains

Piazza di Trinità dei Monti

Luigi XII had this church lying on top of the monumental flight of the Spanish Steps built in 1502 on the ruins of an antique theatre. Inside the church is the masterpiece of Daniele da Volterra, the famous fresco of the Descent from the Cross.

Metro line A Barberini or Spagna

PIAZZA DI SPAGNA

The Spanish Steps

Almost 140 little steps built by the French helped one arrive to their church above-the Trinità dei Monti.

As the Spanish Embassy used to reside at the bottom, the name was given to the plaza. The famous fountain La Barcaccia rests in the centre of the square that was built on orders of Pope Urban the 8th in honour of a vessel that saved many lives in the disastrous Tevere flood of 1598. Receding waters supposedly left the boat stranded exactly there and the fountain has been bubbling and leaking since 1627. Roman's claim that the water has unusual qualities superior taste especially when you cook your vegetables in it and Babington's tea room swore that this fountain dispensed the only water fit for English tea.

The magical waters flow through 8 miles in one of the three ancient aqueducts still in use, the Acqua Virgo Aqueduct which ends in Salvi's Trevi fountain.

Every year, the steps welcome in an important line of fashion with elegant shows striding up and down the steps. The streets growing off the square sprout famous designer shops of all kinds.

Metro Spagna or metro Barberini, it is a short walk up Via Sistina and the Trinity church is on your right.

From the Spanish Steps to Piazza del Popolo take Via Babuino just off the square which ends in Popolo Plaza.

VILLA BORGHESE

Viale S. Paolo d. Brasile

We give thanks to the lush gardens of the Borghese estate. There beneath the labyrinth gardens and plentiful fountains is a biological zoo with zany animals. Miles of green grow up and down mild hills. One of the world's most interesting museums is locked tight behind its gates and cooling trees may be relished during the smothering of the summer's heat.

Bus 88 95 116 490 491 495

Metro line A Flaminio or Spagna

Villa Borghese: Biologic zoo and rollerblades to rent.

GALLERIA BORGHESE

Borghese Gallery

Piazzale del Museo Borghese

Bus 52 or 53 from Via Veneto or San Silvestro and get off on Via Pinciana

Metro line A Spagna, go up the stairs and at top take a left going down Via Trinità dei Monti and another Borghese entrance will be on the right.

Or a brief walk from the top of Via Veneto

GALLERIA NAZIONALE D'ARTE MODERNO

National Gallery of Modern Art

Viale delle Belle Arti 131

This gallery is something special and most visitors come out shining. The gallery houses the most prestigious Renaissance and Baroque paintings in the world. Works by; Raffaelo, Titian, and Caravaggio, sculptures by Bernini and Canova.

Take bus 52 or 53 or 217

Tram 3 or 19

VIA VENETO

This street probably snuck into ever film produced in the 50's and 60's. It was probably walked upon by every film star of the epoch. It was opened in 1889 and was the symbol of the Dolce Vita/Sweet Life. In its ghostly past, and still sparsely today numerous high class hookers walk and wait on the Veneto.

It frolics in lush hotels and historical cafés as well as the Hard Rock Café and is located near the American Embassy. It's the street for the glove shop and its grand selection of pure silk cashmere ties. It possesses one of the two dog fountains in all of Europe. The road's full name is Via Vittorio Veneto and its one to say much of its strange church the Santa Maria della Concezione.
Bus 52 53 63 80EX 95 116 119 630
Metro line A Barberini

SANTA MARIA DELLA CONCEZIONE
Dress appropriately. If you are sightseeing in comfortable shorts, tank tops, sleeveless, mini skirts, or even sandals be aware of the dress-code as church entries require the covering of shoulders and knees.

Section 8

QUIRINALE

Italy's White House
Via XXIV Maggio 16
Tel 06 696271
This building was originally called *Mons Agonalis* and from 1947, this was home for the presidents of the Republic. Before however, it was home to the many popes. When the Italian flag is raised the president is in, when the flag is lowered, he has gone out.
Bus H 60EX 64 70 117 170 640

If you exit the Quirinale at Via del Traforo you will run into Largo del Tritone. Follow Via del Tritone a little ways and take your third left onto Via Stamperia, this road runs into the Trevi Fountain.

FONTANA DI TREVI

The Trevi Fountain
Piazza di Trevi
The mighty Ocean God reigns over the waters of the Trevi in a shell-shaped chariot. The idea was to base it around the seas it celebrates the abundance of wealth and curative powers coming from the sea itself.
The Snake Symbols depicts medicine. Snakes venom was used extensively in medicines by the Romans and Greeks.
The Cornucopia is a symbol of riches and abundance brought in from the new world.
The Two Seahorses symbolize the rough and tempest seas.
The Horse being pulled symbolizes a slow and calm sea.

Built on behalf of Clement the XII by architect Salvi, it was decorated by several artists of Bernini's school. The fountain took 30 years to complete 1732-1762.
The Acqua Virgo the aqueduct from 19 B.C., supplies the Trevi and the whole area with its water. It's the best water for coffee seeing it's low in minerals.
The fountain is not only celebrated for its excellent water, but for the legend that whoever drinks from it I wouldn't drink directly from it or throws three coins in the fountain shall surely return to Rome.
Bus 175 from Piazza Barberini or Termini station.
Off Via del Tritone and Via del Corso

To find Via del Corso from the Trevi you can take one of two streets off of the square: Via Crociferi which crosses over Via S. Maria and onto Via Sabini that is off of Via del Corso or Via D. Muratte which also crosses Via S. Maria, and goes straight out to the main road.

VIA DEL CORSO

This street stretches almost a mile, starting at the Obelisk in Piazza del Popolo and ending at the Vittorio Emanuele II monument. During the 1700's, thanks to the many cafés that lined the Via del Corso, it became the centre of intellectual, artistic and political life. In the mid nineteenth century, a multitude of fashion boutiques, book stores, and newspaper offices sprang up which gave it its present-day character.
Bus from Piazza del Popolo 117 119
Bus from Piazza di Venezia 62 63 81 85 95 117 119 160 175 630

From the Via del Corso to arrive at the Pantheon follow directions carefully. There are several different ways to go from the main road.

Here are a few suggestions:
Via Caravita to Piazza S. Ignazio to Piazza S. Macuto to Via Seminari bearing right into Piazza della Rotonda or Via Pietra to Piazza di Pietra to Via dei Pastini which leads to Piazza della Rotonda.

PANTHEON

Piazza della Rotonda
Tel 06 68300230
Monday-Saturday 8:30am-7:30pm Sunday 9-6pm

The Pantheon was the main religious temple for the Romans. Two huge bronze doors open to the perfect 133ft hole carved into the ceiling and you wonder why there are no windows.
It was consumed by flames in 80 A.D., the worst affliction that it could have suffered. Emperor Hadrian remodelled the entire monument and wiped away Agrippa's original design. Others that took part in its restoration include; Marcus Aurelius and Caracalla.
Emperor Hadrian left one thing intact; the original inscription on the architrave of the door that reads; "M. Agrippa L. F. Cos Tertium Fecit" actually reads: "Marcus Agrippa, son of Lucius, built it. "Interestingly he did not substitute Agrippa for Hadrian. The baths which touch the outer wall of the Pantheon opposite to the colonnade or the porch-like front of the building were left behind.
The Pantheon in all of its royal prestige lies to rest some fallen admirables; Italian kings and Raffaelo.

"I believe I have never met a person in my life that was absolutely devoid of emotion at the sight of the Pantheon. "
Stendhal's - A Roman Journal.

The Pantheon's square Piazza della Rotonda, possess nice outdoor-style restaurants and free gypsy entertainment.
Continuing on to Piazza Navona, you may follow Via Giustiniani and straight onto Via del Salvatore to the main Corso Rinascimento. From here go straight across the street and you are in Piazza Navona.

Bus 30EX 40EX 46 62 63 64 70 81 87 116 116T 186 204 492 628 910

PIAZZA NAVONA

Navona Square

If you've ever seen the Talented Mr. Ripley with Matt Damon, it was in Piazza Navona where he met Freddy.
This square yells Domitanus's name. At one time the square was a Roman Papal forum and underneath Navona are the remains of Domitanus's circus. The surrounding buildings show signs of its ruins and the shape of the piazza is that of a racetrack. Redesigned by Bernini, the finishing touches were applied in 1626.
A little girl's pain lies behind the Church of Agnes in Agony in Navona square. When Saint Agnes was only twelve she refused to marry a pagan man and was sentenced to death. She was dragged through the square nude, the only protection from humiliation she possessed were her immense locks. Navona's hidden meaning is derived from the word Agony; agone-n'agone-navone-navona.

THE FOUNTAIN OF RIVERS 1651

The Nile-The Danube-The Ganges-The Rio della Plata

Does the fountain in Navona square represent the four forces of the world? Sculpted by famous sculpturist Bernini it is better known as La Fontana dei Fiumi or the Fountain of Four Rivers. Today it collects various fountain-hangers with camera's or love on the mind.

It is an artist's lane with classy places to eat and plenty of homemade ice cream. Bus 30EX 40EX 46 62 63 64 70 81 87 116 116T 186 204 492 628 810

For Piazza Navona; after the Vittoriano building or Piazza Venezia, get off at the 3rd bus stop then walk till you see a piazza on your right with a huge statue of Marco Minghetti on Corso Vittorio Emanuele take either street behind it.

Now I will guide you to Campo de' Fiori. On one end of the Piazza you will find Via di Pasquino, or Canestrari go straight over these streets and onto Cuccagna leading you back onto the main road. Just cross Corso V. Emanuele and go down Baullari and this road leads you to Campo de' Fiori.

CAMPO DE' FIORI

Field of Flowers

7am-1:30pm Monday-Saturday
Jekyll and Hyde would both tell you it's not a field of flowers anymore, but WHERE cut flowers are for sale. The square breaths life, full of bright seasonal fruits, nuts, vegetables, and fresh fish which is brought in on Tuesdays and Fridays. At the corner of the piazza behind the flower tent, there is a delightful little pizza/bakery. By nightfall the piazza turns into a mad musical hang out with pubs and youngsters flitting about.

The morbid statue overlooking the square is intelligent philosopher, Giordano (Filippo) Bruno. He searched for The Truth not the truth set up by the church, but his own. One day he started to question the fundamental truth of the catholic religion as he studied magic, astrology, and Aristotle. He also studied religion and graduated in Theology. At the end of 1600, the church couldn't stand his 'free thinking' anymore and Giordano was stripped and stuffed with leather and tied to a pole on which he burned to death slowly.
Bus 30EX 40EX 64 116

Section 9

TERME DI DIOCLEZIANO

Baths of Diocletian

Viale E. de Nicola 79
Tel 06 39967700
9am-7:45pm
Closed Monday

The former baths of Diocletian turned into the church Santa Maria degli Angeli e dei Martiri that could accommodate 3000 bathers simultaneously, about twice as many as the baths of Caracalla set on 32 acres. It was complete with changing rooms, concert halls and sculpture gardens. Now it holds a large collection of pieces from the National Roman Museum.
The Stadium of Diocletian was used for sporting events and athletic contests like running or for anything intellectual. For gladiator fights they had the Coliseum, for chariot races they had Circo Massimo.

If you are leaving the baths, you may visit Saint Maria of the Angels church which is right around the corner in Piazza della Repubblica. If you leave on Via E. Nicola just go up Viale L. Einaudi into the square.
Bus H 16 36 60EX 61 62 84 90EX 175 492 590 910
Metro lines A and B Termini station or line A Reppublica

SANTA MARIA DEGLI ANGELI

Saint Maria of the Angels

Piazza della Repubblica
This fine basilica was built among the ruins of the baths of Diocletian. Michelangelo was given the task as legend notes, for the designing of this church which is dedicated to the many thousands of Christian martyrs who built the baths.

From here if you walk to Via Nazionale which is off the Piazza Repubblica, onto the left side of the street, take the first left onto Via Torino and you'll find the Santa Maria Maggiore Church.

SANTA MARIA MAGGIORE

St. Mary Major Basilica

Piazza Santa Maria Maggiore
Tel 06 483195
Everyday 7am-7pm
This church is considered as one of the great churches of Rome. It is dedicated to our lady St. Mary Major and is the only Roman Basilica in spite of several additional decorations, that's retained its original shape. It houses a series of 5th century biblical mosaics and whimsical miniature marble squares in marvellous colours including gold. Built, as the legend goes after an appearance of the Blessed Virgin in 352 B.C., the basilica is also called Liberiana.
Bus 70 75 84 204 360 590 649 714
Metro-Subway lines A/B Termini or line B Cavour

SANTA PRESSEDE

Look to the floors for mosaics and graffiti's
Via Santa Pressede 9a
Tel 06 4882456

This street is right off Piazza Santa Maria Maggiore-it's close to Via Merulana.

AQUEDUCTS

AQUEDUCT CLAUDIO

Considered the greatest aqueduct builders in the ancient world, the Romans employed soldiers and slaves to build and maintain the water-carrying network so they could bath in Caracalla.
Knowing that polluted water carried disease, the Romans invested huge amounts of money in creating their own water supply. They built aqueducts to carry the water across valleys from where it was piped into public fountains, baths, and the private homes of the wealthiest citizens.

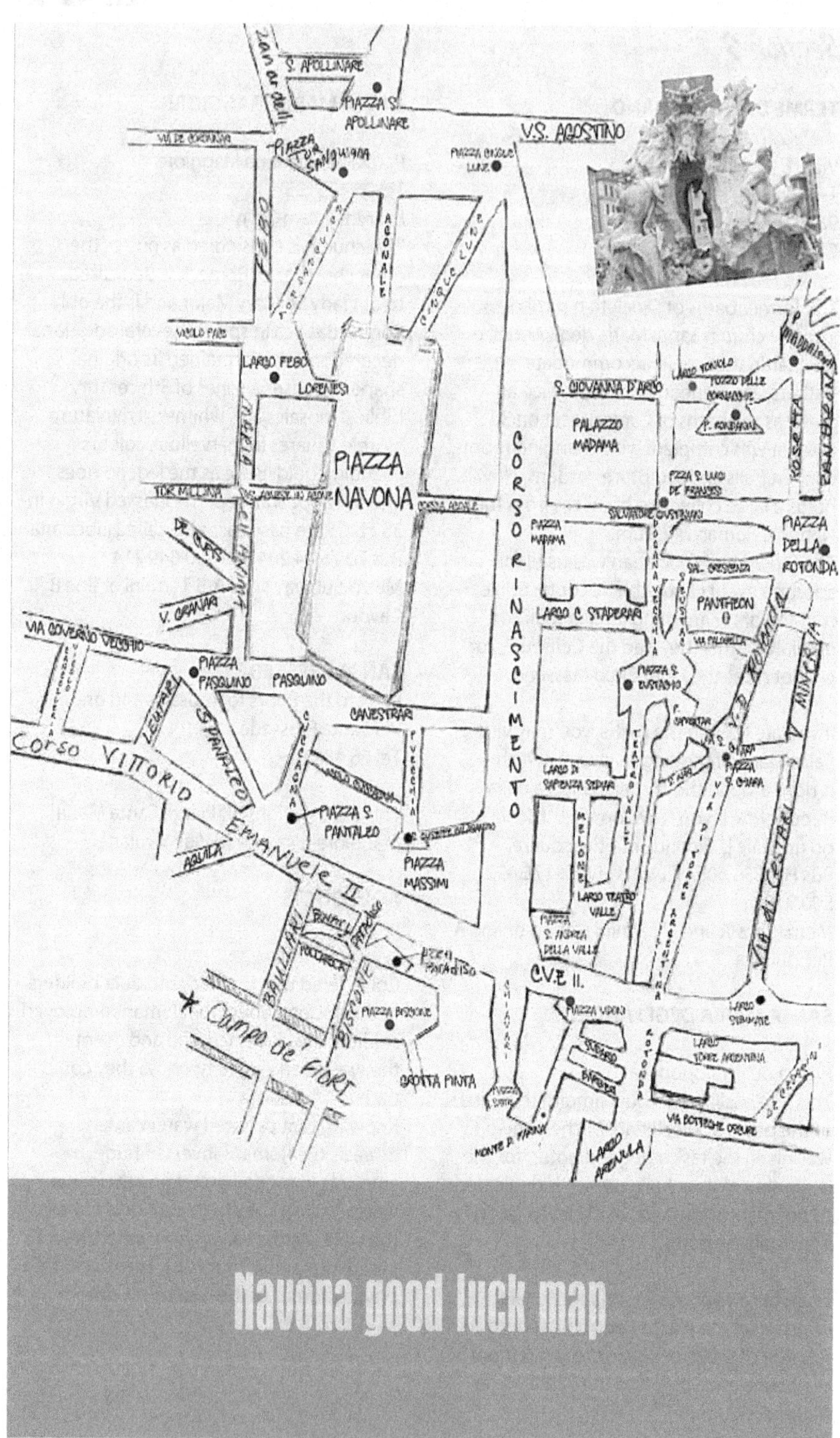

Navona good luck map

Section 10

SAN GIOVANNI IN LATERANO

St. John in Lateran
Piazza San Giovanni in Laterano 4
Tel 06 69886433
Everyday 7am-7pm

San Giovanni is one of the most important saints for the Italians, and this is the most important Basilica in Rome.
The outer wall reads, "SACROSANCTA LATERANENSIS ECCLESIA OMNIUM URBIS ET ORBIS ECCLESIARUM MATER ET CAPUT", "The most Holy Lateran Church, mother and mistress of all churches of the city and the world".
San Giovanni in Lateran was considered the mother church until 1377 when the Vatican was chosen as the papal residence and Rome's first cathedral.

The story behind San Giovanni is quite complex. Through constructions, destructions, fires, earthquakes, invasions and other reconstructions and restorations it was built the first time in 318. The first Christian Emperor Constantine had it erected donating it to the pope.

The area was named Laterano as was taken from the Laterani family whose palace's ruins were covered by the San Giovanni church and after Plauzio Laterano was accused of conspiring against Emperor Nerone and killed.
The Basilica is full of new and old testament episodes. It was Architect Borromini's job to restore the church during 1646-1649 giving it its Baroque look. There are fifteen Baroque statues lining its roof, all of Christ and the saints. In the film "Roman Holiday", - the front wall of San Giovanni (St. John) is featured in the beginning.
It was also used as the backdrop for Rome's and Italy's largest concert of the year on May 1st Primo Maggio which is a free outdoor event.
Just around the corner is the religious shrine of the Holy Stairs and the well-preserved Roman Aurelian Wall
Bus 16 81 85 87 117 186 218 590 650 714 810 850 Tram 3

Section 11

SAN PAOLO BASILICA

St. Paul's
Via Ostiense
About 2km from Via Ostiense you'd find the Basilica of St. Paul. It was built over the burial place of the Apostle of the Gentiles and consecrated in 324. It's the building of the first place of worship over St. Paul's tomb attributed to the Emperor Constantine. A larger basilica was erected by Emperors Valentiniano II, Theodosius and Arcadius. Destroyed by fire in 1823, it was rebuilt on the same foundations and consecrated by Pope Pius IX.
Bus 23 128 670 707 761 766 769
Metro line B San Paolo

Section 12

L'APPIA ANTICA

The Ancient Appian Way
"Regina Viarum"
Tel 06 46952343
Just my favorite romantic road it's serene and has character. Artists and famous faces have their hidden homes up and down this antique street, and it was Rome's first road paved in 312 B.C. by Appio Claudio Cieco. The way is stuffed with catacombs and tombs. Many lives were taken there and the road was lined with victims of a Roman designed torture called crucifixion. 6,000 people were grossly beaten and crucified along the Appia.
Supposedly pine trees were brought in from the north and planted along the Appia to cover a long string of sufferers.
Named Regina Viarum Queen of Roads by the Latin poet Stazio, it was built for connecting Rome to the southern provinces, Africa and the East. Eventually they extended it to the seacoast of Brindisi. There are about 19 different sites to see including churches, catacombs, temples, mausoleums, a castle and aqueduct. The first Christian cemeteries rose along the Appian Way at the end of the first century.

Way at the end of the first century. S. Callisto and S. Sebastian are the most momentous burial grounds discovered here. It was the site where the bodies of Apostles Peter and Paul were housed for a while. The most interesting section of the Appian Way runs from the tomb of Cecilia Metella to Casal Rotondo that is approximately 530km/365 miles long. The way is lined with marble ruins and broken statues, but is now covered by grassy hills.
The arches of a Roman aqueduct line one side and on the horizon glimpses of the Roman Castles emerge. The sea has fascinated many a great poet such as: Orazio, Ovid, Goethe, Byron, Carducci and D'Annunzio.
Metro line A to San Giovanni to bus 218 which follows the Appia Antica
Metro line A to Colli Albani to bus 660
The Appia Antica bus line is called the Archeobus and departs at Piazza Venezia everyday from 10am-5pm for 8€

Section 13

VILLA DORIA PAMPHILJ
Piazza del Collegio Romano 2
Tel 06 6797323
10am-5pm
Closed Thursday
Flooded with formal gardens, meadows, flowerbeds, and grottoes, this villa was transformed into a public park. It's an amazing villa with a glass-type gazebo reminding one of the Sound of Music. Live music is performed during the summer months.
Bus 30EX 40EX 46 63 64 70 81 84 85 87 186 492 628 810 916

Section 14

ZONE I: NOMENTANO

VILLA TORLONIA
CASINO DEI PRINCIPI
The Jewish Catacombs of Vigna Randanini are found along the roads of the villa and the only Jewish cemeteries in use today. French Décor. It may remind one of a large gingerbread house like Hansel and Gretel's. It was home to loner Prince Torlonia.
Tel 06 82059127
Via Nomentana 70
Winter 10am-5pm Summer 10am-7pm
Bus 36 60EX 84 90EX

CASINA DELLE CIVETTE
Little House of the Owls
Villa Torlonia
Tel 06 82059127
Winter 10am-5pm Summer 10am-7pm
Bus 36 60EX 61 62 84 90EX
Metro line B Bologna

Prince Torlonia was a bizarre person who never wanted much to do with people or the outside world with one exception; women he'd entertain in his frescoed bathroom. Floor-length windows opened out to gorgeous views obtainable from the tub. He had a small round room built with a high ceiling where he would meditate and spend time in solitude. The prince garnished the quaint casina or little house with the French touch and the owl was the dominating animal in his décor. This story was handed down by the elderly woman who works in the little house.

All the sites were personally chosen as those of important interest or the most commonly travelled.

Note: many places are closed on Mondays at reduced prices for:
EU citizens
Over 65
Students
Children under 3feet tall
Children under four years old

**The reason I broke them down into sections is because I had wanted to place all destinations in close proximity with each other in the same category. You may start from the top or from the bottom of each section. I also jotted down some section combo's if you're feeling ambitious.*

TRANSPORTATION TO MAIN CITY STREETS	
Via Appia Antica	Bus 118 (218 from san Giovanni in laterano)
Via Appia Nuova	***85 86 87 649 Metro line A*** ***(Colli Albani 87 660 663) Furio Camillo 412***
Via Aurelia	Bus 46 49 and Metro line A (Cornelia)
Viale Aventino	Bus 60 75 81 118 160 175 628 673 715 and Tram 3
Via di Boccea	46 and Metro A (Battistini)
Via Cassia	Bus 224 (at Piazza Cavour)
Via Cavour	Bus 16 70 71 75 84 117 360 649 714 and Metro B
Via Cristoforo Colombo	Bus 160 714715 and Metro A
Via del Corso	***Good street for shopping, touristy and good connecting street. Near to: Trevi F and Pantheon. Connects Piazza Venezia and Piazza del Popolo. Passes Piazza di Spagna.*** Buses from P. del Popolo 117, 119 Buses from P. Venezia: 62 63 81 85 95 117 119 160 175 630
Via Flaminia	Bus 490 495 910 491 (from Piazzale Flaminio 95) Tram 2, 19
Crv. Gianicolense	H 44 170 780 781 Tram 3, 8
Via Governo Vecchio	A walk off Piazza Navona south end. Passes Piazza Pasquino running off it.
Via Merulana	Street good for photo shops and bread shops. Off of P. Santa Maria Maggiore (St. Mary Major). It's walking distance from termini station and ends near P. di Porta San Giovanni 16 714 810 780 781 tram 3
Viale delle Milizie	70 (280 from Piramide Metro B) 490 Metro line A Lepanto tram 19
Via Nazionale	One of the main shopping streets—touristy. Near Piazza Venezia, P. Repubblica and P. Barberini. 40ex 60 64 71 86 170 780 tram 3, 8
Via Nomentana	Historical villas, classy neighborhood 36 84 86 90 211 714
Via Ostiense	Get bus 23 at Vittorio Emanuele or Metro line B Piramide
Via di Pietralata	81 211 443 810 75 Metro B Pietralata
Via Prenestina	81 105 810 409 545 492 Trams 5, 14, 19
Viale Regina Margherita	490 491 495 649 36 84 90 86 910 630 Tram 3, 19
Via Salaria	86 92 217 360 630
Viale delle Terme di Caracalla	Baths of Caracalla 60 75 81 160 175 714
Via Tiburtina	Cemetary Verano 71 492 490 metro B Tiburtina tram 3, 19
Viale di Trastevere	Starts in an artsy neighborhood and passes Porta Portese (famous flea market) ends near Trastevere station- Buses H 780 44 75 H 170 Tram 3, 8
Corso Vittorio Emanuele II	40ex 46 62 63 64 70 81 492 630 780 main street, many shops, passes by P. Navona, Campo de' Fiori
Via Veneto	Bus 52 53 63 80 95 116 119 630

TRANSPORTATION TO PIAZZAS	
Largo Torre Argentina	30 40ex 46 62 63 64 70 81 87 492 630 780 Tram 8
Piazza Augusto Imperatore	Bus 81 117 119 224 628 913 926 Here you'll find the mausoleum of Emperor Augustus
Piazza Barberini	Bus 62 63 95 175 492 630 (80ex in Piazza San Silvestro) Metro A (Barberini) Everything easy 24hr internet café, hard rock café (up Via Veneto running off it). Good restaurants upper class. In P. Barberini, starts Via Tritone shopping street, near Trevi
Piazzale Belle Arti	Tram 2, 3, 19 Bus (926 in Piazza Cavour)
Piazza Bologna	Bus 62 310 Metro B landmark - Huge post office -"Posta"
Piazza Buenos Aires	Bus 63 8 92 630 Tram 3, 19
Piazza Cavour	70 87 492
Piazza Cinquecento - Termini Station	Bus C H 16 36 38 40 64 75 84 86 90 92 105 175 217 310 360 492 649 714 910 Metro A&B
EUR-	Bus 714 Metro B Euro Palasport Man—made lake constructed by Mussolini, ice cream bar, nice for a walk
Piazza del Colosseo	Bus 60 75 81 85 87 175 810 Metro B Coliseum Tram 3 Coliseum areas
Piazza Fiume	Bus 63 (80ex P. San Silvestro) 86 92 217 360 490 491 495 630
Piazzale Flaminio	Bus 95V 490 491 495 Metro A Flaminio There's Piazza del Popolo and Villa Borghese close by large park with historical buildings, museum and zoo
Piazzale Garibaldi- Gianicolo	Bus 115 870
Piazza Navona	Bus 40ex 46 62 64 70 81 87 492 artsy piazza where local sketchers and painters gather. Good ice cream and restaurants—touristy
Piazzale Ostiense	Bus 60 75 95 175 715 716 Metro B (Piramide) Tram 3 Train FM 1, 3, 5 Landmark -Huge Pyramid, connections to the beach (Lido di Ostia)
Piazza del Popolo	Bus 9 117 119 490 491 495 Metro A (Flaminio) Tram 2 Outdoor summer concerts. Near P. di Spagna (shopping district)
Porta Maggiore	Bus 105 Tram 3, 5, 14, 19
Piazza di Porta Pia	36 60 62 84 90 490 491 495
Piazza Porta Portese	Bus 44 75 Tram 3 Famous flea market—here in this piazza
Piazza di Porta S Paolo (piramide)-	Bus 60 75 95 175 715 716 Metro B (piramide) Tram 3 Night clubs
Piazza della Repubblica	Bus H 40ex 60 62 64 84 86 90 170 175 492 910 Metro A (Repubblica)
Piazza Risorgimento (San Pietro)-	Bus 81 492 40ex 62 64 Metro A (Ottaviano) St. Peter's shopping district, touristy Tram 19
Piazza della Rotonda (Pantheon)-	Bus 116 (P. San Silvestro and P. Barberini) nice restaurants, shops, hotels
Piazza San Giovanni Di Dio	Bus H 44 Tram 8 Church of San Giovanni, mother church of the world
Basilica di San Paolo	Bus 23 128 271 670 707 761 766 769 Metro B (San Paolo)
Piazza Santa Maria Maggiore	Bus 70 71 75 84 360 649 714 Tram 5, 14
Piazza S. Sonnino- (Trastevere)	Bus H 23 63 115 271 280 630 780 Tram 8
Piazza di Spagna	Bus 117 119 Metro A (Spagna) Here are the famous Stairs made by the Spaniards, area of finest shopping and famous designers
Piazza Vittorio Emanuele II	Bus 64 360 Metro A (Vittorio Emanuele) Tram 5, 14 This is area now could almost be considered Little China. Little India. There are more than 2 full streets of Chinese shops and restaurants.
Piazza Venezia "Vittoriano"	Bus H 30 40ex 44 46 60 62 63 64 70 81 84 85 87 95 117 119 160 170 175 492 571 715 780 810 850 916

TRANSPORTATION TO MAIN TRAIN STATIONS	
TIBURTINA STATION Stazione Tiburtina	Metro Line B (Tiburtina FS) Bus-C 71 111 163 168 211 409 443 448 490 491 492 495 545 649 Trains FM 1, 2 (Air Terminal)
TERMINI STATION Stazione Termini	Metro Lines A&B (they cross here) Bus-C H MA2 16 36 40 64 75 84 86 90 92 105 170 175 217 310 360 492 649 714 910 Train FM 4, 5, 6, 7 Tram 5, 14
PIAZZA VENEZIA TERMINAL	Landmark - Vittorio Emanuele II Building (Vittoriano) Terminal across from it. Bus-H 30 40 44 46 60 62 63 64 70 81 84 85 87 95 117 119 160 170 175 271 492 571 628 630 715 716 780 781 810 850 916 541
TRASTEVERE STATION	Bus H 170 228 719 766 773 774 780 781 786 871 Train FM 1, 5 Tram 3, 8

TRANSPORTATION TO PUBLIC OFFICES AND MONUMENTS	
Anagrafe - for social security numbers etc. Via L. Petroselli	Bus 23 30 60 44 63 81 95 160 170 280 628 715 781
Biblioteca Nazionale - National Library Pretorio	Bus 310 49 649 Metro B – Pretorio
Bioparco - Zoo Vl. Giardino Zoologico	Bus 52 217 Bio Park 223 910 Tram 3 19
Cappella Sistina - Sistine Chapel Vl. Vaticano	Bus 23 32 49 81 492 907 982 990 Metro A (Ottaviano-San Pietro) Tram 19
Castel S. Angelo - Castle S'angelo	Bus 23 34 40 62 64 280 982
Catacombe S Callisto Via Appia Antica	Bus 118 660 Archeobus from Piazza Venezia everyday 10am-5pm 7. 75€ Info- 06 469-52343
Cimitero del Verano - Verano Cemetary Pl. del Verano	Bus C 71 93 163 443 448 492 Tram 3, 19
Cimitero di Prima Porta - Cemetary	Bus 34 79
Colosseo - Coliseum	Bus 60 75 81 85 87 117 175 673 810 850 Metro B (Colosseo) Caracalla baths nearby, home of Emperor Nerone (Domus Aurea) Fori Imperiali and Roman Forum Bus 52 53 61 63 71 80 81 85 95 116 117 119 160 175 492 628 630 850 Famous Trevi Fountain, San Crispino Natural Ice cream nearby, museum of Pasta
Foro Italico - Forum	Bus 32 48 69 168 186 220 224 232 280 301 446 911
Foro Romano - Roman Forum	Bus 60 75 84 85 87 117 175 810 850 Metro B (Colosseo)

TRANSPORTATION TO PUBLIC OFFICES AND MONUMENTS	
Galleria d' Arte Moderna - Gallery of Modern Art Vl. Belle Arti	Tram 3, 19
Monumento Vittoriano II - Piazza Venezia	Bus H 3040 44 46 60 62 63 64 70 81 84 85 87 95 117 119 160 170 175 492 628 630 715 716 780 810 850 916
Museo della Civilta' Romana - Civil Roman Museum p. Agnelli, 10	Bus 703 707 765 767
Musei Vaticani - Vatican Museums Vl. Vaticano	Bus 23 49 492 907 990
Museo di Villa Giulia - Museum of Villa Giulia Vl. Belle Arti	Tram 3, 19
Piazza Navona	Bus 926 Tram 3, 19
Orto Botanico - Botanical Garden Via Corsini	Bus 30 40 46 62 64 70 81 87 116 492 628 916
Ospedale Bambini Gesu'- Children's Hospital Piazza S. Onofrio	Bus 870
Ospedale Filippo Neri - Hospital Filippo Neri Via Martinotti 20	Bus 546 907 991 997 998 Train Fm3
Ospedale San Giovanni - San Giovanni Hospital Via Amba Aradam 9	Bus 16 81 85 87 117 218 650 673 714 850
Palatino-Palatine	Bus 60 75 81 175 673 Metro B Tram 3
Porta Portese – Flea Market	Bus 23 30 44 75 95 170 280 716 780 781 Tram 3, 8
Questa - Police Headquarters Via S. Vitale 15	Bus 40 60 64 70 71 170
San Giovanni in Laterano	Bus 16 81 85 87 117 186 218 360 650 Tram 3
Santa Maria Maggiore - Saint Mary Major	Bus 40 60 64 70 117 170
San Paolo Basilica- Saint Paul	Bus 23 128 670 707 761 766 769 Metro B (San Paolo)
Stadio Flaminio- Flaminio Stadium Vl. dello Stadio Flaminio	Bus 53 217 910 Tram 2 (take metro line A, Flaminio stop, then outside take a right up ahead take tram 2)
Stadio Olimpico - Olympic Stadium Foro Italico	Bus 32 48 69 220 224 232 280 301 446 911
Stazione Porta S. Paolo	Bus 23 30 60 75 95 118 175 280 715 716 Tram 3
Terme di Caracalla - Vl. d. T. d. Caracalla	Bus 118 628 671 714
Vaticano- Vatican City	Bus 23 32 49 81 492 907 982 990 Metro A Ottaviano
Piazza Risorgimento	34 46 64 98 881 916 982 Train FM 3, 5 Tram 19

TRANSPORTATION TO MAIN CITY STREETS	
Via Appia Antica	Bus 118 (218 from san Giovanni in laterano)
Via Appia Nuova	***85 86 87 649 Metro line A (Colli Albani 87 660 663) Furio Camillo 412***
Via Aurelia	Bus 46 49 and Metro line A (Cornelia)
Viale Aventino	Bus 60 75 81 118 160 175 628 673 715 and Tram 3
Via di Boccea	46 and Metro A (Battistini)
Via Cassia	Bus 224 (at Piazza Cavour)
Via Cavour	Bus 16 70 71 75 84 117 360 649 714 and Metro B
Via Cristoforo Colombo	Bus 160 714715 and Metro A
Via del Corso	***Good street for shopping, touristy and good connecting street. Near to: Trevi F and Pantheon. Connects Piazza Venezia and Piazza del Popolo. Passes Piazza di Spagna.*** Buses from P. del Popolo 117, 119 Buses from P. Venezia: 62 63 81 85 95 117 119 160 175 630
Via Flaminia	Bus 490 495 910 491 (from Piazzale Flaminio 95) Tram 2, 19
Crv. Gianicolense	H 44 170 780 781 Tram 3, 8
Via Governo Vecchio	A walk off Piazza Navona south end. Passes Piazza Pasquino running off it.
Via Merulana	Street good for photo shops and bread shops. Off of P. Santa Maria Maggiore (St. Mary Major). It's walking distance from termini station and ends near P. di Porta San Giovanni 16 714 810 780 781 tram 3
Viale delle Milizie	70 (280 from Piramide Metro B) 490 Metro line A Lepanto tram 19
Via Nazionale	One of the main shopping streets—touristy. Near Piazza Venezia, P. Repubblica and P. Barberini. 40ex 60 64 71 86 170 780 tram 3, 8
Via Nomentana	Historical villas, classy neighborhood 36 84 86 90 211 714
Via Ostiense	Get bus 23 at Vittorio Emanuele or Metro line B Piramide
Via di Pietralata	81 211 443 810 75 Metro B Pietralata
Via Prenestina	81 105 810 409 545 492 Trams 5, 14, 19
Viale Regina Margherita	490 491 495 649 36 84 90 86 910 630 Tram 3, 19

Important Tip:
Often street address's are written using only the last name. For example:
Via V. Veneto= Via Vittorio Veneto note that is it almost always called "Via Veneto"

USEFUL WORDS	
Cimitero	Cemetary
Terme	Baths
Stadio	Stadium

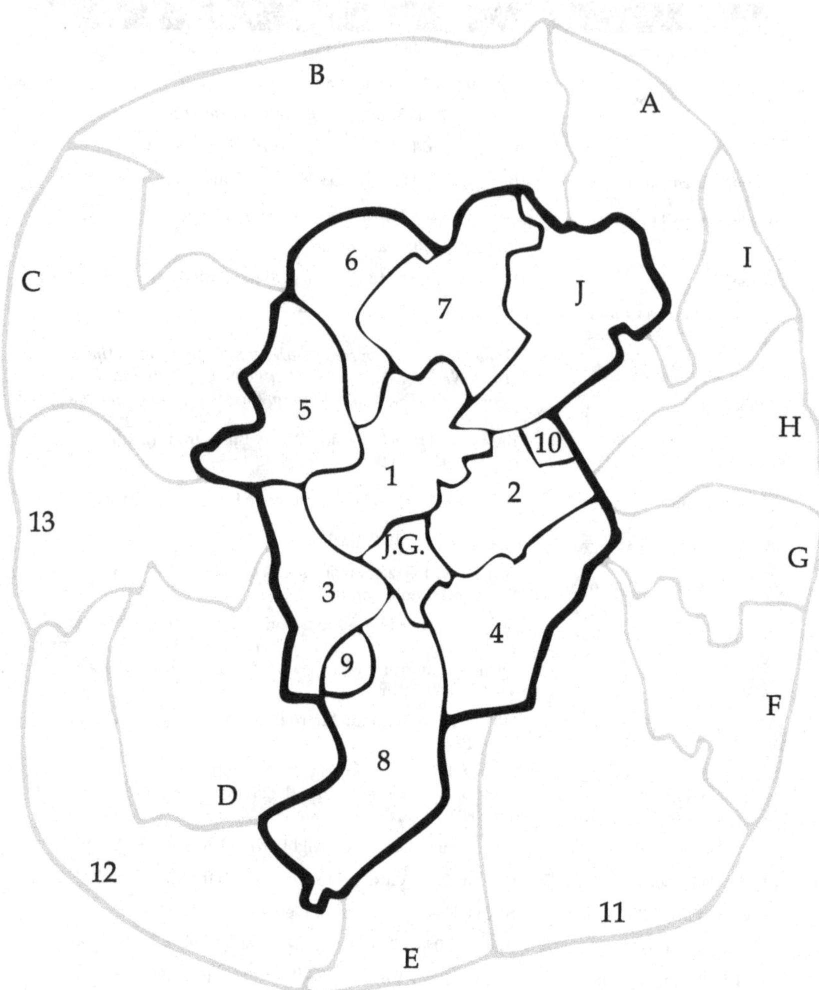

The Zone Map

ZONE 1 - CENTER
ZONE 2 - ESQUILINO
ZONE 3 - TRASTEVERE
ZONE 4 - SAN GIOVANNI
ZONE 5 - PRATI
ZONE 6 - FLAMINIO
ZONE 7 - PARIOLI
ZONE 8 - OSTIENSE
ZONE 9 - TESTACCIO
ZONE 10 - SAN LORENZO
ZONE 11 - APPIO
ZONE 12 - EUR
ZONE 13 - AURELIA
ZONE A - MONTE SACRO
ZONE B - CASSIA
ZONE C - TRIONFALE
ZONE D - MONTEVERDE
ZONE E - LAURENTINO
ZONE F - TUSCOLANO
ZONE G - PRENESTINO
ZONE H - TIBURTINO
ZONE I - NOMENTANO
ZONE J - SALARIO
ZONE K - CASTELLI ROMANI
J.G. - JEWISH GHETTO

The Adventures of The Fontana Sisters

'Made in Italy'

Micol, Zoë, and Giovanna Fontana three lovable dressmakers had fulfilled their apprenticeship. It was time to leave the confinements of their childhood neighbourhood, which now haunted them.

The three of them packed and left it forever setting up a workshop on Via San Sebastianello in Rome near the Spanish square. In this respectable fable, the three sisters had only touched the tip of their magnificent adventure: the adventure of the Fontana sisters and the birth of Made in Italy labels.

In 1939, the three sisters rented an apartment on Via Firenze with three rooms and an apprenticeship with two famous dressmakers: Zecca and Battilocchi.
One day a woman of 'high society' was captivated by the sensational quality of the sister's dressmaking and decided to become one of their clients. Gioia Marconi. She was the daughter of one of the greatest Italian scientists, and inventor of radio waves and telecommunications.
Thanks to this encounter of fate all three went out straight away in search of other notable clients.
The war arrived but the Fontana sisters kept on, in bad and good women always find a moment to be and feel beautiful and they knew this.
Even the Princess Aldobrandini ordered an outfit to be made after curfew. And during those difficult years, it was no problem to simply trade materials for twenty two pounds of potatoes.

Immediately after the war, Rome was transformed completely. The grand Via Veneto appeared and so did luxurious hotels, nightclubs and open air cafés.

The marriage between Tyrone Power and Linda Christian was a magical scene which moved Italy and America internationally going on to build fame in Rome.
The white satin gown Linda wore had waves on the hip with puffy crinkles and was wrapped with a transparent wedding veil. Pearls were dispersed along it like an open galaxy which were embroidered in silver. From then on, marriage with a white gown would become the principle discussion among girls to wed.

It was then that the Fontana sisters became famous in the United States as well as in Italy.
When the 1950's approached and Hollywood was discovering Rome, all was in the palms of Zoë, Micol and Giovanna. They were entrusted to dress the most famous divas on the other side of the ocean: Michel Morgan, Eva Gardner. Then their outfits were shown in the scenes of The Barefoot Countess and The Sun Rises Again.
Those were the year's Italian fashion was born. It was a beautiful period, because it coincided with maximum research and creation.
Italian fashion had to battle with French trends as all of their techniques were superior over Italian ones.
Italian fashion grew regardless, and the wizardry of the three sisters gave way to the Made in Italy label.
Marella Agnelli, and Jacqueline Kennedy were dressed in their clothes, queens were wearing their clothing like Frederica of Greece, and actresses such as Audrey Hepburn, Elizabeth Taylor and Ingrid Bergman who were modelling Fontana Fashions.

Museums, Galleries and Parks

In early springtime, admissions to all public museums generally named *Settimana dei Beni Culturali* are free for a week; ask at the nearest tourist information point.
Museum and art galleries are free to all EU citizens under 18 and over 65.
For 18-25 year olds, there is a 50% discount.
All museums are set up according to the zones map.

Keats-Shelly Memorial House
Relics and portraits of English poets, including Byron
Piazza di Spagna 26
Tel 06 684235
Closed Saturday and Sunday

ZONE 1: HISTORICAL CENTER

Museo Atelier-Canova
Tadolini Museum
Via del Babuino 150 a/b
Tel 06 32110702
Café, cioccolatiera, tea room, wine tasting
Brunch or tea between huge colossal statues

Museo Criminologico di Roma
Rome Crime Museum
Via del Gonfalone 29 off Via Giulia
Monday-Saturday 9am-1pm
www.useocriminologico@giustizia.it

Museo Napoleonico
Reminisces of the great and brave Napoleon's personal items
Via G. Zanardelli 1
Tel 06 6540286
Many things were donated by Count Primoli
(Piazza Navona area)

Museo Nazionale delle Paste Alimentari
National Museum of Pasta
Tel 06 6991119
Piazza Scanderbeq 117, a tiny street
Private museum fee 9€
It used to be the house of Scanderbeg, the Albanian prince
9:30am-5:30pm
• Learn the history of pasta
• See original photos, and antique pasta machines dated to 800 years ago

Museo delle Cere
Rome Wax-works Museum
Piazza SS. Apostoli 67
Tel 06 6796482
9am-8pm everyday
Bus H 40EX 60EX 64 70 170
Metro lines A B Termini or line A Reppublica
www.museodellecere.it

Museo Numismatico della Zecca

Museum of Coins
Palazzo dei Ministeri Finanziari
Via XX Settembre 97
Tel 06 47613317
9am-12:30pm
Closed Sunday and Monday
Metro line A Repubblica
Bus 16 36 60EX 61 62 84 90EX 492 910 38 86 92 217 360
SAM@ipzs.it

The Zecca Museum consists of 20,000 works in: coins, medals, stamp designs and moulds. During the medieval times until today, there has been an abundance of coins produced in Italy and other foreign countries.

Galleria Nazionale d-Arte Antica

National Gallery of Ancient Art in Palazzo Barberini
Via Barberini 18
Palazzo Barberini was designed by Maderno and built on the site of the previous Villa Sforza for Maffeo Barberini. This man became pope with the title of Urban VIII. When Maderno died in 1629, Gian Lorenzo Bernini took control of construction. One of his collaborators was Francesco Borromini. The great hall was decorated by Pietro da Cortona, who worked on it from 1633 to 1639.

The gallery includes works by:

- Giulio Romano
- Raffaello Sanzio
- Perugino
- Gian Lorenzo Bernini
- Tiziano
- Tintoretto
- Caravaggio
- Tiepolo
- Hans Holbein
- N. Poussin

Tel 06 4814591
Bus 52 53 61 62 63 80EX 95116 119 175 204 492 590 630
8:30am-7:30pm
Closed Monday

Museum of Piazza Venezia

Via di Plebiscito 118
Palazzo Venezia was designated as the seat of the museum in 1916, when it was passed on to the State of Italy after serving as the embassy for the Venetian Republic and then the embassy of Austrian.
In 1911, to provide space for the Vittorio Emanuele II monument on the far side of Piazza Venezia, the entire greenhouse of Paul II, which cornered on the main prospect, was moved and reconstructed with all its stones, marble and cloisters to the left side of the building.
The Museum houses thirteenth to eighteenth century paintings, marble and carved-wood sculptures, terracotta, pottery, china, silver, cloths, seals, medals, glassware, tapestries, and enamels.

Casa di Goethe

House of Goethe
Via del Corso 18
Tel 06 32650412

The dramatic and romantic poet German Johann Wolfgang Von Goethe occupied this house from 1778-1786 as he worked on his diary, a book entitled *Viaggio in Italia.* His book lives on as an inspiration as one of the most important writings in Italy.
10am-6pm
Closed Tuesday
www.casadigoethe.it

I Musei di Capitolini

The Capitoline Museums
Piazza del Campidoglio 1
Tel 06 82059127
9am-8pm
Closed Monday

The Capitoline museums are housed in the Palazzo dei Conservatori and Palazzo Nuovo, which face each other across Piazza del Campidoglio. They were built on the Campidoglio hill in a square designed by Michelangelo. Against the backdrop of Palazzo dei Senatori, the museums represent the classic area of Rome's soul.
The Capitoline museums date back to 1471, and may be considered the oldest public collection in the world.
Sixty five busts of Roman Emperors and seventy nine busts of philosophers and poets are part of the collection.

In the room after the "Sala dei Trionfi" you will find "La Lupa Capitolina" the she-wolf nursing the two human babies Romolo and Remo. In the "Galleria dei Orti Lamiani" there are sculptures recuperated from famed gardens.

Important collections
• Aurora con L'Arco-4th century B.C.
• Venere Capitolina-an exceptional replica of the Roman Venere di Cnido 3rd century B.C.

Bus H 30EX 44 46 60EX 62-64 70 75 81 84 85 87 95 160 170 186 630 716 780 810

Galleria Doria Pamphilj
Doria Pamphilj Gallery
Piazza Del Collegio Romano 2
Tel 06 6797323

The Doria Pamphilj Gallery is housed in the palace located on Via del Corso, but the main entrance is in Piazza del Collegio Romano. When the building is open, it is also possible to visit private and public rooms in the palace. The gallery includes works of: Jacopo Tintoretto, Tiziano, Raffaello Sanzio, Correggio, Caravaggio, Guercino, Gian Lorenzo Bernini, Parmigianino, Gaspard Dughet, Jan Brueghel il Vecchio, and Velasquez.
10am-5pm
Closed Thursday
Bus 30EX 40EX 46 63 64 70 75 81 84 85 87 186 492 628 810
Bus H to Trastevere station to bus 31 (Pantheon area)

Bioparco
Giardino Zoologico di Roma
Villa Borghese
Piazzale del Giardino Zoologico 1
Tel 06 3608211
Schedule
October 28th - March 29 9:30am-5pm (Last admittance at 4pm)
March 30th - October 26 9:30am-6pm (Last admittance at 5pm)
April 10th- September 28 (Sat, Sun and Holidays) 9:30am-7pm

The Rome Zoo was born in 1908, and is kept up by an anonymous group called "Anonimous Society for the Zoologic Garden" who financially support it. Their mission entails research, conservation and education. Much care is taken in the protection of endangered species, and most important for them is the enriching cultural experiences provided for visitors. The Biopark is recognized on national and international levels.
Bears, Reptiles, Monkeys, elephants, lions, and more. Wednesdays are free for children under three and the handicapped.
8.50€ adults
6.50€ children 3-12 years
Tram 19
Bus Lines 52 53 217 360 910 926
Metro line A Flaminio
www.Bioparco.it

ZONE 2: ESQUILINO

Museo Storico della Fanteria/Army
Historical Army Museum
Piazza S. Croce in Gerusalemme 9
Tel 06 7027971
9am-1pm everyday except holidays
www.esercito. difesa.it

Shortly after WWII ended, an Italian army commander initiated the museum's construction in 1948. This was in memory of the soldiers that sacrificed their lives. It was inaugurated on November 11th 1959 and remodelled in 1990.
It is divided into three important sections: weapons, flags and uniforms.
The museum contains a library with historical archives, thirty five display rooms and five galleries. Armoured wheeled vehicles are on display from WWII up until modern times. They include: battle tanks, personnel carriers, weapon systems, and a variety of helicopters.

Museo Storico della Liberazione dal Nazismo
The Museum of Liberation
Via Tasso 145
Tel 06 7003866
Tuesday, Thursday and Friday
4pm-7pm Saturday and Sunday 9:30am-12:30pm
Closed Monday and Wednesday

Metro line A Manzoni, only one hundred meters from the Manzoni stop
The museum follows the story of the city's resistance to Nazism during WWII, one of Rome's most tragic periods.

Museo degli Strumenti Musicali
Museum of Musical Instruments
Piazza S Croce in Gerusalemme 9
Tel 06 7014796
The museum has a wonderful assortment of over 3,000 musical instruments with important historical value.
Closed Monday
Tuesday-Sunday 8:30-7:30pm
Ticket booth is open until 7pm
(Porta Maggiore area)

Museo Nazionale Romano
National Roman Museum
Via E De Nicola 78/Piazza dei Cinquecento
Tel 06 39967700
9am-7:45pm
Closed Monday

The National Museum of Rome possesses one of the world's most important archaeological collections. It is housed in three different facilities: the Baths of Diocletian, including the Octagonal Hall, the Palazzo Massimo, and the Palazzo Altemps. The historic headquarters of the museum is the complex of the baths built by Diocletian between the last years of the 3rd century A.D..
The building of the largest baths in the ancient world Terme di Diocleziano included constructing many rooms besides the traditional caldarium, tepidarium and frigidarium (Frigidaire). There was a natatio or frigidarium for swimmers, a large open air swimming pool, meeting rooms, libraries, nympheums, dressing rooms, concert rooms, and rooms for physical exercises.
Bus H 16 36 61 62 84 90EX 175 492 590
Metro line A Repubblica or Termini

ZONE 3: TRASTEVERE

Museum of Folklore
Piazza S. Egidio 1b
Tel 06 5816563
This museum represents the talking statues, mouth of truth and Roman life.

Museo Internazionale del Cinema e dello Spettacolo
International Museum of Cinema and Entertainment
Via Nicolo Bettoni 1
Reservations 06 3700266
See filmmaking equipment, costumes, and artefacts all relating to the film industry.

Orto Botanico
Botanical Gardens
Explore roses, a bamboo forest, and the house of the carnivorous plants. There is a special garden called the Garden of the blind which grows certain plant varieties that entice the senses. Information printed in Braille.
Largo Cristina di Svezia 24
Tel 06 49917106
Tuesday-Saturday 9:30am-6:30pm Winter Tuesday-Saturday 9:30am-5:30pm
Closed in August and on Sunday and Monday
Bus 23 280 870

ZONE 5: PRATI

Museo Storico dell'Arma dei Carabinieri
Historical Musuem of the Carabinieri
Piazza Risorgimento 46
Tel 06 6896696
Tuesday-Sunday 8:30am-12:30pm

In December of 1925, it is located in a 19th century palace.
All the memories and objects of the Carabinieri's Italian Military Police past history was conserved in the museum. Every year, beautiful Carabinieri calendars are produced and highly collectable. The photos are replicas of paintings redesigned by various Italian painters. The calendars are filled with Carabinieri stories accompanied by colourful drawings. The first one was produced in 1929, and they are still being made today. Unfortunately, they are not for sale in stores.
http://www.carabinieri.it/editoria/calendari/indice4.htm

Museo dell'Arte Sanitaria
The Museum of the Art of Health and Well-Being

You will find the museum on Via Lungotevere in Sassia, adjacent to the Saint Spirito hospital.
Presented to you, is the most extraordinary collection of mysterious objects and teachings of magic and medicine.
Here you will experience anatomic monstrosities and primitive surgical instruments, an exceptional patrimony of art history.
This museum was one of the most antique and glorious Roman hospitals. Windows display objects such as; instruments, authentic documents and copies of long itineraries that would slowly redeem medicine, surgery and pharmacology.

It's from the account of a Pope named Innocenzo. He was hired as guardian to a special boy named Federico di Svevia. In 1198, Federico left for Rome on orders of the Saint Spirito of Montepellier and signed on December 1st 1201 to begin his work and receive sick patients in the Santo Spirito hospital.

1204 marked the beginning of the first hospital in Rome. This great Roman institution was reconstructed by a wise priest named Marianodi Alatri and in the first ten years, the monks and friars were the proprior spiritual guides in addition to being doctors. Vases were preserved and filled with snake venom which was used in preparations. Sickness was then resolved with magic and religion. The museum displays collections of little sacred sacks, magical images, magic spells and medicinal herbs. The museum's library contains stories, pamphlets, books and manuscripts on the Art of Health.

Museo del Purgatorio
Museum of Purgatory
Lungotevere Prati 12
Displays photos showing objects and traces of apparitions.
Closed January 1st, December 25th, and August 15th
Every day 7:30am-11:30am/4:30pm-7:30pm
Inside the church of Sacro Cuore del Suffragio (Piazza Cavour area)

Musei Vaticani
The Vatican Museums
Viale Vaticano 100
Tel 06 69884947/06 69884676

Many surprises await you including:

The Room of Eliodoro
Cacciata di Eliodoro dal Tempio, by Raffaello 1511-1512
The Room of the Segnatura
Disputa del Sacramento, by Raffaello 1508-1511

La Scuola dI Atene/
The School of Athens, by Raffaello 1508-1511

- Egyptian Museum
- Gregorian museum of Etruscan Art
- Antiquarium Romanum
- Vase collection
- Gallery of the candelabra
- Gallery of the tapestries
- Room of the Immaculate Conception
- Raphael's rooms collection of modern religious art
- Sistine Chapel apostolic library, Vatican picture library gallery
- Gregorian museum of Profane Art

The Vatican garden's jail fountain *Fontana della Galera* is a wonder. It's a ship from the 16th century, made of Roman stone that spits out fountain water, it's absolutely beautiful. The Vatican gardens are covered with Italian labyrinths.

November-February 8:45am-1:45pm
March-October 8:45am-4:45pm
Saturdays 8:45am-1:45pm
Closed Sundays except the last Sunday of the month
Closed Jan 1st/6th, Feb 11th, March 19th, Easter and the Monday following it, May 1st, June 29th, August 15th, November 8th, , and the 25th/26th of December.
Bus 23 32 34 49 62 64 81 492 913 990 991 999 Tram 19
Metro line A Ottaviano, San Pietro or Cipro/Musei Vaticani

Museum of Ethnology
Christian Museum
Missionary
Carriage Pavilion
Viale Vaticano
Tel 06 69884676/06 69881947

Closed Sundays, Jan 1st/6th, February 11th, March 19th, Easter and the day after the Day of the Angel, May 1st, June 29th, August 15th, November 1st, December 8th, 25th, and 26th
November-February 8:45am-3:45pm
March-October 8:45am-4:45pm
Saturdays and the last Sunday of month 8:45am-1:45pm
Bus 23 32 34 46 49 62 64 81 492 913 990 991 Tram 19
Metro line A Ottaviano

See the *Ancient Roman ruins* as they were. In this museum, the whole city is rebuilt with plastic model reproductions.
9am-7pm
Sun and holidays 9am-1:30pm
Closed Monday

ZONE 7: PARIOLI

Parco di Scultura Contemporanea
Contemporary Sculpture Park
Outdoor arts in Villa Glori
Buses 53 217 910

Museo di Canonica
Canonica Museum
Viale Pietro Canonica 2
Tel 06 8842279
Fax 06 8845702

Est. 1961
In 1927 the building was given to sculptor Pietro Canonica to use as a laboratory. Canonica museum, the museum has conserved his stylist studies, notes, original models and replicas. The exposition is displayed in a total of seven rooms on the ground floor and offers complete images of the creative evolution of the artist, and complete information of the sculpture techniques. On the first floor you can visit his home, of which has been open to the public from 1988, after the death of his wife.

Tues-Sun 9am-7pm;
Holidays 9am-1:30pm
Closed Mondays, Jan 1, May 1 and Christmas Day
Bus 95 490 495 Electric buses 116 Metro Line A Stop Flaminio

Galleria Borghese
Borghese Gallery
Piazzale Scipione Borghese 5 (Villa Borghese)
Tel 06 328101/06199757510
9am-7pm
Closed Monday
The Borghese villa and its small palace were constructed at the beginning of the seventeenth century outside the Aurelian walls between the Porta Pinciana and the no longer existing Porta Salaria in an area then occupied by orchards and vineyards. Scipio Borghese first engaged Flaminio Ponzio and then Vasanzio to build it: it was constructed between 1613 and 1615. It exemplifies the villa belonging to a great Roman family at the beginning of the seventeenth century.
The Museum includes works of:
Raffaello, Antonio Canova, Pietro e Gian Lorenzo Bernini, Giulio Romano, etc
Tram 19
Bus 52 53 95 116 217 910 926

ZONE 10: SAN LORENZO

Museo di Storico della Medicina
Historical Museum of Medicine
University of Rome
Piazziale Aldo Moro 5/Viale dell'Università 34/a
Tel 06 49914445
For Appointments 06 49914487

Founded in1938, by Professor Adalberto Pazzini. Composed of eight sections, illustrates the evolution of medicine through the centuries.
Pharmaceutical collections from Roman times, modern times and contemporary. Collections include; Microscopes, surgical instruments, medicines for

the handicapped, medicine boxes, and other objects.
For appointment
9am-1pm M-F
carla. serarcangeli@ uniroma1.it

ZONE 12: EUR

Museo della Civiltà Romana
Astronomic & Planetarium Museum
Piazza G. Agnelli 10
Tues-Fri 9-2 Sat and Sun 9-7
Show times: Tues-Fri 9:30, 11, 12:30
Sat and Sun's 9:30, 11, 12:30, 3:00, 4:00, 5:30

Planetarium & Astronomic Museum
Tel 06 820 77304
Ticket 6, 20-adults
Reduced Tickets: Children 6 to 18 and those above 65
Free for children fewer than 6
Roman Civil Museum and the two above:
Tickets Adults 8€
Reduced 6€
www.comune. roma.it/ planetario

Museo della Posta and Comunicazioni
Postal Communication Museum
Viale Europa 190
Reservations: 06 59582082
9-1pm M-F
Area-EUR
Entrance Fee 1€
Founded in 1878, when Ernesto D'Amico was general director of the Italian Telegraph. As the years went by, he founded the museum and dedicated it to postal business, next to the telegraph shop.

Museo Dell' Alto Medioevo
Viale Lincoln 3
Tel 06 54228199
Located in Mussolini's fantasyland
Area-EUR
Opened in 1967
Iron Objects Displayed; Swords, knives & shields. Ceramic objects and combs made from bones. The tomb of a rich knight garnished in ornaments of gold, bronze & silver plaques. Medieval Helmet and parts of armour
Tues - Sun 9am-8pm, holidays 9-14
Closed Monday
Bus 714 from Termini stop St. Colombo corner of Piazza Marconi

Early Ages Museum
Viale Lincoln 3
The recently founded Museum (1967) contains archaeological material from excavations and collections relating to the period of time from late Antiquity to the high Middle Ages (from the fourth to the thirteenth centuries.

Museo della Civiltà Romana
The Roman Civilization Museum
Piazza Giovanni Agnelli 10
Tel 06 5926135

ZONE I: NOMENTANO

Museo della Casina delle Civette
Little House of Owls Museum
Via Nomentana 70
Tel 06 442 50072

A Swiss lodge that dates back to 1840 transformations was brought about, at the request of Giovanni Torlonia Jr., between 1917-1920. Giovanni added porticoes and dormer windows. The villa attained the appearance and the name of "Medieval Village". In 1917, a young well-known architect enriched the villa with an incredible profusion of turrets, bow windows, arches, and balconies. The entire complex was decorated with wrought iron, wall murals, majolica, stucco bas-reliefs, inlaid marble and all windows of stained glass with the image of the owl (Civette).
Bus 36 60 84 90
Oct-Mar 9am-5pm Apr-Sept 9am- 7pm Closed Mon
Entrance fee 3 €
Closed Aug 15, May 1, Monday, Dec 25, Jan 1
Metro/Subway Line B stop Bologna

ZONE K: I CASTELLI ROMANI

Outside Rome City

Museo delle Navi Romane
Roman Navy Museum
Via Guidoni 35
Fiumicino Airport Info line
+0039 06 6529192
Just by enter and you will see a whole collection of ancient ships.
Opened in 1979, the museum is situated at the international airport "Leonardo da Vinci". In it there are the keels of 5 Roman ships that date back to the 1st & 3rd century A. D. The ships have been found during excavations while construction of the airport was going on.
Around the museum only a part of the ancient port of Claudio has been left.
Tuesday and Thursdays
9:30am. to 1:30pm and
2:30pm to 4:30pm
Closed: Mondays, Jan 1st, May 1st and Dec 25th
Each first and last Sunday of the month there are guided tours including archaeological areas of Portus. Visitors have to book if they want guided tours other days.

Museo della Fotografica and dell' Arte Visuali
Museum of Photography
Visual Arts

The Photography collection is composed of more than 150 contemporary artists, whom expressing themselves through photography.

Museo dell'Ara Pacis
Lungotevere Augusta
Tel 06 82059127
Bus H 23 44 75 116 280
Trams 3 8
9am-7pm Tue-Sat
9am-2pm Sun Closed Mon, X-mas, New Years Day and May 1

Museo Nazionale di Castel Sant'Angelo
National Museum of Castle Sant'Angelo
Castello 50
Tel 06 39967600
Metro Lepanto
Bus 23 3449 62 64 80 87 492 926 990
9-8pm Tues-Sun
Closed Mon

La Farmacia S. Maria della Scala
The Pharmacy of St. Mary of the Steps

Mysterious potions once concocted in the peculiarity of an old pharmacy that once possessed miraculous herbals. Little men used to be wizards who formulated magical liquids and enchanting potions. From beneath monastery walls these tiny creators came to work in this laboratory, these men played with medicinal plants and turned them into fine liquors and tonics. Figs were put out to dry naturally, and jams made from fruit ripe on the tree. They collected propolis and raw honey from the working bees and sent it to people in search of them. This place was known as "La Farmacia S. Maria della Scala, " and was in Piazza S. Maria della Scala 23. They are now closed up in their old antique monasteries, but the laboratory is here now as a museum.
Looking through their glass shop, we can only dream of bottles filled with red liquids, plants in vases, liquors of every herb, bee essences and the bliss from the energy mixed into each creation.

Particular Churches

Santa Maria dell'Anima
14th century
Via di S. Maria dell'Anima
Sundays 8am-1pm/3pm-7pm
Mass in German
For centuries this church had serviced the German community in Rome.
The name refers to a dome fresco of the Virgin saving souls or anima.
Bus 70 Largo Torre Argentina, Piazza Navona, Via Giolitti-Termini, Piazza Venezia or 492 Piazza Barberini, Piazza Venezia, Tiburtina station, L Torre Argentina

ZONE 1: HISTORICAL CENTER

Santa Maria Dell'Orazione E Morte 16th century
Lungotevere dei Tebaidi 12
Tel 06 68802715
Santa Maria was built by a confraternity that assumed responsibility for entombing abandoned corpses. It extends above a cemetery and was founded to tell about the dead and to give them their Christian burials.
Bus 23 280 116 116T 870
(Campo de' Fiori area)

Santa Maria Sopra Minerva 13th century
Piazza della Minerva 42
9am-7pm
Santa Maria is considered the only Gothic church in Rome and is the city's principal Dominican church.
Bus 64 exit at Largo Torre Argentina

Pass Largo Stimmate a brief square to Via D. Cestari into Piazza della Minerva
Do not overlook the elephant obelisk. L'Elefantino was designed by Bernini, to support the Minerva.

On the outside of the church, numbers and wavy marks represent the level and date of Roman floods, once a common practice.

San Pietro in Vincoli
Saint Peter in Chains
Piazza San Pietro in Vincoli 4
Tel 06 48 82 865
7am-12:30/3:30-6pm
This church is unique in that it homes the chains that Saint Peter carried from Jerusalem to the prison in Rome. Visit the Moses statue designed by Michelangelo which has made this church famous.

THE MOST BEAUTIFUL CHURCHES BUILT DURING THE PERIOD OF EARLY CHRISTIANITY

Churches that were built over pre-existing Roman ruins

***San Clemente in Laterano*
Via San Giovanni in Laterano 95
Tel 06 70451018
If you love mosaics there are three levels to explore here in the 12th century basilica that was built over a 4th century church. The ancient flooring beneath contains a mithraeum or cult chamber of eastern religion which involves sacrifice.

The most antique relics are now especially conserved under the ground in churches and convents like: Santa Prisca, Santa Sabina, and Sant'Alessio. This church contains the Sisinnio one of the most antique cartoons in history, introducing vulgarity to the human race.

***Santo Stefano Rotondo*
Via Santo Stefano Rotondo 7
9am-12noon Monday-Friday
There is an Imperial Roman barrack that lies beneath the flooring of this church. Frescoes wallpaper the walls on the interior and tell stories of the martyrdoms of numerous saints which are exposed in graphic detail.
Metro line B Colosseo
Via Claudia to intersection leading to Via S. S. Rotondo

Sant'Angelo in Pescheria in the Jewish Ghetto
Via del Portico d'Ottavia
Tel 06 488991
Metro line B Colosseo
San Bartolomeo on the Tiber Island
This was built upon the ruins of the Esculapio Temple.

*** Rome's principal churches*

THE ROMAN CHURCH SCHEDULE
Early mornings, 12:30-4pm, 5pm-7pm

SANTA SUSANNA CATHOLIC-AMERICAN CHURCH OF ROME
Via XX September 14/15
Tel 06 4882748/06 42014554
Sunday Service in English 10:30am
Saturday Service 6pm
Bus 60ex 90ex 61 62 84 217* 910*

METHODIST CHURCH
Via del Banco de Santo Spirito 3
In English
Off Corso Vittorio Emanuele II

PONTE S. ANGELO METHODIST CHURCH
Tel 06 6868314

THE JEWISH SYNAGOGUE
Lungotevere Cenci 2
Bus 63

SANT'ALFONSO ALL ESQUILINO
Via Merulana 31
Tel 06 494901
Sunday English Service 4pm
Bus 714* 16*
(Termini Area)
A ten minute walk from Termini Station

CHIESA AMERICANA DI SAN PAOLO
Via Nazionale 15/16
Tel 06 4883339
Bus 64* 170* 40 ex 60 ex
On corner of Via Napoli

CHIESA DI SAN IGNAZIO DI LODOLA
The English mass is in another building to the left of the church
Mass in English-Sundays at 11am and holidays
Bus 175*
Off Via del Corso on the way to the Pantheon

ANGLICANA CHURCH OF ENGLAND/ALL SAINTS OF ROME
English Congregation of South Rome
Via del Babuino 153b
Tel 06 36001881
www.allsaintsrome. orgil

KINGDOM HALL OF JEHOVAH'S WITNESSES
Via della Ferratella in Laterano 41
Public meeting Sunday 10:05am
Study 11:05am
Study Thursday 6pm
Teaching 7:15pm
(San Giovanni Area)

ST. PATRICK'S CHURCH
(Roman Catholic)
Via Bocompagni 31
Tel 06 4203121
Bus 52 53 63 80ex 630 910*

S. FRANCESCO SAVERIO DELLA CAROVITA
(Roman Catholic)
Via del Caravita 7
Tel 06 5791363

S. ISIDORO CHURCH
(Roman Catholic)
Via degli Artisti 41
Tel 06 488 5359

S. SILVESTRO CHURCH
(Roman Catholic)
Piazza S. Silvestro 1
Tel 06 6797775

THE ROME BUDDHIST VIHARA
Via Mandas 2
Tel 06 22460091

ROME BAPTIST CHURCH
Piazza S. Lorenzo in Lucina 35
Tel 06 6876211

INTERNATIONAL CHRISTIAN FELLOWSHIP
Via Venti Settembre 88
Tel 06 4825865

CHRISTIAN SCIENCE SERVICE
Via del Babuino 159
Tel 06 3014425

POPE SERVICES
Pope Benedetto-Joesph Ratzinger 2005
(the 266th pope)
Sunday mornings 12pm
Wednesdays 10am

CONFESSIONS
Available in English, at these locations:
San Pietro/Saint Peter's
Santa Maria Maggiore/Mary Major
San Giovanni in Laterano/St. John in Lateran
San Paolo/St. Paul's

QUAKER CHURCH SOCIETY OF FRIENDS
Via Balbo 4

GREEK ORTHODOX
S. S. Vincenzo e Anatasio
Via Sardegna 153

ARGENTINA
S. Maria Addolorata
Viale Regina Margherita 81
Tel 06 84401301

CANADA
Nostra Signora del Santissimo Sacramento
Via Giovanni Battista de Rossi 46

ENGLAND
San Silvestro in Capite
Piazza San Silvestro
Tel 06 6797775

FRANCE
S. Luigi dei Francesi
Piazza San Luigi dei Francesi and
Via Santa Giovanna D'Arco

GERMANY
S. Maria dell'Anima
Piazza Santa Maria della Pace 20

GREECE
S. Atanasio
Via de Babuino 149

IRELAND
S. Clemente/Via San Giovanni in Laterano
S. Patrizio/Via BonCompagni 31
San Isidoro/Via degli Artisti 41
San Agata del Goti/Via Mazzarino

MEXICO
Nostra Signora de Guadalupe/San Filippo Martire
Via Aurelia 675

NORWAY
Altar of St. Olav
Via del Corso 437
Tel 06 6878335

PHILIPPINES
Santa Pudenziana
Via Urbana 160
Tel 06 4814622

PORTUGAL
Sant'Antonio dei Portoghesi
Via dei Portoghesi 2
Tel 06 68802496

SCOTLAND
Via XX Settembre 7

SPAIN
S. Maria de Mon Serrato degli Spagnoli
Via de Monserrato

SWEDEN
S. Brigida
Piazza Farnese 96
(Campo de' Fiori Area)

BEAUTIFUL BLESSINGS

Every 17th of January in many churches and squares, cats, dogs, birds or any pet is welcomed in for a blessing. Sant' Eusebio is one place which blesses beloved animals for the year.

Internet access

ZONE 1: HISTORICAL CENTER

EVERYTHING EASY
Via Barberini 2/16
250 PCs
Everyday 8am-2am
Metro line A Barberini
English Speaking
Bus 60EX 61 62 84 90EX 175 492

TREVI-NET cyber cafè
Via in Arcione 103
Tel 06 69922320
Open every day with 37 PCs
Monday-Friday 11-11pm
Saturday 4pm-11pm
Sunday 4-11pm
www.trevinet.com
(Trevi fountain area)

INTERNET TRAIN ROME
Via Gaeta 256
(Termini station area)

ZONE 3: TRASTEVERE

LETTERE CAFFÈ
The first franchising of its nature
Live concerts, coffee bar, tea parlor, poetry literature, book presentations and internet point
www.letterecaffe. org

INTERNET CAFÈ MR. ENTER
Via Pietro Paleocapa 11
Tel 06 55389278
Open nightly after 8pm
Closed Monday
http://web. tiscali.it/MrEnter/

TRASTEVERE INTERNET
Piazza Sonnino 27
Tel 06 58333316
Everyday 8am-midnight
Globalservice@mclink.it
International phone booths and cards
P. O. boxes
Packing and wrapping

ZONE 5: PRATI

STARNET
Borgo S. Spirito18
Monday-Saturday 9am-9pm
Saturday 9am-9pm
Sunday 11am-9pm

ZONE K: CASTELLI ROMANI

GENIUS POINT
Via di Villa Borghese 11
Tel 06 94017086
Cleanly and great service about 2€ an hour. They also carry stationary, gift items, and computer accessories

From the main square in Frascati 'Piazza Roma' there is a street with the Gran Caffe Bar on the right and a bank is on the left. Take Via C. Battisti passing the square with the church on your right go down Via Matteotti and it's about the second street on the right called Via Villa Borghese. The shop is on the right half way down...

Information

Tourist Points in Rome

ZONE 1: HISTORICAL CENTER

FONTANA DI TREVI
Via Minghetti
Tel 06 6782988

FORI IMPERIALI
Piazza del Tempio della Pace
Tel 06 69924307

LARGO CARLO GOLDONI
Tel 06 68136061
On the corner of Via del Corso
and Via Condotti
Off Piazza di Spagna

NAVONA
Piazza delle Cinque Lune
Tel 06 8809240

VIA NAZIONALE
Palazzo delle Esposizioni
Tel 06 47824525

ZONE 2: ESQUILINO

STAZIONE TERMINI
Binario/Platform 4
Tel 06 48906300
8am-9pm

STAZIONE TERMINI
Piazza dei Cinquecento
Tel 06 47825194

SANTA MARIA MAGGIORE
Via dell'Olmata
Tel 06 4740955

ZONE 3: TRASTEVERE

Trastevere
Piazza Sonnino
Tel 06 58333457

ZONE 4: SAN GIOVANNI

Piazza San Giovanni in Laterano
Tel 06 77203535

ZONE 5: PRATI

CASTEL SANT'ANGELO
Piazza Pia
Tel 06 68809707

These Centers will provide you with the following Information and more:

- Maps of Rome
- Individual subject brochures
- Tickets to events
- Special package deals
- Tickets to museums

TOURIST CENTER OFFICE
English speakers
Tel 06 36004399
9am-7:30pm

ZONE 5: PRATI

Reservations Center
Via di S. Maria alle Fornaci 8d
Tel 06 6390409

CHIAMAROMA
24-hour information line for events and services in Rome
060606

Juno and the payphones

An Italian phone number can be any number of digits, ex. 06 4957 or 06 456. 7123.10 don't expect a three number area code and a seven digit phone number. Dots are used to separate numbers not slashes. When in Italy, dial the area code first, even if you're in the same city. In Rome, you must dial 06 first then the rest. When dialing cell phone numbers do not use the 06 area code. Such numbers usually begin with:
340, 347, 349 Vodafone
335, 333, 338 Tim
320 Wind
Calling Tim to Tim or Vodafone to Vodafone is cheaper than say calling from Vodafone to a Tim.

From Italy to the US and Canada dial 001, then the country code and number.
US and Canada to Italy dial 011then 39 for the country code and two digit town code.

The main telephone company is Telecom Italia. There are two other smaller companies also used in Italy: Infostrada and Teledue.

The old-style phones are orange and black; they take the same special cards and worked with cash, the old Italian Lire.
The new style phones are silver, accepting phone cards schede telefoniche, you cannot use cash with these.
Purchase at:
Tabacchi shops or newspaper stands
2.50-10€

ROMA RING TONES

Busy - Consecutive quick beeps
Wrong number - loud fast beeps
Dial tone - when you pick up the phone, rings 2 times pause... 2 times pause, 2 times pause....

Useful Number: 412 yellow page listings

USING PAYPHONE CARD

Before placing the special phone cards into the payphones you must break off the corner tab. Insert it, strip side down. After you insert the card, dial. When the screen reads Confermo press ok if you're sure.

International Calling Cards and Telephone Cards

Great International Phone Cards
100 units
Europa - purple and green card
150-180 min (3 hrs) to USA and Canada
6 hours within Europe

Edicard electronic card
For anywhere ask for your destination
For Europe and the U. S. - calls from a fixed phone last 3 hours for €5 or 6 hrs for 10€.

They sell them in bars or Tabacchi shops where they print lotto/Lottery tickets

EuropaCard
To USA and Canada from Rome:
Using cell phone: 15 minutes
Fixed phone: 3 hrs.
Payphone: 40 min.

Buy at: magazine stands, newsstands, and telephone shops

Cell Phone Recharge Card
Ricarica
10€, 25€, 50€, 100€

** Some payphones at Termini station accept coins.*

USEFUL WORDS		
Fuori servizio	Out of Order	fuor-ree sair-veez- ee-oh
Confermo	Confirmed	cone-fair-mow
Arrivederci	So long, cheerio	ah-ree-vay-dare-chee
Collegato	Connected	coal-lee-got-toe
Appendere linea	Hang up	ah- pen- dare-ray
Local payphones	Telefono Pubblico	tail-lay-phone-no poob-lee-coh

HELPFUL NUMBERS IN ITALY
MCI 172.1022
AT&T 172.1011
SPRINT 172.1877

CELL PHONE COMPANIES IN ITALY
Vodafone
Tim
Wind

Cell Phone Shop-BROS
Corso Vittorio Emanuele II 93A-95
Tel 06 68802888
9:30am-7:30pm

Outside Access codes
USA and Canada to Italy 011 39 two digit town code and number or cell without town code
City code -Rome 06
Italy to USA and Canada 001 area code and phone number

Pay-By-Minute International Telephone Shops

ZONE 2: ESQUILINO

Masterphone
Via Principe Amedeo 65
Tel 06 69200630
(Termini area)

Phone Points
8:30am-9:30pm
Via Solferino 10
Via Carlo Alberto 12

Aexis TeleCom
9am-10pm
Via Merulana 44-45
Off Piazza Santa Maria Maggiore

ZONE 2: EQUILINO

INTERNATIONAL MEDICAL CENTRE
Via Giovanni Amendola 7
Tel 06 4882371

Nights and weekends
Tel 06 4884051
English spoken
Hotel visits
24hrs
Across from Termini station

BAR CAVALLINO Pony Bar
Coffee bar
Piazza Venezia on the corner
Espresso, liquor, pastries
24hrs

CAFFETTERIA LA COLONNA
Emanuele Filiberto 239/241
Tabacchi shop, coffee bar
Selling a variety of things
24hrs

ZONE 5: PRATI

DOLCE MANIERA
(A Sweet Manner)
Via Barletta 29
Bus 492 or Metro line A (Ottaviano)
If you happen to pass Via Barletta and are lured towards the perfumes of pastries and pizzas you have located the last cornucopia alive in our modern day. Around the clock frenzied workers bake. Down the spiny stairwell into the cavern crowds are waiting and others are squeezing their way back up while freeing their fingers of fresh cream. It's a gold mine and harmless for wallets.

ZONE 2: ESQUILINO

CONAD at Termini
Located downstairs in the Forum Termini mall.

ZONE H: TIBURTINO

CONAD at Tiburtina station
This shop is not so appealing at night but you will find most everything here.
Closed only between 11pm-midnight

In Rome, 24 hr supermarkets are referred to as drugstores or Farmacie.

ZONE 5: PRATI

CONAD CLODIO
Via Golametto 4a, close to Piazzale Clodio, is a ten minute walk from the Vatican.
Pharmacies rotate and not all of them are open at the same time.
Antibiotics are sold over the counter, but it's not the law.
There is an additional 4€ extra charge at night.

QUELLI DELLA NOTTE- (Night Owls)
Via Leone IV
Bus 492 or Metro line A (Ottaviano-St. Peter's area)

24 HOUR NEWSTANDS

ZONE 2: ESQUILINO

RIONE CASTRO PRETORIO
Via G. Giolitti
(Termini area)

ZONE 1: HISTORICAL CENTER

RIONE COLONNA
Piazza Colonna-Via S. Maria
Off Via del Corso

RIONE LUDOVISI
Via Veneto
(Barberini area)

QUARTIERE PARIOLI
Piazza Ungheria

RIONE TRASTEVERE
Piazza Sonnino/Piazza Mastai

Edicolla's are the tiny houses depicting the Madonna or St. Joseph which adorn the corners of countless buildings around Rome.

Preparations

Voltage Requirements: 230 volts 50 cycles
Most of the European countries use the same voltage as Italy.

FOR 120 V APPLIANCES

You will need a voltage converter if your appliance is not designed to work (dual voltage) with 230 volts electricity. It is better to purchase one before you leave. If you hook up your appliance without a converter you will cook it.
Italian appliances have round prongs. The larger pronged plugs are used for bigger appliances such as washers and stoves. You will more then likely need a plug adapter which has the flat prongs holes for your appliance, and round prongs for the socket connection. You will find them in the Ferramenta.

Australia	240 V	50 Hz
Canada	120 V	60 Hz
China, People's Republic of	220 V	50 Hz
Egypt	220 V	50 Hz
Greece	220 V	50 Hz
Monaco	127/220 V	50 Hz
Morocco	127/220 V*	50 Hz
Nepal	230 V	50 Hz
New Zealand	230 V	50 Hz
South Africa	220/230 V*	50 Hz
United States of America	120 V	60 Hz
Virgin Islands (British and U. S.)	115V	60 Hz
Philippines	220 V	60 Hz

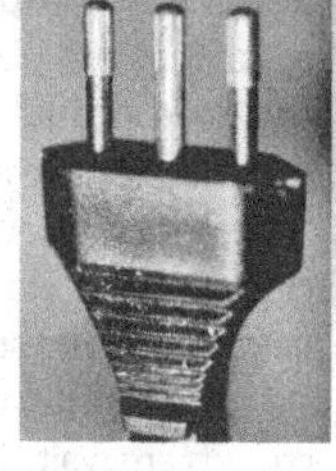

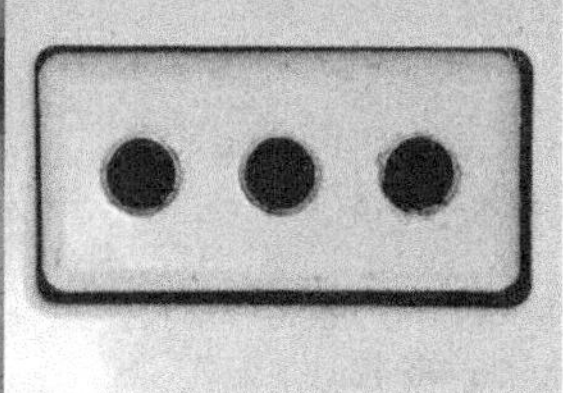

SOME ITEMS TO BRING:

- A security pouch that fits underneath clothing, but if you are acute a regular purse will do.
- Comfortable shoes without spiked heels
- A hat for the sun, as sunblock causes skin cancer
- Ibuprofen - you can pick up Brufen in Italy or lavender to sniff in its place.
- Earplugs - you'll realize that Italy is quite the lively place.
- Licorice - it helps me with low BP when it's too hot. Tabu is a good pure licorice.
- An extra duffle bag for bringing gifts back.

ANTI-BACTERIAL HANDWIPES
1/2 cup of vodka
20 drops of lavender essential oil
20 drops of tea tree oil
10 drops of bergamot essential oil
10 drops of citronella essential oil
Place all ingredients into a small glass bottle, shake it, and then let stand for five days
Cut up old clothing into tiny squares and spray on your anti-bacterial
Keep them in plastic zip lock bags

SPARE CONTACT LENSES
Tissues - you will find many bathrooms ran out of paper.
Clothes that keep you cool. Rome is hot, sticky and humid in July and August
Slippers - for the iced marble Italian flooring, read the poem; Barefoot on flat floors.

THE TABBACHI SHOP
They may have most things that you may need in a hurry like bus tickets, pens, film, gifts, soaps, shampoos, q-tips, razors, mailing envelopes, and stamps if you need to mail something home.
Go to the post office if it doesn't fit in the tiny red boxes on the streets.

Hardware shop	Ferramenta	Fair-rrah-men-tah
Plug adapter	Adattatore	Ah-dah-tah-tore-ray

Aromatherapy for travellers

PREVENTING JET LAG

Drink plenty of liquids and try to avoid alcohol.
Do not eat unless you are very hungry.
Wear loose clothing and switch to open shoes to prevent swelling.
Try to get up and walk a lot.

**Eucalyptus oil will prevent pain as the plane descends*

NERVE CALMING

In a dropper bottle:
1 tsp of lavender oil
1/2 tsp of bergamot essential oil
1/2 tsp of geranium essential oil
35 drops of sandalwood essential oil
10 drops of chamomile essential oil
Store it for five days, then sprinkle it as needed onto a handkerchief or tissue and inhale.

NERVES AND EXHAUSTION

55 drops of lavender essential oil
55 drops of geranium essential oil
35 drops of grapefruit essential oil
1 tsp of vodka
Store for five days
Drip 1-2 drops onto a warm facecloth and gently rub it across your face or on the back of your neck.

Recipes inspired by the Essential Health Bible by Nerys Purchon

Things that Italians don't

Laundry rooms and garbage grinders
Ice machines and clothes reminders
Stuffed into a lost space
Never found or leaving a trace

A culture difficult to modernize
Old sticks in the mud you face
Just a glimpse of disorganized
People in this case

Free of charge is the wind
This is where their minds have been
They worry about bills of woe
And prefer a harsh wind or chilly blow

They perfect the art of clothes hanging,
In paintings on threads spun and dangling

Ice cubes in a tray?
Cold chunks in a drink is a world away
How about that bidet?
The fallen sink besides the floor,
Vital to hygiene, a quick wash and more

Many things Italians don't
Everyone else will when they won't

Roman Bathrooms

Roman bathrooms can develop quite the puzzle. They are speckled all around the city and may greet you by surprise. Unless you are permitted to use one in the local coffee bar, it may proof cumbersome to find one. Bathroom dwellers provide supplies and bathrooms may be kept be clean if they are tipped. Turkish-style bathrooms are still available in Rome. The dark holes in the floor send most into another dimension and some devices are so odd that if instructions were mounted on the wall, we still may not figure them out.

The search for a flushing device, what an awful adventure. You may look for one of the following: a lever or a dangling string, a panel, a thin knob or button in the wall, in the floor, or hanging in front of you. Some people just surrender in frustration.

Convenience is not always a high commodity toilets are continuously found without seats. A small toiletry bag filled with soap, paper, a mirror, and a disposable toilet seat complete with instruction booklet would be the answer to our prayers.

FLUSHING MODELS

The Push Flush - a small round silver metal knob in wall the size of a quarter
The Panel Flush - just push in the panel strip on the left
Tab Flush - look for a small silver knob usually the size of a pen cap on the top part of the toilet on the wall and push it up
The Pull String Flush - just pull

WATER FAUCETS

Pedals on the floor under the sink
A normal model on the sink itself
Automatic modern types

DOORS OF MONSIEUR		
Uomini	Men	
La Toilette per Uomini	Men's toilet	
Signori	Gentlemen	
DOORS OF MADAM		
Donne	Women	
La Toilette per Le Donne	Women's toilet	
Signore	Ladies	
USEFUL WORDS AND EXPRESSIONS		
Free	Libero	lee-bear-row
Occupied	Occupato	oh-coo-pah-toe
Out of Order	Fuori servizio	foo-or-ree ser-vitz-ē-oh
Toilet paper	Carta igenica	car-tah ē-jenny-cah
Soap	Sapone	sah-poe-nay
Water	Acqua	ah-coo-ah
Tampon	Tampone	tom-pone-nay
Where can I find the bathroom?	Dove posso trovare il bagno?	
May I use the bathroom?	Posso usare la stanza da bagno?	

Fitness and Beauty Farm

ZONE 1: HISTORICAL CENTER

Rome Sports Centre

The sports centre entrance you may find from the Spagna metro underground or from outside Villa Borghese at the end of Via Veneto and across the street just beyond the arched Roman walls.

Upon entering the centre, you'll find an elegant lobby with a staff dressed classically, and a grand waiting area to the right. They provide an aerobics and sauna room, and the woman's locker room is vast and obsessively clean.

A huge open space in the centre is the café area complete with juice bar which serves carrot/celery juice and orange spremutas. The eating area is comfortable, and the varies rooms around it include free weights and racket ball. Down the stairs to the left, a wonderful courtyard allows you to sit outside in a plant surrounded area. Lining the window to this courtyard is an internet bar with a row of computers. This club has been managed by an American actor for years.

Viale Galoppatoio 33
Down stairs on the corner of Villa Borghese and the top of Via Veneto
Tel 06 3201667 American trainer
Health foods

ZONE 2: ESQUILINO

Fitness First

Via G. Giolitti
Tel 06 478 26300
The building is a part of the Termini station outside.

ZONE B: CASSIA

Veio Country Club

Via di Grottarossa 1148
Tel 06 336 16400
fax 06 336 28106
Tram 2 to Piazza A. Mancini then take bus 301 to Via Grottarossa

USEFUL WORDS	
Train	Treno
Soccer	Calcio
Stadium	Stadio
Gym	Palestra

Mr. Postman

Post offices handle telegrams, mail, bills and money transfers.

Postal information line 160

Historical Center - Post Offices

ZONE 1: HISTORICAL CENTER

MAILBOXES ETC.
Via Barberini
Tel 06 6892053
English speaking
(Piazza Barberini-Via Veneto Area)

POST OFFICE
Via Arenula 4

POST OFFICE
Corso Vittorio Emmanuele II 331

POST OFFICE
Piazza San Silvestro 19
Monday-Friday
8:25am-7:40pm
Saturday 8:25am-11:50am

POST OFFICE
Via Delle Vite 116
Tel 06 6786618
(Piazza di Spagna Area)

ZONE 2: ESQUILINO

POST OFFICE
Via Marsala 77
Tel 06 4451917
(Termini Area)

ZONE 5: PRATI

POST OFFICE
Via del Porta Angelica
Monday-Friday
8:30am-6:30pm
Saturday 8:30am-1pm
(San Pietro Area)

America, Japan and Canada stamp 0.85 €
Australia stamp 1€
Priority Prioritario 1.50 €

Within Europe 0.65 €
Priority Mail within Italy 0.62€

Where to Purchase Stamps: Post offices, tabacchi shops and at the front desk of some hotels

Blue Mailboxes - Priority and international mail
Red Mailboxes-Regular mail
The left side slot is for Provinces of Rome, the right side for All Destinations

The Banco Posta may be for you if you need a bank account in Italy.
It works as a bank with debit card, but is run by the state and is not private like banks making it secure with a 75€ a year tax. To keep one in Italy, there are no requirements except a Social Security number or Codice Fiscale which is free to obtain. You may use it to transfer money or take out money anywhere in the world. Go to any post office with a passport and ask to *aprire un conto corrente.*

The Codice Fiscale is obtained at various offices around Rome with a valid passport
Via Ippolito Nievo 36
Tel 06 583191
www.poste.it

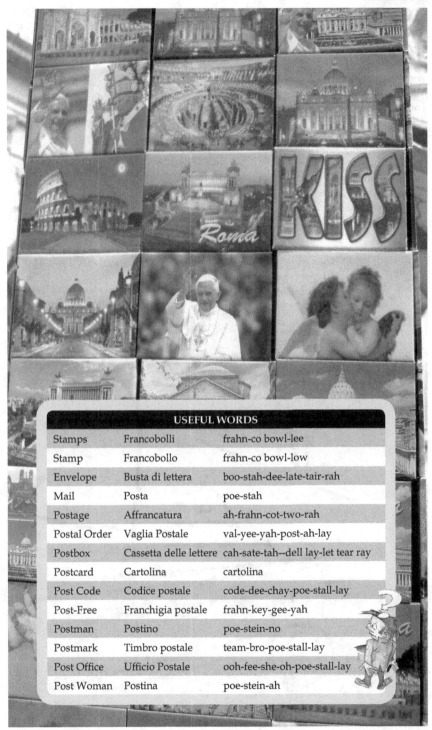

USEFUL WORDS		
Stamps	Francobolli	frahn-co bowl-lee
Stamp	Francobollo	frahn-co bowl-low
Envelope	Busta di lettera	boo-stah-dee-late-tair-rah
Mail	Posta	poe-stah
Postage	Affrancatura	ah-frahn-cot-two-rah
Postal Order	Vaglia Postale	val-yee-yah-post-ah-lay
Postbox	Cassetta delle lettere	cah-sate-tah--dell lay-let tear ray
Postcard	Cartolina	cartolina
Post Code	Codice postale	code-dee-chay-poe-stall-lay
Post-Free	Franchigia postale	frahn-key-gee-yah
Postman	Postino	poe-stein-no
Postmark	Timbro postale	team-bro-poe-stall-lay
Post Office	Ufficio Postale	ooh-fee-she-oh-poe-stall-lay
Post Woman	Postina	poe-stein-ah

Why not get married in Rome?

GIOVANNI MA-
RIO MATALO-
NI EMMA SER-
PIERI SPOSI RO-
MA 1·FEBBRA-
JO 1906

Rome Surroundings
Via Conti di Tuscolo 12
Frascati ROMA
Tel +39 06 94289989
Fax +39 06 94015241
info@romesurroundings.it

Just get Married
www.weddings-in-rome.net
weddings@justgetmarried.com
weddings@justgetmarried.com

Italian Language Instruction

Scuola D'Italiano
Via Nazionale 204
Tel. + 39 06 4746914
Fax +39 06 47826164
Metro Line A Repubblica
www.scudit.net

Scuola Leonardo da Vinci
Piazza dell'Orologio 7
Telefax + 39 06 68219084
Roma@scuolaleonardo.com
www.scuolaleonardo.com

Rome Language Center
Tel +39 06 446 3891
Fax +39 06 446 2876
info@romelanguages.com
www.romelanguages.com

Arco di Druso
Via Tunisi 4
Tel +39 06 39750984
Fax +39 06 39761819
www.arcodidruso.com

Torre di Babele
Via Cosenza 7
Tel +39 06 44252578
Fax +39 06 44251972
info@torredibabele.com
www.torredibabele.com

Istituto Italiano
Via Machiavelli 33
Tel + 3906 70452138
Fax + 39 06 7008512
istital@uni.net
www.istitutoitaliano.com

Ciao Italia
Via delle Frasche 5
Telefax +39 06 4814084
Metro line A exit Repubblica
info@ciao-italia.it
www.ciao-italia.it

Dilit International House
Via Marghera 22
Tel +39 06 4462592
Fax +39 06 4440888
www.dilit.it

A quote

**If you are distressed
by anything external,
the pain is not due to the thing itself,
but to your estimate of it;
and this you have the power
to revoke at any moment.**

Marcus Aurelius
121-180

Foreign universities

ZONE 4: SAN GIOVANNI

CRISTALLOTERPIA-AUTOCURA
School of Crystal Comunication
Via Principe Eugenio 106f
Doorbell 4
Tel 347 4215722/338 7511620
Relation between the atomic structure of crystals and galaxies
Sacred geometry and the interior evolution of man
The subtle anatomy of quartz and calcite
The characteristics of the crystals for personal use
www.web. tiscali.it/lapietradiluce

COOKING, SCULPTURE AND WATERCOLOR COURSES
Hotel Ristorante Adriano
Via di Villa Adriana 194
Tel 07 74535028
Tivoli
www.hoteladriano.it

FOREIGN UNIVERSITIES IN ROME

Cornell University
Via Dei Barbieri 6
Tel + 39 06 6897070
Fax +39 06 68199227
cornell@nexus.it

Iowa State University
Via Arco della Ciambella 19
Tel +39 06 68808552

John Cabot University
Via della Lungara 233
Tel +39 06 6819121
Fax +39 06 6832088

Pennsylvania State University
Dept. of Architecture Rome Program
Piazza del Collegio Romano 1A
Tel +39 06 6790420
Fax +39 06 6788945

St John's University
Via Santa Maria Mediatrice 24
Oratorio San Pietro
Tel +39 06 636 937
Fax +39 06 636901

Rhode Island School of Design
Piazza Cenci 56
Tel +39 06 68802490
Fax +39 06 6875848

University of Arkansas
Via dei Leutari 20
Tel +39 06 6833298
Fax +39 06 68807106
arcrome@nexus.it

Saint Mary's College
Corso Vittorio Emanuele II 110
Tel +39 06 68804752
Fax +39 06 68864852

Temple University Rome
Lungotevere Ar. Da Brescia 15
Tel +39 06 3202808
Fax +39 06 3202583

Trinità College
Cesare Barbieri Center
Clivo dei Publicii 2
Tel +39 06 5757184
Fax +39 06 5750456

University of Colorado at Boulder
College of Architecture and Planning
c/o University of Washington, Rome Centre
Palazzo Pio
Piazza del Biscione 95
Tel +39 06 6868807
Fax +39 06 68802849

IDIOMATIC		
To die broken-hearted	Morire di crepacuore	more-rear-ray dee cray-pah-quar-ray
Meek as a lamb	Manso come una pecora	mahn-zoe coh-may pay-core-rah
To come out well	Riuscire a buon fine	ree-oo-sheer-ray ah bwon fee-nay
Yeah sure I do	Sfido!	sfee-dough
Anything more beautiful	Niente di più bello	knee-en-tay dee pew bay-low
I am exhausted	Non ne posso più	known nay poe-sew pew
In the usual place	Al solito posto	ahl soul-lee-toe post-toe
Darn you	Mannaggia a te!	mahn-nah gee-ah ah tay!
So much so that	Tanto che	tahn-toe k
It is none of our business	Non sono affari nostril	known sew-no ah-far-ree no-stree
A total mix-up	Impicciato come un pulcino nella stoppa	eem-pea-chah-toe coh-may oon pooch-een-no nell-lah stow-pah
Summing things up	In fin dei conti	een feen day cone-tea
If worst comes to worst	Alla peggio del peggio	ahl-lah pay-joe dell pay-joe
It's just too bad for them	Guai a loro	goo-why ah lore-row
Without a doubt	Senza dubbio	sense-ah do-bee-oh
The cat leads a fine life	Il gatto fa una bella vita	eel gah-toe fah oon-nah bail-lah vee-tah
He seems to me like a man with little brains	Mi sembra un uomo di poco cervello	me same-brah oon woe-mow dee poe-coh chair-vell-low
To lay yourself out to ridicule	Mettersi in ridicolo	mate-tear-sea een reed-dee-coh-low
To go into a frenzy	Andare in bestia	on-dahr-ray een baste-stee-ah
It's not worth an iota	Non vale un'acca	known vah-lay oon-ah-cah
In the twinkling of an eye	In un batter d'occhio	een oon bah-tear doe-key-oh
The appointed hour	L'ora fissata	lore-rah fee-sah-tah
Or thereabouts	O giù di lì	oh jew dee lee
Knock on wood	Toccare ferro (touch iron)	toe-car-ray fair-row
I don't have the slightest idea	Non ho la minima idea	known o lah mean-knee-mah e-day-ah
You have guts	Hai fegato	eye-fay-gah-toe
I'll take the chance	Correrò il rischio	core-rare-row eel risk-key oh
I don't blame you	Non ti biasimo	known-tea-bee-ah-sea-mow
I gave up hope	Ho perso la speranza	oh pair-sow lah spare-rahn-tsah
It's awful	È tremendo	eh tray-men-doe
Everything's straightened out	Tutto sistemato	to-toe sea-stem-mah-toe
Little white lie	Una strataggemma	oon-nah strah-tah-gem-mah

	IDIOMATIC	
He's feeling sorry for himself	Lui si commisera	louie sea-comb-me-say-rah
It's out of the question	È fuori discussione	eh fwor-ree dee-scoo-see-own-nay
He didn't move a muscle	Non ha mosso un muscolo	known ah moe-sew oon moose-coh-low
No hard feelings	Senza rancore	sane-tsah rahn-coh-ray
You just gave me the chills	Mi fai gelare il sangue	me fi jail-lar-ray eel sahn-gway
Don't bother	Non ti scomodare	known tea scoh-mow-dahr-ray
Does it seem like it to you?	Ti sembra?	tea-same-bra?
We have a deal?	Siamo d'accordo?	see-ahm-mow dah-cord-doe?
Mind your own business	Fatti i fatti tuoi	fah-tea e fah-tea twoy
I'm fed up	Sono stufo	sew-no stew-foe
I give up	Io rinuncio	è-oh ree-noon-cho
What's so funny?	Che c'è di buffo?	k- chay dee boo-foe?
Don't waste my time	Non sprecare mio tempo	known spray-car-ray me-oh tame-poe
It's never too late	Non è mai troppo tardi	known eh my trow-poe tar-dee
I didn't notice	Non ci ho fatto caso	known chee oh fah-toe cah-zoe
What does that have to do with it?	Che c'entra?	k chen-trah
I'm spaced out	Sono rintronato	sew-no reen-trown-nah-toe
Can you do me a favor?	Mi fai una cortesia?	me fah-eye oon-nah core- tay-see-ah?
A little at a time	Un pò alla volta	oon poe ah-lah vowl-tah
There's no hurry	Non c'è fretta	known chay fray-tah
I didn't do it on purpose	Non l'ho fatto aposta	known low fah-toe ah-poe-stah
It doesn't matter	Non importa	known eem-pore-tah
In my opinion	Secondo me	say-cone-doe may
Is it my fault?	E colpa mia?	eh coal-pah me-ah?
I don't give a care	Non mi frega niente	known me fray-gah knee-en-tay
I don't feel like it	Non mi va	known me vah
Do you mind?	Ti dispiace?	tea dee spee-ah-chay?
Did you make plans?	Hai preso un impegno?	eye pray-zoh oon eem-pain-yo?
Yeah, whatever, why not?	Si, perchè no	sea, pear-k no?
Wow it's hot!	Scòtta	scoh-tah!
Nosy	Un fica naso	oon fee-cah nah-zoh
I'm out of here	Me ne vado	may-nay vah-doe
People never cease to amaze you	Le gente non smetterà mai di sorprenderti	lay jen-tay known smate-tear-rah my dee sew-pren-der-tea

Italian Hands with a Pen

Through pleasure or strain
Simple curiosity or slight pain

Italian letters derange on estranged plains
Are forms that rearrange without refrain

We try to decipher guess and imagine
Yet with Italian hands you just can't fathom

Letters tilt forwards, backwards on rather strange angles
Is it an A or a triangle?
Is it an a or somewhat of a tangle?
The gs are confused upon the os where they dangle

Out from schools with correct incision
Then flitting around without precision.

Interpretation is our task at hand
Though written in English we'd a bright clan

To comprehend words in foreign-hand-written
Swells us whirls us at last we've been smitten

Their letters are created to make an example
To last to hold for us to trample

Singing to us and luring us away
They bring us down into dismay

Italians make letters with grand expression
Continuing strokes in unknown directions

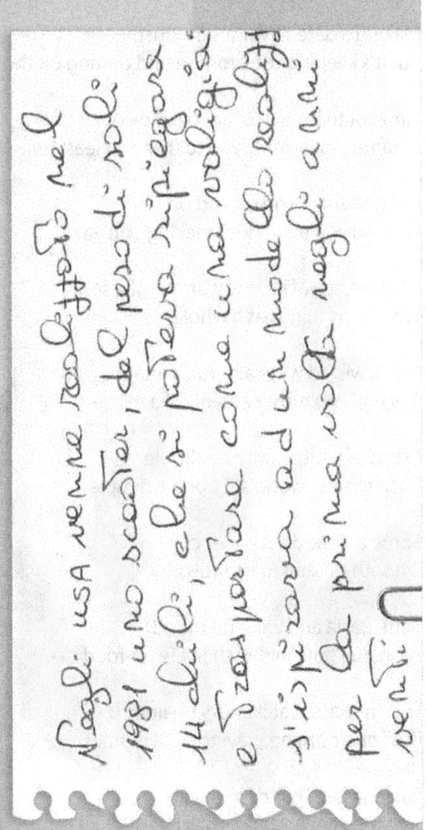
Negli USA venne realizzato nel
1981 uno scooter, del peso di soli
14 chili, che si poteva ripiegare
e trasportare come una valigia:
si ispirava ad un modello realizzat
per la prima volta molti anni
venti

Romans a proud breed brazen race
Taken in by such as leather and lace

Vanity plays on these sorts
Unimpressed by their own cultural space of course

Non-aware and seemly far away
Bug-eyed sunglasses above cleavage on display

Their scooters jet putting to and fro
Remember: Versace Cavalli Valentino

The endeavours of driving curtail as we read
Stop! to the approaching red light will they take heed?

What is this! These people are of a charade
Just a drop of love and their devotion cannot be weighed

Traced from Romans way back in time
Ironically given the mould but somehow less divine

Making a date never seems unsmooth
But it's keeping the promise and getting on the move

Time for them is like the roll of dice
A game that tempts you to throw at least twice

It just seems to go on and on
Leaving you to wonder making you yawn

It's the spice of life the warmth of a soul
Wondrous things as a whole

Their twisted ways and rules unabode
Sincerely no most certainly alla mode

Crests of white pure and simple
Their minuet world set upon a dimple

Some are caddy acute or coy
Smooth rhythm masterful ploy

Caffè pasta and wine for mood
All in due time within their life for food

Lost in space wet laundry on lines
Realizing nothing playing with rhymes

Rapid jesters' hands in the air
Join the conversation, shall I dare?

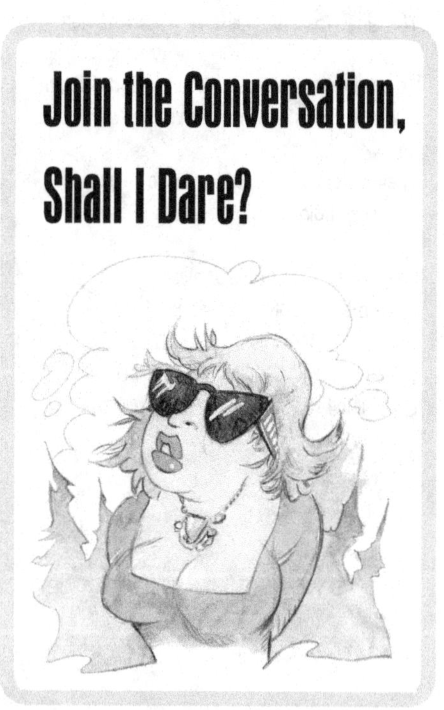
Join the Conversation,
Shall I Dare?

Ads

WANTED IN ROME MAGAZINE

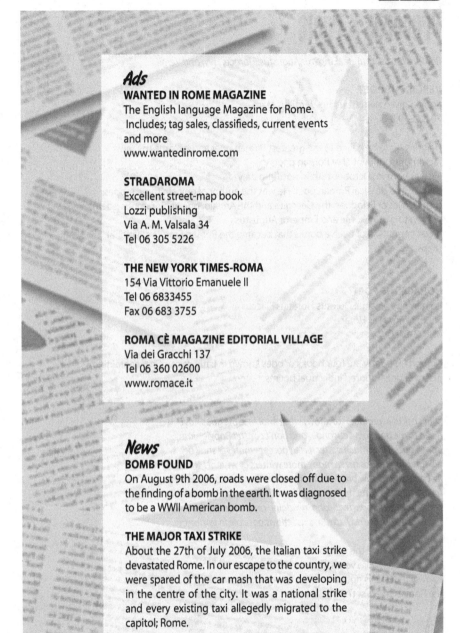

The English language Magazine for Rome.
Includes; tag sales, classifieds, current events and more
www.wantedinrome.com

STRADAROMA

Excellent street-map book
Lozzi publishing
Via A. M. Valsala 34
Tel 06 305 5226

THE NEW YORK TIMES-ROMA

154 Via Vittorio Emanuele II
Tel 06 6833455
Fax 06 683 3755

ROMA CÈ MAGAZINE EDITORIAL VILLAGE

Via dei Gracchi 137
Tel 06 360 02600
www.romace.it

News

BOMB FOUND

On August 9th 2006, roads were closed off due to the finding of a bomb in the earth. It was diagnosed to be a WWII American bomb.

THE MAJOR TAXI STRIKE

About the 27th of July 2006, the Italian taxi strike devastated Rome. In our escape to the country, we were spared of the car mash that was developing in the centre of the city. It was a national strike and every existing taxi allegedly migrated to the capitol; Rome.

Proverbs & Poets

Romans Intellects under Emperor Augustus: Horace, Livy, and Vergil

VERGIL THE POET
Roman given name: Publius Vergilius Maro
70 B.C.-19 B.C.

He grew up to be hailed as the greatest Roman poet and became the most famous and influential of Roman poets
He was born on October 15th in northern Italy
Vergil was a classical Roman poet. He was the author of epics in three modes: the Bucolics or Eclogues, the Georgics and the Aeneid, one of his famous poems written to glorify Rome and Emperor Augustus.
It was comprised of twelve books that became the Roman Empire's national rhapsody.

HORACE THE POET
Roman given name: Quintus Horatius Flaccus
Simply known as Horace
65 B.C.-8 B.C.

Among his poetry are four books of odes known in Latin as carmina, containing just over one hundred individual poems.

ODE 1. 11
Don't ask (it's forbidden to know) what final fate the gods have
given to me and you, Leuconoe, and don't consult Babylonian
horoscopes. How much better it is to accept whatever shall be,
whether Jupiter has given many more winters or whether this is the
last one, which now breaks the force of the Tuscan sea against the
facing cliffs. Be wise, strain the wine, and trim distant hope within
short limits. While we're talking, grudging time will already
have fled: seize the day, trusting as little as possible in tomorrow.

And are you sure the girl you love
This maid on whom you have your heart set
Is lowly that she is not of
the Roman smart set?

LIVY THE HISTORIAN
Roman given name: Titus Livius
59 B.C.-17 A.D.

Livy's writing style was poetic and archaic in contrast to Caesar's and Cicero's styles. Also, he often wrote from the Romans' opponent's point of view in order to accent the Romans' virtues in their conquest of Italy and the Mediterranean. In keeping with his poetic tendencies, he did little to distinguish between fact and fiction. Although he frequently plagiarized previous authors, he hoped that moral lessons from the past would serve to advance the Roman society of his day.

Roman proverbs

Roman Li Proverbi sò come er Vangelo
Italian I proverbi sono some il Vangelo
English Proverbs are like a gospel

Roman Indove serio vorsuto, corre e stacce
Italian Dove sei desiderato, corri e rimani
English Where you are wanted, you run there and stay

Roman Dormece sopra e poi porta risposta
Italian Prima di rispondere, dormici sopra
English Before answering, sleep on it first

Roman Ama L'amico tuo cor zu' difetto
Italian Ama il tuo amico con i suoi difetti
English Love your friend, also with his defects

Roman La vanosità è un arbero che fa quarche fiore e gnente frutti
Italian La vanità è un albero che fa qualche fiore e nessun frutto
English Vanity is like a tree that has a few flowers, but no fruit

Roman A quarcheduno piace mètte er lutto all'orinale
Italian L'originalità non è mai morta
English Originality will never die

Roman Parlà vale un grosso, statte zitto un papetto
Italian Il silenzio è D'oro
English Silence is gold

Filing a Complaint:

Stations

ZONE 1: HISTORICAL CENTER

Via Vittorio Veneto Station - Zone 1
(Piazza Barberini) - Via Bocompagni 31 06 481-9865

Viminale Station Zone 1
Via XXIV Maggio 23 06 678-2854

Celio Station - Zone 1
(Colosseo)- Via Annia 44 06 709-6375

Piazza Farnese Station - Zone 1
(Campo de' Fiori) Via Trinità dè Pellegrini 34 06 686-5115

Piazza Venezia Station - Zone 1
V. C. Battisti 6 06 679-0444

ZONE 2: ESQUILINO

Termini Station - Zone 2
(Inside Termini Station top floor)
Via Marsala 71 06 473-06318

Macao Station - Zone 2
(Termini) - Via Mentana 6 06 447-41900

Piazza Dante Station - Zone 2
(Between Santa Maria Maggiore & San Giovanni in Laterano) Via Tasso 12
06 772-00069

ZONE 3: TRASTEVERE

Gianicolense Station - Zone 3
(Trastevere) - Via G. di Colloredo 15
06 582-09419

Porta Portese Station - Zone 3
(Trastevere) - Via Monti 29 b 06 581-2073

Trastevere Station - Zone 3
Via E. Morosini 24
06 585-96700

ZONE 4: SAN GIOVANNI

San Giovanni Station - Zone 4
(San Giovanni In Laterno - Near Sunday flea market)
Via Britannia 35 06 77206232

ZONE 5: PRATI

San Pietro Station - Zone 5
Via Muzio Clementi 39 06 5859660

ZONE 6: FLAMINIO

Ponte Milvio Station - Zone 6
(Olimpic Stadium & International Youth Hostel) Via Flaminia Vecchia 472
06 333-3651

ZONE 8: OSTIENSE

Aventino Station - Zone 8
(Terme di Caracalla)- Via Felice Nerini 26
06 574-6996

ZONE 10: SAN LORENZO

San Lorenzo Station
(Pub Zone) - Via dei Volsci 112 06 445-6785

ZONE 11

San Sebastiano Station - Zone 11
Via Appia Antica 218 A 06 780-3906

ZONE 12: EUR

Eur Station
Viale Asia 66 06 542-7481

ZONE I

Piazza Bologna Station
Via Antonio Gallonio 2 06 442-36409
Metro Line B: Bologna

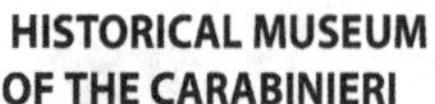

HISTORICAL MUSEUM OF THE CARABINIERI

Museo Storico dell'Arma dei Carabinieri
Piazza Risorgimento 46
06 689-6696
Open Tue- Sun 8:30am-12:30

Open in December 1925, the 19th century palace is still in it's orginal state.
All the memories, and objects left behind that make up the past history of the Carabinieri (Italian Military Police).
Every year the military police produce beautifully artistic calendars that are highly collectable, photos are replicas of true paintings by various italian painters. The calendars are full of Carabinieri stories accompanied by colorful paintings. They started in 1929 and still make them today. Unfortunately they are not in any stores nor for sale, I guess that's why that are so valuable to the people they are precious. They only way to get one would be to know someone who is a part of the Italian Military Police. Take a look:
Website http://www.carabinieri.it/editoria/calendari/indice4.htm

Police

Municipal Police
Virgili Urbani
Uniform: navy and white helmets
Summer uniform: white and white helmets
Job description: handle city traffic, and other city tasks
May have badges that display the languages spoken

Carabinieri
Elegant Armani uniforms: black, red stripes on pant legs
Job description: theft, serious crimes, demonstrations, military and federal affairs

Polizia di Stato
State Police National Police
Uniform: navy blue jackets, light blue pants
Job description: deal with other police and administrative matters

Main Headquarters for Carabinieri Police and Military
Piazza S. Lorenzo in Lucina 6
Off Via Del Corso and close to
Piazza del Popolo
Tel 06 58594500

HEALTH RELATED LAWS

- Abortion is Legal - up to 3 months
- Antibiotics sometimes sold over counter, but law is by prescription
- Smoking prohibited in public establishments as of January 10 2005

MINOR-RELATED LAWS

- License age: 18
- Cigarette purchases: age18 - not strictly enforced

ANIMALS

- Italian no-kill law: it is illegal in Italy to put a companion animal to death - cats and dogs

ALCOHOLIC LAWS

Drinking and Driving Law- enforced

- Limit 0.5% Blood al content - takes 1 glass of liquor for some
- 1st offense - a15 day license suspension,
- 2nd offense - 2 months
- Limit 50cl of beer to consume in coffee bar or you must take it to go
- Drinking age 18 - not strictly enforced
- Open Container Law - not strictly enforced

Auto-stops (shops) along the highways: after 10pm - no purchases of alcohol

DRIVING

- Seatbelt laws - enforced Fine 65€
- Highway Hitch-Hiking: Auto stop' is Illegal
- Prohibited along main roads and highways, Italians will rarely stop

DRUG-RELATED LAWS

- Against the law to sell drugs - if someone is found with a substantial amount, they will be accused of pushing drugs
- Legal to use drugs - if found using drugs, they'll confiscate them, but will not press charges

Military Time Chart

STANDART TIME	MILITARY TIME	STANDART TIME	MILITARY TIME
1:00am	1.00	1:00pm	13.00
2:00am	2.00	2:00pm	14.00
3:00am	3.00	3:00pm	15.00
4:00am	4.00	4:00pm	16.00
5:00am	5.00	5:00pm	17.00
6:00am	6.00	6:00pm	18.00
7:00am	7.00	7:00pm	19.00
8:00am	8.00	8:00pm	20.00
9:00am	9.00	9:00pm	21.00
10:00am	10.00	10:00pm	22.00
11:00am	11.00	11:00pm	23.00
12:00pm Noon	12.00	12:00am Mid	24.00

Health Information

ZONE 2: ESQUILINO

International Medical Center
Via Giovanni Amendola 7
Tel 06 4882371

Nights and Weekends
Tel 06 4884051
English Spoken
Hotel Visits
24 hrs

ZONE K: CASTELLI ROMANI

Homeopathic Doctor Dr Francesco Casu
Via Don Minzoni 8
Tel 06 9323295
Closed Saturday and Thursday evenings
Albano Laziale

ZONE 5: PRATI

San Spirito Hospital for Children
Lungotevere Sassia 1
Tel 06 68351
Emergencies
Tel 06 462371

G. Eastman Dental Hospital
Viale Regina 287
Tel 06 844831
English Spoken

ZONE G: PRENESTINO

Rome American Hospital
Via Emilio Longoni 59
Tel 06 2285062
Tel 06 2285064

Emergency Rooms

ZONE 3: TRASTEVERE

San Camillo
Tel 06 58701
(Circ. Gianicolense - Trastevere)

ZONE 4: SAN GIOVANNI

San Giovanni
Tel 06 77051
Via Amba Aradam 8
Metro Line A

ZONE 5: PRATI

San Pietro
Via Cassia
Tel 06 33581

ZONE 6: FLAMINIO

San Giacomo
Tel 06 36261
(Piazza del Popolo area)

ZONE I: NOMENTANO

Policlinico
Viale Policlinico
Tel 06 4462341
24 hour hotline 06 462341
Metro Line B Policlinico

EMERGENCY NUMBERS

- Ambulance 118
- Italian red cross ambulance - Tel 065510
- Chemist's open on holidays - Tel 06 228941
- Urgent blood transfusion- Tel 06 4456375
- San Giovanni-Tel 06 77055563
- Helicopter ambulance- Tel 06 5344478 or 06 58702696
- Permanent first aid station - Tel 06 4826741 0658201030
- Centre against drugs intoxication Gemelli - Tel 06 3054343

ANIMALS

- Pronto Intervento Veterinario/Animal Ambulance Tel 06 58238488
- Ambulance Vet Tel 06 5810078

FUNGAL CONCERNS/ TUMORS

English Spoken
Dr. Tullio Simoncini
www.cancerisafungus.com

IAMAT

Contain lists of English Spoken Doctors Worldwide
Tel 716 7544883

USEFUL WORDS		
Allergies	Allergie	ahl-lair-gee-ay
Asthma	Asma	ah-smah
Blood pressure	Pressione Sanguigna	pray-see-own-ay sahn-gwee-nya
Fever	Febbre	fay-brey
Infection	Infezione	een-fates-see-own-nay
Heart Disease	Malattie di cuore	mahl-leh-tea-ay dee quor-ray
Sore Throat	Mal di Gola	mahl-dee-go-la
Stomache Ache	Mal di Pancia	mahl-dee-pahn-cha
Faint	Svenire	sven-ear-ray
Dehydration	Disidratazione	drah-tah-ts-ee-own-ay
Head injury	Dirigere la lesione	dee-ree-jer-ray lah lay-sea-own-nay
Diabetes	Diabete	dee-ah-bay-tay
Cold	Raffreddore	rah-frah-door-ray
Sunstroke	Insolazione	e-sow-lots-ee-own-ay
Surgery	Chirurgia	key-rewer-gee-ah
Emergency Room	Pronto Soccorso	prone-toe sow-course-sow

WOMEN'S CONCERNS		
Yeast infection	L'Infezione Lievito	lynn-feck-tsee-own-nay lee-ay-vee-toe
Abortion	L'Aborto	lah-boar-toe
Birth control	Controllo di Nascita	cone-troll-low dee nah-she-tah

Termometro/Thermometer

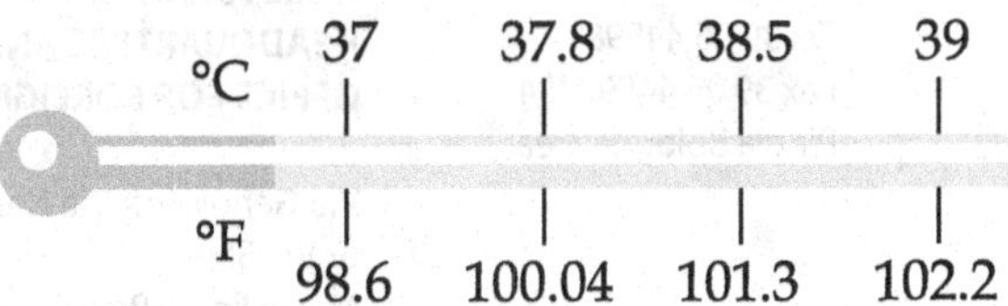

Your Embassy in Rome

ZONE 1: HISTORICAL CENTER

Embassy of Brazil
Piazza Navona 14
Tel 39 06 683981
Fax 39 06 6867858

Embassy of Great Britain
Via XX Settembre 80a
Tel 39 06 4825441
Bus 16 36 60EX 61 62 84 86 90EX 217 360 910

Embassy of India
Via XX Settembre 5
Tel 39 06 488 4642/4884643
Fax 39 06 4819539

United States Embassy
Via Vittorio Veneto 119
Tel 39 06 46741
Fax 39 06 4882672
Bus 52 53 63 80EX 95 116 119 630

Embassy of Japan
Via Quintino Sella 60
Tel 39 06 42014552

Embassy of Argentina
Piazza dell' Esquilino 2
Tel 39 06 4742551/ 474 2552
Fax 39 06 4819787

*Dial without the 39 when in Italy

ZONE 2: EQUILINO

Embassy of Germany
Via S. Martino della Battaglia 4
Tel 06 492131

Embassy of Israel
Via Michele Mercati 14
Tel 39 06 36198500
Fax 39 06 36198555

ZONE 7: PARIOLI

Embassy of Korea
Via Barnaba Oriani 30
Tel 39 06 8088769

Embassy of the Philippines
Viale delle Medaglie D'oro 112
Tel 39 06 39746621

ZONE 13: AURELIO

Canadian Embassy
Via Giovanni Battista de Rossi 27
Tel 39 06 445981
Fax 39 06 44598754
Piazza Bologna area

ZONE I: NOMENTANA

Embassy of New Zealand
Via Zara 28
Tel 39 06 44029283081
Fax 39 06 4402984

Embassy of Mexico
Via Lazzaro Spallanzani 16
Tel 39 06 441151
Fax 39 06 440387

Embassy of China
Via Bruxelles 56
Tel 39 06 884 8186/8413458
Fax 39 06 8442275

ZONE J: SALARIA

Embassy of South Africa
Via Tanaro 14/16
Tel 39 06 8419794

Embassy of Australia
Via Alessandria 215
Tel 39 06 8542721

QUESTURA/POLICE HEADQUARTERS AND OFFICE FOR FOREIGNERS

Via Genova off Via Nazionale or Via Salavati
Metro line A Repubblica

- Interpreters of all languages
- Visa information
- File police reports

Thefts

CREDIT CARD AND TRAVELER CHECK THEFT REPORT TO:

Toll-free In Italy
Amex-800 872 000
Visa-800 874 155
MC-800 870 866 - Traveler's Checks - call the U.S. collect at 001-212-974-5696 (24hrs)

ALSO REPORT IT TO:

The Italian Public Security Authorities:
Toll-free In Italy
Amex-800 073 973
Visa-800 877 232
MC-800 870 866

Go to the closest police head quarters on the list.
Go to your Embassy - visit the tourist info office.

Amex
Cancel stolen/lost Credit Cards
Tel 06 72900347
7am-1pm everyday of the week
For a new card file a police report with:

- Social Security Number
- Home phone number
- Issuing office

DINERS CLUB:
Italy Toll Free Number: 800-864-064 (24hrs)
DISCOVER CREDIT CARD:
U. S. collect at 001-801-902-3100 (24hrs)

MASTERCARD-MASTERCARD II, DIAMOND CARD, UNION CARD, EUROCARD
Italy Toll Free Number: 800-870-866 (24-hrs) or U. S. collect at 001-914-249-2000 or 001-314-275-6690

VISA INTERNATIONAL:
Toll Free Italy: 800-877-232/800-874-155/800-819-014 (24hrs)

Thomas Cook
Toll-free in Italy
800 872 050

CITIBANK
Report loss/theft and obtain clearance for replacement
Toll-free Italy
800 877 223

RESTITUTION FROM TRAIN THEFTS

Trenitalia and Ferrovie dello Stato (state trains) have an insurance policy covering limited types of thefts. On InterCity or EuroStar trains claims can be filed if bags were stored in the baggage areas at the head of the car (not above the seats). Or if the theft occurred on a night train in a sleeper car/couchette and the traveller was in the room with the door locked at the time.
To file a claim, the traveller must present a copy of the police report and a copy of his ticket or Eurail pass to either a train station ticket counter or by sending the documentation to a Customer Service Representative at: Trenitalia 'Rapporti con I Clienti,' (Client Relations) in Piazza della Croce Rossa 1.

EMERGENCY NUMBERS

Dial 112 - Carabinieri: it is a free call from any phone and English is spoken more often here.
113: Police

USEFUL WORDS

Multa (penalty)	Accosta	La Droga	Drogato
Ticket	Pull over	Drugs	Drug addict

Butti la roba per terra	Da finestrino	Sei in arresto
Littering	Littering from a car	Your under arrest

The Carabinieri calendars came to life in 1929, when one of the grandest collections was published. Several Italians collect them and the only way to obtain them is if you know someone. Diverse artists have contributed their personalities and creative intelligence for these artistic military calendars which are the most prestigious in the world.
www.carabinieri.it

The Gypsies

This section was written to weed out the rebellious gypsies, it was not meant to criticize the entire gypsy race. Among every culture we find good and bad and unfortunately we need to be educated on the bad to prevent harm and violation.

THE TOP 5 REASONS PEOPLE ARE ROBBED BY GYPSIES

1. They do not recognize them
2. They do not pay attention
3. They don't take charge of the situation
4. Fear paralyzes them
5. They have no knowledge of the gypsies

TRUE GYPSY WORDS

Hokkani Boro means The Great Trick
Hakk'ni Panki means Trickery
Congratulations to the gypsies for giving us this definition: *Hanky Panky*
Vardo means Wagon or Caravan
Gadjo (Gàh-joe) means a Non-Gypsy
Pen Dukkerin means Fortunetelling

THE GYPSY OASIS OF ROME:

- Termini station and surrounding areas
- Tiburtina station and area
- On buses 64 and 492
- In subway cars
- Porta Portese flea market
- On Via del Corso
- Up Via Nazionale
- Around San Pietro
- Around Via Condotti (Piazza di Spagna)
- Piazza del Popolo
- Campidoglio

GYPSY DESCRIPTIONS:

- Women in long skirts and sandals with socks
- Women with long black usually unclean hair, light-dark complexions
- Women carrying babies
- Woman holding big slabs of cardboard in tourist areas
- They usually don't speak English
- The children are very clever, quick, and expert pickpockets working in pairs
- Gypsies appear on subway cars playing violins and accordions for money
- Gypsies generally push you hard and put their hands into your pockets as you fall back
- They may appear sweet to you, until you refuse them money
- They are also the ones that you see sitting on the streets with begging signs
- Gypsies congregate in tourist areas, subways, outside markets, crowded ones
- Gypsies snatch: luggage, purses or anything of value. Watch your belongings if eating outside

There have been horrific episodes on countless occasions of gypsies following tourist tours; it's a playground for them. They follow the groups with big pieces of cardboard which they use to cover their hands while they dig into your belongings. So preoccupied and excited by the trip, travelers can be oblivious of the wolves drooling behind. They prey on victims in over-crowded buses too.

Letting them know we are onto them by demonstration would avoid further actions.

These gypsies are mostly woman and children. The men generally play violins on the subway or other musical instruments in plazas and some are incredibly talented.

They are great actors some pretending to be blind-others are really blind-and young ladies become bend over cripples struggling around the Coliseum and Via Sacra.

Signs to watch out for: nervousness, rushing, rudeness, if intuitive tells us that the situation does not feel right, it probably isn't.

SHOUT WHATEVER WORDS FEEL MORE COMFORTABLE		
Help!	Aiuto!	ah- u toe
Thief!	Ladro!	lah-drow
Get out of here! Go away!	Via!	vee ah

PHONE BOOTH HORROR; A TRUE OCCURENCE

There was a woman in a phone booth screaming.

Obscure claws began groping her and as her eyes filled with fear, they sopped her cheeks. She was a simple tourist trying her best to understand the Italian instructions given on the phone. Not even in the cellar of her mind did she think about being mugged in that tight fitting phone booth that day in July.

She was being observed. Was she sent there by chance or by fate?

Now in a state of confusion, pins and needles started jabbing her. She had never been to Europe let alone Italy and was not only being watched, but surrounded. Stifling heartbeats made her blouse pulse; she was hot, flushed and frightened.

Within a transparent phone booth possessing a mere thumb of space, a woman looked up into three faces. Gypsies were covering the outer edges and glaring in on her. She squirmed a bit and dropped the receiver which hit her knee bone. It then bounced off the glass and left itself to dangle. They entered the glass booth and roughly fondled her and wrestled with her pockets. A few began to fling scant objects to the others outside.

Then her luck changed, as someone came to assist her. The gypsy's aggressiveness stirred anger in a man who settled to watch from afar. A fight broke out and the gypsies fled.

This horrified woman was indeed rescued and left with an interesting lesson to think about.

Time Zones

WORLD CLOCK - FUSO ORARIO			
Rome Time:	Argentina: Buenos Aires -4	Finland +1	New Zealand +11
Amsterdam	Athens +1	Glasgow -1	Peru -6
Berlin	Arizona -8	Hawaii -11	Perth +7
Budapest	Alaska -10	Hong Kong +7	Portugal -1
Madrid	Bermuda -5	India +5	Panama -6
Paris	Barbados -5	Ireland -1	Phillipines +7
Prague	Bahamas -6	Israel +1	Rio de Janeiro, Sao Paulo -4
Sweden	Beijing +7	Iceland -1	South Africa +1
Switzerland	Brazil (West) -6	Indonesia +6	Sydney +9
Vienna	Canada, BC -6	Jamaica -6	Singapore +7
	Canada: NewBrunswick -5	Japan +8	Tasmania +10
	Canada: Ontario, Quebec -6	Korea +8	Thailand +6
	China +7	Kenya +2	Taiwan +7
	Costa Rica -7	Lima -6	Turkey +1
	Cuba -6	London -1	Uruguay -4
	Cyprus +1	Martinque -5	USA East -6
	Egypt: Cairo +1	Morocco: Casablanca -1	USA Central -7
	Caracas -5	Mali -1	USA Middle -8
	Ecuador -6	Mexico City -7	USA Pacific -9
	El Salvador -7	Moscow +2	Vietnam +6
	Fiji +11	Melbourne +9	Wales -1
			Zimbabwe +1

Tips

COFFEE BARS

Coffee or caffé bars have the knack of overcharging tourists. A cappuccino or espresso is no more than 2€.
Check the wall menus or ask for the pricing first.
These type of bars are the places for coffee and sandwiches panini. Alcohol is also served, though an Italian's idea of a drink is an Aperitivo before lunch or dinner. When ordering in the bar take note that there is a price difference for standing at the bar versus sitting down at a table, prices swell at the tables.

In coffee bars, you usually pay and order at the cashier then hand in your receipt to the barman and tell him what you've ordered.

RESTAURANTS

Waiters have a tendency to make special table deliveries. Bread or a side dish can be brought clumsily and left unannounced. Remember to refuse what you do not want to pay for. Roma loves the alla cart principle.
Most restaurants open or reopen around 7-7:30pm, so if you're hungry most coffee bars are still open during this time and serve tramezzini light sandwiches.

- Often Italians don't write down the order, mostly trust the customer to help add it up at the end by memory
- Service charges are added to your restaurant bill are normal, if 15% is added to your bill to cover charges an additional tip isn't expected
- Doggy bags are never requested

ASKING FOR DIRECTIONS IS ALWAYS AN ADVENTURE

After asking various people where the <blank> is, you'll find one who shrugs, another who's amazed he doesn't know, a policemen that knows but won't tell, and yet another fellow who tells and doesn't really know. Finally, there are those that know and tell you the exact opposite out of spite. Asking a police officer for directions is your absolute best bet as locals usually can't tell directions any better than a foreigner can.

Bus

If you validate your bus ticket in the ticket machine, check to see if the date is current. It's no surprise that I validated mine only to find out it was one year behind. If you mention this problem, the driver will probably shrug and say oh well, another words, who cares.

Sales & Bargains

Summer Sales begin around July 13 and end in the beginning of September. Winter Sales run from January 8-February 18th. This is a national directive and each town announces the sales during this time. Also note that some stores stay open during lunch hours while others are closed for pausa pranzo.

Romans & Holidays

In August, remember that most people about 85% leave the city, and go to their homes by the sea or in the mountains where it's cool, so most places of business are at a stand still for the month.

PAUSA PRANZO-LUNCH BREAK

Lunch breaks are long lasting. Forget the 30 minute race courses most of us take for digesting our food. For Italians three and a half hour breaks every day is an old tradition. In the afternoon shops rest somewhere during these hours: 1pm-4:30pm. In downtown Rome, timetables are modernizing a bit and remain open.

Water & Ice

A strange little story about the ice factor... Mark Twain discussed the differences between Americans in the south and Americans from the north in one of his books. In particular, their preference or lack thereof of adding ice to their drinks. Northerners were considered similar to the Europeans. He reminded the reader that Europeans didn't put ice in their drinks, because they believed it was damaging to the health.

Tap water in Rome is safe and tastes good. The white build-up you may witness is nothing but the large calcium content. Rome has very hard water.
Do fill up your plastic bottles and canteens at public fountains. The water runs from ancient Roman aqueducts, delivering pure water that is drinkable.
Beware though of; non potabile water not fit to drink.

Ice is difficult to find, as Italians do not request it. You may start preparing yourself to drink your drinks warm or maybe open up an ice making business?

BEING CAREFUL

Be careful not to confuse street names with the names of bridges ponte or piazzas. Even if the name is similar, check the codes (via, viale, ponte, corso) they may not even be in the same vicinity. For example: Piazza Cavour versus Via Cavour.
Rome in general is a safe city aside from pickpockets and beggars.

Do's

- Cover your shoulders and knees at the Vatican and San Pietro, allowing yourself 4-6 hours
- You may wish to keep a sarong in your pack or you may find peddlers that will sell you paper thin pants for 10€
- Check for train strikes before buying tickets because no refunds will be issued
- Take advantage of the Tax-Free shopping and always bargain, you can save up to 50%
- Take the train to the airport; it'll cost you 80% less than taking a taxi or shuttle bus. From metro line A Punto Lungo, you can take the train at Tuscolano station that costs practically nothing
- Be aggressive and wise when crossing the street
- Say good morning, good evening, hello and good-bye, those are good cultural manners
- You can buy tickets for museums and other tourist places in packaged deals in tourist information points
- Tickets for the Coliseum may be purchased going directly to Via Sacra, the tight road next to L'Arco Constantine and off the square of the Coliseum.

Don'ts

- Don't ever show anyone your money or ID. If asked for it on the street this is a con
- Don't wear a money belt where you can visibly see it
- Don't leave your bags or purse unattended in touristy areas, especially if eating outside
- Don't look at or talk to the gypsies
- Don't buy beverages or fruits at the kiosks outside, you'll pay five times more than at any supermarket
- You don't need to tip more than 15% on top of the service charge at a restaurant
- You usually cannot leave a tip on a credit card
- Don't enter the metro, tram or bus without validating your ticket in the machine a.s.a.p.
- If you get pictures developed, do not have them serviced around Termini station, someone once paid 48€ for 2 rolls of film development when normally you would pay 9-14€

SOME GENERAL ADVICE

- Cigarettes can be purchased after hours in machines found on some tabacchi shop doors. There is one in Barberini Square and in Piazza Repubblica on Via Vittorio E. Orlando. Remember: there's no smoking allowed in public places.
- Small hotels and pensions usually take cash only.
- Phone numbers in Rome can vary from 4-9 digits long.

Deaf Island

There probably are other ways to get to the Island, like passing the bridge of friendly faces who offer us sandals and purses.

If we walk over Ponte Cestio from the Trastevere side-there are only two bridges that permit entry to the island-then directly over the bridge the Piazza Fatebenefratelli or the do well brothers square we'd have accessed the Island. The square is connected to an elder called Ponte Fabricio bridge and one may easily return to the centre by foot from here.

Many a time has been spent looking down on the river and even more time down below by the water. Sometimes coloured bottles caught up in continuous swirling pools. Warm days were spent within the walls of the Sant'Angelo Castle or down the passageway stairs to the island from the Fatebenefratelli square.

A generous bike path runs on both sides of the river and though we never had the chance to run it to see how far it went, we'd admire the joggers that just came and went, as cyclists passed them.

Sitting under the bridge was where outside noises were deafened by the crashing and rushing of the water below. The water speaks and is alive and anyone that studies the water will tell you so too.

Deaf Island is one place in the city that is out of the city because the traffic above is dulled into fainted murmurs and slow motioned silent scenes. Reading in the shade of the sun is what most artists do.

Riverboats pass every now and then and are sometimes filled to the railings-they peddle about quietly and leave the water thrashing behind.

When the sun is hot, sunbathers swarm all along the curved walls of the cement hill. There is one spot closer to the children's hospital where a patch of grass and trees shade parts of the strand that is frequented by lovers of literature.

Shade is also brought in by the bridge's overpass. For when the temperature rises, it rescues sitters as does the breeze of the rushing waters.

Sometimes we'd dose off and dream relaxed by the sounds of deaf Island.

Billy goats would come to graze in the grass that winds around the hospital, with beards hanging, horns curved.

Then the riverboat would come back again and we'd see such a pretty woman with a shoulder cape tied at the chest and a bonnet tied around her face, as she waved. Some of the women's gloves were fingerless. There were men with hats of vivid shapes like up-side down vases and worn widened bands.

On Deaf Island the solitude can cause anything to happen.

Oh, Nerone

On my knees I scrapped through the dirt with my hands and nails. I was walking with some other people, but I stopped there and they continued. I closed my eyes and thanked God to myself that my feet joined ancient Roman sandals. Sifting and rubbing I remembered the sand on that seashore in Cape Cod, only it was white. The exhilaration I felt was overwhelming and then I felt something odd in my fingers, I held it up curiously. It was a medallion, a Roman coin with a deep past. One side shown half of an animal, where the other side part of an olive tree and one corner was worn off. It was small and paper thin. It worked its way to the surface and I'd hoped its energy would tell me a thousand tales.

I had no idea that the ground under the world's greatest arena was so terribly uneven, bad habits of the ancient people who kept building one structure on top of the other. With the Coliseum's high altitude one could breathe simultaneously with Vespasian its inventor, now long gone but his spirit soared all around it. The earth was intriguing now, what else could I find hidden deep under the surface of the ground? There must be millions of objects still condensed within the soil, pasted into tightly-packed mounds of earth that only beg to be released or found by some common person like me. The barbarians sacked the Coliseum 446 years later, but didn't have time to gather coins because they were too busy peeling off the bronze clamps from the stones that secured it.

I wondered off on my own and was no need for a map. I saw Via Labicana from afar running out from the Coliseum and a black iron gate with curved stairs around it. That black entrance was what drew me to into immense greenery. There I found a structure behind bars, such an obscure place for a cave and it had its own entrance. There were timetables on the gate which couldn't read a second later. The cave was changing into a liveable haven. It unfolded in front of my eyes, that ancient villa, how it was meant to be. Just then the iron bars continued to recede, and the cave-like structure kept taking on another forms. Now I was hearing voices, and could pick up movement from the other side. I affixed my eyes on a figure barely visible. Now my imagination began to run wild. I couldn't quite make out what was there, but I spotted a figure not just any man, but one with muscles and bronzed. The man had a body like a Greek God statue.

Suddenly I lit up and the entire world had gone. I wanted a rational explanation for this, but nothing was available. What was happening?

As he turned his head I could see bits of an arm or leg from behind part of the stone palace. He was moving ever so slightly, but I could make out the fact that he was nude, and perhaps someone important. I couldn't care about the how, what or why, but I just knew that I wanted to know him. I had a yearning desire to know him. I wanted him to notice me. It came upon me so fast that if it wasn't real now, I knew I would surrender to insanity. I fought through desire, emotion, longing, curiosity, risk and dementia.

What if I couldn't touch him or caress him? What if he could caress me? Maybe a magic spell was cast, well; thank the wicked witch who chose me as her anchor.

I wanted to call his name, but what was his name? as though I knew for sure that it was he, Emperor Nerone. I was familiar with the location and the story and according to my readings this was the home of the young handsome, psychopathic, but brilliant Emperor. This was the House of Gold, but was I losing my mind? He vanished so long ago, 68 A.D. actually, and he committed suicide in Sempione

The Temple of the Sun" as found in the ancient tour guide (16th century) no longer exists on the hill. (Nero was represented as the sun god Sol, by Pliny who saw a resemblance.)

SETTIMA. 85

lazzetto, e giardino dell'Sforza, col nuouo Conuento di Monache dette Turchine, fondato dalla Prencipessa Borghese;

Parte del Tempio del Sole.

e più oltre la deuotissima, e bellissima Chiesa di S. Martino de'Monti, di S. Matteo in Merulana, ò in Mariana, di santa Croce in Gierusalemme.

Nella Vigna vicina à questa Chiesa è vn Tempio creduto dalla maggior parte degli antiquarij la Basilica di Caio, e di Lucio, edificatagli da Augusto; ma per non esser struttura di Basilica, credo sia il Tempio d'Ercole Callaico fatto da Bruto, e detto il Callutio per corrottione di Callaico, e non di Caio, e Lutio, come scriue il Fuluio. si conferma ciò per esser di mattoni, che di questi testifica Plinio nel capitolo 14. del libro 35. esser stato fabricato detto Tempio, e per essersi ritro-

F 3

square where his ghost to appears regularly. Did he also come to visit his home from time to time? From what I could see he was flesh and blood, not shadowy nor transparent. This in itself intrigued me to the point of no return. Maybe in another life I was someone close to him or maybe I was only capable of seeing him and not communicating with him. He was present in another dimension and untouchable this was enough to make me suffer plenty. If I only knew what I could do and what I couldn't do within the laws of that dimension this would suffice, temporarily.

I sat half sad as if a child. I'd accept meeting with him even with limitations, even to just look at him face to face, even if we never uttered a word.

Balancing along the Iron Gate pathway, I longed to cling to it for a while so to catch glimpses of him through the long-speared metals. The sun was compromising with weak rays that gave me just the right lighting which emphasized the lovable parts.

"Notice me, just this once, notice me. Nerone... ". I cried a whisper.

I realized that I must work with extreme discretion; somehow I shouldn't let him notice me.

But, he did.

Was this supposed to work? His era and mine coming together with the possibility of interacting? Was the spell's recipe to melt the dimension's walls, this night?

He smiled.

I half-smiled and half froze, unsure of what we were doing. He wrapped himself in a crème cloth at the waist and continued to look. That was when I stepped back and lost balance. Behind me, a small indentation waited in the ground and I was forced backwards. I felt myself hit the soil and fathomed to crack my head on the tree trunk below me, Oh Nerone.

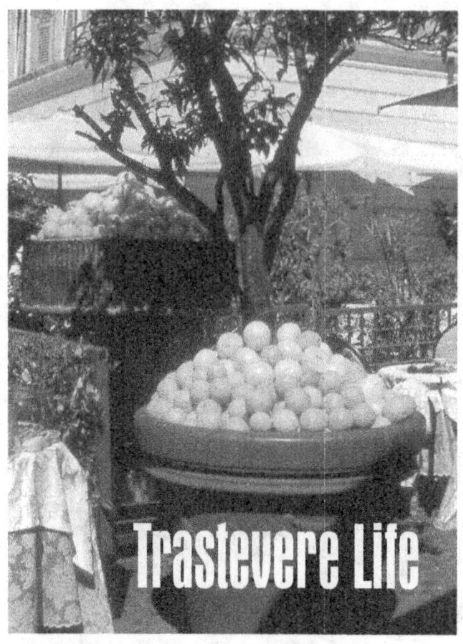

The swells of jasmine and musk seemed to be related to Trastevere; somehow one couldn't get away from it.
It welcomed strangers and the strangest and wafted through bedroom linens then back out the balcony window. It was the only thing that could press itself through the twisted up alleyways they call vicoletti's.

Down into the squares it showed up passing by as Jazz would sound, and clowns would scream out Italian expressions. No one noticed it, only the art of the neighbourhood or the man on the corner with his bagpipes and six puppies yelping by his hip.
A wavy-haired man caught the attention of every passer, with strands blowing North, East, South and back again. They watched his fingers dance and pluck some unknown contraption he designed himself and called the music machine. Poles and cans and strings and hammers and everything found in the junkyard were still good and all fixed together by a wizard of the Trastevere streets.
Notions of musicians from the 21st century annoyed him and he told everyone how true players used to exist and possess talent, and there was nothing of that sort nowadays.
I should tell you that he wore nothing on his feet, no shoes, no flip flops nor boots of any kind. He used them too for strumming and they needed to be bared, kept in their current state.
It wasn't a quiet day, people rushing and looking downwards and backwards, Italian words being shouted here and there, and there was music coming from five street players per via.
The sunny days make the perfume warm up in the air, and the people swarm around the huge fountain in the square.

Magical places do exist in Trastevere, as do haunted churches. La Farmacia S. Maria della Scala was once a quiet magical pharmacy of mysterious potions and miraculous herbals, a place where monks were wizards and formulated sorcerous liquids. It was for men to scurry about in robes and concoct medicinal plants recipes which turned out fine liquors, elixirs and tonics. Figs hung all over drying and jams were made from ripen fruits off the trees and stored in the cupboards. From the front window passers-by could make out shelves with rows of red bottles, liquors of every sort of herb, and bee essences from the looking glass opposite it. The antique monastery was a magic factory laboratory and is now a museum in Piazza S. Maria della Scala 23.

Saint Clement,
the monk and the oldest cartoon

San Clemente was a Roman bishop, the third successor of Peter from '88 to '97 A.D. and author of Lettera ai Corinzi a remarkable historical works. San Clemente died a martyr's death and was in exile in Asia during the reign of Trojan. And sadly, the origins of San Clemente went lost during medieval times.

A basilica discovered in 1859, lay beneath the church itself. San Clemente was built over the previous basilica which caught fire and left many levels. Down the stairs to the lower level, anyone could enter the older basilica.

But the peculiarity about this particular place was that a certain kind of fresco lies hidden within it. It's one that is considered the most antique cartoon in history and even the earliest expression of the tautest vulgarities ever known.

The fresco depicts two servants dragging a pillar being lashed and screamed at: Trahite, fili de le pute! or Tirate, figli di puttana! worse yet, pull, you sons of a bitch. It's an interesting Catholic representation. There is one of the oldest antique documents in the Italian language of vulgarity.

Some time back in the fifties or sixties, an Irish monk met with a guest for a tour of the San Clemente church. His dramatic expressions made this story become a part of my writing. It was his first visit to this church, and where unexpected ironies took place.

The Irish monk greeted him at the entrance and welcomed him in. No doubt it was cold and damp below the church, so the monk emphasized this by saying,

"No, you don't want to go down there. "

And when the guest asked why not, the monk replied,

"Because it's as cold as a witch's tit. "

He now guided his guest to a small room that was furnished with one desk alone, and he paused.

"Ok, wait a minute"he said as stuck his head out the door for a clearing.

"Hurry come over here, he said, you'll need this. "And from one of the drawers he was pulling out a glass bottle then handed it to the man. As he held it up, he saw the colour of blood. Swallowing a knob, he felt the sweat come and to amuse the monk, took the glass and started drinking from it. A fire ripped through his throat and he felt it burn everything inside his body.

The monk explained that it was a whisky made from potato peels.

Under the church a small river or fiumiciattolo ran its course like a miniature waterfall. It also ran between an Imperial Roman house transformed into a mitreo or temple, the same place where the alleyway separated it from the building of Zecca.

The guest admired the rushing flow and he bent his head down to see it beneath the grates.

When he returned from his underground journey, he never felt so cold in his life. But then he remembered the blood coloured whisky was hidden in the desk drawer. And in he went after it, stealing another swig of potato drink. Immediately after, the cold faded and he had needed to open his jacket as he walked out.

The water Rome receives comes from Tivoli and runs through the Roman aqueducts all over the city. In Roman times too much water was flowing into the city so, it was made to flow out of gorgeous fountains that decorated instead of wasting it into the Tevere River.

The Call to Aquaverde

A man made a telephone call to the water services in Rome. He had a problem with the water in his pipes, it didn't reach the house.
The phone rang at the Aquaverde Company.
"Aquaverde, the water stopped running in my house, are you having problems? Your company must check more often to make sure the water is running or not."

When he finished the man on the other end responded carefully;
'Are you finished? He said. Well, I only have one thing to say, Aquaverde has been running for 3,000 years, so why don't you go and check your own pipes."

And when he did, he discovered that Aquaverde was right.

The Romans Saw Them As Gods

The Egyptians saw them as Gods. Rome brought them in because they stole everything from everyone they conquered that was; important, meaningful, beautiful, curing, strong, and genius. As we can see, their concept was quite effective. They were felines or cats and Rome was always full of them.

Romans today though, have the habit of caring for them only to abandon them when summer vacations start sentencing most all of them to an early death.

In 1929, Largo Torre Argentina developed a cat sanctuary inside the ruins of the temple. It has now become a home to several of them including Caesar's place of doom.

There's a set of stairs on the corner, where anyone may slip down and share a bit love.

Dodging the tram tracks in the middle of Piazza Argentina, the Largo Argentina theatre is free for a peek. At showtime elegant wardrobes strut about the theatre as fans are endowed with tux and cocktails. The whole demonstration gives the feeling of relief from the hardships of life and thoughts.

The square has an elegant air and in the farthest corner there's Largo Arenula then Via Arenula which guides you to Trastevere just over the bridge. Leaving this square by hanging a left at the beginning of Via Arenula, you'd be in Jewish pastry heaven.

One time an elegant lady stood on a plank waiting for the bus. She was right in the middle of Largo Arenula where beautiful graffiti works decorated the tram's belly, back and behind. A lonely lamp post looked to her in approval with its hand-crafted curves and iron-works of brilliance. There she stood in dark strappy shoes, clasped with silver buckles. Her calf-length skirt exposed her legs, all chequered and a mixture of whiteness soaked throughout black. It was a particular material born of blushed ruffles. She wore earrings of good quality, swirls which complimented the pattern of her skirt. She must have come from the theatre with hair all twirled up dark and shiny.

The Romans saw them as Gods too.

Soap Inventors

It's Possible, And Anything Is Probable

We didn't have the pleasure to ask a Roman face to face if they invented the soap, but they left us to wonder and with this story to ponder.
The word soap has the same sound as the word is seems to have originated from: Sapone. The word sapone comes from the "Mountain of Sapo", or "Mont Sapo" and is the result from the story that rests behind it.

In the ancient Roman days the Romans used to climb the Mont Sapo hill and sacrifice animals upon an altar. During rainfalls, animal's ashes were washed down the side of the hill and into the Tevere or Tiber River.

This river posed for a basin and was used by Roman women in which to wash their clothes. Here, the animal ashes mixed into the water causing an unknown chemical reaction to take place without their knowing. This coupling produced the chemical"lye. "Lye is the main ingredient in soaps and without lye; "soap" would not exist.
Soon the Roman women began noticing, a bubbling while rubbing the clothes together, and these strange flakes in the water were producing cleansing effects never before seen. Thus, the new mix invented; soap.

Roman and Italian Cuisine

The most delightful part of travelling to Italy is tasting proper Italian cuisine. With use of quality ingredients to make simple recipes and consumed while in season Italian food is also healthy.
The quality of ingredients depends on a variety of important factors: the soil, if the plants grow in a healthy natural environment, the water, how meats and animals are treated and fed, and the climate too.
A good majority of Italian vegetables are grown by families who sell them at stands on the streets. Remember the good ole days? Wholesome organic ingredients can be found everywhere.
Foods in Italy for the most part are still free of preservatives, colorants, processing, and genetically modified meats, fruits and vegetables. If anything modified is sold, Italian law says that they must be labelled.

You'll know the difference with meat that has been raised properly, not given antibiotics, hormones, nor packaged diseased. This is how life was for the Romans, and many places conserve this tradition, serving it like two thousand years ago.

I will introduce you to some ways of eating and preparations used in Italy. It seems to be that simplicity has taken the front seat in their secret to preparing many dishes.

Certain dominate spices wouldn't be added to a recipe with capers, because both have very distinct tastes. Parmigiano or Pecorino is sprinkled over certain types of pasta's only. For example, pasta's made with lentils or legumes, fish or seafood are not consumed with grated cheese. Vegetable-based sauces are never served with cheese, neither is pasta made with olives and capers, a typically Sicilian recipe. All other types of pastas are served with grated cheeses, including pesto, a condiment made with: basil, olive oil, garlic, and pinoli or pine nuts.

Pizza? Romans even though not from Naples, have their own type of thin crusted pizza. You will see plenty of shops calling themselves pizza al taglio or pizza by the slice. There are varieties of pizza slices to choose from like potato or chicory and sausage and the Roman's eat the slices folded in half.

We use white wine when preparing seafood, and red wine in meat sauces or ragu.

PASTA

Gone are the days of dropping semi-hot sauce onto lumpy glued spaghetti. You struggle to smile while eating a dish of partially nude pasta, with the rest drown in sauce, and then you think, maybe there's another way?

Italians drain the pasta then pour it back into the sauce pan with the sauce then mix it well and heat it a bit more. It is then immediately served. Some add a dash of extra-virgin olive oil or pepperoncino oil hot pepper. Pasta is not refrigerated, it's always made fresh. It is not made then dipped into hot water to warm it up. Fresh parsley is added at the end on spaghetti and clams or porcini mushroom pasta and seafood pastas.

SALADS

Salads are simple too. Generally are lightly covered in olive with a dash of white vinegar, fresh lemon or a drop of Balsamic for a sweet taste and salt and that's it. You will not find ready dressings or pre-made mixes in a test tube. In general the base of all Italian salads is olive oil and vinegar with salt, (it can slightly change from person to person, some add fresh garlic in addition or cheese etc). It's important though to use extra virgin (Raw) olive oil and the freshest lemons.

GARLIC VS. ONION

Garlic is used in tiny amounts when making white sauces like porcini mushroom pasta and seafood pastas. Onion is added to meat sauces such as Ragù, or egg and bacon sauce, Carbonara.

WINE

Wine of course is a staple in the Italian diet like bread is. Some types are red, rosè and white, dry, sweet or spumante.

TYPICAL SOUPS

Tortellini in brood - meat filled pasta in chicken broth

Escarole e fagioli - escarole and white bean soup

Pasta e fagioli - mixed pastas with tomato and white beans

Stracciatella alla Romano - chicken broth with spinach, egg, and Parmigiano cheese

Reading an Italian menu can be challenging if it hasn't been translated into English already. Most often you will not see side dishes or vegetables included with the main course, and most of the time the menus are a la carte.

There are tourist menu's menu turistico and fixed menu's menu fisso and I suggest the latter not the former.

In Italy, you will rarely find children's menus. Nuts are often used in sauces, as well as many desserts, so if you allergic, ask if you see: noci, mandarle, or arachidi on the list of ingredients.

APERITIVO-BEFORE DINNER DRINKS

Before dinner appetite stimulants come in orange, red or white and are bubbly, slightly bitter, non-alcoholic or alcoholic.

Fresh Herbs

In Italy, rarely do you walk away from a local grocer that does not hand you or at least ask you if you would like some fresh herbs for cooking. Herbs are so commonly used in Italian kitchens that they give them away and are always available. Oregano (origano) is used in tomato sauces and on pizzas. Fresh basil is widely used on pizza too, also in tomato sauces, and for making pesto. Don't forget bruschetta, and eggplant dishes, caprese salads. Alloro (bay leaf) is used with meats such as liver. Garofano (Cloves) is often put in ragu sauces. And °1 is pepperoncino, hot spicy pepper.

ANTIPASTI-HOR D'URVRES

Prosciutto crudo and melone - raw cured ham with fresh sweet cantaloupe
Bruschetta - grilled Italian bread topped with fresh cherry tomatoes and basil or olive pâté.
Olive ascolone - breaded fried little green olives stuffed with tuna
Verdure fritte - mushroom, pepper, onion, zucchini, artichokes or zucchini flowers are bathed in egg wash floured and then fried.
Verdure alla griglia - grilled vegetables usually eggplant melanzane, red bell peppers and onions.
Olives - olive dolce are sweet fresh unsalted olives
Sun-dried tomatoes
Fresh mozzarella (moz-air rail-lah)
Coppa sotto olio - tiny sausages, capers, hot pepper, mixed olives, fresh parsley and prosciutto or lonza pork shoulder meat marinated in olive oil
Coppa Sott'olio - tiny sausages made from wild boar
Marinated artichokes
Calamari - breaded squid fried in oil
Scamorza - melted smoked cheese
Acciughe - anchovies in oil

JOYS OF THE HOUSE

There are many quaint eateries in Rome that do not have a menu at all, shall call them Joys of the House? Another term for it in Italian is menu fisso. The price is fixed for the entire meal including dessert. They will automatically bring out the courses and you need not ask for anything.

SALT ALERT:

Italians cook with a lot of salt, if you cannot eat salt let them know! ***Senza Sale!*** (sen-sah sahl-lay)

Quick Menu example

Antipasto samples;
- Bruschetta (Broo-skett-tah) with Pomodori tomatoes, funghi mushrooms, prosciutto
- Calamari - fried salted squid

Primo - first, also called primi piatti or first course, is usually pasta or soup
Secondo - second, also called secondi piatti or second course or entrées, is usually meat or fish
- Abbacchio - roasted baby lamb
- Bistecca - steak
- Pollo - chicken dish
- Vitello - veal
- Manzo - beef
- Vitello/vitellone - veal
- Maiale - pork
- Pecora - sheep
- Wild boar - cinghiale
- Orata - gilthead sea bream
- Pesce spada - swordfish

Contorni (cone-tore-knee) side dishes
- Roasted potatoes patate arrosto
- Grilled vegetables verdure alla griglia
- Cicoria spinaci or insalata chicory, spinach or salad

Frutta (froo-tah) - fruit
- Italians like to eat pears, apples, pineapples, and oranges after a meal, and often peel them.

ITALIAN DESSERTS

Dolci (dole-chee) -Sweets
- Tiramisù
- Panna cotta
- Frutti di Bosco con panna - fresh wild berries and cream
- Cantucci e vin santo - hard biscuits to dip in wine

**The best desserts are types fatta in casa, homemade*

Caffè/Espresso (ay-spray-so)

ALCOHOLIC DRINKS

Most Italians are happy with house wines, which are usually sulphate-free, making a difference in the taste.

- Vino
- Grappa
- Amaro

ITALIANS AND SWEETS

Sweets aren't even sweet-Italians and sweets are like mixing oil and water. The majority of sweets are brought home and eaten on special occasions.

Once I thought I'd ask the little old ladies in town for a great dessert recipe. What old Roman lady wouldn't know one? Which of them didn't bake lot of sweets? Nevertheless, I was outwitted! None of the eight ladies, knew a sugared recipe. Strangely they told me, "we don't bake enough sweets to remember". Were they not queen of desserts?

DESSERT AND DESSERT WINES

Zabaione is similar to egg-nog. It is made with 95%, alcohol, Marsala wine, whole milk, sugar, 4 egg yolks, and a vanilla bean.
Tartufo (tar-two-foe) - Ice cream covered in a powdered cocoa made to resemble truffles
Crème brulè
Torta (tore-tah) - cake
Budino (boo-dee-no) - pudding
Frutto di Bosco colla Panna - wild berries with cream
Passito di Malvasia (Lazio) - a great sweet dessert wine

SOME ROMAN DISH TERMS
Coda alla Vaccinara (co-dah ahl-lah vah-chin-nar-rah) Roman oxtail stew
Gnocchi alla Romana (gn-yo-key) Yellow pasta flour cooked in milk with butter, cheese, egg yolks and breadcrumbs
Filetti di Baccalà (fee-let-tea dee bah- cah- lah) Deep fried cod fish with bread crumbs
Fiori di zucca (fee-or-ree dee zoo-cah) Zucchini flowers stuffed with anchovies and mozzarella then deep fried
Trippa alla Romana (treep-pah ahl-lah row-mahn-nah) Roman tripe stew with fresh mint and Pecorino Romano cheese
Saltimbocca alla Romana (saul-teem-bow-kah) Thin veal cutlets with prosciutto ham, sage and Marsala, a sweet Sicilian wine
Panzanella (pahn-zahn-nell-lah) Stale bread smothered with fresh cherry tomatoes, olive oil, balsamic vinegar, minced onion, cucumber, fresh basil and salt. You find them at food festivals, they are typically Roman
Pajata (pie-yah-tah) Specific dish made from calf intestines

Come il cacio sui maccheroni (like cheese on macaroni) - just about perfect

Starci come il cavolo a merenda (to be a cabbage at snack time) - to be utterly out of place

WINE VOCABULARY

Nostrano - local
Esteri - foreign
Vin rosato - rosè
Vino rosso - red
Vino bianco - white
Spumante/frizzante - bubbly wines
Vini da dessert - sweet dessert wines

Puntarelle

the Roman Salad

Puntarelle is a Roman semi-bitter vegetable found during the sunrise of December until spring on streets with grocer's stands. Unstripped bundles are everywhere and pre-washed puntarelle are sold in plastic bags for a little extra. They grow in thick bunches with a substantial bottom that holds dark green leaf-like growths protruding from the stark white parts.

If buying them in their natural state, you must thinly slice them lengthwise and place them into cold water. The cold water will cause them to curl, but not until they are soaked for hours - best overnight. These curls are eaten raw as a salad and dressed in extra virgin olive oil, white vinegar, minced anchovies and garlic. You may substitute the vinegar for lemon if you prefer.

Recipe:
1 head of puntarelle
5-8 anchovy fillets
2 cloves of garlic
Extra virgin olive oil
Lemon juice of 1/2 lemon
Salt
Fresh ground pepper

Blend all ingredients in a blender or mash with a mortar and pestle, and then add the oil and lemon.
Pour this onto the puntarelle and let it stand for 10-15 minutes to allow the flavours to come to life.

The Roman World Recipe Book

Romans have their own dialect that most Italians can't even understand. It's just like most of Italy, but here are some of the differences between "Italian" and "Roman" in a cooking sense let's take a look:

ENGLISH	ITALIAN	ROMAN
Cocoa	Cacao	Cacavo!
Sweets	Dolci	Dorci!
Parsley	Prezzemolo	Erbetta!
Beans	Fagioli	Facioli!
Eat	Mangiare	Magnà!
Cookie, doughnut, cake	Ciambella	Ciammella!
Zucchini	Zucchina	Cuccomo!
Date	Dattero	Dattolo!
Macaroni	Maccheroni	Maccaroni!
Oil	Olio	Ojo!
Honey	Miele	Mèle!
Oregano	Origano	Regolo!
Mozzarella	Mozzarella	Provatura!
Sausage	Salsiccia	Sarziccia!
Rosemary	Rosmarino	Trosmarino!
Celery	Sedano	Sellero!

Since the most important aspect of Rome or of Italy in general is eating and enjoying food, I thought this section should be pronounced! A lot of these recipes I found from old Roman recipe books and from the Roman people themselves.

Anti-Pasti Apettizers

CROSTINI ALLA PONTICIANA

8 slices of homemade or crusty bread
30g butter
150g Mozzarella
100g prosciutto
150g mushrooms
Salt and pepper

Fry the bread slices in butter, salt, pepper, cover with a slice of mozzarella, then prosciutto ham, and the mushroom slices Place in oven for a few minutes.. and eat immediately.

PANZANELLA

Casereccio bread from Genzano in the Castelli Romani or the closet to Italian bread you can find
4 ripe round tomatoes
1-2 tbsp white wine vinegar
Extra-virgin olive oil
Fresh basil
Salt

Wet the bread slices in water *(if your bread is already very soft and you cannot find good Italian bread, just skim them in water quickly).
Cut tomatoes in thick slices place on bread. Add salt and drops of vinegar. Add enough olive oil and one fresh basil leaf.

PIZZA ALLA ROMANA-ROMAN-STYLE PIZZA

Bread dough
500g peeled tomatoes
300g Mozzarella cheese
80g Pecorino Romano cheese
2-3 salted anchovies
1-2 tbsp fresh diced basil
Extra-Virgin olive oil
Salt and pepper

Place the bread dough on a baking sheet and unite with some olive oil.
Roll out with hands.
Add cut up tomatoes without seeds, anchovies, mozzarella, basil and pecorino, salt and pepper.
Spray on more olive oil.
Place in oven for 20-25 minutes!

SUPPLI ALLA ROMANA-FRIED RICE BALLS

500g rice
200g chicken livers
20g butter
3 eggs
50g grated Parmigiano
Dash cinnamon
Beef broth
Salt
200g beef from ragù sauce
Bread crumbs
1-2 Lemon rinds, grated

Cook rice in beef broth until all the broth is absorbed. Add chicken livers and beef from a ragù sauce, egg yolks and Parmigiano cheese.
Add a dash of cinnamon and lemon rind.
Work in well.
Now form the supplì with the cooked rice by shaping it into an oval.
Pass in egg wash then in the bread crumbs. Fry in boiling oil.

Typical Pastas

PASTA BUCATINI ALLA AMATRICIANA

A tomato sauce flavored with pancetta (Italian bacon), onion, white wine, salt and pepper and Pecorino Romano cheese.

PASTA ALLA GRIGLIA

A Roman pasta dish flavored with pancetta, onion, white wine, salt and pepper, and Pecorino Romano cheese.

PASTA ALL'ARRABBIATA
(means hot and mad)

A tomato sauce with a base of olive oil and hot peppers, served with penne pasta.

PASTA ALLA CARBONARA

A sauce made with onion, pancetta and raw egg, finished off with a pecorino Romano cheese, salt and pepper.

FETTUCCINE CON I FUNGHI PORCINI

A light pasta made with porcini mushrooms, white wine, garlic, fresh parsley and olive oil.

Essere una pasta (batter) d'uomo
TO BE GENTLE AND KIND

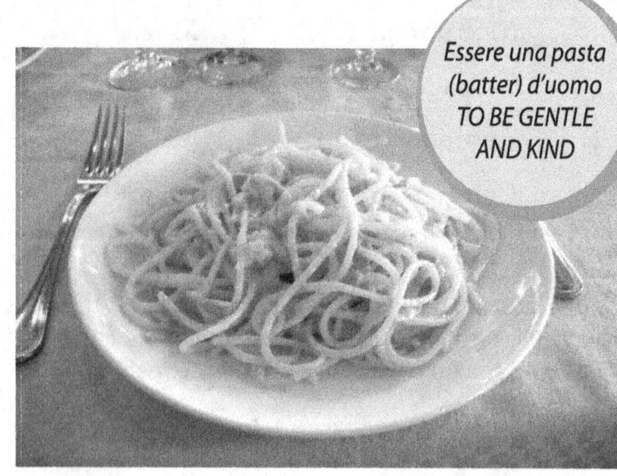

Pasta & Broth

BEEF OR CHICKEN BROTH

150g flour
50g semolina
3 eggs
Nutmeg
80g Pecorino Romano cheese

Work together the flour, semolina, eggs, and a dash of nutmeg until solid.
Flour your surface.
Cut up into small pieces, and let sit to dry.
Boil your broth.
Add the pasta let boil for about 15-20 minutes on medium heat.
Serve with Pecorino cheese.

PASTA & POTATOES

4-5 potatoes
Spoonful lard or animal fat
50g pork
1 medium onion
1 parsley stalk
Salt and pepper
Tubular pasta's
Pecorino Romano cheese

In terracotta baking dish, sauté the pork with a little fat, onion and parsley.
Add the water and potatoes, salt and pepper.
When the potatoes are done, add additional water to cook the pasta.
Serve with Pecorino Romano.

MACCHERONI CON LA RICOTTA-MACARONI WITH RICOTTA

400g maccheroni
300g fresh ricotta
400g peeled tomatoes
1 spoonful of fresh basil
1 clove garlic
Extra-virgin olive oil
Salt and pepper
60g Parmigiano cheese

In a saucepan cooking on medium heat sauté diced garlic and tomatoes in oil, and then add your basil, salt and pepper. When the sauce reduces add it the pasta, and toss.
Mix in the ricotta, 2 spoonfuls of hot water, and Parmigiano cheese.

POLENTA

It's quite popular in the Castelli Romani at festivals

400g large grain corn flour
120g fat
Salt

In a copper pot (preferably) boil fat in 1-2l of salted water. Sprinkle on the corn flour slowly and mix thoroughly with a wooden spoon. Let cook for 50 minutes stirring constantly. When it parts from the sides, turn off flame and spread it out on the counter to let it cool. Serve with hot tomato sauce made with pork or sausage or serve plain with fresh extra-virgin olive oil, Parmigiano cheese, salt and pepper.

PORK SAUCE FOR POLENTA

300g corn flour
800g pork thigh
1 cup of beef broth
100g fat from prosciutto
1/2 onion
A slice of carrot and celery
Olive oil
800g tomato sauce or purée
7 peppercorns
1 clove
10g cumin seed
80g Pecorino Romano cheese
Salt and pepper

Press the pork pieces into flour and let it sauté in oil
Add the prosciutto fat, onion, carrot and celery
Add in the spices; dash of marjoram, black peppercorns, cloves and cumin. Now add the broth and cook until the meat is tender. Next, add in the tomato purée, and salt.
Top polenta with sauce and serve meat as a second.

BUCATINI ALL'AMATRICIANA

400g bucatini pasta
100g guanciale affumicato smoked pig's cheek
40g cubed pancetta Italian bacon
6 ripe tomatoes
1 onion
Pecorino Romano cheese
White wine
Olive oil
Hot pepper, diced
Salt and pepper

In a saucepan sauté the onion and hot pepper in olive oil. Add the guanciale and the pancetta. Add the wine, then the tomatoes, salt and pepper. Mix well with a wooden spoon and cover. Cook for 30 minutes. Toss with pasta and serve hot with Rosatello Cerveteri wine.

PENNETTE ALL'ARRABBIATA

400g penne pasta
500g tomatoes
Garlic
Parsley
Hot pepper, diced

Dice the garlic and slowly sauté in oil. Add an abundance of hot pepper Add in the tomatoes and cook for 30 minutes. Add salt and pour in the pasta with the sauce and toss. Serve with fresh parsley.

LA CARBONARA

What is it? the Carbonara dish was easy to create, heavy enough, and contained protein and plenty of carbohydrates. It didn't cost much to make either. It was loaded with black pepper, as a modern metaphor would explain. The specks of coal would inevitably flake off into plates of pasta and it ended up resembling black coal. Where did La Carbonara recipe come from? Some say Carbonara is a town, a mining village. Some say the dish was invented by the secret society 'Carbonari.' Yet another story says this dish dates back only to 1945, when American soldiers came to Rome at the end of WWII. In the Roman trattorie they kept asking for eggs with bacon and noodles typical Chinese spaghetti that was in fashion in America. The Roman chefs during that time satisfied the soldiers by serving them pig cheeks with fried eggs and a plate of plain spaghetti which ended up tasting bland. Transforming this tasteless dish into something tasty, the American soldiers mixed everything together and unknowingly created la Carbonara.

There seems to be many variations of this pasta dish, some with cream, wine, or parsley and some with or without butter or garlic. Some use Pecorino Romano cheese, and some Parmigiano. I personally prefer the onion over the garlic and the Parmigiano over the Pecorino, but you can make it however you choose. Here is one recipe to try.

RIGATONI/SPAGHETTI ALLA CARBONARA

400g spaghetti or rigatoni
80g smoked pancetta (Italian bacon)
3 eggs
1/2 onion
2 tsp Pecorino Romano cheese
Salt and lots of pepper
30g butter
Olive oil
1-2 cups of white wine (optional add in with bacon)
Fresh cream (optional)

Cut up the pancetta and onion and let it sauté with a little olive oil and butter. Make a mixture of the following; two egg yolks, Pecorino, salt and pepper. Drain the butter from the bacon. Add the cream to the bacon and the egg mixture. Strain pasta and blend in with mixture while still hot. I love it with lots of pepper and Bianco di Frascati white wine.

GNOCCHI ALLA ROMANA-SEMOLINA DUMPLINGS BAKED WITH BUTTER AND CHEESE

Milk
Semolina flour
80g flour
2 egg yolks
Salt
Bread crumbs
Parmigiano cheese

Pre-heat the oven to 200°C and heat up some milk in a saucepan. When it's ready to boil drop in the pasta flour semolina, and mix vigorously. Continue to cook it constantly stirring on low heat for about 10 minutes. When it forms a polenta, a dense consistency, remove it from the heat. Now add 80g of butter, salt, and two egg yolks, and half of the breadcrumbs. Mixing vigorously, taste to make sure the amount of salt is to your desire. Place the dough on a flat surface that is dampened with water. With the help of a metal spatula, (that is dampened) roll out the dough out to about 1cm high creating a form that is about 4-7 cm in width. Cut the gnocchi and place into a buttered baking dish of 30cm. Sprinkle with the rest of the breadcrumbs and pieces of butter and grated Parmigiano cheese. Bake until the gnocchi are warmed up and the cheese adheres. At this point turn off the oven and turn on the broiler, and broil for two minutes or until they are golden.

PASTA ALLA CHECCA

400g farfalle pasta
200g Mozzarella
100g sweet Roman Caciotta (a fresh semi-soft mild cheese)
4 ripe tomatoes
Basil
Olive oil
Salt and pepper

Chop the caciotta, tomatoes and mozzarella into cubes. Cook.
Prepare a pot to boil the pasta. In a dish place the mozzarella, Ccaciotta, tomatoes, fresh basil, olive oil, salt and pepper. When the pasta is al dente drain it quickly.
Mix the pasta together with all other ingredients and serve with:
Bianco Frizzantino di Velletri white wine.

GNOCCHI DI PATATE CON PUNTE DI MAIALE-
POTATO DUMPLINGS WITH PORK SAUCE

400g potatoes
250g flour
1 egg
Salt
1/2 kilo pork
4 tbsp of tomato sauce
1/2 onion
1-2 red hot peppers
White wine
Oil

Dumplings:
1. Immerge potatoes into cold water in a pot and let them cook with the skins on.
Peel them while still hot and then set aside. Add flour, egg and a dash of salt, working together with the hands. Pull now into a long thin cylinder shape.
Cut into tocchetti 8cm and lightly dust with flour. Carve a hole in each centre with thumb.

Sauce:
1. Place pork points into a pan with a drop of oil, and sliced onion. Sauté until lightly browned. Add a little white wine. As soon as it reduces, add the tomato, hot pepper, and dash of salt. Cook over low heat for 1 hour, stirring occasionally.
2. Add the gnocchi to boiling water, and cook until soft (few minutes) then strain.
Mix well with sauce and serve.

Vegetables

FUNGHI BRODETTATI-
PORCINI MUSHROOMS WITH BROTH

800g porcini mushrooms
130g butter
1 tbsp flour
1 tbsp of beef stock
2 egg yolks
1 lemon
1 tbsp of fresh chopped parsley
1/2 cup dry white wine
Toasted bread
Salt and pepper

Clean the porcini well, dry and slice. In a saucepan place 50g of butter, and when it's well heated, add the porcini mushrooms. Add salt and pepper and cook over high heat. As soon as the liquid thickens add a little flour and wine. Mix well.
After the wine evaporates, add in one cup of hot water and beef stock. Let cook it for 30 minutes. When it becomes dense take it off the heat and add in the lemon juice and 2 egg yolks, parsley and a little butter. Mix, then cover and let cook for another 5 minutes. Serve with toasted bread fried in butter.

FAGIOLI ALLA ROMANA-
BEANS ALLA ROMANA

400g white beans, pre-soaked overnight
1 onion
3 salted anchovies
30g butter
1 tsp of extra-virgin olive oil
Nutmeg
Salt and pepper

Let beans lightly boil in salted water. When tender place in casserole dish. In a bowl place the anchovy fillets, spoonful of olive oil and some of the water left from the beans. Now fry the onion in butter and add pepper and a dash of nutmeg. Combine the anchovy, onion, and beans. Now let the liquid evaporate over a low heat, stirring occasionally.
Serve hot.

BROCCOLI STRASCINATI-
BROCCOLI RABE

2.2 lb broccoletti broccoli rabe
70g cooking fat
100g prosciutto crudo
2 cloves garlic
Salt and pepper

Clean broccoli in salted water. In frying pan, let the garlic sauté with the fat, then adding the broccoli. Mix with wooden spoon. Add salt and pepper.
Always squashing them with the wooden spoon. Now add the prosciutto ham, cut up in strips. Let add flavour then serve right away.

CARCIOFI ALLA ROMANA-
ASPARAGUS ALLA ROMANA

4 large artichokes
1 lemon
Parsley
Olive oil
Garlic
Mentucci Romana mint
Salt and pepper

Clean the artichokes well, cut off the hard parts and shave the stalks (cutting about 5cm from the head). Peel the petals three full times around advice from a Roman woman. Smash top of head on a cutting board to open. Stuff with: parsley, garlic, fresh mint, oil, salt and pepper. Place them in a tall baking pan standing them up closely together. Drizzle a spoonful of olive oil over them and fill with one inch of water, cover. Bake in the oven one hour at 160°C.

CICORIA STRASCINATA-
WILD CHICORY

1kg (2.2 lb) Chicory selvatica wild
Garlic
Salt and pepper
Olive oil

Wash the chicory well, drain and add salt. Place in a pan with garlic and olive oil and mix. Add pepper or hot pepper and sauté 5 minutes. Serve hot.

Second course recipes

PORCHETTA ALLA ROMANA-
PORK THE ROMAN WAY

2 1/2 lb pork
A branch of sage
1/4 tsp fennel seeds
Fresh mint
4 tbsp extra-virgin olive oil
1/2 cup vinegar
1 cup dry of white wine
1 clove
Salt and pepper

In a baking pan add; oil, garlic, salt and pepper, mint, white wine and fennel seeds. Sauté then add pieces of pork and let cook a few hours. Every now and baste it with hot boiling water.

Romans and Salt

The Italians live in connection with Sale Grosso. They swore that this coarse salt had a different flavour than refined salt. The ancient Romans used to eat coarse salt garnished in herbs and olive oil, as their diets were lacking in sodium.

ABBACCHIO ALLA
CACCIATORA

2.2 lb/1kg young lamb
Cooking fat or olive oil
2 cloves garlic
1 rosemary branch
2 sage leaves
Salt and pepper
1/2 tbsp flour
2-3 salted anchovies

Cut the lamb into pieces and rinse well. Let them brown in the cooking fat on high heat, adding salt, pepper, garlic, sage, rosemary, vinegar and 1/2 cup of water. Mix well and let it cook covered on low heat for 45 minutes. Squash the anchovies with a fork and add a little of the meat broth to it, then combine it with the meat. Finish cooking. Serve with Rosso Acilia red wine.

TRIPPA ALLA ROMANA
(Calves intestines)

About trippa: the story says that trippa was eaten after the war as every part of the animal was consumed on the account that food was not only scarce, but also expensive. So food scraps formed new recipes in the Roman household.

Diced veal
1kg (2.2 lb) tripe
1celery stalk
1 carrot
1onion
1 cup red wine
Fresh mint
2-3 tbsp tomato sauce made with prosciutto
Pecorino Romano cheese, grated
Extra-virgin olive oil
Salt and pepper

Cut the tripe into strips. Rinse them in fresh water and place in a casserole dish with a little salted water.
Prepare a ragù sauce:
A sauce you can make with veal, pork, bacon finely diced, 1 glass of red wine, 2-3 tbsp of tomato sauce, salt and pepper.
Sauté in oil; tripe stripes, celery, and diced carrot for a few minutes. Add ragù sauce, salt and pepper. Cook 30 minutes covered on low heat.
Serve hot, adding fresh mint and the Pecorino Romano cheese. Serve with Zagarolo wine.

POLENTA DI FARRO DI TARTUFO-
SPELT WITH TARTUFO CREME

200g spelt
80g black tartufo
50g sausage
50g olive oil
50gr butter
1l broth
Celery stalk
Hot pepper

Cook spelt in 1liter of broth for 45 minutes and add one celery stalk.
Truffle/tartufo crème:
Rinse truffles in clean water and grind or dice. Combine with butter melted in a double boiler and oil. Add sausage, salt and hot pepper. Serve with spelt.

SALTIMBOCCA ALLA ROMANA

8 veal fillets
8 sage leaves
4 slices raw prosciutto (not too thin)
50g butter
1/2 cup dry white wine
Salt

Lay out the veal and place a sage leave and slice of Proscuitto in each centre. Roll and spear with a toothpick to hold into place. Sauté butter in large pot. Place in saltimbocca and allow them to brown on both sides on high heat. Sprinkle with salt and white wine. Allow to cook for 5 minutes.

CROCCHETTE DI SPINACI ALLA ROMANA-
ROMAN SPINACH CROCHETTES

2 lb spinach
200g fresh ricotta made with goat's milk whenever possible
100g grated Parmigiano cheese
2 eggs
Nutmeg
50g butter
Salt
Flour
Extra-virgin olive oil

Wash the spinach well and drain. Melt butter in a pan and sauté spinach for a few minutes. In a bowl mix the ricotta, spinach, Parmigiano, dash of nutmeg and salt. Make croquettes with the mixture. Coat them with flour, and beaten egg mixture (eggs and a dash of salt). Fry in boiling oil. Serve hot.

Roman desserts

FRAPPE- FRIED DOUGH BISCUITS

200g flour
50g butter
2 eggs
100g sugar
Salt
150g fat strutto
100g powdered sugar zucchero di velo

Mix together: flour, 1 egg, 1 yolk, sugar and a dash of salt. Roll out the dough very thinly and cut into wide strips. Deep fry them in the fat, drain, and cover in powdered sugar.

TRADITIONAL PANGIALLO

300g yellow raisins
200g almonds
200g walnuts
200g hazelnuts
100g pinoli nuts
100g flour
200g honey
150g cocoa
50g grated chocolate

Dice up all ingredients. Heat honey over a low flame. Place all ingredients into a plastic basin and mix with wooden spoon until it forms a thick consistence. Form small bread shapes and place in the oven cooking it for 30 minutes.

*This recipe was given to me by the old Roman ladies in Rocca Priora around Christmas time. This dessert is made for the holidays and originally from the hills of Rome. P. S. It is delicious

MARITOZZI CON LA PANNA-MARITOZZI WITH CREAM

600g flour
200g raisins
100g sugar
100g pinoli pine nuts
100g candied fruits cedro candito
100g bread dough
3/4 cup olive oil
4 eggs
Salt

Combine into a bread dough: 200g flour, 2 eggs, and a dash of salt. Leave it in a warm place to stand for 8 hours. When it's nice and risen, add in 400g of flour, 2 eggs, and 80g of oil, sugar, a dash of salt and warm water. Work the dough not allowing it to become excessively hard. Lightly butter a wooden plate or baking dish. Shape the dough into ovals and place them far enough apart so they don't touch. Add: pinoli, raisins, and the candied orange into each oval. Let sit for another 6 hours.

After that, cook in the oven on high heat. Take out of oven, and paint on sugar (dissolved in water) with vanilla and split open and add fresh lightly sweetened cream or chocolate cream.

Quick recipe

TIRAMISÙ
(tira-pick mi-me su-up)

A sponge cake soaked in espresso
400g lady fingers
4 eggs
100 g sugar
350g mascarpone cheese
6 espresso cups of espresso
Bitter cocoa

Separate the yolks from the egg whites. Add the sugar and beat until thick. Add your mascarpone. Add the eggs whites and delicately fold in. In a deep tray or baking dish, make one layer of lady fingers. Brush on sugared espresso, and spread on one layer of the prepared cream. Layer until ingredients are used up and top with sifted cocoa.

OMLETTE ITALIANO

Eggs
Salt and pepper
Zucchini
Olive oil to cook

No Milk
No Butter
That may be the French recipe...?

SIMPLE PASTA DOUGH

150g whole wheat flour
150g white flour
3 eggs
Dash of salt

Work in ingredients; knead with flour and roll several times until it obtains the same thickness all over. Cut to desired shapes making sure they are all the same size.

Sugar cubes are soaked in lemon peel, sage or mint leaves with alcohol and taken after dinner for digestion purposes

A SIMPLE PIZZA DOUGH
250g white flour
250g wheat flour
1 egg
1 tbsp olive oil
Dash of salt
20g yeast dissolved in 1/8 cup of warm water
Sift flour forming a mountain in a bowl. Add salt, egg, and oil.
Add in the yeast. If need be, add more warm water.
Let the consistency become elastic and keep kneading. After, place it in a bowl and sprinkle with flour then cover it with damp cloth. Let stand for 1 hour. Knead it again and let it sit one half hour more. Roll dough out nice and thin and top with oil or anything you choose. Set the oven to the maximum temperature and cook until crispy.

Liquor recipes

GRAPPA-RHUBARB AND CLOVE
1l grappa
2 rhubarb roots
1/2 lemon zest
3 clove buds
Cinnamon
3 tbsp sugar
Clean the rhubarb roots well and smash them in a mortal with a pestle.
Place them in a tightly closed container and cover them in sugar.
Leave for two days letting them marinate.
Now add the clove buds, a piece of cinnamon bark, a lemon peel, and the grappa. Leave to infuse in a dark cool place like the basement for 3 weeks and shake often
Filter and let sit another 3 months before drinking.

GRAPPA- WILD ROSE
1l of dry grappa
A handful of rose hip fruits
Clean the fruits of the skins and recover and place the pulp and smash into the grappa. Place in a container with a tight closure. Leave to soak for 3 weeks in a warm place shaking it every once in a while. Filter and place in bottles for 3 months before tasting. It is a light liver tonic.

GRAPPA-DIGESTIVE
2l dry grappa
40g sugar
4 tbsp honey
10 juniper berries
10g dried gentian root
1 branch of absinth (wormwood)
1 branch of rue
5 wild mint leaves
5g cinnamon bark
After you have accurately cleaned the berries, leaves and roots, place them into a container to infuse with the grappa, honey, and cinnamon bark.
Close the container tightly, and put aside for at least 40 days, then filter and bottle.

In the 1800's absinth became popular in France. It was the typical drink of forefront troops.

LIMONCELLO ANTICO-ANTIQUE LEMON LIQUOR
10 lemons
2 cups of 95°alcohol
350g sugar
1 1/2 cups of purified water
Wash the lemons, dry and peel them. Place the peels in an air-tight jar, pour in the alcohol and close. Leave to infuse for one week. After this time, filter the infusion. Boil the sugar and water for 5 minutes the let it cool. Mix the lemon liquor with the sugar syrup and place it in a closed glass jar to rest for another week. Filter it once again then pour into bottles and place aside for 40 days.

CENTERBE-ITALIAN HERB LIQUOR
1liter grappa (a type of brandy)
500g sugar
10 pine needles
20 juniper berries
1 lemon zest
1 orange zest
China root
Rhubarb root
Gentian root
5 clove buds
Camomile
1 arnica flower
1 tiny slice of celery
Add one branch of any of the following herbs;
Sage, basil, parsley, rosemary, bay leaf, mint, melissa, or wild fennel
Along with the zest of the lemon and orange, place the herbs in alcohol to infuse for 35 days. After the 35 days filter. Boil sugar in 1liter of water, then filter and place in a sealed bottle for one month.

This is only one of the infinite recipes for preparing Centerbe, antique traditional liquor. Every house made their own original flavours that were kept a secret.

HARD TO FIND ITEMS
Poppy seed filling, brown sugar, molasses, cranberries, barley, graham crackers, relish, peanut butter, cans of baking powder and maple syrup. I've seen only in large grocery stores or in natural food shops.

Cooking Conversion charts

15 g	1/2 oz
30 g	1 oz
50 g	1/12 oz
60 g	2 oz
90 g	3 oz
100 g	3 1/2 oz
125 g	4 oz
150 g	5 oz
185 g	6 oz
200 g	7 oz
250 g	8 oz
280 g	9 oz
300 g	10 oz
500 g	16 oz
1 kg	32 oz

1 ml	1/5 tsp
5 ml	1 tsp
15 ml	1 tbsp
30 ml	1/8 cup
60 ml	1/4 cup
80 ml	1/3 cup
125 ml	1/2 cup
150 ml	2/3 cup
175 ml	3/4 cup
250 ml	1 cup
375 ml	1 1/2 cups
500 ml	2 cups
450 g	1 lb
1 kg	2, 2 lb

COOKING MEASUREMENTS	
Temperatures in degrees	
Fahrenheit (°F)	Celsius (°C)
32	0
212	100
250	120
275	140
300	150
325	160
350	180
375	190
400	200
425	220
450	230
475	240
500	260

Spelt

"Farro"or spelt is a cereal that's only recently been rediscovered dating back to thousands of years. Not having bread, the ancient Romans used it a great deal, as it was very resistant to decay and easier to store. In a place called Licenza, pasta made with spelt can be found everywhere. There is even a sagra delle sagne e farro, homemade pasta made with spelt flour and dressed with a simple peperoncino (hot pepper) sauce.

Cadere dalla padella nella brace = "to fall from the pan into the cinders" = to worsen one's own situation

---

Nuts for Nuts

Italy is the land for nuts, nuts of every type, size and shape.

The shells are unique and the nuts themselves are divine if they are found in the wild. Autumn is gorgeous and just the right time for nut harvesting. If you are nuts for nuts, welcome to the nut kingdom of Rome.

Nuts are abundant in the Castelli Romani towns, as they surround the area predominately chestnuts. If you must pay for them at the local market, you must be nuts yourself.

I will give you an example. Just walking down the lane where I reside I can find; hazelnuts, chestnuts, walnuts and pine nuts. During a good wind, walnuts start to bounce off my terrace, yet not enough to keep me through the winter and chestnuts are everywhere. I must fill a large basket in a few days for my winter supply, every season. The squirrels do the same. These trees line the lane by the hospital, fill the forests and are in my neighbour's backyard.

As I pick them up from under the leaves in early October, I can see them bounce off the pavement; I felt them bounce off my head. You must watch out for the spiky pods they come disguised in, it reminds one of a porcupine, and a cactus to the touch. It's enough to rub them under your shoes to pop out the tender dwellers. If they've popped out themselves, you may need to stoop down in the leaves or woods with garden gloves to gather them.

I wait for this time of the year, for it is my favourite. Olives too are ripe during this time as are; grapes, figs and other thoughts of Mother Nature.

Walnuts are easier to gather than the prickly pods of the chestnuts. They grow in green sacks that turn black after a while. You need to turn the grass over to find them, if they're not sitting in front of you. If they are too light-weight, this usually indicates that they are dried up inside. But after a while one becomes an expert and don't even need to open them up to check them.

Pine nuts are fun and can be worth your while because they cost an arm and a leg. These are easy to find since they are housed inside the robust pinecone. You may gather the ones already fallen to the ground--yet are difficult to find because the shells are dusted in a black coating and they are tiny. You may pry them out of their cones or even shake them out, with a little luck.

Nevertheless, nuts are full of vitamin E, protein, and mono-unsaturated fats. They are great in desserts and in sauces.

Your Pasta Glossary

LONG PASTA'S

Bavette thinner than fettuccine
Bucatini long thick hollow strands
Cappellini angel hair
Filini slightly curved thin tubes
Fresine thinner but similar to fettuccine
Lasagne long wide flat pasta
Linguine long thin flat pasta
Pappardelle long wide flat egg pasta
Spaghettini thin spaghetti
Spaghetti long skinny round pasta
Spaghettoni thick spaghetti
Trenette long flat thin pasta (half width of fettuccine)

SMALL PASTA'S

Anellini small rings
Ave Maria similar to short ditalini rings
Chifferini rigati fat elbows
Campanelle look like tiny waffle cones
Ditalini Rigati tiny lined tubes
Farfalle rotonde rounded butterfly shapes
Occhi di Pernice tiny tubes Occhini
Orecchiette ear-shaped
Orzo tiny almonds
Pepe bucato (hollowed pepper) tiny cans
Perline tiny tiny shells
Piombi little balls
Quadrucci similar shape to gnocchi small square
Risone little rice shaped pastas
Ruote small wheels
Semi di melone melon seeds
Stelline small stars

CUT PASTA'S

Cavatappi corkscrews
Gemelli twists
Gramigna skinny curly worms
Lumaconi giganti bent short large tubes
Maccheroni long skinny tubulare pasta like bucatini's
Mafalde flat medium length pastas
Penne cut tubes
Penne rigate larger penne with lines
Rocchetti open hollow segments
Sigarette ziti slightly curved smooth tubes

SHORT PASTA'S

Chifferi rigati conchiglie shells
Denti d'elefante elephants teeth
Dischi volanti look like snail shells
Eliche tightly wound spirals
Fusilli loose spirals
Gnocchi potato and flour drops
Gomiti elbows
Mezzi cocci small shells
Sedanini short tubes
Tortiglioni medium smooth tubes

OTHER PASTA'S

Caramelle classic candies shaped pasta's stuffed
Farfalle butterflies
Gramigna little wormlike
Racchette tennis rackets

STUFFED PASTA'S

Panzarotto half moon stuffed pasta's
Mezzelune half moons stuffed
Tortellino round stuffed pasta with hole in middle
Ravioli square stuffed pastas
Ravioloni larger square stuffed pastas
Agnolotti rectangular stuffed pasta

PASTA DISHES
Pasta al' forno-baked pasta
Pasta all'uovo-egg pasta
Pasta ripiena-stuffed pasta

It's possible to colour pasta to obtain different tastes, enrich it, or to add nutritional value. You can use the pulp or juices from vegetables like; tomato, spinach, artichokes, borragine, squash, or carrots. You can also use ingredients other then vegetables like; grated cheese, spices, saffron, and even cocoa. You may even tint the pasta, blue for example with a blue liqueur, in this case use only the whites of the eggs, as yolks would alter the final colour you're looking to obtain. With these pastas, be as simple as possible with sauces, such as a light butter and Parmigiano cheese.

The Thomas Jefferson pasta story
It is said that Thomas Jefferson the third president of the United States 1801-1809, was the smuggling president. He brought pastasciutta bagged dried pasta's, mascarpone cheese, and gorgonzola back to his country hidden in a military bisaccia. He was a cultured individual indeed, and knew the exact point of maturation of grains, the level of humidity needed for hay, and didn't ignore the secrets for good fabrication and conservation of cheeses. He had to create havoc to transport a big press or mixer to create pasta. Most probably if it wasn't for Jefferson and all of his intelligent smugglings, the pasta wouldn't have arrived in the U.S. till centuries later.

Pasta producers in the Lazio region

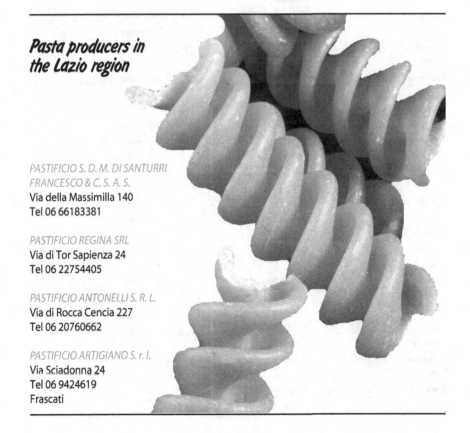

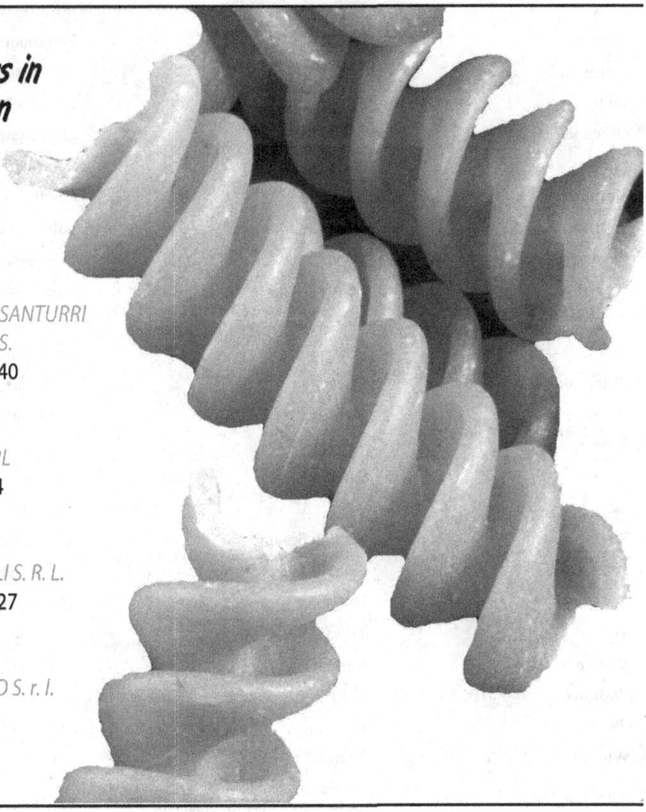

PASTIFICIO S. D. M. DI SANTURRI FRANCESCO & C. S. A. S.
Via della Massimilla 140
Tel 06 66183381

PASTIFICIO REGINA SRL
Via di Tor Sapienza 24
Tel 06 22754405

PASTIFICIO ANTONELLI S. R. L.
Via di Rocca Cencia 227
Tel 06 20760662

PASTIFICIO ARTIGIANO S. r. l.
Via Sciadonna 24
Tel 06 9424619
Frascati

NUTS, SPICES AND GRAINS		
Bay Leaf	Alloro	ah-lore-row
Almonds	Mandorle	mahn-door- lay
Aniseed	Anice	ahn-knee-chay
Basil	Basilico	bah-sill-lee-coh
Brazil nut	Noce del Brasile	no-chay dell bra-seàl-lay
Bran	Crusca	crew-skah
Buckwheat	Grano Saraceno	grahn-no sar-rah-chain-no
Bulgar Wheat	Bulgar	bool-ghar
Chesnuts	Castagne	cah-stahn-yeah
Cinnamon	Cannella	cahn-nell-lah
Cashew nut	Noce di acagiu'	no-chay dee ah-cah-jew
Cocoa	Cacao	cah-cow
Coconut	Cocco	coh-coh
Dill	Aneto	ah-nate-toe
Farro	Spelt	fah-row
Fennel	Finocchio	feen-no-key-oh
Garlic	Aglio	ahl-yo
Ginger	Zenzero	zane-zer-row
Hazelnuts	Nocciole	no-cho-lay
Kamut	Kamut	kah-moot
Marjoram	Maiorana	my-oh-rahn-nah
Millet	Miglio	me-lee-oh
Oregano	Origano	oh-ree-gahn-no
Mint	Menta	main-tah
Nutmeg	Noce moscata	no-chay moe-scah-tah
Paprika	Paprika	pah-pree-cah
Parsley	Prezzemolo	prets-say-moe-low
Peanuts	Le Arachidi	ah-rah-key-dee
Pepper	Pepe	pày-pay
Pinoli	Pine nuts	peen-knoll-lee
Pistacchio	Pistacchio	pea-stah-key-oh
Rosemary	Rosmarino	rose-marine-oh
Saffron	Zafferano	zah-fair-rahn-no
Sage	Salvia	sahl-"v"-ah
Salt	Sale	sahl-lay
Sesame Seeds	Semi di Sesamo	say-me dee say-sah-moe
Poppy seeds	Semi di Papavero	say-me dee pah-pah-ver-row
Tarragon	Dragoncello	drah-go-n-chell-low
Thyme	Timo	team-mow
Vanilla	Vaniglia	vah-kneel-yah
Walnuts	Noci	no-chee
Flour	Farina	fah-reen-ah
Wheat	Grano	grahn-no
Semolino/Semolino Intergrale	Similar to the "Farina" and "wheatina" for breakfast cereals	sea-mow-lee-noh

FRUIT/LA FRUTTA		
Apple	Mela	male-lah
Apricot	Albicocca	ahl-bee-coke-ah
Avocado	Avocado	ah-voh-cad-doe
Banana	Banana	bah-nahn-nah
Blackberries	More	moh-rey
Blueberry	Mirtillo	mere-teal-low
Cantaloupe	Melone	male-loan-nay
Cherries	Ciliegie	chill-lee-age-gee
Cherries, sour	Amarena	ah-mahr-reign-nah
Citrus	Agrume	ah-groom-may
Cranberries don't exist		
Currants	Ribes	ree-bays
Gooseberry	Uva spina	oo-vah speen-nah
Grapefruit	Pompelmo	polm-pale-mow
Grapes	Uva	oo-vah
Figs	Fichi	fee-key
Kiwi	Kiwi	key-wee
Lemon	Limone	lee-moan-nay
Lime	Limo	lee-mow
Mandarin	Mandarino	mahn-dar-reen-no
Melon	Melone	male-loan-nay
Marasca	Sour plum	mahr-rah-skah
Mulberry	More di gelso	more-rey dee jail-so
Nectarine	Pesca noce	pay-skah no-chay
Orange	Arancia	ah-rahn-cha
Papaya	Papaia	pah-pie-ya
Peach	Pesca	pay-skah
Pear	Pera	pay-rah
Persimmons	Cachi	cah-key
Pineapple	Ananas	on-nah-nahs
Plum yellow	Susine	sue-seen-nay
Pomegrante	Melograno	male-low-grahn-no
Prugne	Plums	prune-yeah
Prugne Secca	Prunes	proon-yea say-cah
Raspberries	Lamponi	lahm-pony
Raisin	Uva passa	oo-va pah-sah
Strawberries	Fragole	frah-goal-lay
Visciole	Black sour cherries	vee-show-lay
Watermelon	Cocomero/Anguria	cocoa-mair-rah

VEGETABLES/VERDURE		
Artichoke	Carciofo	car-cho-foe
Asparagus	Asparago	ah-spar-rah-gee
Dried beans	Fagioli	fah-gee-"o"-lee
Beets	Barbabietole	barba-bee-ate-toe-lay
Broccoli rabe	Broccoletti	broke-coh-late-tea
Broccoli Rabe (Roman)	Cavolbroccolo	cah-voe-broke-coh-low
Brussel sprouts	Cavolini di Bruxelles	cah-voe-lee-knee
Cabbage	Cavolo (cappuccio)	cah-voe-low
Cabbage curly green	Verza	ver-zah
Califlower	Cavolfiore	cah-vol-fee-or-rey
Carrot	Carota	car-row-tah
Celery	Sedano	say-dahn-no
Chickpeas	Ceci	chay-chee
Chicory	Cicoria	chee-core-ree-ah
Corn	Mais	mice
Cucumber	Cetriolo	chay-tree-oh-low
Eggplant	Melanzana	male-lahn-zahn-nah
Endive	Indivia	een-dee-vee-ah
Green beans	Fagiolini	fah-joe-lee-knee
Italian wide green beans	Corallo	core-rah-low
Romaine Lettuce	Lattuga	lah-two-gah
Lettuce round head soft leaves	Cappuccina	cop-poo-cheena
Mushrooms	Funghi	foon-ghee
Onion	Cipolla	chee-pole-lah
Peas	Piselli	pea-sell-lee
Potatoes	Patate	pah-tah-tay
Pumpkin	Zucca	zoo-cah
Radishes	Ravanelli	rah-vahn-nail-lee
Red cabbage	Cavolo rosso	cah-voh-low row-so
Shallots	Scalogne	scah-loan-yeah
Spinach	Spinaci	speen-nah-chee
Sweet potato	Patate Americane	pah-tah-te ah-mair-ree-cahn-nay
Tomato	Pomodoro	poh-mow-door-oh
Turnip	Cavolo rapa	cah-voe-low rah-pah
Zucchini	Zucchine	zoo-cheen-nay
Zucchini flowers	Fiori di zucca	fee-or-ree dee zoo-cah

Puntarelle is a thin green plant, with long white and dark green stems. They are curled in cold water and eatten like salad.

MEATS/CARNE		
Beef	Manzo	mahn-zoe
Bresaola-dried beef seasoned with oil lemon and pepper, very lean. The best is made from horsemeat		
Chicken	Pollo	pole-low
Cured ham	Prosciutto crudo	pro-shoot-toe crew-doe
Duck	Anatra	ahn-nah-trah
Guts	Frattaglie	frah-tahl-yea
Ham	Prosciutto	pro-shoot-toe
Hare	Lepre	lay-pray
Lamb	Agnello	ahn-yell-low
Liver	Fegato	fay-gah-toe
Pheasant	Fagiano	fah-john-no
Pork	Maiale	my-ahl-lay
Quail	Quaglia	qwa-lee-yah
Rabbit	Coniglio	corn-kneel-yo
Salami	Salume	sah-loom-may
Sausage	Salsiccia	sahl-see-cha
Young lamb	Abbacchio	ah-bah-key-oh
Tripe	Trippa	tree-pah
Wild boar	Cinghiale	cheeng-ahl-lay
Goose	Oca	oh-cah
Horse meat	Carne equina	car-nay a-queen-nah
Baby goat	Capretto	cah-prey-toe
Mutton	Montone	moan-tone-nay
Sheep	Pecora	pay-core-rah
Veal	Vitello	vee-tell-low
Venison	Cervo	chair-voh
Meatballs	Polpette	pole-pet-tay
Hot dog	Wurstel	woor-stel
Pork chops	Bracioloa	bra-cho-lah
Breast	Petto	pay-toe
Fillet	Filetto	fee-late-toe
Kebabs	Spiedini	spee-a-dee-knee
Loin	Lombata/Lonzo	lohm-bah-tah
Poultry	Pollame	pole-lahm-may
Ribs	Costolette	coast-toe-lay-tay
Intestines	Pagliata	pah-yee-ah-tah
Roast	Arrosto	ah-row-stow
Sirloin Cone-trow	Contro filetto	fee-let-toe
Sparerib	Costolotta di maiale	coast-toll-late-tah dee my-ahl-lay
Steak	Bistecca	bee-stay-cah
Game	Selvaggina or cacciagione	sale-vah-gina
Bacon	Pancetta	pahn-chay-tah

Chianina is considered the best beef in Italy

FISH/PESCE		
Anchovies	Alici	ahl-lee-chee
Anchovies in oil	Asciughe	ah-shoo-gay
Anguilla	Fresh water eel	on-gwee-lah
Bream	Orata	oh-rah-tah
Capitone	Salt-water eel	cah-pete-tone-nay
Clams	Vongole	vohn-go-lay
Cod	Merluzzo	mair-loots-oh
Crab	Granchio	grahn-key-oh
Crayfish	Aragosta	ah-rah-ghost-stah
Halibut	Alibut	ah-lee-boot
Herring	Aringa	ah-reen-gah
Lobster	Aragosta	ah-rah-ghost-stah
Lumache	Snails	lou-mah-k
Mackerel	Sgombro	sgome-bro
Mussels	Cozze	coats-say
Octopus	Polipo	pole-lee-poh
Oysters	Ostriche	oh-stree-k
Perch	Pesce persico	pay-shay pair-see-coh
Prawns	Gamberoni	gahm-bear-rohn-ney
Salmon	Salmone	sal-moan-ney
Sardine	Sardine	sahr-dean-ney
Scallops	Scaloppine	scah-low-peen-nay
Seafood	Frutti di mare	froo-tea dee mahr-ray
Shellfish	Molluschi	mole-lou-ski
Shrimp	Scampi	scahm-pea
Squid	Calamaro	cah-lah-mahr-row
Trout	Trota	troh-tah
Tuna	Tonno	tone-no

IL VIARINO

Triana Mompeo, Rieti

Tel (*39) 07 65469010

• Miniature Olive Oil Manufacturing Farm

They serve you bruschetta toasted in over a fire, while you may glance through transparent windows into the olive oil-making rooms. They explain the procedures of the oil olive-making process, and vapours mist the room with its essence. The oil is genuine. A one litre bottle is only 7€, a five litre 35€. They also ship all over the world.

SWEETS/I DOLCI		
Cookies/biscuits	Biscotti	
Hazelnut macaroons	Brutti ma Buoni	
Dounut	Ciambella	cham-bell-lah
Cake	Torta	tore-tah
Pie/Tart	Crostata	crow-stah-tah
Nougat	Torrone	tore-rohn ney
Ice Cream	Gelato	jail-lot-toe
Small stuffed pasteries	Pasticcini	pah-stee-chone-knee
Easter Sweet Bread	Panetone	pahn-ney-tone-ney
Budino	Pudding	boo-dean-no
Breakfast crossiant	Cornetto/brioche	corn-net-toe

COOKING VARIATIONS

Rare	Poco cotto	poe-coh coat-toe
Medium-rare	Non troppo cotto	known troh-poe coat-toe
Well-done	Ben cotto	ben coat-toe
Almost raw	Cotto pochissimo	coat-toe poe-key-see-mow
Raw	Crudo	crew-dough
Smoked	Affumicato	ah-foom-me-cah-toe
Roasted	Arrosto	ah-row-stow
Grilled	alla Griglia	ahl-lah gree-yah

LIQUOIR AND WINE

Maraschino (mah-rah-ski-no)	a cherry liqueur
Cremovo	a wine made with an aroma of Marsala and egg yolks, fantastic
Liquore Parampa'mpoli	a sweet liqueur made with distilled wine, sugar, espresso and honey, drink hot
Infuso di Visciole	a sour black cherry liquor, highly recommended
Fragolino	a sweet wine made with wild strawberries, bubbly and common in Rome

SALUMI

Capocollo	a spicy salame flavoured with fennel seeds, black pepper and garlic
Salamini di Cinghiale	tiny salami's made from wild boar, recommended

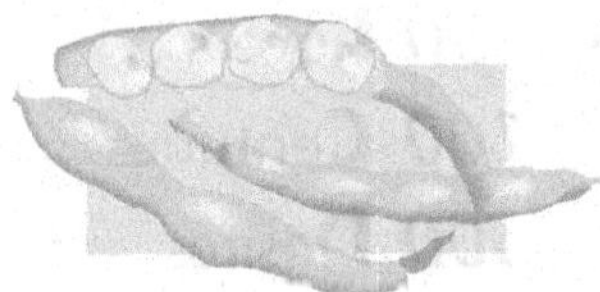

FAVE BEANS are eaten raw right out of the shells with slices of fresh pecorino cheese.

Volete un 'altro?	Would you like another?
Volete qualcosa da bere?	Would you like something to drink?
Che cosa prendete?	What would you like to order?
Avete già ordinato?	Have you ordered already?
Buon Appetito!	Enjoy your meal!
Siete pronti a ordinare?	Are you ready to order?

Roman female names	*Roman male names*
Adriana	Adriano
Antonia	Antonio
Aurora	Augusto
Cecilia	Claudio
Claudia	Cesare
Crispina	Clemente
Cristina	Crescenzo
Emilia	Fabio
Flavia	Giulio
Giulia	Gregorio
Gustina	Leone
Lucilla	Luciano
Lucinda	Marcello
Marcella	Nero
Martina	Orazio
Marzia	Paolo
Patrizia	Remo
Prisca	Sergio
Tiziana	Silvano
Valeria	Valentino
Vittoria	Vittorio

Romanumerals

If a smaller number comes after a larger number, add the value: **XI = 11**
If a smaller number comes before a larger number, subtract the value: **IX = 9**

XIX	19	*1*	**I**magination
XXL	30	*5*	**V**irtues
LIX	59	*10*	**X**'s
XVIII	18	*50*	**L**overs
XCIX	99	*100*	**C**enturies
DCCIXIV	713	*500*	**D**esires
MDCCCCLXIX	1969	*1,000*	**M**istakes

298

Games

Game players will need their Italian-English dictionary to successfully complete the crosswords puzzles. Some answers are in Italian and some are in English. The anagrams are made up of comical nonsense phrases that when mixed up, become a person place or thing. Some answers you may find within the book, and some you must test yourself with. Enjoy them.

crosswords game 1

crosswords game 1

Horizontal

1. The airport code for Rome's Fiumicino
5. Rome (It.)
8. They take your money
9. Roman fashion designer
12. Mickey Mouse's Rome
15. Italy's skin
18. Musical instrument
19. A well-known Roman dictator
22. Dean's initials
23. Sweet & Gabana
25. Star of "A Roman Holiday"
27. An apostle buried under the altar in Vatican City
29. People (It.)
30. Independent State
32. Code for special wine
33. Japanese pay in
35. Abbr. N.A.T.O. license plate
38. Rome's flow
39. Delicate
40. Hard to find type water
42. Remo's kin
44. Main street (It.)
47. Roman actor A.S.
50. Grattachecche
52. Sun to colour
53. How many great Churches of Rome?
56. 1st Roman Emperor
58. The original Roman language
59. Oil (It.)
62. A red sweet spumante
64. System of measurement
66. Sweet and rhymes with corta
67. Italy (int.)
68. Venetian boat
69. Town with a falling tower
72. Australian island
73. Cooked earth
75. House of ice
76. Actor (It.)
77. Pesto country

Vertical

2. Rome's Hollywood (It.)
3. Gold (It.)
4. A cured meat (It.)
6. Quaker
7. *Maria
10. Arte (En.)
11. Caffè is...
13. Sea (It.)
14. Most renowned poet of all times whose face is on the two euro coin
16. Something that was, and isn't anymore
17. A colour of the Rome soccer team
20. Cell messages
21. Initials of Poe
24. (Skirt) rhyming with donna (It.)
25. Roman cheese
26. Città (En.)
28. Adam's side-kick
29. Potato pasta
31. Si
34. This minute
36. Fairy tale (It.)
37. Roman poet 65-8 B.C.
38. Largo * Argentina
41. Home sweet home (It.)
43. Old Italian money
44. National religion
45. Orange outsides
46. Not off
48. Jewish jeans
49. 369 stand in Rome
51. First of Isabella
54. San Gennaro's hometown (It.)
55. Remains
57. Rhymes with Cristina, by Michelangelo
59. Perfectly preserved city, * Antica
60. Region below Tuscany
61. Religious leader
63. Cannoli cheese
64. One of two great masterpieces- Leopardian/Michelangelo
65. Plaza of the Pantheon
70. Italian island
71. Most famous Brigitte *
74. Go in

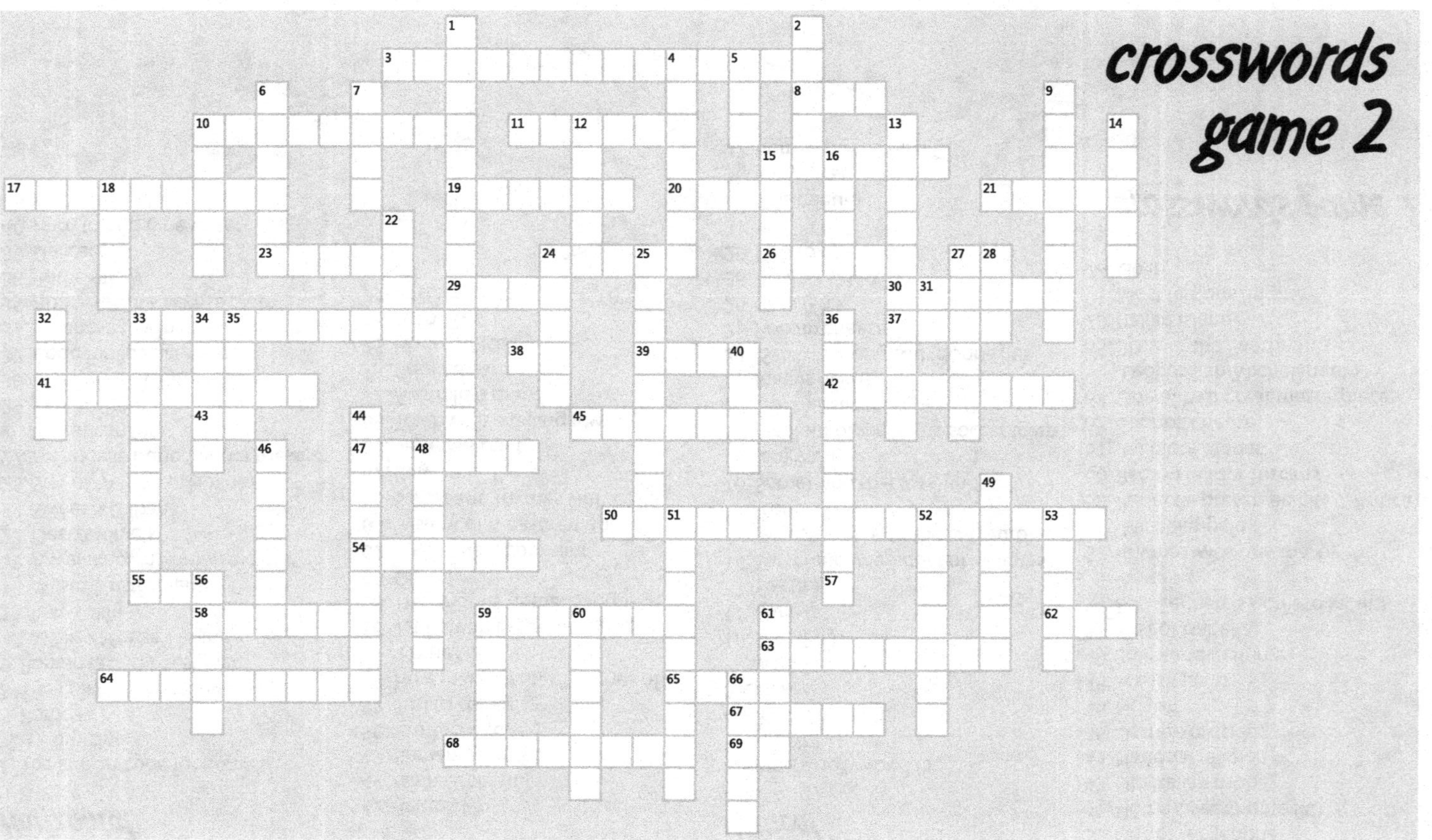
crosswords
game 2

crosswords game 2

Horizontal

3. Cinque Terre, Portofino, San Remo
8. Uncle (It.)
10. The Italian breakfast-Capuccino and *
11. Take out the shrimps digestive tract
15. Italian sport
17. An Italian in China
19. Italian clothing label
20. Thin lemon peel
21. Abominal pains
23. Isle of the Bahamas
24. Home of Parmigiano
26. Before an explanation
27. Frank Sinatra int.
29. Camera film
30. Great tenor Enrico *
33. Greatest Italian- Jazz musician
37. Paradise of Eve
38. The borders of Connecticut
39. Going through it fast
41. Italian car A. R.
42. The speed at which something moves
43. The American state of Rhode Island
45. A judge killed by Mafia in Sicily
47. Town in Lazio region
50. Last king "rei" in Italy
54. Creative, birthday end of Feburary
55. Closing of a movie
57. Look out! (abbr.)
58. The Greatest
59. Rocky land
62. An alcoholic drink made from distilled molasses
63. Italian airlines
64. Rome wasn't built in a day
65. Auto's in London
67. Inventor of the ice cream cone * Marchioni
68. Great Italian poet Giacomo *
69. Salerno (abbr.)

Vertical

1. Roman Volcanic Villages
2. Region Rome
4. Famous Carnival City
5. Zone of Rome
6. People (It.)
7. From Grapes
9. Actor Red
10. Funny face
12. The inventor of electricity, Alessandro *
13. A liquor made with lemons or oranges
14. Most important for success
15. Character; wood
16. Rad
18. Chicago baseball
22. Dream big, start small (int.)
24. Disney dog
25. Father-in-law to Sophia Loren, Benito *
27. Francais
28. Sole
32. Procrastination
33. Lifeline of wine
34. More than to love
35. Home of wild strawberries
36. Beatle's city
40. Most famous female singer in Italy
44. Beautiful Egyptian business woman
46. French fragrance
48. Game with lots of coloured spots
49. The true mozzarella
51. Sicily's original name
52. Appearing like angels
53. They are never true
56. Flemish
59. The perfect number
60. Type of western Indian music
61. Staple of Italy
66. Something we cannot stop taking

Games - Answers

number 1

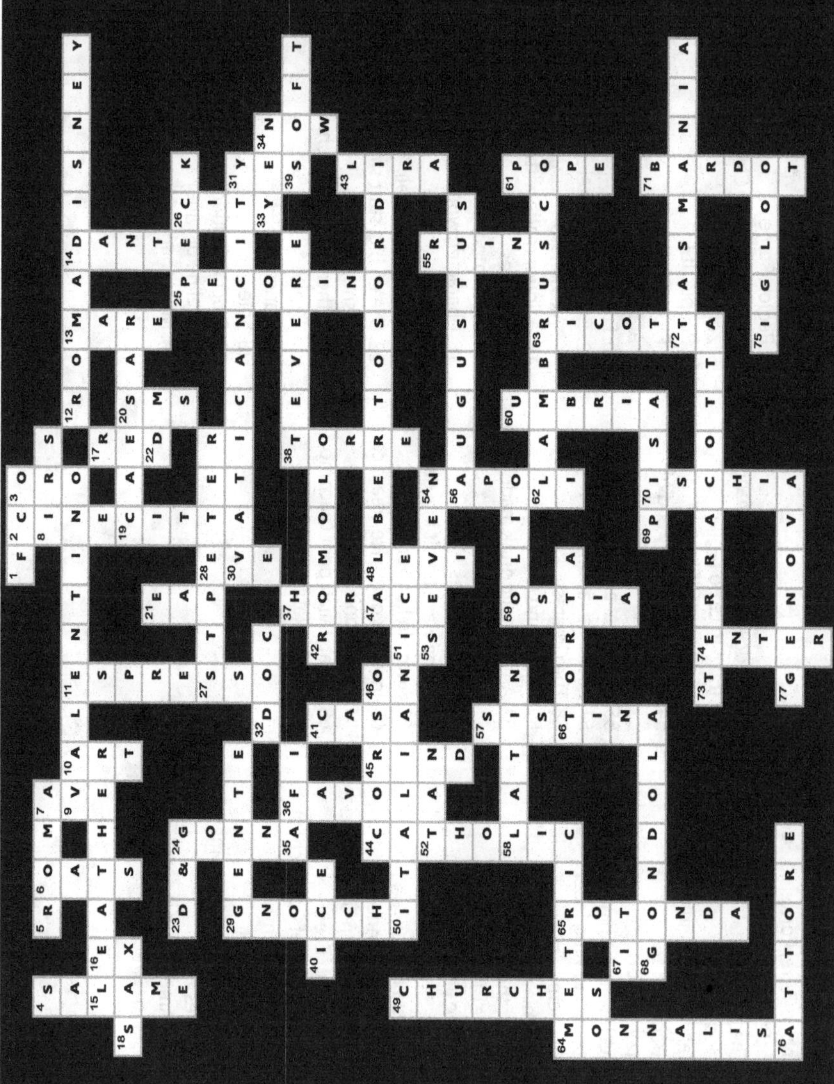

number 2

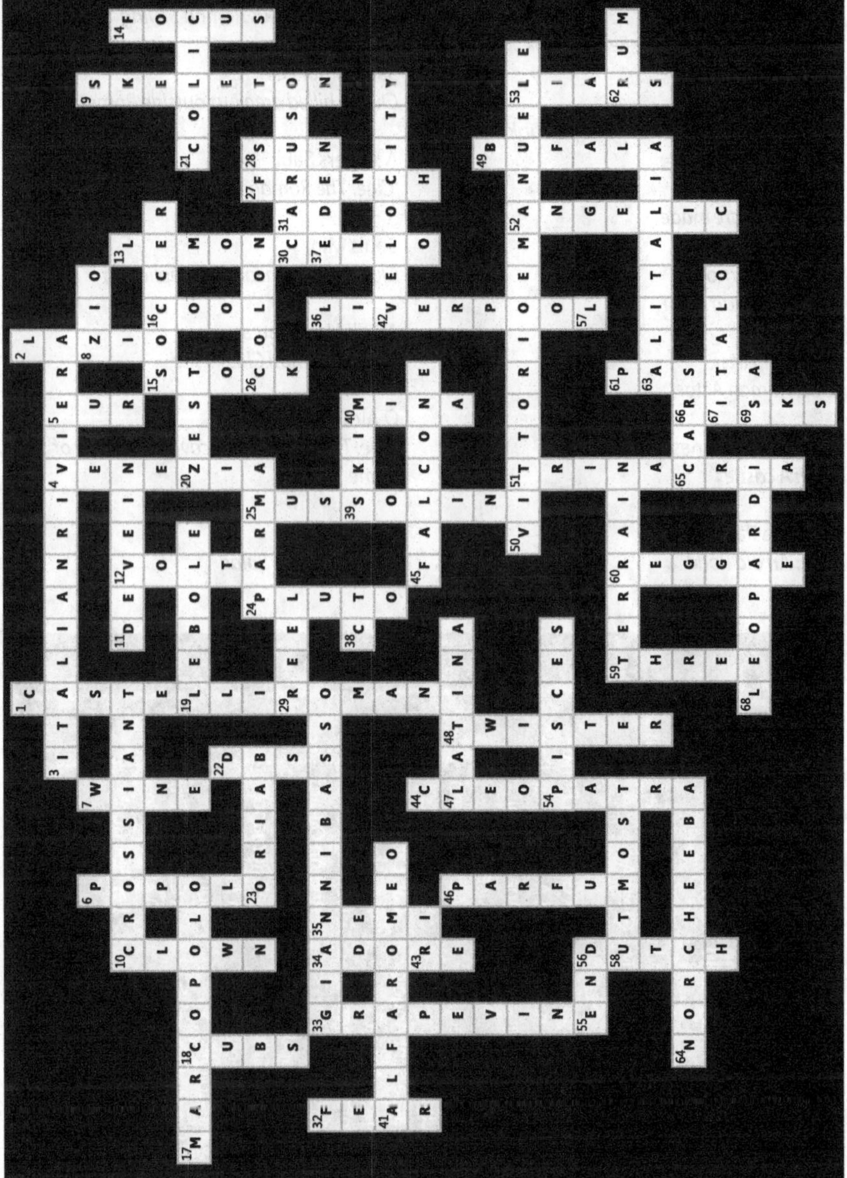

1 CASTELLIROMANI
2 LAZIO
3 ITALIANRIVIERA
4 VENEZIA
5 EUR
6 POPOLO
7 WINE
8 ZIO
9 SKELETON
10 CLOWN / CROSSIANT
11 DEVEIN
12 VOLTA
13 LEMONCELLO
14 FOCUS
15 STOCK / SOCCER
16 COOL
17 MARCOPOLO
18 CUBS
19 LEBOLE
20 ZEST
21 COLIC
24 PLUTO / PARMA
25 MUSSOLINI
26 COLON
27 FRENCH
28 SUN
29 REEL
30 CARUSO
31 AD
32 FEAR
33 GRAPEVINE / GIANNIBASSO
34 ADORE
35 NEMI
36 LIVERPOOL
37 EDEN
39 SKIM
40 MINA
41 ALFAROMEO
42 VELOCITY
44 CLEOPATRA
45 FALCONE
46 PARFUM
47 LATINA
48 TWISTER
49 BUFALA
50 VITTORIOEMANUELE
51 TRINACRIA
52 ANGELIC
53 LIARS
54 PISCES
55 END
56 DUTCH
58 UTMOST
59 THREE / TERRAIN
60 REGGAE
61 PASTA
62 RUM
63 ALITALIA
64 NORCHEEBA
65 CARS
66 RISKS
67 ITALO
68 LEOPARDI

Roman Anagrams

A Gourmets Pursue
Clue: An Emperor

A Acrobats Rap Ran
Clue: A Pasta dish in the Recipe book

Anal Amoral
Clue: part of a dish title- in recipe book

Nice Attic
Clue: Films are made

Mad in Inferno
Clue: A Roman Actor

Bloodier Arts
Clue: Roman Actor

Can Eat Gallstones
Clue: A castle

A Capita Pain
Clue: An old Road

Neuronal Swarm
Clue: Digits

And An Oilbird
Clue: A Roman Prince and building in Frascati

Aim uno: Dumpcart
Clue: The famous Roman Saying

Salt Romances
Clue: A hilled area just outside Rome

A Juicers Saul
Clue: The Roman Dictator

Souls Mini
Clue: Hitler's Italian Accomplice

A Cab Halo Flatcars
Clue: A Roman Classic site

O Almond Roomer!
Clue: The Two who discovered the city of Rome

Let Peal Run!
Clue: A Roman Salad

Roman Anagrams Answers

The Romans referred to the study of anagrams as; *"ARS MAGNA"*, "The Great Art"

A Gourmets Pursue	Emperor Augustus
A Acrobats Rap Ran	Pasta Carbornara
Anal Amoral	Alla Romana
Nice Attic	Cinecittà
Mad in Inferno	Nino Manfredi
Bloodier Arts	Alberto Sordi
Can Eat Gallstones	Castle Sant'Angelo
A Capita Pain	Appia Antica
Neuronal Swarm	Roman Numerals
And An Oilbird	Aldobrandini
Aim uno: Dumpcart	Roma Caput Mundi
Salt Romances	Roman Castles
A Juicers Saul	Julius Caesar
Souls Mini	Mussolini
A Cab Halo Flatcars	Baths of Caracalla
O Almond Roomer!	Romolo and Remo
Let Peal Run!	Puntarelle

Anagrams

COMEDIES
Tower my pant
Kitties oh me lo
Herbs dit
Hinges Hint
Whizzed far too - *(1939)*
Metro Tuner
Smothering all it is
Rethink then pep
Latex Bran O
Gee Math
Suitable Flu If I
Headmistress Rum Mag Mind
Panther Matte
Gentler Ones
Jealous ok Rich
Overeats Chef Fee
Fraction Hot Ant - *(1958)*
Fairy Madly - *(1964)*
Grove It - *(1958)*
Twisty or Seeds - *(1961)*
Egyptian Blue es - *(1959)*
Chief to Hat Cat - *(1955)*
Raw Stars - *(1977)*
Always Cone Pop - *(1979)*
Advising Dry Miss I - *(1989)*
Fooled Gals - *(1990)*
Festoon Caw Man - *(1992)*
Whodunit Ill Gong - *(1997)*
Mouthwash Enter - *(1998)*
Crayons en en
Riots Tale
Infancies corn
Faints ark ran
Fern oh dry
Brainiest el net
Awoken will i
Parkas he see
Vet van chin gong
Larvas idol ad
Basics polo pa
Ah pearl

WRITERS
The king pens
Heckler runny fib
Hob in odor
Swirl cellar
Twin karma
Jambs Wand Lie
Cute Boomers
Fencers Bat Runt

ACTORS CHARACTERS
Diva Day Discs
Blue ill call
Speller trees
Jewelry sir
Skinny pooh than
Kale cry gel
Cologne grey oe
Blueberry ban (Flintstones)
Run errand o (Looney tunes)
Elf mud red (Looney Tunes)

EDIBLE FLOWERS
Wolfs Rune
Donna Deli
Blame poploss
Nice Gala
Unlaced La
Mocha Lime
Silly Idea
Isnidely Hags
Dialogs La
Slouchy Knee
Such Sibi
Everland
Lacs Li
Peanut is
Sores
Grandpas No
Up Silt
Loves It
Few Floras

CARTOONS
Pet by boot - *(1940)*
Tutu Ell Ill - *(1943)*
Utterly Ailed - *(1947)*
Yogis the Mum - *(1955)*
Fella Farm Afar - *(1956)*
Jell Check Eke - *(1956)*
Flax Tech Tie - *(1958)*
Cloudberry He Hunk - *(1958)*
Pudgy we Tad - *(1960)*
Gram Moo - *(1960)*
Unwell Bilk - *(1961)*
Bogie Ray - *(1961)*
Joss Net - *(1962)*
Marsala It - *(1962)*
Belly I Tea Bee - *(1963)*
Nudged or - *(1964)*
Poetry Hip Hoop - *(1964)*
Silhouetted Haler Inn - *(1964)*
Horsemint melt not - *(1965)*
Vanda ark art - *(1966)*
Orchll Deus - *(1967)*
Juggler Ghee Foe Ton - *(1967)*
Gosh Poor Egg - *(1968)*
Gatherers Tomb Troll - *(1970)*
Fanny Ok Thump - *(1971)*
A Left Brat - *(1972)*
Hyperactive Hinge Hi - *(1973)*
Hooky Gong Phone - *(1974)*
Jar Jab Web - *(1976)*
Vaccinate am nap - *(1977)*
Yo Drop - *(1979)*
Measured Nog - *(1981)*
Introspected Gag - *(1983)*
Etch If Half - *(1984)*
Crab Erase - *(1985)*
Deaf Girl - *(1988)*
Jibe cute eel - *(1989)*
Rattlebox Rosy Read - *(1996)*
Navy John Orb - *(1997)*
Doc Tag - *(1998)*
Yo Beep
Sty Notion
Capers

HITCHCOCK
Evidently Ash Ash - *(1938)*
I i Jam Canna - *(1939), Maureen O'Hara*
Cab Cere - *(1940), Joan Fontaine and Lawrence Oliver*
Confronting Roper Seed - *(1940), Joel McCrea*
Cousin Sip - *(1941), Cary Grant and Joan Fontaine*
O Flea Bit - *(1944)*
Pollens Bud - *(1945), Gregory Peck and Ingrid Bergman*
O Irons Out - *(1946), Cary Grant and Ingrid Bergman*
A Fancied Pear - *(1947), Gregory Peck*
Unpriced Rancor - *(1949)*
Fright Gates - *(1950)*
Astringents Ran Oar - *(1951)*
If Scones *(1953), Montgomery Cliff*
Afro Rim Muddler - *(1954)*
Widower Ran - *(1954), James Stewart and Grace Kelly*
Mother Gnawn *(1956), Henry Fonda*
Throb Twenty Horns - *(1959), Cary Grant*
I Namer - *(1964), Sean Connery*
Unicorn Tart - *(1966), Paul Newman and Julie Andrews*
Zap To! *(1969)*
Motif Pally - *(1976), Karen Black*

Anagram Answers

iufyskf
haesry
bewiyg
rbsdd
fhahdg
fkjasdf
kjsadhf
skjdfh

Orchil Deus . . . . Herculoids
Juggler Ghee Foe Ton . . . . . . George of the Jungle
Gosh Poor Egg . . . . Go go Gophers
Gatherers Tomb Troll . . . . Harlem Globtrotters
Fanny Ok Thump . . . . Funky Phantom
A Left Brat . . . . Fat Albert
Hyperactive Hinge Hi . . . . Inch High Private Eye
Hooky Gong Phone . . . . Hong Kong Phooey
Jar Jab Web . . . . Jabberjaw
Vaccinate am nap . . . . Captain Caveman
Yo Drop . . . . Droopy
Measured Nog . . . . Dangermouse
Introspected Gag . . . . Inspector Gadget
Etch If Half . . . . Heathcliff
Crab Erase . . . . Carebears
Deaf Girl . . . . Garfield
Jibe cute eel . . . . Beetle Juice
Rattlebox Rosy Read . . . . Dexter's Laboratory
Navy John Orb . . . . Johnny Bravo
Doc Tag . . . . CatDog
Yo Beep . . . . Popeye
Sty Notion . . . . Tiny Toons
Capers . . . . Casper

HITCHCOCK

Evidently Ash Ash . . . . The Lady Vanishes
i i Jam Canna . . . . Jamaica Inn
Cab Cere . . . . Rebecca
Confronting Roper Seed . . Foreign Correspondent
Cousin Sip . . . . Suspicion
O Flea Bit . . . . Lifeboat
Pollens Bud . . . . Spellbound
O Irons Out . . . . Notorious
A Fancied Pear . . . . Paradine Case
Unpriced Rancor . . . . Under Capricorn
Fright Gates . . . . Stage Fright
Astringents Ran Oar . . . . Strangers on a Train
If Scones . . . . I Confess
Afro Rim Muddler . . . . Dial M For Murder
Widower Ran . . . . Rear Window
Mother Gnawn . . . . The Wrong Man
Throb Twenty Horns . . . . North by Northwest
I Namer . . . . Marnie
Unicorn Tart . . . . Torn Curtain
Zap To! . . . . Topaz
Motif Pally . . . . Family Plot

COMEDIES

Tower my pant.................... Pretty Woman
Kitties oh me lo .... Some like it Hot
Herbs dit............................. The Birds
Hinges Hint .... The Shining
Whizzed far too .... The wizard of Oz
Metro Tuner .... Return to me
Smothering all it is .... Gorillas in the Mist
Rethink then pep................ The Pink Panther
Latex Bran O .... A Bronx Tale
Gee Math .... The Game
Suitable Flu If I .... A beautiful Life
Headmistress Rum Mag Mind A Midsummer Night's Dream
Panther Matte..................... The Apartment
Gentler Ones........................ Solent Green
Jealous ok Rich................... Jailhouse Rock
Overeats Chef Fee........ The Three Faces of Eve
Fraction Hot Ant .... Cat On a Hot Tin Roof
Fairy Madly .... My Fair Lady
Grove It.................................. Vertigo
Twisty or Seeds .... Westside Story
Egyptian Blue es .... Sleeping Beauty
Chief to Hat Cat .... To Catch a Thief
Raw Stars .... Star Wars
Always Cone Pop................ Apocalypse Now
Advising Dry Miss i .... Driving Miss Daisy
Fooled Gals .... GoodFellas
Festoon Caw Man .... Scent of a Woman
Fret Him................................ The Firm
Whodunit Ill Gong............ Good Will Hunting
Mouthwash Enter .... The Trueman Show
Crayons en en...................... Sean Connery
Riots Tale .... Aristotle
Infancies corn...................... Connie Francis
Faints ark ran .... Frank Sinatra
Fern oh dry .... Henry Ford
Brainiest el net .... Albert Einstein
Awoken will i........................ Willie Wonka
Parkas he see .... Shakespeare
Vet van chin gong............. Vincent Van Gogh
larvas idol ad .... Salvador Dali
Basics polo pa...................... Pablo Picasso
Ah pearl .... Raphael

WRITERS

The king pens...................... Stephen King
Heckler runny fib............... Huckleberry Finn
Hob in odor.......................... Robin Hood
Swirl cellar o .... Lewis Carroll
Twin karma .... Mark Twain
Jambs Wand Lie.................. James Baldwin
Cute Boomers........................ Umberto Eco
Fencers Bat Runt .... Frances Burnett

ACTORS CHARACTERS

Diva Day Discs .... David Cassidy
Blue ill call .... Lucille Ball
Speller trees .... Peter Sellers
Jewelry sir .... Jerry Lewis
Skinny pooh than .... Anthony Hopkins
Kale cry gel .... Grace Kelly
Cologne grey oe .... George Clooney
Blueberry ban...................... Barney Rubble
Run errand o........................ Road Runner
Elf mud red .... Elmer Fudd

EDIBLE FLOWERS

Sunflower............................ Wolfs Rune
Dandelion .... Donna Deli
Apple Blossom.................... Blame poploss
Angelica .... Nice Gala
Calendula.............................. Unlaced La
Chamomile .... Mocha Lime
Day Lilies .... Silly Idea
English Daisy....................... Isnidely Hags
Gladiolas.............................. Dialogs La
Honeysuckle........................ Slouchy Knee
Hibiscus .... Such Sibi
Lavender .... Everland
Lilacs .... Lacs Li
Petunias .... Peanut is
Roses .... Sores
Snapdragon .... Grandpas No
Tulips...................................... Up Silt
Violets.................................... Loves It
Safflower .... Few Floras

CARTOONS

Pet by boot .... Betty Boop
Tutu Ell Ill .... Little Lulu
Utterly Ailed .... Little Audrey
Yogis the Mum.................... Mighty Mouse
Fella Farm Afar..................... Farmer Alfalfa
Jell Check Eke..................... Heckle & Jeckle
Flax Tech Tie .... Felix the Cat
Cloudberry He Hunk......... Huckleberry Hound
Pudgy we Tad...................... Deputy Dawg
Gram Moo .... Mr. Magoo
Unwell Bilk............................ Bullwinkle
Bogie Ray .... Yogi Bear
Joss Net .... Jetsons
Marsala It .... Lariat Sam
Belly I Tea Bee...................... Beetle Bailey
Nudged or .... Underdog
Poetry Hip Hoop .... Hoppity Hooper
Silhouetted Haler Inn...... Linus the Lionhearted
Horsemint melt not .... Milton the Monster
Vanda ark art....................... Ant & Aardvark

Romanames

```
            O
          N A T
        E F I D S
      R E S B V R U
    O L C R A A G I G
  N I F U L I R A D A U
E C R T K Z E I O I C N A
E X O N I G R M Z R E O O
O A T R O E E E E M U T M
U N T R L R R S A N E A O
Q A I A D C C S I R T I L
P O V T U E S A R H N E O
P L I L N I Y L O O E A K
  X E Z M E I I T A S F
    O O A S L N T S I
      I N R A A I A
        P E O O V
          P K I
            A
```

Adriano
Antonio
Appio
Augusto
Aurora
Bruto
Cassio
Clemente
Crescenzo
Felice
Flavia
Gregório
Leone
Lucrezia
Massimo
Messalina
Nerone
Orazio
Patrizia
Remo
Valentino
Valeria
Vittoria
Vittorio

Romatones

Arancio
Bianco
Bleu Oltremare
Bleu Prussia
Celeste
Giallo Chiaro
Giallo Limone
Giallo Scuro
Grigio Cenere
Marrone
Nero
Ocra Rossa
Rosa
Rosso Carminio
Rosso Porpora
Seppia
Terria di Siena
Verde Chiaro
Verde Scuro
Verde Smeralde
Violetto

```
V
Q E D
Z R Q
D I D D Y
Q U E O L
E C Z C K M V
U V K H H Q P
T Q E G I T V A A
A O R I A I E X J
C V N D U R A I P J A
Q E B E N O R R A M E
P R R X S I S Y W G W T F
O W D E M P S T Z U C Y Y
B E R E N E C O I G I R G M T
E G N S U R L C T D E G X J F
Y V O I C N A R A O M A B M K E N
A B L E U O L T R E M A R E A K A
L M T I T R M D C M S N Y L R B R A V
T Y D B S O Q E C I L E O O H E B C H
N P J I I E G N R A N T B P M P J T M J V
X G G I A L L O C H I A R O P I K L A W Z
U M Q O H N E C W E T O O S M A I L R P V A O
C H M I U C C B L E U P R U S S I A O H I A W
V G I A L L O S C U R O C M A Y O K K K L O O O C
K Q X R M R E M W R S R F N F O R R T U F L L I N
O L M D W G O V I Q S P R V W X M I T A D V E A Y W M
H J A G T D T P Z O M J E X P Q Q A Y X R G T M I D A
F B I S A S S Z J R P U X N B X R S E M Z G C T Y K G C N
H R S U R T H M N H Y W X X T P A I Z A W B Z O A D K L W
```

Colors

Blue	Blu	*Lilac*	Lilla
Azure	Azzurro	*Red*	Rosso (Row sew)
Sky Blue	Celeste	*Green*	Verde
Lime	Green	*Dark Green*	Verde Scuro
Sea green	Acquaverde	*Purple*	Viola
White	Bianco	*Gray*	Grigio
Off White	Bianco Sporco	*Tan*	Marrone chiaro
Gold	Oro	*Beige*	Beige
Silver	Argento	*Bruno*	Dark Brown
Yellow	Giallo	*Maroon*	Marrone
Black	Nero	*Fuscla*	Fuxsia
Brown	Marrone	*Orange*	Aroncione
Pink	Rosa (Row zah)		

World of Italian Disney

Why did I decide that a book on Rome needing to have a small section on Disney? Disney plays a large role in the Italian culture.
Because, Disney is timeless among Italian children, its left its imprint upon their hearts. I have listed the Italian Disney characters for those who are curious. There is a Disney shop on Via del Corso, up towards Piazza del Popolo.

DISNEY CHARACTERS			
ENGLISH	ITALIAN	ENGLISH	ITALIAN
The Aristocrats	Aristogatti	Huey Dewey & Louie	Qui, Quo & Qua
Beagle Boys	Banda Bassotti	Lil Bad Wolf	Lupetto
Big bad wolf	Ezechiele	Little Helper	Edi
Black Pete	Pietro Gambadilegno	Ludwig von Drake	Pico de Paperis
Brigitta McBridge	Brigitta	Magica de Spell	Amelia
Chief O'hara	Commissario Basettoni	Micky Mouse	Topolino
Chip & Dale	Cip e Ciop	Minnie Mouse	Minnie (also Minni and Topolina)
Clarabelle Cow	Clarabella	Morty & Ferdie Fieldmouse	Tip e Tap
Daisy Duck	Paperina	Paperinik	Paperinik
Detective Casey	Manetta	Peter Pan	Peter Pan
Donald Duck	Paperino	Pluto	Pluto
Dugan Duck	Pennino	Scrooge McDuck	Paperon de Paperoni (also Zio Paperone)
Eega Beeva	Eta Beta	Snow White	Bianca Neve
Ellsworth Bhezer	Gancio	The Phantom Blot	Macchia Nera
Fethry Duck	Paperoga	John Rockerduck	Rockerduck
Flintheart Glomgold	Cuordipietra Famedoro	The Three Little Pigs	Tre Porcellini
Gladstone Gander	Gastone Paperone	TInker Bell	Campanellino
Glittering Goldie	Doretta Doremi	Winnie the Pooh	Winnie the Pooh
Goofy	Pippo	The Junior Woodchucks	Giovani Marmotte
Grandma Duck	Nonna Papera	Witch Hazel	Nocciola
Gus Goose	Ciccio	Ducksburg	Paperopoli
Gyro Gearloose	Archimede Pitagorico	Mouseton	Topolinia
Horace Horsecollar	Orazio	Goosetown	Ocopoli

The Easiest Italian Pronounciations in the World

PLACES		
Albergo	*Hotel*	Ahl-bear-go
Alimentari	*Grocerystore*	Alee-mane-tah-ree
Banca	*Bank*	Bahn-ca
Birreria	*Brewery*	Bee-ray-ree-yah
Calzoleria	*Shoestore*	Cal-tso-lare-ree-ah
Dentista	*Dentist*	Dane-tea-sta
Enoteca	*Vintage Wine Shop*	Ay-no-tay-cah
Erboristeria	*Healthfood Store*	Air-bore-ree-stay-ree-ah
Farmacia	*Pharmacy*	Far-mah-chee-ah
Ferramenta	*Hardware Shop*	Fair-rah-main-tah
Frutteria	*Fruitstand*	Froot-tear-ree-ah
Gelateria	*Ice Cream Parlor*	jay-la-tear-ee-ah
Gioielleria	*Jewelery Shop*	Joy-ale-lare-ree-ah
Lavanderia	*Laundry Mat*	La-vahn-dare-ree-ah
Libreria	*Bookstore*	Leeb-ray-ree-ah
Mercato	*Market*	Mair-cah-toh
Museo	*Museum*	Moo-say-oh
Ospedale	*Hospital*	Oh-spa-dal-lay
Osteria	*Tavern/Sm. Restaurant*	Oust-stare-rea
Panificio	*Bread Bakery*	Pahn-knee-fee-coh
Paninoteca	*Sandwhich Shop*	Pahn-kneen-know-tech-cah
Parco	*Park*	Par-coh
Parrucchiere	*Hair Salon*	Pah-rue-key-yer-ray
Pasticceria	*Pastry Shop*	Pah-stee-chair-ree-ah
Pelletteria	*Leathershop*	Pel-lay-tear-ree-ah
Questura	*Police Head Quarters*	Quest-oo-rah
Ristorante	*Restaurant*	Ree-sto-rahn-tay
Rosticceria	*Roasted poultry Shop*	Stadio- Stadium
Stah-dee-oh	*Tabaccaio*	Tah-bach-eye -oh
Teatro	*Theatre*	Tay-ah-tro
Tintoria	*Dry Cleaners*	Teen-tore-ree-ah
Centro Benessere	*Wellness Center*	Solarium

QUESTIONS		
I don't understand	*Non (ho) Capisco*	Nohn- Cah- pea-sko
Thank you	*Grazie*	Grah-ts-ee-ay
Are you open?	*Sei aperto?*	Say-ah-pear-toe?
May I have the bill?	*Posso avere Il conto?*	Poe-so ah-ver-re eel Cone-toh
How much does it cost?	*Quanto costa?*	Qwan-toh coh-stah
Where is....	*Dov' è...*	Doe-vay
It 's too much	*Costa troppo*	Coh-stah troh- poe
It's very expensive	*E' molto caro*	Ay mole-toh cah-roh
Do you speak English?	*Parli L'inglese?*	Pahr-lee Lean-glaze say?
Good evening	*Buona sera*	Bwo-nah Say-rah
I'm sorry	*Scusa*	Scoo-sah
I'm sorry about what I've done	*Scusami*	Scoo-sah-me
I don't know	*Non lo so*	No- low-so
Okay	*Va bene*	Vah ben-ay
Good morning	*Buon Giorno.*	Bwon gee-oar-no
How are you?	*Come stai?*	Coh-may sty?
May I?	*Posso?*	Poe-so?
Pardon me	*Permesso*	Pear-may-so
May I have...	*Posso avere ...*	Poe-so Ah-ver-ray

Say quickly! Try to roll R's! Trick, open your mouth wider!
Pronounce vowels like this:
A = ah E = a I = e O = oh U = ooo

Hi	*Salve*	Sahl-vay
What time is it?	*Che ora è?*	K- oh-rah eh?
I'm looking for...	*Sto cercando....*	Stow chair-kàhn-doe...
Are you joking?	*Scherzi?*	Scare-ts-ee?
May I see...?	*Posso vedere...?*	Poe-so veh-deh-ray
What does that mean?	*Cosa significa?*	Coh-sah see-knee-fee-cah?
I want...	*Voglio...*	Voe-lee-yo...
I would like...	*Vorrei...*	Voe-r-Ray. .
Go away!	*Via!/Vai Via!*	Vah-eye!/Vah-eye/Vee-ah!
Excuse me	*Mi Scusi*	Me- skoo-sea
I don't believe it	*Non ci credo*	Nohn chee cray-doe
I don't trust you	*Non ti fidi*	Nohn tea fee-dee
I'm not sure	*Non sono sicuro*	Nohn so-no sea-coo-roh
Help me!	*Aiuto!*	Ah-u-toe!
Thief!	*Ladro!*	Lah-drow!
May I try it on?	*Posso provarlo?*	Poe-so pro-var-low?
I'm finished	*Ho finito*	O fee-knee-toe
I like it	*Mi piace*	Me pea-ah-chay
Everythings fine	*Tutto bene*	Too-toe ben-nay
It's very good	*E' molto buono*	Eh mole-toe bwon-no
Your very kind	*Sei molto gentile*	Say mole-toe jen-tee-lay
I love Rome	*Amo Roma*	ah-moe Row-mah
Where is the police station?	*Dov' è la Questura?*	Doe-vay lah quest-oo-rah?
Where can I find you?	*Dove posso trovarti?*	Doe-vay poe-so troh-vah-r-vee
THINGS		
One Ticket	*un Biglietto*	Oon Beel-yee-eh-toe
Two Tickets	*Due Biglietti*	Do -ay Beel-yee-eh-tee
Military Police	*Carabinieri*	Cah-rah-been-year-ree
Main Street	*Corso*	Coor-so
Street	*Via*	Vee-ah
Stamp	*Francobollo*	Fran-coh-bowl-low
Station	*Stazione*	Sta-ts-ee-own-ay
Church	*Chiesa*	Key-ay-sah
Bus stop, train stop	*Fermata*	Fair-mah-tah
Line	*Linea*	Lean-ee-ah
Exit	*Uscita*	Oo-she-tah
Avenue	*Viale*	Vee-all-lay
Closed	*Chiuso*	Key-oo-so
Platform	*Binario*	Been-are-ee-oh
Arrival	*Arrivo*	Ah-ree-voh
Bus	*Autobus*	Ou-toe-boos
Door won't open	*Porta Guasta*	Pour-tah Goo-ah-sta
Delay	*Ritardo*	Ree-tar-doe
Timetable	*Orario*	Oh-rah-rio
Train	*Treno*	Tray-no
Open	*Aperto*	Ah-pear-toe
Envelope	*Busta da lettera*	Boo-sta dah let-tear-rah
Mail	*Posta*	Po-stah
Mailbox	*La cassetta postale*	Lah Cah-sate-tah Poe-stall-lay
Strike	*Sciopero*	Show-pear-row
A ride/Lift	*Passaggio*	Pah-sah-joe
A walk	*Una Passeggiata*	Oo-nah pah-say-jah-tah

Open your Mouth Wide!

HAVING FUN PRONOUNCING ITALIAN

Pronouncing the Italian language can be somewhat of a chore especially if the language is completely foreign to you.

A small secret is to be aware of the shape of your mouth. It seems you'll need to open your mouth wider then usual for the word to sound correct. The positioning of your tongue is important. (you may want to do this in private) It needs to stay clear of the teeth! But if you don't care to, disregard all that I'm telling you here. This tip is essential because you'll find, that it's difficult for Italians to understand what you are saying otherwise. You shall feel strange, yes, you will! But don't worry, after repeating the same words over and again, this dread will pass and it'll become more natural. So repeat repeat and repeat! And try and express yourself more dramatically.

They should (AND DON'T) teach these methods wherever they teach the Italian language it is just as important as learning the phrases!

Here's How

Your R's, S's & T's will give you away each and every time (if it's not the 1,000 other hints that won't) if your mother tongue English. The Italians will pick up on the hissing sound that spits out with the letters. When they pronounce them, the sound is completely clean and clear, it takes so much practice and awareness, so don't fret, just love your accent and be bold! When pronouncing words with "T" the trick is, this, instead of placing your tongue between your teeth when saying the letter T - go ahead, say "T" you'll hear the air that comes out? Now try placing your tongue on the roof of your mouth, and say "T", hear a difference?

The S is a challenge. Say "soon" hear a hiss? Italians don't have it. Try now by saying soon with your tongue on the palate of your mouth, the hiss is much less visible. But, if you want to perfect the language, you must cancel out all your hard years of habitual tongue-to-teeth-talking.

The R. There are many people that will never be capable of rolling the letter R.

These people are not physically capable of doing it, so if you are one of them, you can say that you learned to talk from "Stanlio e Olio". That is..."Laurel & Hardy" in Italian. They are dubbed but seem to keep their thick American accent with them, they can't seem to roll their R's either. This letter uses the upper part of the mouth also, but in a vibrating motion. It is pronounced as"erre"or Air-rray.

Words with one "R" have a simple roll. Words containing "RR" need to be rolled even more so. For example, "F-A-R-R-O" here the roll is strong, the R is strong. Fah-rrrrrrow.

As for "F-A-R-O" it has a different sound. Fah-row, with accent more on the first part. In farro, you hear almost nothing but the R's!

THE ITALIAN ALPHABET

A ah	**B** b	**C** chee	**D** d	**E** a
F f-ay	**G** g	**H** ah-kah	**I** e	**J** eloonga
K kappa	**L** l-ay	**M** m-ay	**N** n-ay	**O** o
P p	**Q** coo	**R** air-ray	**S** s-ay	**T** t
U oo	**V** voo	**Y** ipsilon	**Z** zet-ta	

The traditional Italian Alphabet is composed of 21 characters. The modernly adopted letters are as follows: J, K, Y W, X
Vowels: A, E, I, O, U

PRACTICE THESE FOR MOUTH FORM:

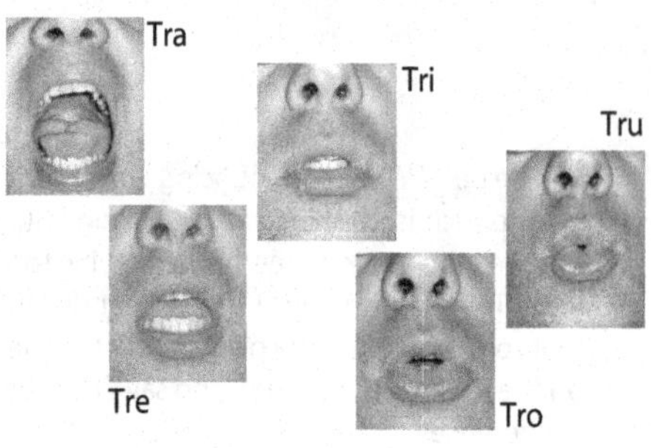

ITALIAN TONGUE TWISTERS

- Chi porta in porto le porte, parta dai porti e porti in porto le porte aperte.
(Who brings in harbours the doors, departs from the harbours and bring in harbours the open doors.)
- Tre tigri contro tre tigri. Trentatré tigri contro trentatré tigri.
(Three tigers against three tigers. Thirty-three tigers against thirty-three tigers.)

DAYS OF THE WEEK

Monday	Lunedì	Loon-à-dee
Tuesday	Martedì	Mahr-tay-dee
Wednesday	Mercoledì	Mair-coh-lay-dee
Thursday	Giovedì	Joe-vay-dee
Friday	Venerdì	Vane-nair-dee
Saturday	Sabato	Sah-bah-toe
Sunday	Domenica	Doe-main-knee-cah

(All accents are on the end of the days except for Saturday and Sunday.)

MONTHS OF THE YEAR

January	Genaio	Jen-nì-oh
Febuary	Febraio	Fay-brii-oh
March	Marzo	Mahr-ts-so
April	Aprile	Ah-pree-lay
May	Maggio	Mah-joe
June	Giugno	June-yo
July	Gulio	Lou-lee-oh
August	Agosto	Ah-ghost-toe
September	Settembre	Say-tame-bray
October	Ottobre	Oh-toe-bray
November	Novembre	No-vame-bray
December	Dicembre	Dee-chame-bray

NUMBERS

1	Uno	Oo-noh
5	Cinque	Cheen-Quay
10	Dieci	Dee-A-Chee
20	Venti	Vane-Tee
30	Trenta	Train-Tah
40	Quaranta	Core-Rahn-tah
50	Cinquanta	Cheen-Qwan-tah
60	Sessanta	Say-sahn-tah
70	Settanta	Say-tahn-tah
80	Ottanta	Oh-Tahn-Tah
90	Novanta	No-Vahn-Tah
100	Cento	Chen-Toe
200	Duecento	Due-ay Chen-Toe
500	Cinquecento	Cheen-Qway Chen-Toe
1,000	Mille	Meal-lay
10,000	Mila	Dee-ay-chee Me-lah
50,000	Mila	Cheen-Qwan-tah-Me-lah

Alimentari (ali-men-terry)

Grocery shop and deli, generally open 7am-1:30pm/5pm-8pm every day except Thursday afternoon and Sunday A good way to go, if you are looking to eat cheap with a fresh sub made with italian cold cuts and cheeses.

Bar

Known almost everywhere in the world as "cafes". This is where you go to get your caffè (espresso) and cappuccino. They also have ready made sandwhiches, and serve alcohol and fruit frappes!

Enoteca (ain-no-take-ah)

Typically a wine shop, bottles of wine are sold, but often they offer an array of wine sampling.

Gelateria jail-lot-tear-ree-ah

Follow the dripping cones and cups to one of these places offering Italy 's unique version of ice cream, gelato. Common practice is to get three different flavours and a dollop of whipped cream (panna) on top. Good old fashioned cioccolato and vaniglia are always satisfying, and fruit flavors like fragola (strawberry) and pesca (peach) are to die for in the hotter months, but don't be afraid to try out the Italian specialties of baci, gianduia, and zabaglione. Mmm! Depending on the size of your cup or cone, 2.50€-5€.

Grattachecca (grah-tah-"k"-cah)

A summer-only phenomenon--you'll find these kiosks set up in different parts of the city, often close to the Tiber, offering shaved ice with various flavored syrups squeezed over. 1.50€-3€.

Pizzeria pea-ts-air-ree-ah

Yes, that's right. Pizza here. Usually only open for dinner, from 8pm or so. Decor may be spare, but a good forno a legna (brick oven) is all you really need anyway! Pizzas will normally cost from € 6-7 for a simple margherita, a bit more for a more complex pizza like the capricciosa.

Pub/Birreria bee-bear-Ree-ah

Like a British pub or American "bar", these have become extraordinarlly popular in Rome. A variety of beers on tap, plus cocktails and other alcoholic beverages. A pint of beer is around 4-5€, cocktails 6-7€; glasses of wine 1.50-3€; prices are usually lower in the early evening, when there's some kind of happy hour or drink special. There is also a sub-category of pubs called "disco-pubs", which typically offer lower lights, higher prices, and a DJ.

Trattoria, Ristorante, Hostaria

All names for places to sit down and eat lunch or dinner. They offer a selection of appetizers (antipasti), pasta dishes (primi piatti), meat or fish dishes (secondi piatti), and side dishes (contorni). If you order one course plus house wine, you can sometimes pay as little as 10€ per person, but 15€ is more realistic. A decent-sized meal, including house wine, will cost about 20€-30€. A five-course extravaganza, with all the trimmings, will set you back at least 40€. As a general rule, try to avoid restaurants where the menu is available in more than five languages or, worse yet, where the menu has photographs of all the different dishes.

Trattoria (trah-tore-ree-ah)

Trattoria are family-owned ordinary eateries that are often the best choice for authenic Roman food. Remember the checkered tablecloths?

Tabbachi Shop

A stop shop for gum, smokes, envelopes, newspapers magazines, candies, pens, shampoos, bus-train and cell phone cards.

My Journal

Places to Remember

Number ______

Address ______

Special Interest ______

Number ______

Address ______

Special Interest ______

Number ______

Address ______

Special Interest ______

Number ______

Address ______

Special Interest ______

Number ______

Address ______

Special Interest ______

Number ______

Address ______

Special Interest ______

Number

Address

Special Interest

Number

Address

Special Interest

Number

Address

Special Interest

Number

Address

Special Interest

Number

Address

Special Interest

Number

Address

Special Interest

Number

Address

Special Interest

People to Remember

Name ______________________________

Address ______________________________

Telephone ______________ Country ______________

Email ______________________________

Name ______________________________

Address ______________________________

Telephone ______________ Country ______________

Email ______________________________

Name ______________________________

Address ______________________________

Telephone ______________ Country ______________

Email ______________________________

Name ______________________________

Address ______________________________

Telephone ______________ Country ______________

Email ______________________________

Name ______________________________

Address ______________________________

Telephone ______________ Country ______________

Email ______________________________

Name ______________________________

Address ______________________________

Telephone ______________ Country ______________

Email ______________________________

Name

Address

Telephone Country

Email

Name

Address

Telephone Country

Email

Name

Address

Telephone Country

Email

Name

Address

Telephone Country

Email

Name

Address

Telephone Country

Email

Name

Address

Telephone Country

Email

My Thoughts...

Web

www.

www.

www.

www.

www.

www.

www.

www.

www.

www.

www.

www.

www.

www.

www.

www.

www.

www.

www.

www.

www.

www.

www

www.

Gift Lists

Name	Gift Idea	Gift Shop	Price	Done

Favorite Italian Foods

Daily Journal

DAY 1

What to bring ______________________

What to see ______________________

Appointments ______________________

Money spent ______________________

DAY 2

What to bring ______________________

What to see ______________________

Appointments ______________________

Money spent ______________________

DAY 3

What to bring ______________________

What to see ______________________

Appointments ______________________

Money spent ______________________

DAY 4

What to bring ______________________

What to see ______________________

Appointments ______________________

Money spent ______________________

DAY 5

What to bring ______________________

What to see ______________________

Appointments ______________________

Money spent ______________________

DAY 6

What to bring ______________________________

What to see ______________________________

Appointments ______________________________

Money spent ______________________________

DAY 7

What to bring ______________________________

What to see ______________________________

Appointments ______________________________

Money spent ______________________________

DAY 8

What to bring ______________________________

What to see ______________________________

Appointments ______________________________

Money spent ______________________________

DAY 9

What to bring ______________________________

What to see ______________________________

Appointments ______________________________

Money spent ______________________________

DAY 10

What to bring ______________________________

What to see ______________________________

Appointments ______________________________

Money spent ______________________________

A Place so Fond

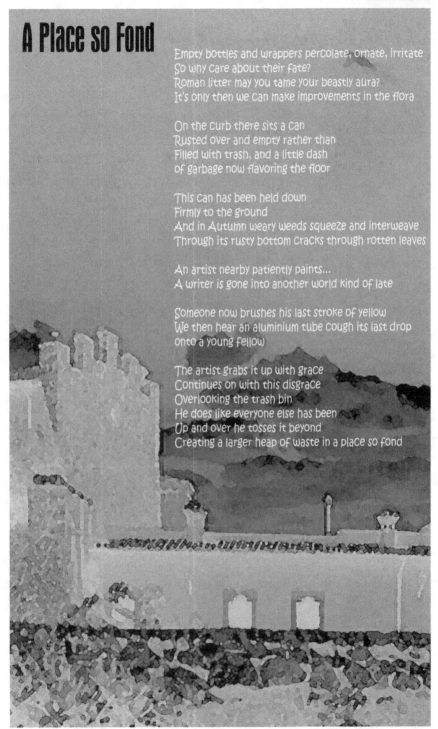

Empty bottles and wrappers percolate, ornate, irritate
So why care about their fate?
Roman litter may you tame your beastly aura?
It's only then we can make improvements in the flora

On the curb there sits a can
Rusted over and empty rather than
Filled with trash, and a little dash
of garbage now flavoring the floor

This can has been held down
Firmly to the ground
And in Autumn weary weeds squeeze and interweave
Through its rusty bottom cracks through rotten leaves

An artist nearby patiently paints...
A writer is gone into another world kind of late

Someone now brushes his last stroke of yellow
We then hear an aluminium tube cough its last drop
onto a young fellow

The artist grabs it up with grace
Continues on with this disgrace
Overlooking the trash bin
He does like everyone else has been
Up and over he tosses it beyond
Creating a larger heap of waste in a place so fond

ROMA
METRO-BUS
MAP - PLAN - MAPA
ALL BUS - SUBWAY - TRAM ROUTES
Fuori le pro
LA FABBRICA di Cio
Leon
dal 1857
CIOCCOLATO DARK CHOCOLATE
FONDENTE
CONCATO IN CONCA PIANA
OLTRE 60 ORE
74%
CACAO
ROMA STORE
Marcella
Giorgio
TreviNet Piece
Chiosco "La Selvotta"
...il suo unive
VILLA TO
LOTTERIA ITALIA 2003
Primo Premio 6 Milioni di Euro
€3,00
6 Gennaio 2004
1157370-02
Arancione
Orme

di Cioccolato
1857
HAPPY RENT
XII edizione
2006
FESTIVAL
I grandi artisti di oggi nelle molteplici espressioni della chitarra classica
Direzione artistica: M° Stefano Raponi
leggo.it
Lotteria di Natale 2006
vinci Alfa 147
TUSC
Città
Tuscolana
a diffusione gratuita
Scuola
Cicerone al silicone
Niente di sicuro
tra i banchi
Grottaferrata
Affare Traiano:
dell'assessore
Monte Porzio
Maggioranza
alle polemiche
Sanità
Ciampino
Altro che C
Arancione
mercoledì 3 a martedì 9 novembre
da COLORADO CAFÈ
Al via il MedFilm Festival
Keith Jarret al Parco della Musica
Wayne Shorter per il Roma Jazz Festival all'Auditorium
Stefano Arienti al Maxxi
I monologhi di William Yang al Palladium
I Motus e Le vie dei Festival al Teatro del Lido
Coriolano con all'Argentina
Maurizio
Battista
dal 4 al 21 Novembre
Teatro dei Satiri
via di Grottapinta, 18

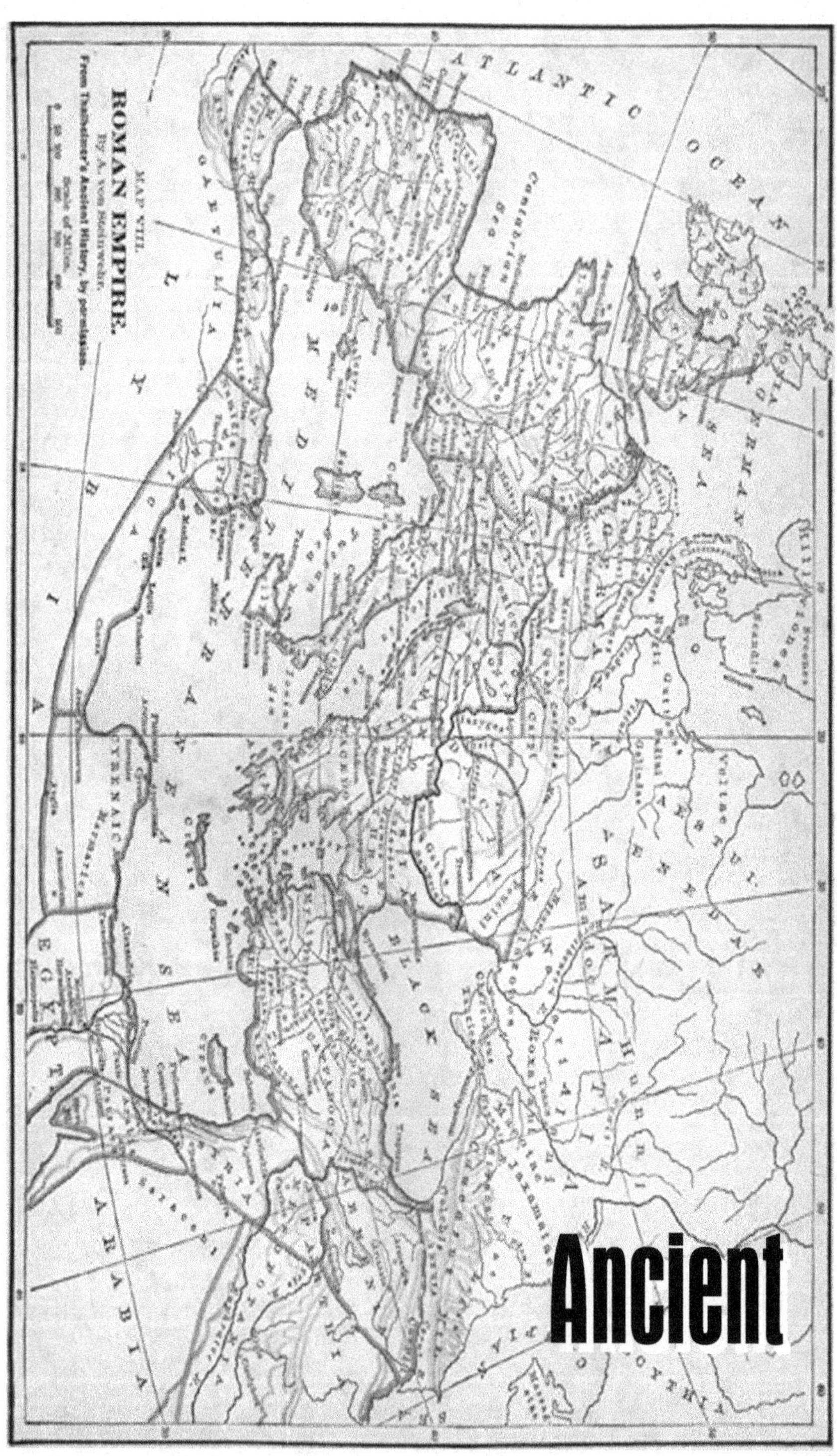
MAP VIII.
ROMAN EMPIRE.
ATLANTIC OCEAN
BLACK SEA
EGYPT
ARABIA
Ancient

PART 7

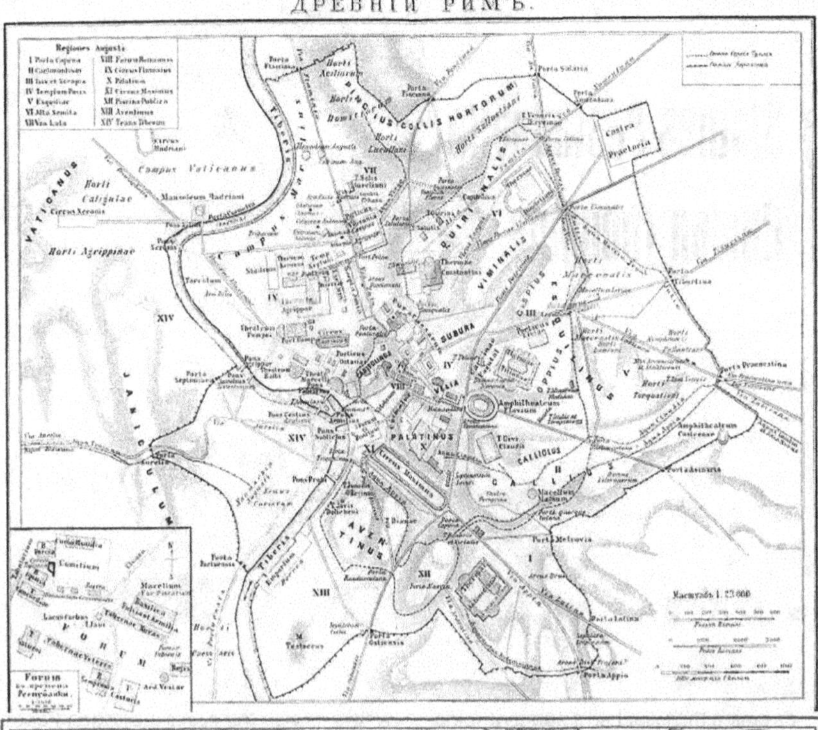
ДРЕВНІЙ РИМЪ.
Regiones Augusti
Campus Vaticanus
Horti Agrippinae
Mausoleum Hadriani
Castra Praetoria
Horti Sallustiani
SUBURA
VIMINALIS
PALATINUS
AVENTINUS
Circus Maximus
Amphitheatrum Flavium
CAELIOLUS
M. Testaceus
Porta Salaria
Porta Praenestina
Porta Asinaria
Porta Latina
Porta Appia
Porta Metrovia
Porta Ostiensis
Porta Portuensis
Campus Martius
COLLIS HORTORUM
QUIRINALIS
JANICULUM
FORUM

maps of Rome

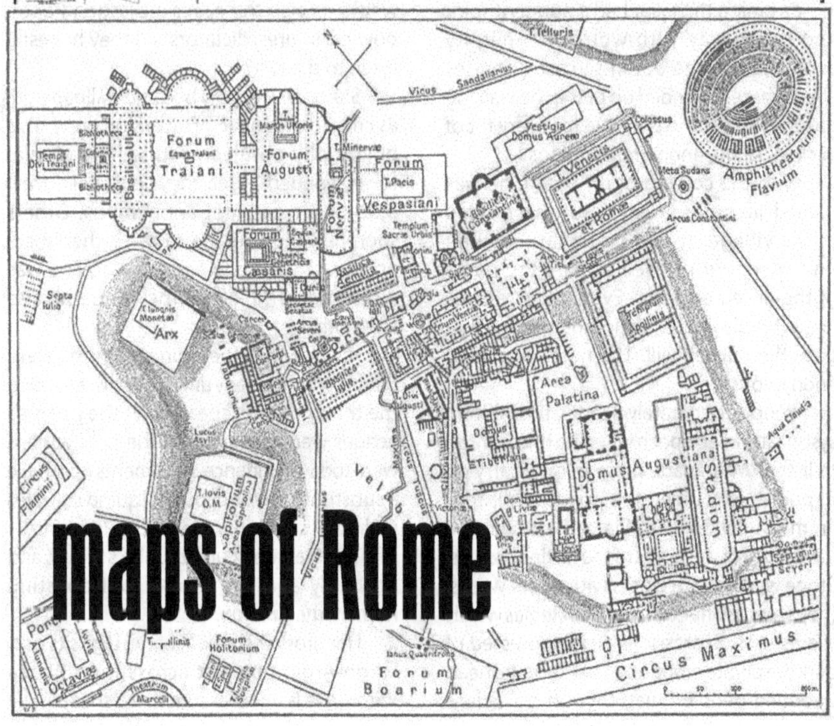
Vicus Sandalarius
T. Telluris
Forum Traiani
Basilica Ulpia
Bibliotheca
Templ. Divi Traiani
Forum Augusti
T. Minervae
Forum Nervae
Forum Vespasiani
T. Pacis
Forum Caesaris
Templum Sacrae Urbis
Basilica Constantini
Vestigia Domus Aureae
Colossus
T. Veneris et Romae
Meta Sudans
Amphitheatrum Flavium
Arcus Constantini
Basilica Aemilia
Septa Iulia
Arx
Basilica Iulia
Area Palatina
Templum Apollinis
Domus Tiberiana
Domus Augustiana
Stadion
Aqua Claudia
Lucus Asyli
Circus Flaminii
T. Iovis O.M.
Capitolium
Velabrum
Forum Holitorium
Ianus Quadrifrons
Forum Boarium
Circus Maximus
Porticus Octaviae
Theatrum Marcelli
Septizonium Severi

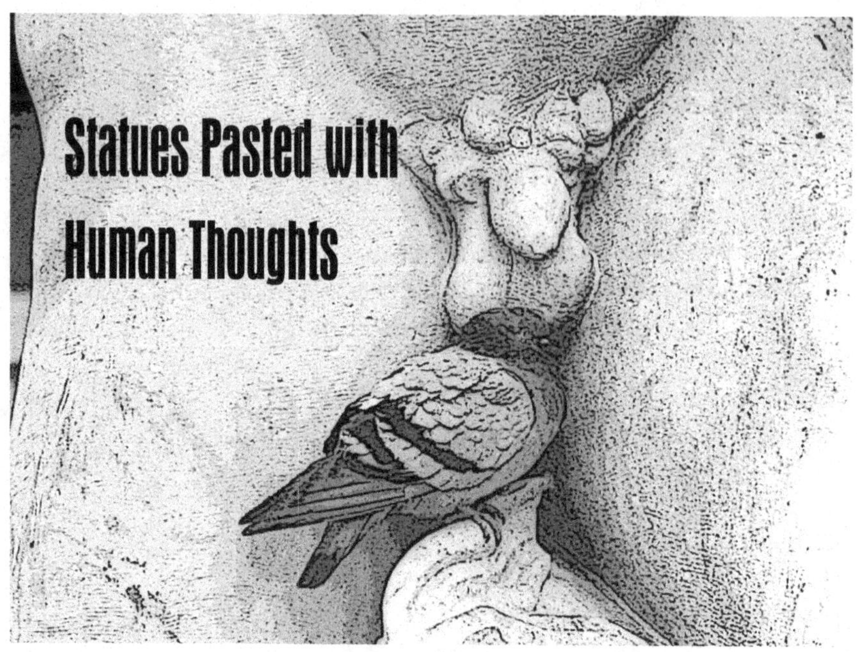

Statues Pasted with Human Thoughts

Pasquino the tailor had a pungent spirit and rough way with words. His mighty expressions came out in sarcastic phrases everywhere. He ended up being the walking gazette. He was responsible for every bit of wicked action, anonymous doings.

With the coming of his death, he was named after the ancient statue that resided in his village. It was one that was half mutilated, but pleased to bare the name of the deceased tailor. Every night wicked lanky people posted their thoughts onto its base-their last ill-will. The notes remained anonymous.

People desperately needed this venting system it was an epoch when no one wanted to listen. What made these people carry on in public, why didn't the politicians listen? From Via del Corso to Piazza Pasquino, we have proof of the births of the talking statues. Stone was life with words with paper words; they were as effective and piercing as words themselves. Expressions were expressed of dark desperate emotions. Fear kept the head swooned people quiet, though politicians would receive the eager messages. Popes, political figures, dictators did they honestly listen to the rest?

Statues eventually became wallpapered, as cries for the need of attention grew. This philosophy positively rubbed off all over town, wonderful idea, they could voice their opinions, were kept anonymous. Others soon had the courage to leave their mark on one of the stone figures. Pasquino was a real man and left us the statue named after him.

In the end, the stoned figures were bludgeoned so many times, guards removing the thoughts with spears, that the people's echoes were violated and the hollow scars were today's evidence. Arguments now have a substitute method, but Pasquino still lives on in that small space in Piazza Pasquino.

The Madame Lucrezia, she's a bust and probably another strong soul boasting human imagination.

Her brother statue"Abate Luigi"sits past Largo Argentina just across from Piazza Vidoni. He is another symbol to speech.

The graphic designer of this book, José Elias, would like to express a few words:

"Hello!
Jackelin discovered me via internet. Thank you very much! What a great opportunity you've given me. And it's not only for the project, in whose success I believe in so much, but also in granting me a page of my own, one where I could share a bit of myself.

I was born in Brazil, in December of 1965. Since 1986, when I finished a bachelor's course at the university, I was linked with the arts and communication, text, drawing, advertisement and marketing.
I spent one year in art school and in 2000, attended a specialization course for Marketing Management.
Beyond my profession, I am a passionate lover of music. I played bass guitar for two bands in Brazil between 1988 and 1994, which I'd love to rekindle sometime in the future.
Now married, I am a father living with my family in Germany and endlessly happy!"

My brief portfolio you may find here:
zeelias 65portfolio. blogspot.com
To reach me please send an e-mail to:
zeelias65@gmail.com

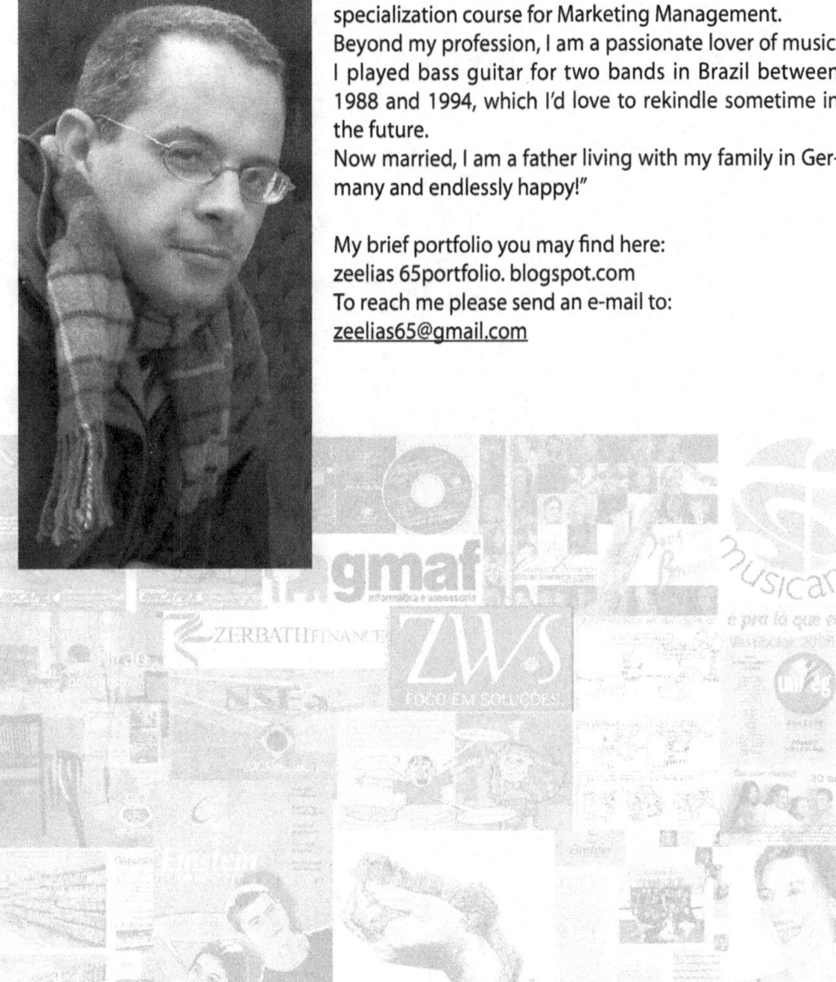